D1351476

Marketing Places Europe

Marketing Places Europe

How to attract investments, industries, residents and visitors to cities, communities, regions and nations in Europe

Philip Kotler
Christer Asplund
Irving Rein
Donald H Haider

FINANCIAL TIMES
PRENTICE HALL

For
European decision-makers in their capacities as creative placemarketers

PEARSON EDUCATION LIMITED

HEAD OFFICE:
Edinburgh Gate
Harlow CM20 2JE
Tel: +44 (0)1279 623623
Fax: +44 (0)1279 431059

London Office:
128 Long Acre, London WC2E 9AN
Tel: +44 (0)171 447 2000
Fax: +44 (0)171 240 5771
Website: www.business-minds.com

First published in Great Britain 1999

ISBN 0 273 64442 4

British Library Cataloguing in Publication Data
A CIP catalogue record for this book can be obtained from the British Library.

10 9 8 7 6 5 4 3 2 1

Typeset by Northern Phototypesetting Co Ltd, Bolton
Printed and bound in Italy by Rotolito Lombarda

The Publishers' policy is to use paper manufactured from sustainable forests.

Contents

Preface ix
Acknowledgements xi

1 The marketing challenge in Europe 1
A bottom-up approach to the European growth challenge 3
Placemarketing outside Europe 6
What is Europe? 8
Conclusions 11

2 European places in trouble 13
What is happening to places? 13
Why do places land in trouble? 16
What are places doing to solve their problems? 23
What should places be doing to solve their problems? 25
Conclusions 28

3 How places market themselves 29
What are the main target markets of placemarketers? 30
How do placemarketers market their place? 51
Who are the major placemarketers? 66
Conclusions 73

4 How place-buyers make their choices 75
Steps in the place-buying process 75
Additional factors influencing place decision-making 80
Influence of place-rating information 89
Conclusions 96

5 Place auditing and strategic market planning 99
Four approaches to place development 101
The strategic market planning process 106
The two abilities: strategy and implementation 123
Conclusions 124

6 **Strategies for place improvement** 125

Place as character – aesthetic urban design 126
Infrastructure improvement 130
Basic service provider: protection of people and property, social security and education 137
Attractions 140
People 153
Conclusions 154

7 **Designing the place's image** 159

What determines a place's image? 160
How can a place's image be measured? 162
What are the guidelines for designing a place's image? 167
What tools are available for communicating an image? 169
How can a place correct a negative image? 172
Conclusions 176

8 **Distributing the place's image and messages** 177

Clarifying the target audience and desired behaviour 177
Choosing the broad influence tools 178
Selecting advertising media channels 187
Selecting the specific media vehicles 194
Deciding on media timing 196
Evaluating media results 197
Managing conflicting media sources and messages 199
Conclusions 200

9 **Attracting tourism and hospitality business markets** 201

Tourism market 201
Business hospitality market 219
Conclusions 222

10 **Attracting, retaining and expanding business** 225

Attracting businesses from elsewhere 226
Retaining and expanding existing businesses 237
Promoting small businesses and fostering new business start-ups 239
Conclusions 241

11 Expanding exports and stimulating foreign investment 243

How important are exports to a place's economy? 245
Assessing a place's export potential 246
Ways to assist companies in promoting exports 247
Exploiting the place-of-origin image 253
Conclusions 257

12 Attracting residents 259

Why resident attraction is important in placemarketing 260
Defining the population groups to attract 264
Conclusions 269

13 Organising for change 271

What key challenges are places facing? 271
How must places respond to these challenges? 275
The necessity of marketing places in Europe 286

Notes 289
Index 297

Preface

Today's communities and regions of Europe are engaged in a continuous and significant battle to create more jobs and greater local prosperity. Their citizens and businesses expect this of their communities. To create more opportunities, communities must have skills in attracting investors, business, residents, and visitors. Yet, it would be a mistake to think that success lies in mayoral cheerleading, more government subsidies, larger place advertising expenditures in *The Economist* magazine, or more local politicians making sales calls on prospects.

Places, like products and services, need to be marketed in a sophisticated way. Each community must define its special features and effectively communicate its competitive advantages to the 'prospects and customers' whose support it seeks. This is not an easy task. To develop a competitive advantage, places need to consider their past, present, and future. They must inventory their strengths and weaknesses and their major opportunities and threats. They must identify those other communities with whom they compete for resources and find ways to differentiate and position themselves to stand out in the minds of their target markets.

Make no mistake about it: European communities are in active competition with each other for jobs, investments, residents and visitors. We have seen some market leading communities and regions lose their economic dominance and vitality as a result of shifts in market forces. We believe that in the future other major communities could suffer the same fate because of complacency and a lack of skilled market planning. And we expect that some less prominent places today will emerge tomorrow as strong economic contenders due to adopting sophisticated strategic market planning.

In this book, we present a planning framework that can be used by mayors, regional planners and their staffs, and leading local businesses to identify what might constitute winning directions for developing their respective communities. The framework considers major issues – evaluation of competition, dynamics of buyer-seller relations, the role of marketing infrastructure, the creation and distribution of effective communications and images, and other themes. We illustrate the framework with several hundred examples of European places engaged in various strategies to meet the competitive challenge. Some places that we describe illustrate major successes achieved through applying the principles of placemarketing. Other places illustrate the dilemmas or missteps that places have made in trying to compete for resources.

All European communities *cannot* prosper in the next millennium. There will be winners and losers. Some places may prosper through luck, accident, or initially strong endowments without applying strategic market planning principles. But market forces keep changing and don't forgive the complacent. We believe that the places that seriously apply the principles of strategic market planning will build a better future for their citizens and local businesses than those places that leave their future to chance or inertia. We view this book as providing a roadmap to guide places in creating stronger and better communities throughout Europe.

Philip Kotler
Christer Asplund
Irving Rein
Donald H Haider

Acknowledgements

Inspiration for this book stems from many local and regional actors – public and private – throughout Europe. Their struggle to improve place attraction has resulted in a profound knowledge base waiting to be structured and diffused to others.

The cross-Atlantic dialogue preceding this book has added a new dimension to what is taking place in Europe. New and exciting comparative aspects have emerged when European and American placemarketing has been studied in more detail.

The authors wish to thank the Foundation of Marketing Technology Center (MTC) and EuroFutures – both based in Stockholm – for granting support to Christer Asplund, which enabled him to travel to sites of European place excellence and spend time writing. We are also indebted to Professor Bengt Sahlberg, European Tourism Research Institute (ETOUR), for valuable inspiration as well as granting support, and the whole staff of EuroFutures, who have participated with enthusiasm as well as providing research support.

A number of people at Northwestern University, Evanston, Illinois, were invaluable to the production of this book. We are grateful to Jacquie Dalton and Brian Fink who provided valuable assistance in researching, editing, and organising the manuscript; Michael Cohen who researched and wrote case studies which were important to the development of the manuscript; Rachel Blank and Vijay Tellis-Nayak who skilfully edited the manuscript; and Cathy Fink who edited and developed cases.

1

The marketing challenge in Europe

What places will be successful in Europe? The opportunities have never been greater. The unified Europe will comprise the largest market in the world. For the responsive place – community, city or region – new competitive forces will invigorate and produce new partnerships and star performers.

This book argues that in this changing and challenging environment, places need to adopt a strategic marketing plan to take advantage of the new configuration. Strategic market planning is not a one-shot attempt to solve a crisis or a financial shortfall, but an ongoing process to enable places to face and adapt to the ever-evolving world marketplace. A place dedicated to an overall marketing plan will have developed a template that is flexible and avoids hasty and ill-conceived quick-fixes.

There are five issues that will shape a place's marketing performance in the European marketplace. The *first* is the necessity of place excellence in Europe. Europe has some of the strongest branded places in the world. Whether one considers the tourism magnetism of Paris, the automotive strength of southern Germany, or the financial prowess of London, the brand equity of these places is enormous. Europe has a reputation for history and culture unrivalled in any other continent. Furthermore, these vast resources include not only castles, but also skilled workforces, important clusters of industries, and a rich diversity of people and languages. There are in fact thousands of places in Europe that enjoy superiority in some area of placemarketing. The challenge of Europe is to create a tent big enough to support the branded places and encourage new players to build place excellence. For the first time, places in Europe, large and small, will share an overriding identity through common currency, governance and law.

The *second* issue relates to the conflicting megatrends towards, on the one hand, localism and regionalism in Europe (known as *divergence*) and, on the other hand, harmonising rules and standards in Europe (known as *convergence*).

Europe is decentralising into a 'Europe of regions'. At the same time, Europe has launched one of the most important convergence projects: the introduction in 1999 of the single currency, the euro. The term 'Euroland' was used to brand the single currency countries and quickly became the subject of a media-driven linguistic controversy. Once fully implemented, this convergence project will open a market that will overtake the USA in terms of GDP. Paradoxically, this huge market will create an endless number of opportunities for individual places. The Commission of the European Communities acknowledged this paradox in the following way: 'Cohesion and diversity are not conflicting objectives, but can be mutually reinforcing.'[1]

A *third* issue is that places are increasingly responsible for their own marketing. Local places will be empowered to find strategies that stand out in a marketplace crammed with competitors. This challenge is the natural outcome of a Europe that is highly competitive and locally based. The winners under these rules will organise their places to maximise their marketing impact. Places will turn to self-audits or commission audits, seek outside monies for goals, build meaningful buyer/seller relationships, market and manage their infrastructure, and skilfully promote their products. All these marketing efforts may appear overwhelming to particularly small or historically under-marketed places. However, place success stories abound all over Europe, as strong leadership and systematic marketing applications often overcome size and location problems.

The *fourth* issue is the integration of information technology – the infostructure – into the marketing plan. The pace of technology is so rapid that it enables even the smallest place to access new markets. Many places will face the dilemma of deciding when to buy into technologies and at what costs. Technology greatly increases the opportunities for communities to grow. For example, location is now a negotiable consideration for many industries and services. Technology enables places worldwide, for the first time, to compete on a level playingfield for a large number of jobs that were previously confined to major markets.

The *fifth* issue concerns the importance of managing the communication process. The marketing of places involves image-making, promotion and information distribution. Technology has facilitated the use of the Internet, fax and desktop publishing, but all these breakthroughs demand the management of communication skills and strategies. Many places will be developing image campaigns, writing proposals and speaking over a wide variety of media. All these responsibilities demand an understanding of how the communication strategy is integral to the overall marketing plan.

All of these issues are now set in a competitive context that can only be characterised as intense. There are many more places that are willing and capable of developing place strategies. In Europe alone there are over 102,000 communities, 1,000 regions and millions of places. The influence of the multinational companies and the emergence of the worldwide market impels every community to assess its identity. The global economy with its unrelenting movement towards interconnected goods and services creates a greater urgency for excellence and a higher standard of performance for all places. Rosabeth Moss Kanter in her book, *World Class: Thriving Locally in the Global Economy*, implores places to upgrade their education and training systems, export efforts, and all of their critical place encounters to meet the global challenge.[2] The higher standards require that communities recognise their strengths and weaknesses and systematically upgrade their services and products.

A bottom-up approach to the European growth challenge

For the purpose of developing a European concept of placemarketing, our focus follows a 'bottom-up' process of how places, communities and regions manage to compete in the new, globalised economy. We have researched how scores of individual places in Euroland are managing to improve their competitiveness and secure economic growth. While Europe as a whole is facing formidable growth problems, there are European 'hotspots' which can teach other places how to achieve a positive growth spiral. Such lessons are vital since the old scourge, 'Euro-sclerosis', is haunting Europe. Unemployent rates of 10–20 per cent are common in different European countries and regions. Yet many of their capitals refuse – or do not know how – to take the steps that may free the continent's energy for long-term economic growth.

Back in 1993 the Commission of the European Communities introduced its White Paper called *Growth, Competitiveness, Employment: The Challenges and Ways Forward into the 21st Century* in the following way: 'This White Paper sets out to foster debate and to assist decision-making – at decentralised, national, or Community level – so as to lay foundations for sustainable development of the European economies, thereby enabling them to improve their competitiveness and create the millions of jobs that are needed.'[3] The document reflected the cautionary testament of the Commission's former chairman Jacques Delors about the worrying signals concerning low growth and high unemployment. He painted this picture of economic stagnation:

1. The European economy's potential rate of growth has shrunk from around 4 per cent to around 2.5 per cent a year.
2. Unemployment has been rising from cycle to cycle.
3. Europe's competitive position in relation to the USA and Japan has deteriorated in terms of employment and share of export markets.

These macro-observations form the European challenge expressed from Brussels. However, the challenge is no longer limited to the current member states of the European Union comprising the 'internal market' of Europe and 372 million consumers – but eventually an expanded market of 500 million after enlargement.[4] With already 16 million enterprises this market represents the largest economic entity in the world. The problems are felt from the Urals to Portugal, from Rome to the Kola Peninsula. The questions are: How should Europeans improve their investment climate? Which new methods should be tried in order to create new jobs? As questions of this type are more often raised, one can notice an increased European interest and openness towards new solutions often worked out on a local or regional level.

A 1996 document, *Employment in Europe*, from the European Commission warns: 'The pace of change in Europe causes insecurity among people. It can cause our institutions, sometimes, to look like puzzled spectators, rather than the managers of change.'[5] Such insecurity is even more obvious when being confronted with later OECD (1997) macro statistics in Figure 1.1. The jobless queues are now reaching record levels in Europe.

The European insecurity, the puzzled spectators and the problems of managing change are obvious on a *macro* level. On the other hand, there is another structure on the *micro* level that suggests how to manage change. One can find thousands of positive growth communities and dynamic local clusters that are unevenly spread all over the European continent. For example, 9 million jobs were created in Europe between 1986 and 1990. However, these newly

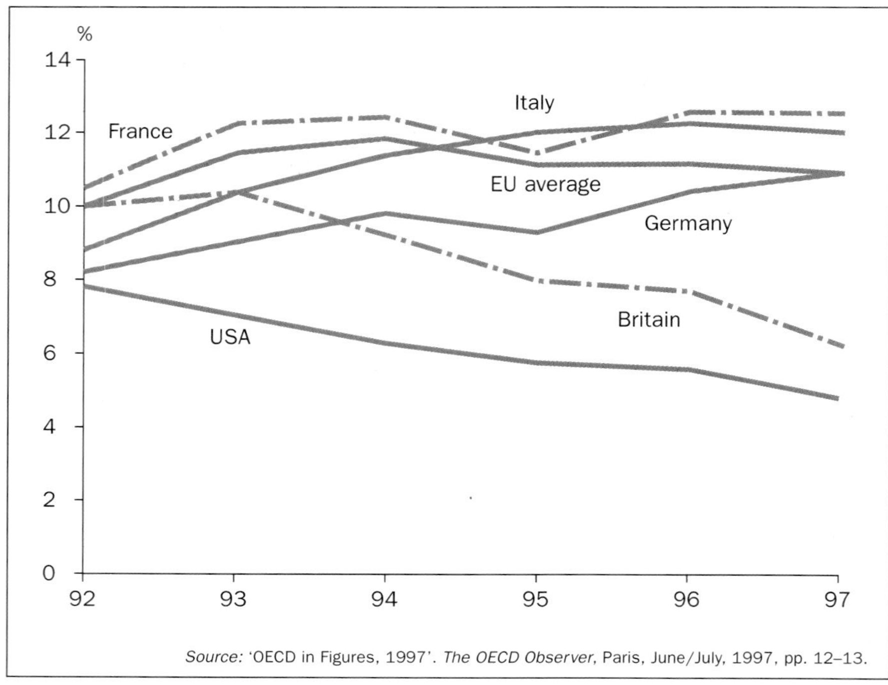

Source: 'OECD in Figures, 1997'. *The OECD Observer*, Paris, June/July, 1997, pp. 12–13.

Fig 1.1 ◆ Unemployment on macro levels

created jobs were often related to new businesses started in fast-growing places where they create an attractive cluster climate. Many winning places are the generators of these new businesses and are not suffering from the structural problems described in the Brussels White Paper and many other macro observations. These high-achieving places can provide European communities, cities, and regions positive examples of how to maintain effective place-marketing strategies.

The overall unemployment situation in Europe should not overshadow the fact that many successful places are confronted with problems to attract employable people. This raises a long-term challenge: over the next twenty years Europe runs the risk of massive decrease of the labour force. This challenge was addressed in 1998 by the European Commission in a report called *Towards a Society for All Ages*,[6] which concluded: 1) The number of young people is quickly decreasing in many nations and regions (–11 million). In certain parts of Germany, Italy, Spain, and France young people make up only 25 per cent of the total population. Simultaneously, the ageing population is shifting more and more into retirement. Facing these trends, many European places end up in a new situation where not unemployment but the lack of employable people – is felt as the number one obstacle. Even in this new situation, strategic market planning is the answer. Attracting residents may well become as common as attracting investments.

Economic analyses on macro levels, such as nations and mega-regions, tend to overlook the complex realities underlying the development of local strategies for growth. The broad sweep, symbolised by the classic European investment 'banana' (Figure 1.2, p. 6), prevents our discovering how a growth dynamic is created and flourishes. In traditional post-war thinking, Europe was regarded as a high-growth 'banana' which started in northern Italy or the so-called Sun Belt of southern France, moved north towards Austria/Switzerland, encompassed southern Germany and Paris, and ended in south-east London.

Today, the 'banana map' is no more. Instead one can see a new *cluster growth map*' of Europe (Figure 1.3, p. 7). One discovers many significant as well as unexpected clusters of excellence spread all over Europe. The Cluster Map indicates that successful measures have been taken within a specific European city, community or region. Responding to competitive pressures, these places have developed strategies to increase their attractiveness to investors, industries, residents and visitors.

In this book, we examine and describe strategies which European communities have implemented to achieve a stronger position in the European placemarket. Many European places with weak place identity can reverse their decline and experience a rebirth and revitalisation through the process of strategic market planning.

Fig 1.2 ◆ The Classic European 'banana map'

Placemarketing outside Europe

Many places outside of Europe have achieved significant identity and growth through applying the principles of strategic market planning. Among them is Singapore which aims to reach Switzerland's living standard by the end of the century. Singaporean leaders have developed Singapore into a set of core competences whose unique selling propositions include: '*The Best Airport in the World*', '*Half the World's Computer Disk Drives are Made here*', '*World's Second-busiest Port*.' Singapore has also staked out a position as a regional '*Brain Capital*', '*Financial Capital*,' and '*Medical Capital*.'

The city of Bangalore, the new 'Software City' in India, is another telling example from Asia. Many high-tech firms, including IBM and Microsoft, have contracted for millions of lines of code to be written by highly qualified Indian software firms.

In the USA, cities such as St Paul, Indianapolis and Baltimore are prospering after a period of stagnation. The state of North Carolina, which forty years ago was the second poorest state of the USA, today provides an exceptionally

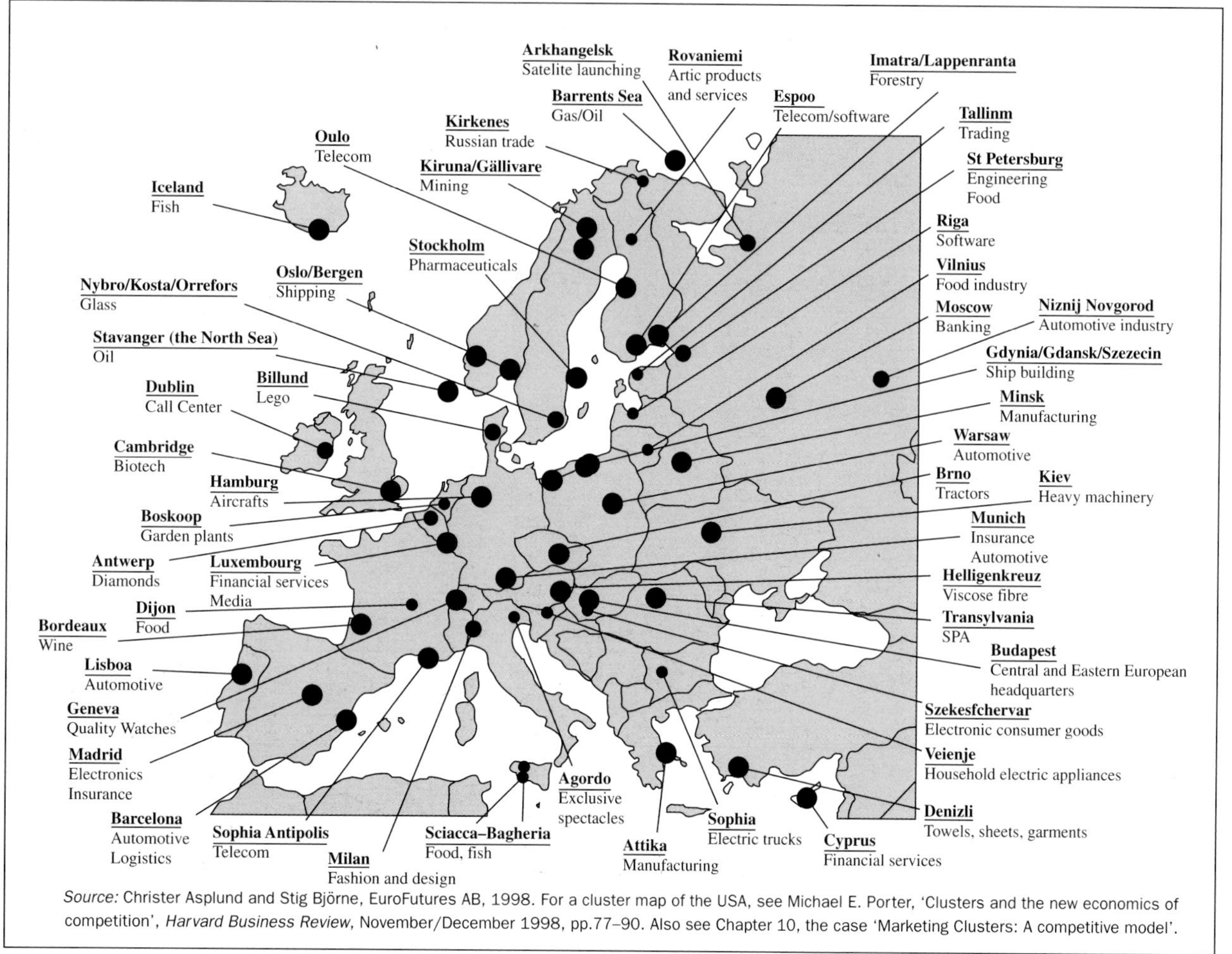

Source: Christer Asplund and Stig Björne, EuroFutures AB, 1998. For a cluster map of the USA, see Michael E. Porter, 'Clusters and the new economics of competition', *Harvard Business Review*, November/December 1998, pp.77–90. Also see Chapter 10, the case 'Marketing Clusters: A competitive model'.

Fig 1.3 ◆ Selected European clusters

attractive business climate. Many European regional and business managers are visiting North Carolina and its successful cities of Durham, Chapel Hill and Raleigh to experience first-hand their strategic placemarketing.

In Latin America, the Brazilian city of Curitiba has won many international awards for its various attraction programmes. New urban transit systems, innovative quality of life plans, high level education, even a waste recycling campaign comprise important elements of a co-ordinated strategic market plan. As a result, foreign inward investments – often from Europe – have boomed and new clusters of industries are emerging.

An example of the radical shifts in the fortunes of places is shown by the decision of IBM to choose four surprising cities to constitute its 'round-the-clock development cycle': Beijing in China, Bangalore in India, Minsk in Belarus and Riga in Latvia. Twenty years ago, the list would probably have included London or Brussels. In a rapidly changing worldwide market, there is opportunity for places to develop a niche and reposition their mix of workers and businesses.

What is Europe?

We will discuss Europe not only as the fifteen member states of the European Union but also as the European continent which covers an area of 10,505,000 km^2. The area extends from the Urals to Portugal and from Rome to the Kola Peninsula. The eastern border is along the foot of the Ural Mountains and along the boundary of Kazakhstan to the Caspian Sea. Turkey is usually regarded as a part of Europe, as are Cyprus, the islands of Madeira, the Azores and the Canary Islands.

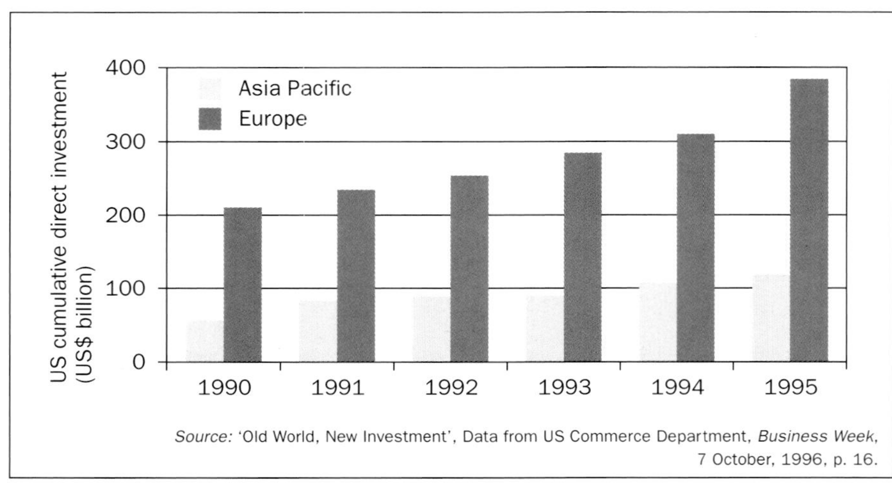

Source: 'Old World, New Investment', Data from US Commerce Department, *Business Week*, 7 October, 1996, p. 16.

Fig 1.4 ◆ Where American investment dollars go

Table 1.1 ◆ Communities in the fifteen states of the EU

Country	*Number of communities*	*Average number of citizens*
France	36,433	1,600
Germany	16,068	5,000
Italy	8,066	7,200
Spain	8,056	4,700
Greece	5,922	1,700
Austria	2,301	3,200
Netherlands	647	23,200
Belgium	589	17,000
UK	480	120,000
Finland	461	10,900
Sweden	289	29,800
Denmark	276	18,800
Portugal	205	32,000
Luxemburg	118	2,900
Ireland	84	41,700
Total in EU states	**79,995**	

Source: Anders Lidstrom, *Community Systems in Europe*, Publica, Stockholm, 1996, p. 152, and updated 1999.

This vast geographical area – at its greatest length 4,340 km – encompasses a market of more than 800 million inhabitants with about sixty different languages. Although, Europe covers only 4 per cent of the total global area, it contains 14 per cent of the population. Altogether it makes up the biggest market in the world in terms of purchasing power. Many investors have been drawn to the economic potential of this market. Over the past six years, American companies alone have ploughed some US$150 billion into Europe and nearly doubled America's investment base to US$364 billion. In fact, the European market has, contrary to conventional wisdom, managed to attract a much higher proportion of American investments than the economies in Asia (Figure 1.4).

Based on our definition of Europe we are talking about more than 100,000 communities. Table 1.1 illustrates Europe's 'mass army' of local units.

As indicated in Table 1.1, there are about 80,000 communities within the fifteen member states of the European Union. In the three non-EU member countries – Switzerland, Norway and Iceland – one finds as many as 3,000 (Switzerland), 454 (Norway) and 196 (Iceland) communities, some of which are extremely small in terms of inhabitants.

In Central and Eastern Europe – but excluding Russia, Ukraine and

Belarus, where there are no comparable community-level statistics – we can add roughly another 19,000 communities to our European casting list. Thus, with these figures and limitations in mind, Europe contains 102,645 communities. And each community has its own image, problems and positioning possibilities.

Above the local level, Europe contains more than 800 regions. Given all this, the EU has decided to recognise the regional dimension. At the EU heads of state conference in Maastricht in December 1991, member countries agreed to form a region committee with an advisory brief. Representatives of regions and communities would play a formal role in the EU's decision-making process. This agreement was supported by the Assembly of European Regions (AER) and the Council of European Municipalities and Regions (CEMR). The outcome was called the Committee of the Regions, and it is made up of 222 full members drawn from local and regional authorities within member states of the EU. The Committee acts as 'the natural guarantor of subsidiarity, the principle that decisions should be taken by public authorities at a level as close as possible to the citizen. The Committee wants this principle to be applied at all institutional levels: European bodies and institutions, member states, regions, and local authorities.'[7]

The principle of subsidiarity focuses on the struggle throughout Europe to form diversity, preserve local traditions and operate through self-rule. As an example, consider the British government's proposal in July 1997 to devolve power from Westminster to a 129-member body to be called a 'parliament' in Edinburgh, Scotland. Other European units – cities, communities and regions – are trying to develop their own strategies for the future. Millions of local and regional decision-makers are involved. The common denominator today is the struggle for more jobs. Naturally, expectations increase when new investments and positive job-creation efforts are announced on the market.

Many cities, communities and regions have managed to attract new investments, which have created success stories that in turn provide stimulation to other places. Public interest in a story seems to be even greater if a region has managed to outbid another region. When, in 1996, BMW decided to invest in north Warwickshire in the UK, instead of Austria, it created headlines because US$600 million were to be spent on this greenfield project.

Additional investments are now pouring into Europe and the trends are promising:

1. The flow of foreign direct investments (FDI) to the countries of Western Europe accounted for 30–50 per cent of global inflow of FDI during the 1990s. Foreign investors find it important to be well established in the internal market.[8]
2. A more deregulated European market is now open for new companies and investors which has created a restructuring boom. Previous monopolies

are disappearing, for example, in the fields of telecommunications, energy and railways, leaving room for new initiatives and enterprises. A restructuring boom is following.

3. Privatisation, especially in Eastern Europe, opens opportunities for new investors.
4. A large number of mega-investments are regularly announced in the European business press. This information quickly spreads among local and regional decision-makers. Consider the 1997 announcement of investment in South Wales by the South Korean electronics company the LG Group, which was said to reach a level of US$2.65 billion and to create 6,100 jobs. The Welsh Development Agency adds: 'The LG Group is joining 360 other foreign companies such as Sony and Toyota in choosing Wales for their European investment.'[9]

Conclusions

The challenge to excel in the European and global marketplace has never been greater. In the past, Europe has not been without placemarketing strategies. However, those past strategies have been characterised by heavy public subsidies, limited public/private partnerships, public officials without any commercial experience, and much use of non-innovative endeavours. These approaches no longer work. An accelerating pace of change will result in winners and losers all over Europe. The ultimate threat is a global economy with world-class competition, fewer restrictions and unexpected events. Inevitably, these new factors create enormous opportunities for the local decision-makers who are willing to face two basic questions:

1. How can we be successful in the European arena in attracting investments, residents, and visitors?
2. Where can we find successful marketing strategies to guide our own planning?

The next chapter identifies the problems and solutions that places face in global competition.

2

European places in trouble

What is happening to places?

Almost all European places are experiencing problems, but some more than others. The situations fall along a continuum. At the most desperate extreme are places that are *dying or are chronically depressed*. Many such places have emerged in Europe as a result of recent decades of economic crises and industrial restructuring. These depressed places lack even the internal resources to launch a recovery. Some small places and cities have lost their major industry or business and are plagued with high unemployment, boarded-up shops and abandoned property. As a consequence, people and businesses migrate and leave a weakened tax base from which the community is supposed to fund schools and many other public services. In too many cases, crime and drugs take over the life of these places and further accelerate the decline. Charleroi in the region of Wallonia, Belgium, with its lost coal and steel cluster, is a vivid illustration of a ravaged place. In this case the city has sadly managed to become notorious for its depressed situation with high unemployment and crime. Reversing such a reputation on the placemarket can take decades.

There are also *acutely depressed* places that nonetheless have some potential for revival. Places such as Liverpool in the UK, Seville in Spain – the site of the World Expo 1992, and Gothenburg on the Swedish west coast, have experienced hard times. While the bad news is that their debts and problems keep worsening, the good news is that these places possess historical, cultural, commercial and perhaps even political assets that could support a turnaround if the right leadership and vision should emerge.

Other places have *boom and bust characteristics*. These places, as a result of their mix of industries and growth companies, are highly sensitive to business cycle movements. Luxembourg is a European example of a place that after the Second World War shifted focus from steel production to bank and insurance services and media. This cluster created the concept of Luxembourg as

'*Mediaport Europe*'.[1] Steel production in Luxembourg in 1970 represented almost one-third of its GNP; by 1996 steel production represented only 7 per cent, and two-thirds of the steel jobs had disappeared.[2] Today bank, insurance and media dominate employment among Luxembourg's 400,000 residents. Attractive tax regulations make this package even more desirable in the marketplace. Yet one may well ask what will happen with Luxembourg's bank and insurance commitments in light of the development of increasingly shared economic policies in Europe. The EMU and new harmonised tax rules threaten to upset Luxembourg's future development. Several other financial centres in Europe – for instance Frankfurt, London and now also Dublin and Prague – threaten to take over market segments from Luxembourg. And there is increasing competition from unlikely places such as Malta where Malta Financial Service Centre markets itself as a place with a '*World-class Climate*'. The message from Malta is: '*Where Money Works Harder*'[3] – a value-added position combining a warm sun and cold euros.

On the brighter side of Europe, we find many places that have undergone *healthy transformations*. These places have devised effective placemarketing plans to create new conditions that improve their attractiveness. Glasgow in Scotland transformed itself from a gritty industrial city into a museum destination reflected in the slogan '*An Arts Capital of Europe*'. Using the arts metaphor as an anchor, Glasgow went even further by renovating its old industrial structures into new ones. Two examples of major European transformations are Sheffield and Frankfurt (see Exhibit 2.1 and 2.2).

Stripping in Sheffield

EXHIBIT 2.1

In the 1997 film *The Full Monty* a group of out-of-work Sheffield, England, steelworkers resorted to stripteasing to restore their self-image. The men were victims of the steel industry's decline in the 1970s and 1980s. While not a completely accurate reflection of Sheffield's decline, the film version dramatised what can happen to workers' lives when a place fails to maintain its job base. The film struck a comic nerve and became a major world hit. Choosing Sheffield as the location made the film's theme doubly powerful.

The long established name of Sheffield cutlery had served not only as a powerful brand image but also as an important marketing asset for the town. Representing a 700 year old history of tradition and quality, the worldwide strength of the Sheffield name has served the city as one of its only defences against global competition and industry decline. Once home to three hundred cutlery companies, Sheffield's strength in this industry has been diminished as competition and historic trends have reduced this number to twelve. Since the late 1950s, an estimated 28,000 jobs have been eliminated.

The cutlery industry had long relied on the twin marketing strategy of brand image and product quality to boost sagging sales; however, this alone was not enough. To remain competitive in the global marketplace, manufacturers had to adapt to the mass market. Manufacturer Richardson Sheffield has based its strategy on technological innovation by selling the popular Laser brands as a high quality and mass-market product. Arthur Price of

England positions itself at the market's high end by employing a strategy that appeals to a younger market – selling designer-led cutlery with coloured handles in department store outlets.

Today, following a series of infrastructure renovations and improvements, Sheffield is on the rise. Employing a long-term transformation strategy including job retraining; rebuilding sewers, roads, docks and plants; and the broadening of manufacturing and service industries, has made Sheffield a late-1990s success story. The Sheffield Development Corporation spearheaded the launching of 18,000 new jobs and £638m of private investments. David Hall, chief executive of Firth Rixon, a metal processing business, summarised the transformation: 'When the city was dying, we didn't want to know. We would not have stayed if the city had not regenerated. We have six factories in the UK and two in the US. We moved our headquarters to Manchester but returned to Sheffield because we can now be proud of the place.'[1]

Sources: 1. Ian Hamilton Fazey, 'An effective example of industrial regeneration', *Financial Times*, 28 February 1997 (Lexis Nexis).
Richard Wolffe, 'Comfort zone built on branding', *Financial Times*, 28 February 1997 (Lexis Nexis).

From 'Krankfurt' to 'Bankfurt' – Frankfurt positions itself as Europe's financial capital

EXHIBIT 2.2

When it comes to finding a unique selling proposition, Frankfurt has taken on an ambitious approach. Rather than market itself around its wealth of history and culture or its reputation as a European trade fair centre, Frankfurt has set loftier goals: it seeks to become *the financial capital of Europe.*

Frankfurt is already well positioned to stake such a claim. Frankfurt is home to over 400 banks (over half are foreign), 770 insurance companies, a stock market that accounts for 70 per cent of Germany's stock and bond turnover, and Europe's busiest airport. The city employs over 50,000 people in the banking and credit sector alone. Since Germany's reunification, Frankfurt has challenged London for Europe's top spot by undertaking a series of government-sponsored reforms which the futures and equity markets appreciate. Imposing supervisory control against insider trading, lifting reserve requirements and encouraging private German companies to list on the exchange have all worked to make Frankfurt more attractive to investors. State-of-the-art electronic trading methods speed trades and signal to the market that Frankfurt is seeking every edge to be competitive.

Moreover, Frankfurt's competitive advantage is the single European currency. Many European companies will be compelled to locate, invest and list themselves in Frankfurt, home to the new European Central Bank, which offers a favourable exchange rate for the redenomination of shares. Evidence of the strategy's success is reflected in the merger plans of the London and Frankfurt stock exchanges. In early 1999 the Frankfurt-based Eurex became the world's busiest futures exchange when its trading volume exceeded that of the Chicago Board of Trade. And as long as Britain remains absent from European financial unification, Frankfurt's position can only improve.

Behind all of Frankfurt's financial positioning lies an important marketing strategy. Frankfurt put forth a broad vision on a global scale, then capitalised on the strength of its ▶

▶ pre-existing resources through careful government planning to move towards that goal. The future success of Frankfurt now lies with the city's commercial and financial planners; these leaders will determine the success of both the European currency and Frankfurt's financial dominance.

Sources: Frankfurt tourism information, Internet: http://cityinfo.nacamar.de/city/frankfurt/e_commercial.html; Oliver August, 'Don't Mention the Euro as Germany prepares for E-Day to dawn in city'. *The Times*, 15 July 1997 (Lexis Nexis); Kenneth Keefe, 'Frankfurt: the gateway to capital, commerce, and communication in the new Europe', *Business America*, 26 July–9 August 1993, pp. 14–15 (Lexis Nexis); Greg Burns, 'Eurex volume pops up above Board of Trade's', *Chicago Tribune*, 9 February 1999, p. 3.

Many places in Eastern Europe, such as Prague, Warsaw and Budapest, fall into this category of healthy transformation. The business opportunities following their transformations have been substantial. For example, the housing renovation market in Poland, which for the moment is the biggest in Europe, reached a volume of £2.1 billion in 1996, and it is expected to triple in less than ten years.[4]

Finally, some places deserve the title of *favoured few*. They enjoy a strong position and continue to attract businesspeople, new residents and visitors. Some European places such as Venice, Florence, Paris and Vienna have done this for centuries; but there are always newcomers. The small Jutland community of Billund in Denmark has the lowest taxes in the country and is home to the well-known Legoland. Still, even these favoured few face threats like congestion, pollution and crime.

Why do places land in trouble?

The European continent with its many competing communities, regions and nations is now experiencing extreme economic turbulence. This turbulence is often called the European 'place wars', or 'Standort gegen Standort' in German. One can identify two basic dimensions. First, every place is subject to *internal* growth and decline cycles. Second, every place may experience *external* shocks and forces beyond its control.

Internal forces leading places into trouble

Many places experience a period of growth followed by a period of decline, and the fluctuations may be repeated several times. The growth period inevitably ends because growth lays the seeds of its own destruction. The decline period will also end, but for different reasons. The processes underlying growth and decline dynamics can occur independently of the business cycle stage. However, these processes may be accelerated by sudden changes in the economic climate.

Figure 2.1 illustrates a well-documented *place-growth dynamic*. Imagine a place that is initially attractive. It might be blessed with expanding industries, an exceptional climate, natural beauty, or a remarkable historical heritage.

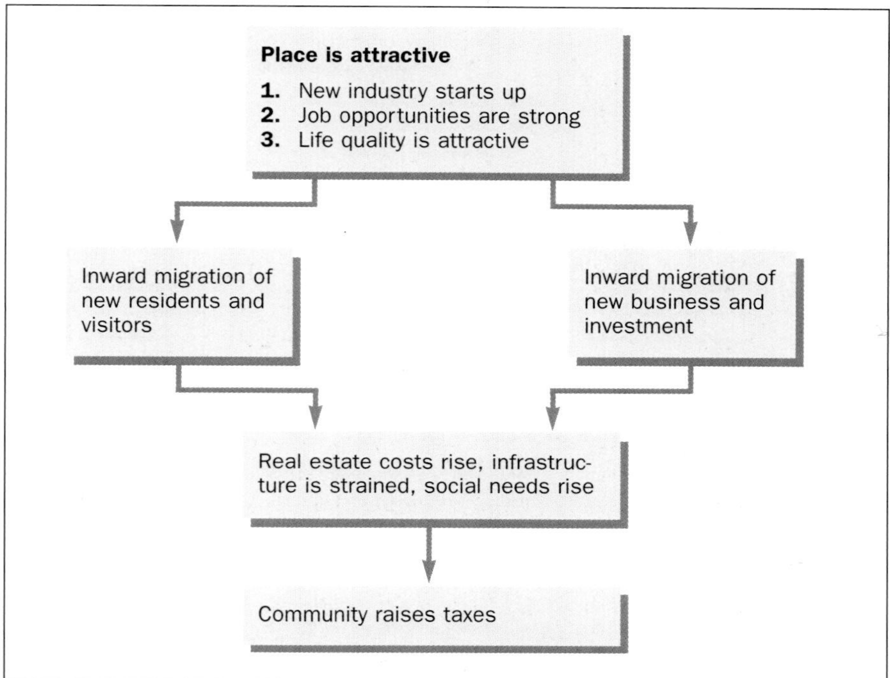

Fig 2.1 ◆ Place-growth dynamics

Assuming that job opportunities are strong and the quality of life is appealing, this place inevitably attracts new residents, visitors, business firms and investments. The inward migration of people and resources raises housing and real estate prices and strains the existing infrastructure and social service budget. We recognise this process from observing many European cities such as Paris and London. The city will typically raise taxes on residents and businesses to pay for the needed expansion of transportation, communication, energy and social resources. Some residents and businesses begin to move out of the city to lower their costs; therefore the tax base is reduced. Ironically, the very state of being an attractive place may unleash forces that ultimately unravel the attractiveness of a place.

As a place begins to lose its attractiveness, forces are released that worsen the situation (see place-decay dynamics in Figure 2.2). A major company or organisation in a specific community might falter or depart. Jobs decline and real estate prices fall. Soon the infrastructure deteriorates. These developments accelerate the outward migration of residents and businesses. Banks tighten credit and bankruptcies rise. Joblessness leads to more crime and drug abuse, and social needs increase. The image of the place becomes further tarnished. The community raises taxes to maintain or improve the infrastructure and to meet social needs, but the higher taxes only accelerate the out-migration of resources.

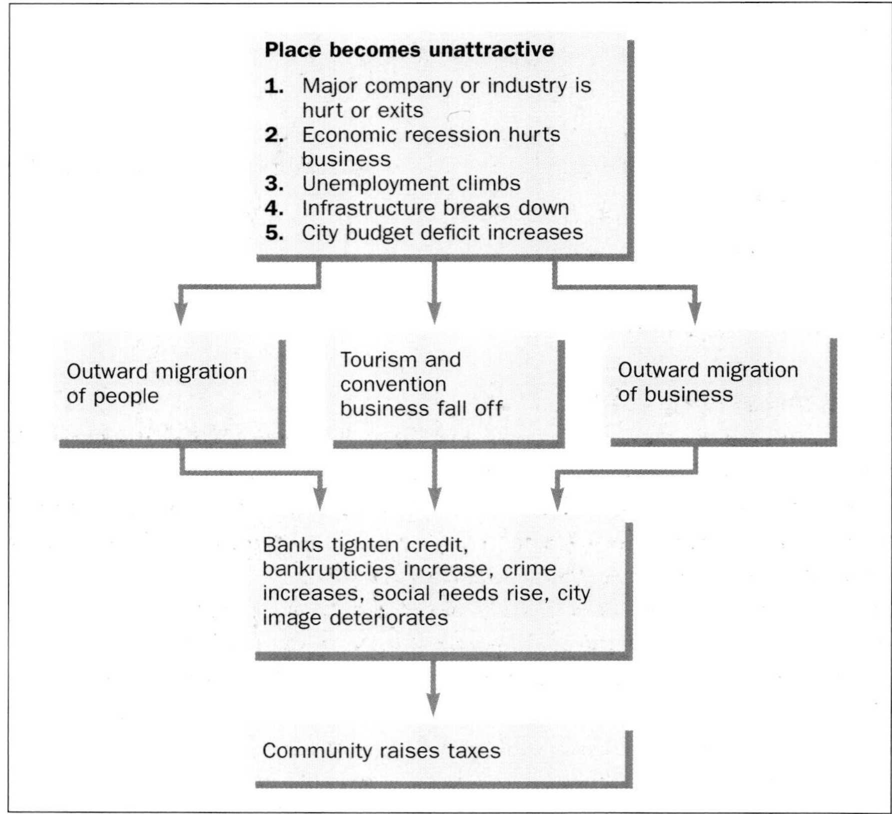

Fig 2.2 ◆ Place-decay dynamics

Unfortunately, the European map depicts numerous place decay examples. Consider the beautiful French region of Auvergne at the heart of the Massif Central. It began to decay in the 1980s after benefiting from a thirty-year period of growth. During the 1980s, the agricultural sector experienced a downturn, and the huge tyre manufacturer Michelin (20,100 employees) announced substantial job cuts. No contingency strategy was prepared, and the region failed to provide political unity and leadership that could sustain a new growth direction and image. Young people started to move out; 10,000 residents left during the 1980s; 23,000 jobs disappeared between 1982 and 1990. Unemployment increased, especially among women and those under 25. Early retirement was enforced, and one-third of the jobless remained unemployed for a year or more.[5] All of these problems have resulted in public deficits, bad image and a need to raise taxes. The challenge for Auvergne is to halt this decay process and to outline a growth strategy that can strengthen new industries. Since the region is the second most important spa region in France, efforts are now being directed towards the improvement of the tourism industry.

External forces leading places into trouble

Places are also shaken by major forces in the external environment over which they have no control. The three major forces upsetting the economic equilibrium of communities are:

1. Rapid technological change
2. Global competition
3. Political power shifts

Rapid technological change

In the nineteenth century, Europe was the centre of the Industrial Revolution. English cities such as Manchester, Sheffield and Liverpool enjoyed immense wealth. But the industries on which they were based soon migrated to other areas with more favourable economics. During most of the twentieth century, the great automobile factories of Germany were located near natural and worker resources. Today, new technologies and manufacturing innovations allow vehicles of the same quality to be produced not only in Eastern and Southern Europe, but also in Alabama and Mexico. No matter the place of origin, these vehicles have a special European feel that motorists in other countries recognise as a differentiated attribute.

On the threshold of the twenty-first century, all of Europe is discussing how to exploit the new information technologies. Places and communities throughout the continent are trying to identify their information technology (IT) position. Many European nations, regions, and communities are eagerly looking for a unique role to play in this information society. When companies such as Canon advocates '*Work–Where–You–Want*', it stimulates the race to compete. The region of Wales, for example, has managed to establish thousands of new jobs in the IT field. The Silicon Glen in Scotland is another site where over 500 software companies have emerged. And according to the European Commission, the Minitel has created 350,000 new jobs in France.

Thousands of European-based projects and programmes have been launched in order to stimulate the application of new technologies. Top-level seminars in Europe promote new possibilities under themes like '*information society: on the threshold of the new millennium*' and in far-reaching proposals like teleworking, distance learning and road traffic management which are offered by Martin Bangemann, Commissioner for Industry, Information Technology and Telecommunications of the European Commission. The city of Stockholm has taken up Bangemann's proposals in an IT policy called 'The Bangemann Challenge' where the city argues in the following terms: 'Stockholm challenges all other cities in Europe half its size or larger',[6] claiming it will lead the implementation of all recommendations stated in the Bangemann Report. An ever-increasing number of local decision-makers are taking part in these meetings. The questions are action-oriented: How shall we act in order to join the club of peak performers? What is our unique IT image going to be?

Places are now beginning to feel the full impact of the revolution in technology and communication. The old notion that only mega-cities such as London or Frankfurt can lead in finance or information services is no longer valid. These services could just as well turn up in Prague, Dublin or Krakow. Internationally high-ranked cities may eventually find themselves facing serious competition from smaller places like, for example, Silicon Glen in Scotland. The map of European hotspots is full of surprises owing to new technologies that are seized by localities seeking to build a strategy for growth.

Global competition

Cities and regions in Europe are not only competing with each other but also facing competition from other global locations. Europe's textile and electronics industries have been seriously damaged by global competitors from the Far East. Today, for example, Kuala Lumpur is setting itself up as a '*Multimedia Super Corridor*' with over 16,000 employees working in this new Asian version of Silicon Valley. The government of Dubai announced a new '*Plan for Growth*' (see Figure 2.3) which builds on the momentum of the 700 international companies that have established themselves in Dubai over the past four years. This remote country offers a tax-free market – with no corporate or income taxes – and no foreign exchange controls, along with an expanding market. European places must now compete for investments and production with places as far away as Kuala Lumpur, Dubai and others.

According to an Organization for Economic Co-operation and Development (OECD) study, globalisation leads to greater specialisation of regions and places. The OECD data demonstrate that incoming foreign investment reinforces patterns of regional specialisation in 60–70 per cent of cases.[7] This implies that regions geared towards a particular industry have a higher chance of attracting further specialized investment. Thus, an important task for regional policy-makers is to clarify which industries they should support in accordance with their relative strengths and weaknesses.

For the first time, some of the smallest European cities and regions are competing in a global marketplace. Following the Second World War, Europe

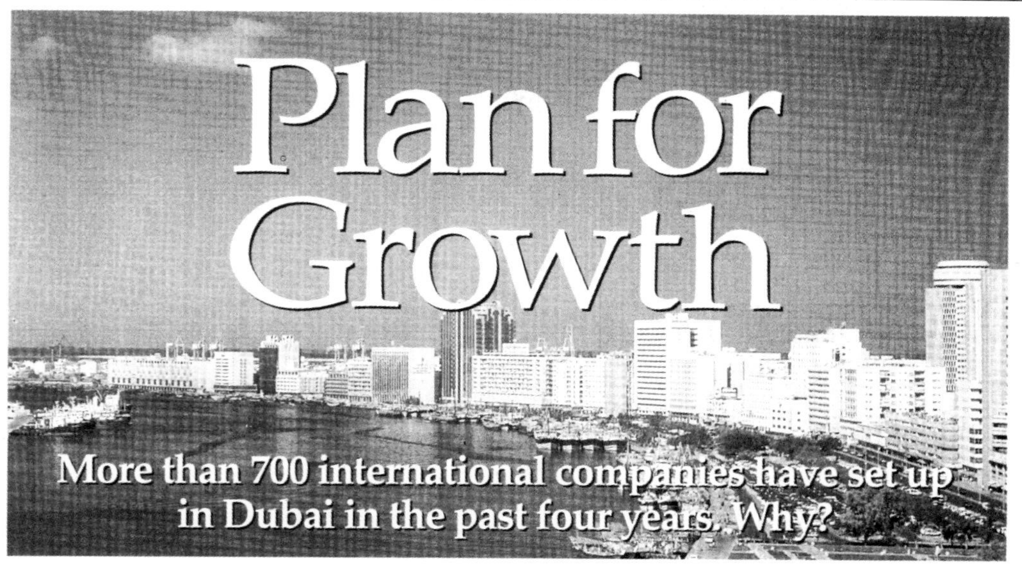

The Potential

- **A large market** - gateway to a region with $150+ billion annual imports.
- **A growing market** - Dubai's imports doubled since 1990; strong regional economic growth expected.
- **A prosperous market** - strategic location at the heart of one of the world's richest regions.
- **An expanding market** - trading hub for emerging economies in the Middle East, CIS, Central Asia, the subcontinent and Africa.
- **A diversified market** - wide import requirements; opportunities for suppliers of most products.

The Incentives

- **A tax free market** - no corporate or income taxes.
- **A liberal market** - no trade barriers; no foreign exchange controls; low or zero import duties; 100% foreign ownership in the Jebel Ali and Airport Free Zones.
- **An efficient market** - state-of-the-art telecommunications; first class infrastructure facilities.
- **An established market** - well developed banking and services sector; regional conference and exhibition centre.
- **An accessible market** - served by 120 shipping lines and 80 airlines.
- **A cosmopolitan market** - superb quality of life and accommodation; top class education, health and recreation facilities.

Decide on Dubai

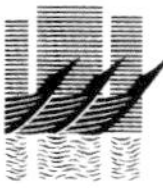

GOVERNMENT OF DUBAI
DEPARTMENT OF TOURISM AND COMMERCE MARKETING

125 Pall Mall, London SW1Y 5EA, U.K. Brochure line (24 hours) Tel: (0171) 839-0581

Source: *The Economist*, 5 April, 1997.

Fig 2.3 ◆ Plan for growth

focused on urban and business reconstruction. The Marshall Plan, which focused on sixteen Western European nations, increased reconstruction resources and simultaneously magnified the struggle between East and West. At the time a *global* strategy was not so important, as local and national issues overshadowed place decisions.

The fall of the Berlin Wall and the growing internal market, stimulated by the Common Market, have intensified the amount of place competition. With the promise of all kinds of benefits, places have sought out and courted corporations to locate in their areas. Places needed to show their best face in terms of reliable and cost-effective labour supply, attractive housing and educational opportunities, friendly government treatment and stability, and whatever else may have been assessed to maximise attractiveness.

Political power shifts

Extensive debates about the appropriate role of government intervention into troubled places and industries have been on the rise at all levels of the public sector – city, community, regional, national and European – owing to technological advances and global competition. The European unemployment situation is one factor that has raised public interest in government intervention – but how and of what type?

On a European level, an important intervention is coming from the EU's regional funds. We should not underestimate the importance of this effort. It sets the standard for all of Europe. There are three structural funds: the European Regional Development Fund (ERDF), the European Social Fund (ESF) and the European Agriculture Guidance and Guarantee Fund (EAGGF). A willingness of the funds to intervene is mirrored in the fact that these three funds alone have increased substantially, from ECU 7 billion, or 19 per cent of the EU budget in 1987, to ECU 23 billion or 30 per cent of the EU 1995 budget. According to the EU itself, the goal is to increase this type of effort and bring the structural funds up to 33 per cent of the EU 1999 budget.[8]

Development priorities include promoting the manufacturing sector, modernising infrastructures for communications, telecommunications, energy and water supplies, research and development, vocational training, business services, and so on. Intervention in the market is, in other words, as considerable in its breadth of activity as in its economic resources. In this regard, EU politics have been a major player in the allocation of resources, consequently places must plan for such a powerful and resolute force. The EU importance in place development is reflected in the fact that a large number of regions have established their own offices in Brussels.

On a *national level* there are many sophisticated intervention programmes to encourage new behaviours both regionally and locally. Great Britain's Conservative revolution under Margaret Thatcher set in motion a complete reorientation towards a less regulated and more market-oriented economy – as in her support of the well-endowed Welsh Development Agency. Two decades later, under the slogan '*Labour is Good for Business*', the Labour Party is back in power with Tony Blair. Acknowledging the forces of change, Blair asserts: 'Change is the blood and bones of the British – we are by nature and tradition innovators, adventurers, pioneers.'[9]

On a *local and regional level*, where problems and opportunities are found in concrete form, the political landscape can quickly change. Old personalities can disappear and new ones emerge. A review of the European experience indicates that the most important factor is the capacity of new leadership, more than their 'political colours', to see the necessities and opportunities latent in the global market and to press for a local alignment with these opportunities.

Europe lives in a political climate where increased decentralisation is encouraging local and regional bodies to make decisions. Tony Blair, for example, presented a proposal to Parliament to establish a network of regional development agencies. In this climate the dialogue between local public officials and local business managers is critical. Ideally, the dialogue will continue regardless of changes in the national and local political leadership.

What are places doing to solve their problems?

Troubled places exhibit a variety of responses when confronting their problems. The *first and least desirable response* is to do little in the hope that problems will diminish on their own. Some places even consider their individual situations as a 'divine destiny'. A common pattern is to scramble for more economic resources from the central government or Brussels (or both). Portugal has received massive funding for a number of projects that may appear promising but which, in the long run, lack connectivity and long-term benefits. Such places may see subsidies as their only solution. Their cry is: 'We want our fair share of the pie!' In the end the place's image is built around the key concepts of crisis, unemployment and welfare payments. During the past decade, thousands of European communities and regions embarked on this road. There is even a risk that European regional policies on a national level or from Brussels stimulate this type of response.

The *second response*, in contrast to the first, consists of an ever-increasing number of places husbanding their financial resources while at the same time working out aggressive growth programmes to attract industry, investments and visitors. The aggressive growth programmes consist of grant offerings and other financial incentives to lure investors. The German state of Saxony awarded over US$1 billion in grants to land three highly-sought-after investments. The US semiconductor firm Advanced Micro Devices received a

US$544 million grant and in return built a US$1.9 billion plant. Siemens chose Saxony instead of the UK for the same reason.

Today, many European communities offer competing incentive packages. Unfortunately, these packages represent promotion programmes rather than systematic marketing programmes. Marketing would call for more comprehensive problem diagnosis and planning, of which promotion is only a small part.[10]

A *third response* focuses on developing sophisticated informal measures to prevent businesses moving away from their current place. When an enterprise signals place discontent to local, regional or national decision-makers, intensive discussions often follow in an attempt to find an agreeable solution. At this point it is often too late. In 1997, Ericsson, the Swedish telecommunications giant, announced its plans to move headquarters with a staff of four hundred out of Stockholm and into London. Lars Ramqvist, Ericsson's CEO at that time, complained that Ericsson found it difficult to recruit staff to Sweden owing to Sweden's high personal taxes. Since Ericsson is seen as a crown jewel, the threat caused an intense debate. Although Ramqvist's plans were immediately criticised (especially by Social Democrats) less than twenty-four hours after the Ericsson announcement, the minister of commerce (also a Social Democrat) explained that he was prepared to introduce a special tax reduction for expatriates. However, the Ericsson discontent was so great that a decision was made in 1998 to move the company's headquarters to London.

A *fourth response* is to compete by investing in expensive attractions in the area. The project could be a new cultural centre (for example Centre Pompidou in Paris), a World Expo (for example Seville in Spain) a huge congress centre (as in Leipzig), or a Disneyland Paris. This type of approach is generally characterised by piecemeal *ad hoc* actions that seek a single solution for multifaceted problems. Unfortunately, some of these *ad hoc* investments, as in Seville's case, generate more costs than income. There is a risk in Europe today that this fourth approach may be increasingly seen as the panacea to a place's ills. Desperate local decision-makers tend to rely on *ad hoc* projects that offer no long-term strategy and give a false sense of hope.

A *fifth response* is to undertake strategic market-oriented planning. Here a top-level commission is appointed with mixed representation from the public and private sectors. Together the members examine the place's current and potential strengths, weaknesses, threats and opportunities. They work towards establishing a long-term vision of what the community could be and is capable of achieving in the long run. The period may be defined in terms of five to twenty years. This type of response, strategic market planning, is not limited to just the larger and more resourceful geographical entities. Small and even very troubled places need to take the path as well.

What should places be doing to solve their problems?

A central proposition in this book is that European communities and regions are under heavy pressure owing to competition in both the world market and the European internal market. Places are competing for investors, experts and visitors in a climate which could best be described in terms of a place war. This competition has intensified as Eastern Europe moves into the placemarket arena. Viewing Eastern Europe as an attractive investment alternative to Western Europe, leading carmakers have invested heavily throughout Eastern Europe in new plants. And the general attractiveness is quickly changing. In a survey conducted by real estate consultants Healey and Baker, more than five hundred executives from top European companies were asked about their firm's most likely locations for future European *expansion*.[11] The surveyed executives cited Warsaw, Prague, Moscow and Budapest.

In this turbulent European environment, each place is challenged to deliver something truly superior or *unique* for the marketplace. A place's desire to secure a unique position and positive image in the huge European market is a crucial part of strategic placemarketing. Each place must formulate a combination of offerings and benefits that can meet the expectations of a broad number of investors, new businesses and visitors.

Placemarketing, at its core, embraces four activities:

1. Developing a strong and attractive positioning and image for the community.
2. Setting attractive incentives for current and potential buyers and users of goods and services.
3. Delivering a place's products and services in an efficient, accessible way.
4. Promoting the place's attractiveness and benefits so potential users are fully aware of the distinctive advantages of the place.

Too often, communities fall into the trap of concentrating on only one or two of these marketing activities, often concentrating on the promotion functions. They may spend money on expensive advertisements or an unfocused slogan without first doing the diagnostics and planning.

A fairly common European model is to organise a *planning group* made up of local and/or regional officials from the public sector. Sometimes an external consultant is contracted in order to provide an outsider's perspective and a broader view. However, in order to be successful the planning group should involve representatives from the local business community from the very beginning of the process. Sound planning requires the inclusion of commercial knowledge from early on because collaboration between the public and private sectors is a prerequisite for future success.

When comparing European and American models, one finds that local businesspeople in Europe are less frequently involved in the regional planning process. In the USA a mix between public and private representatives has existed for decades, for example the Economic Development Partnership of Alabama, Arkansas Electric Cooperative Corporation or New York's Empire State Business Alliance. This interactive model includes business partners such as local banks, real estate companies, the local electricity company, telecoms companies, water suppliers and so on. It is inevitable that these types of alliance will continue to emerge in Europe as well.

The planning group's charge is threefold:

1. It must define and diagnose the community's condition. The major strengths and weaknesses of the community should be identified along with major opportunities and threats. (SWOT analysis: see Chapter 5, Place Auditing and Strategic Market Planning, pp. 111–115.)
2. It must develop a vision of long-term solutions based on a realistic assessment of the community's problems. This vision must be founded on a combination of factors that are unique and commercially viable, upon which a value-added process can be started.
3. It must develop a long-term plan of action that involves several intermediate stages of investment and transformation. This so-called *value-added process* takes time. The most successful cases are developed over a 10–15 year period.

Strategic placemarketing involves a number of elements that are shown in Figure 2.4.

The value-added process of a sustained community involves four major marketing steps. *First*, the process must assure that basic services are provided and infrastructure maintained to the satisfaction of citizens, businesses and visitors. *Second*, the place may need new attractions to sustain current business and public support as well as to attract new investments, businesses or people. *Third*, the place needs to communicate its features and benefits through a vigorous image and communication programme. *Fourth*, the place must generate support from its citizens, leaders and established institutions to make the place hospitable and even enthusiastic about attracting new companies, investments and visitors to the community.

These four marketing factors affect the place's success in attracting and satisfying its five potential target markets:

1. Producers of goods and services
2. Corporate headquarters and regional offices
3. Outside investment and export markets
4. Tourism and hospitality
5. New residents

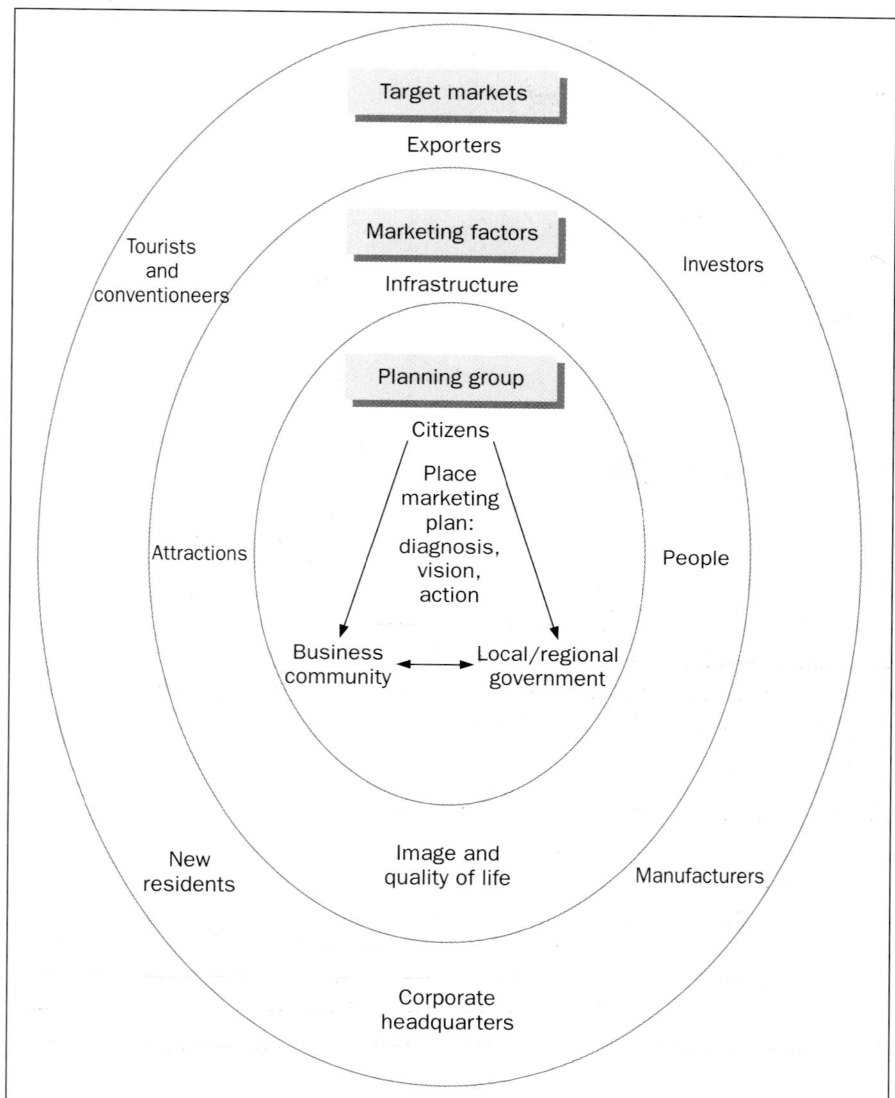

Fig 2.4 ◆ Levels of placemarketing

In the final analysis, the fortunes of places depend on the collaboration of the public and private sectors. European places must learn to build better teamwork among local public units and business firms as well as voluntary and civic associations. Unlike purely business or commercial product marketing, placemarketing requires the active support of public and private agencies, interest groups and citizens. Successful European places will be those that are most skilful in developing collaboration among all players.

A place's potential depends to a lesser degree on location, climate and natural resources than it does on its human will, skill, energy, values and organisation. For example, the possibilities for Norwegian Kirkenes on the top of Europe or Seville in Southern Europe depend increasingly on the places' capability to carry out the following tasks:

1. Interpreting what is happening in the broad environment.
2. Understanding the needs, wants and behaviour choices of specific internal and external constituencies.
3. Knowing the major strengths and weaknesses of the place.
4. Building a realistic and commercially viable vision of what the place can be.
5. Creating a plan of action to complement the vision.
6. Building internal consensus and effective organisation for operational activities.
7. Evaluating the progress being achieved with the action plan.

The smaller and more peripheral the place, the more professional the place must be in handling these tasks.

Conclusions

Place competition in Europe has never been more intense. The market in Europe comprises more than 100,000 communities that in many cases are in head-to-head competition over visitors and business attraction. To complicate matters, Europe is shrinking from a communication point of view, and global competition is growing. The winning places must develop a strong and attractive package of benefits. The rapidly changing market place means that European communities must deliver products that will appeal to carefully targeted audiences. In the next chapter we examine strategies that are designed to reach selected markets.

3

How places market themselves

If we follow today's European press, there is a clear observation to be drawn: places are increasingly competing with other places to attract investments, businesses and visitors. Between 5 and 10 per cent of today's advertising space in newspapers such as the *Financial Times* is devoted to marketing places, regions and nations. In addition, special surveys describing regions and places in detail are published regularly.

The marketing of places has become a leading economic activity. Consider a few examples:

1. The French community of Lille had been seen traditionally as a mining community. This was still true in the 1980s when Lille embarked on the Channel Tunnel project as part of a new strategy to market the community. The strategy resulted in the development of Lille as one of Europe's largest business and commercial centres. As a result of the FFr 5.3 billion investment, the city positions 'itself as offering first-class offices, communication and distribution facilities to companies that want high-speed access to northern Europe's markets.'[1] Today Lille, with Mayor Pierre Mauroy as a driving force, is marketed as 'Euralille,' and a French regional competition chose it, after Paris, as the French place most prepared for the year 2000.

2. The German state of Saarland markets administrative efficiency: 'In contrast to other German states, there is no administrative level between the community and the state government. This assures that business initiative does not get bogged down in bureaucracy.'[2] It is also marketed as a gateway to Germany and France with the slogan: '*In the Very Heart of the European Market*'. The German/French industrial and commercial infrastructure of the area forms an important value proposition. As a result, many foreign investors have selected Saarland. For example:

   The Chamberlain Group (Elmhurst, Illinois) is producing garage door openers; Western Atlas (Beverly Hills, California) is selling industrial automation systems; Johnson Controls (Milwaukee, Wisconsin) has opened a new plant; Winnebago Industries (Forest City, Iowa) is now producing mobile homes in Saarland; the German media giant Bertelsmann has started a joint venture with America Online and is setting up a European competence centre for customer service; and the mail-order company Land's End, Inc. has selected Saarland for its German call-centre.[3]

3. As noted earlier, business enterprises can play an important role in placemarketing. One example is Midland Electricity in Britain. Owing to the increased inward investment in the Midlands, which has led to greater demands for electricity, the company has established itself as an important force in marketing the area. Another variation on this theme is the global company ABB and its role in marketing the '*Greater Zurich Region*'. In the example shown in Figure 3.1, ABB invites you to the '*Paradise of the Greater Zurich Area*'. In spite of being global – or perhaps just because of that – ABB feels a need to identify itself with specific regions. Former CEO of ABB, Percy Barnevik, called this a 'multidomestic' approach.

Economic development has long been a priority of places, communities, regions and nations. A good example is the Hansa League, which at its peak in the thirteenth century covered basically the Baltic Sea region and included more than seventy commercial cities. The Hansa cities of that time generated several marketing actions, especially co-ordination and co-operation. However, there is a wide gap between a collection of actions and systematic placemarketing strategies. Only in the past decade have a few European places shifted from a narrow view of economic development to a broad set of strategies to attract new businesses, retain old ones, develop overseas network, build tourism and attract outside investors. A growing number of places are transforming their *ad hoc* economic campaigns into sophisticated marketing strategies designed to build competitive advantages, create a strong identity, target specific buyers and position the community's resources to respond to specialised buyer needs and desires.

Organising a programme to develop and market a place requires a thorough grasp of target markets. In this chapter, we address three questions: (1) What are the main target markets of placemarketers? (2) How do placemarketers market their place? (3) Who are the major placemarketers?

What are the main target markets of placemarketers?

Places are interested in a particular growth that can contribute to more 'real' jobs and add to the tax base of the place. It is desirable, however, to distinguish

Source: Site Selection, August, 1996.

Fig 3.1 ◆ Welcome to paradise

between the three specific categories of people and businesses that might be drawn to a place:

1. People and businesses worth attracting.
2. People and businesses that are acceptable but do not need to be targeted specifically.
3. People and businesses to avoid or discourage.

Too often, places fail to define whom they want to attract or distinguish among the three categories. Some places have expertly defined their targets – see Exhibit 3.1

There's no business like snow business

EXHIBIT 3.1

What could possibly draw an international market to vacation north of the Arctic Circle in Swedish Lapland? How about the marriage of romance and bone-chilling cold in the unique Jukkasjarvi Ice Hotel. Ready for the public on 1 December and open until after Easter (when it is melted and floats away), the Ice Hotel – the world's largest igloo – is constructed annually with 2,000 tons of snow and 1,000 tons of ice. Showcasing a chapel and a luxury bridal suite, the Ice Hotel has become popular as a one-of-a-kind honeymoon spot for couples who seek a cold-start to their union. Additional attractions include a gallery of ice sculptures, the Absolut Ice Bar, a restaurant, an ice-sauna, and a 'close-up' view of the Northern Lights. Activities offered in connection with the stay include dog-sledding, skiing, helicopter rides, and a two-day snowmobile safari. After spending a night in the Ice Hotel, all visitors receive a survival certificate testifying to their accomplishment in the Arctic Circle.

The Jukkasjarvi Ice Hotel demonstrates an innovative twist on concept integration (tying all the diverse elements into one central theme). By creating a central attraction that encompasses everything that Jukkasjarvi has to offer, the Ice Hotel provides a strong tourism base to an area that otherwise would seem to be a very unlikely vacation destination. By using Japanese ice-artists as a visibility building attraction, the hotel first targeted Japanese tourists, then branched out to a select international market.

According to owner Yngve Bergqvist, the Ice Hotel has 5,000 overnight stays, and 30,000 visitors pay a fee simply to enter. The Ice Hotel demonstrates that a unique sales concept combined with regional concept integration can build a thriving tourist base anywhere – even in the Arctic Circle.

Sources: www.norrbotten.se; www.laplandguide.com; Interview with Yngve Bergqvist, 27 August 1998.

Consider a place such as Florence, Italy that, like Jukkasjarvi, thrives on tourist expenditures. Possessing one of the world's greatest treasure houses of Renaissance art, Florence attracts visitors who want to experience its art, history and cultural life. Yet even this market is a complex one which consists of many different nationalities, ages and income groups: professional groups such as art curators; European historians and their professional associations and conventions; students of Michelangelo, Donatello and other great masters of painting and sculpture; perhaps even business firms in the fields of art supply, paint manufacturing and the graphic arts. This link between the original target group, art-tourists, and more business-like target groups such as design and fashion visitors is now being exploited in Florence.

The potential in the French region of Burgundy is another example to consider. This region has achieved a global reputation in gastronomy and wine, especially for the famous Chablis wines and Dijon mustard. Burgundy exploits its gastronomic image by aggressively marketing to the national and international food industry. In 1997 the region launched the European Centre of Taste Sciences through the University of Burgundy. In a parallel move, research contacts are being established with companies such as Nestlé, Unilever, and Pernod Ricard. Professor Stylianos Nicolaidis, head of the new institute, understands why companies want to connect with Burgundy: 'because it would cost them ten times as much to do this research on their own'.[4]

Now let us examine in detail the four broad target markets of placemarketers in Table 3.1.

Table 3.1 ◆ The four main target markets of placemarketers

1. Visitors	• Business visitors (attending a business meeting or convention, reconnoitering a site, coming to buy or sell something) • Non-business visitors (tourists and travellers)
2. Residents and employees	• Professionals (scientists, physicians, etc.) • Skilled employees • Teleworkers • Wealthy individuals • Investors • Entrepreneurs • Unskilled workers • Senior citizens and pensioners
3. Business and industry	• Heavy industry • 'Clean' industry assembly, high-tech, service companies, etc. • Entrepreneurs
4. Export markets	• Other localities within the domestic markets • International markets

Visitors

The visitors market has expanded both in Europe and globally during the past few decades. It is estimated that the introduction of a single European currency will curb costs and increase European travel and tourism. The greater transparency of air fares as well as hotel rates will force down prices.[5]

The term *travel and tourism* is chosen by the World Travel and Tourism Council (WTTC) to cover both business and leisure markets, domestic and international. This economy sector is already responsible, directly and indirectly, for more than 10 per cent of global GDP and investment. Today, Europe accounts for 35 per cent of global travel and tourism GDP and 38 million travel and tourism related jobs. A closer look at Europe shows that 19 million of these jobs are found within the European Union. The employment prospects in this sector are predicted to increase by some 10 per cent within the EU during the next decade. Eastern Europe employment opportunities account for 37 per cent of the new jobs available.[6]

Furthermore, in specific European nations, regions and places, the travel and tourism sector contributes disproportionately high receipts. In 1995, France had the highest gross receipts from visitors (ECU 19.2 billion) followed by Italy (ECU 18.8 billion) and Spain (ECU 16.5 billion).[7] In 1997, France, Finland and Greece all recorded a 10 per cent increase in nights spent by non-residents.[8]

These national macro figures disguise the micro hotspots which depend almost entirely on their performance in the visitors market. The local economies of places such as Venice (Italy), Salzburg (Austria), Spa (Belgium) and Skagen (Denmark) are based totally on revenue generated from visitors. These places are in a permanent struggle to improve their travel and tourism value. Their strategic objective must be to protect, maintain and improve their position.

The visitors market consists of two broad groups: business and non-business visitors. For placemarketers it is important to prepare to meet these two distinct markets. *Business visitors* congregate in a place to attend a business meeting or convention, to reconnoitre a site, or to buy or sell something. *Non-business visitors* include tourists who want to see the place and travellers who are visiting family and friends. Within these two groups there are a number of important sub-target groups that need to be carefully prioritised.

Unfortunately there is a lack of target prioritising. Tourist brochures are usually sent everywhere to anyone, and one standardised publicity campaign follows another. Instead of employing a professionally developed marketing strategy, placemarketers invest increasing amounts of resources in new tourist brochures or place advertisements without carefully considering market needs and differences.

The concept of *destination development* calls for a place to develop a systematic and long-term marketing strategy directed towards nurturing and developing the natural and potential attributes of the area or region. A central priority in developing such a strategy is to identify the specific target group to which the area should direct its resources.

A destination must continuously create new value. This requires a *value-added process* in which additional benefits are developed to appeal to increasingly specific target groups. The smaller the destination, the more important it becomes to offer something of unique and genuine value. A quick trip around Europe via the Internet already reveals some progress towards specific target group definitions. Some examples are presented in Table 3.2.

The list in Table 3.2 can be long or short, depending on the patience, time and money that the tourist is able to use for exploration. In spite of the fact that Europe has over 100,000 communities, there is always the possibility of identifying a unique combination for each community. Target groups can range from the smallest hobby-interested groups (for example European yodel

Table 3.2 ◆ Specific target groups and resulting appeals

Target group	*Appeals*
Sport fishermen	Fly fishing in Northern European rivers in combination with outdoor living
IT interested	Visit to the CeBIT conference in Hannover where 600,000 people usually participate
Wine lovers	Wine tasting tours starting in French Colmar, 'The Capital of Alsace Wine'
Fashion designers, buyers and related groups	Fashion shows in Milan and Paris
Café lovers and tourists	Visit to Vienna and its traditional café culture
Connoisseurs of fine Italian food	Fine dining tours in Toscani
Beer enthusiasts	Oktoberfest in Munich
Golf enthusiasts	New golf courses with special attributes like Europe's most northerly (Bjorkliden 156 miles north of the Arctic Circle), highest in altitude (Isola, north of Nice, at 2,000 metres)
Physicians	Participation with colleagues in Stockholm's yearly International Physicians' Conference (IPC)
Rose garden enthusiasts	European tour of world famous rose gardens: Rome's Municipal Rose Garden, St Anne's Park in Dublin, Valbyparken in Copenhagen, Parc de la Tête d'Or in Lyons
Train and rail travel enthusiasts	Tour on Switzerland's small alpine railways
Yodellers	Visit to the Yodel Festival in Thun, Switzerland
Children	Family tours of Legoland in Billund, Denmark

Source: Christer Asplund, 'The USP market', *EuroFutures*, Swedbank, Stockholm, 1999.

enthusiasts) to the largest groups (the over 30,000,000 organised European sport fishing enthusiasts) whose hobby interests have great economic potential.

Hannover has done a successful job in targeting and attracting business-people and IT enthusiasts to its annual CeBIT conference. The conference attracts over 600,000 visitors to Hannover and over 7,000 exhibitors. The skilful hosting of this target group can lead to secondary rewards such as the establishment of expert and specialised businesses in the Hannover region. These secondary effects are promoted clearly in Hannover's slogan: '*The World of Technology Revolves Around Hannover*' (Figure 3.2).

In the past decade an interesting phenomenon or megatrend in travel and tourism in Europe has emerged. Places and companies are increasingly high-

Source: Advertisement. *Financial Times*, 16 March 1998.

Fig 3.2 ◆ 'The world of technology revolves around Hannover'

lighting the 'European dimension' in marketing strategies. The current European integration is an obvious explanation of this phenomenon and marketers are seizing the opportunity to articulate a definitive European position. Some examples within the travel and tourism industry are: '*Top of Europe*' (a number of Northern European regions in Norway and Sweden), '*EUROpportunity*' (Austria), EuroTunnel (the tunnel between UK and France), EuroStar (the high-speed train between London and Paris), EuroClass' and 'EuroBonus' (European Airlines), EuroToques (a promotion organisation for European chefs), '*Europe's Cultural City*' (Stockholm 1998), EuroCard (a leading European creditcard), and their magazine '*Euro World*' (often describing European places), Europcar (a car-rental company), EuroLines (Europe's Express Coach Network), Euralille (a new business-centre in the French city of Lille), '*Europe's Largest Trade Mart*' (in Utrecht), '*Arts Capital of Europe*' (Glasgow) and the NBC TV's daily broadcasting, '*What's On in Europe*', a pan-European event service. The long-running Eurovision Song Contest, organised by the European Broadcasting Union, can also be defined as a competition between European places. In 'Mini-Europe', outside Brussels, one can have a convenient tour around Europe in only a few hours. In 1998 more than 3 million visitors walked through the park with its models of 'Europe's Nicest Places'. Places are eager to capitalise on any opportunity for a quick placemarketing fix by using the common market slant as a hook that appeals to the large European market.

These examples show how the assets of a place are used as marketing attributes both by the community itself as well as by commercial enterprises. This strategy has everything to do with the search for an identity. A community or region must create and send 'identity signals' for companies in the travel and tourism industry to easily recognise, understand and communicate to others.

Residents and employees

A second target market for places is residents and employees. During some post-war decades a number of European countries employed a strategy to attract foreign low-skilled labour. Germany, France and Sweden actively recruited foreign low-skilled labour from Italy, Turkey, Algeria and Morocco. Today, priorities are quite different. As European unemployment has increased, the strategy is to recruit highly competent and skilled labour. The search for civil engineers, researchers, multilinguists, inventors, wealthy and healthy seniors, and stable tax-paying residents is an important megatrend.

This strategy takes many forms. An example is the little Swedish community of Oxelosund that began its promotion campaign with 'Citizens Wanted!' At the core of the offer were attractive living places, high quality of life and strategic steps to make the community more attractive. The community even encouraged interested parties looking for more information to call the locally elected mayor at home. This unusual approach to communicating with the market attracted many responses from interested people.

Another example appeared in promotions in London Underground stations. The city of Milton Keynes profiled itself for the young, professional, well-educated people and families that could see the disadvantages of big-city living (see Figure 3.3.) Milton Keynes, a town bathed in greenery, is located an hour's train ride outside central London. It was created in the 1960s and continues to develop with modern workplaces and manifold individualised living alternatives. The integration of up-scale living and working conditions is the primary message that Milton Keynes markets.

The Milton Keynes example makes it clear that placemarketers must determine the mindset of their target group if they want to sell a productive lifestyle and milieu, not just a piece of property. The cosmetics manufacturer Revlon stated this marketing strategy: '*I don't sell lipstick – I sell hope.*' You have to sell the right concept. Milton Keynes is not just selling houses to residents – it's selling a desirable lifestyle.

Milton Keynes is not alone. Many communities that lie just outside large cities offer an alternative lifestyle to the negative aspects of big-city living. The city of Rieti, 50 miles north east of Rome in the Lazio region, is now selling itself as a tranquil alternative for Romans: '*A superb quality of life in a peaceful setting where one can shake off stress.*' The mayor, Antonio Cicchetti, claims Rieti offers not only quality of life but also quality of work: 'American, German, and Japanese high-tech firms find the skilled labour pool they need for electronics and fibre optic manufacturing operations.'[9]

An American guide to small town excellence sums up the main message by asking: 'Are you fed up with big-city living? Would you like to start a new life in a place with clean air, safe streets, good schools, and friendly neighbors? If so, here are one hundred all-American small towns where you can find your dream!'[10] This type of concept-building in placemarketing is spreading across Europe. New residential dreams in certain target groups can be realised. Sometimes, as in the case of Milton Keynes or Arabianranta just outside Helsinki, the residential aspect has been the driving force of marketing strategy. Selling new domestic dreams will increase as the IT highway widens and reaches European homes. Businesses, families and local decision-makers in European cities such as Paris, Vienna and Stockholm are considering what *teleworking* can mean from a residential living point of view, and a new target market is being created: teleworkers.

To attract families, placemarketers should be aware of several subgroups:

1. Families without children
2. Families with small children
3. Families with pre-teen and teenage children
4. Families with children who have moved out of the house ('empty nest' families)

Source: Milton Keynes Marketing Limited, 1992.

Fig 3.3 ◆ The young and professional profile of Milton Keynes is marketed

Each target group has specific characteristics and needs. For example, some communities build and emphasise fine schools. Education quality appeals to families with young children and teenagers but is less appealing to empty nesters.

If the community wants to attract special language groups, it can offer and promote special language teaching. The language theme can appear in many different levels with completely unexpected perspectives. Figure 3.4 is an example from Schleswig-Holstein that seeks to attract skilled Japanese professionals by offering to build a Japanese school in Halstenbek.

Even within larger cities, different districts have their own residential marketing strategies. For example, each district in Paris does its own targeting. Léonard Weil, of the real estate firm Hamptons International, notes: 'On the Left Bank the most popular districts for foreign buyers are the 5th, 6th and 7th which have the *chic* of old Paris. One is in the centre of town and in the centre *des plaisirs*. Also popular is the 15th, which is becoming steadily more *chic*.'[11] Such targeted messages are available via specialised magazines, for example *Propriétés de France* or *L'immobilier en France*. But this is only the beginning of selectivity: each Parisian district can communicate its own appealing characteristics directly to the global market via the Internet marketplace. Not surprisingly, house prices reflect the appeal of the district.

Business and industry

Attracting business, industry and economic investment constitutes a third target market category. This category has the longest tradition and is also the hottest market today. This is understandable given the extremely high level of job destruction taking place in Europe. With almost 20 million unemployed within the European Union alone it is logical that the *business and industry* target market should attract the amount of attention it does.

At the same time this target market has begun to place growing demands on European placemarketers. Businesses are becoming increasingly professional in their place-buying or place-hunting. As a consequence, an increasing number of consulting companies offer their services to companies seeking places in which to invest. In some cases, banks and real estate brokers co-operate to provide services to place-buyers. Special 'location advisory services' are organised. These services include, for example, location strategy development, labour market evaluations, operating cost and conditions comparisons, business tax comparisons, real estate searches, incentives, negotiations and even relocation project management. The increasing number of European place ranking lists which have appeared of late is evidence of this quickly rising volume of knowledge. Regions and nations are ranked in all possible dimensions one can imagine (see Chapter 4).

Several tools are used by places to meet the growing placemarket needs of

Schleswig-Holstein has many faces.

Schleswig-Holstein – Germany's northern-most state – provides a positive, highly diversified environment for companies that want to grow and flourish. Strategically located between the Baltic and North Sea at the cross-roads of major trading routes to Scandinavia and the Baltic region, Schleswig-Holstein has a long tradition of supporting international business. And of being open to people and ideas from around the world. Hospitality and internationality are priorities in Schleswig-Holstein. Just two good reasons why we are building a Japanese school in Halstenbek. Have a look at Schleswig-Holstein. We welcome new faces.

Economic Development Corporation of Schleswig-Holstein,
Lorentzendamm 43, D-24103 Kiel, Germany
Telephone (4 31) 5 93 39-17, Fax (4 31) 55 51 78

Schleswig-Holstein
Committed to Healthy Growth

Source: Corporate Location, November/December, 1994.

Fig 3.4 ◆ 'Schleswig-Holstein has many faces'

businesses. *Investment seminars* are arranged in almost every country. One country or region after another is producing *road shows* in high-priority target markets. Almost all European countries today have established free-of-charge *inward investment agencies*. One of the forerunners of these was the French national DATAR, Invest in France. Other national organisations are found in IDA Ireland, Invest in Britain, and Netherlands Foreign Investment Agency. Eastern Europe is moving in the same direction, with the creation of the Romanian Development Agency and the Slovak National Agency for Foreign Investment and Development. Sometimes the work may be organised as part of the Ministry of Economy as in Croatia where investment services are handled by the Ministry of Privatisation and Property Management.

As if these national initiatives were not enough, numerous *regional and local* investment agencies have been formed. These are rich in variety, as are their differing economic and personnel resources. The following are some examples:

Regional investment agencies:

- Saarland Economic Promotion, in the German state of Saarland
- West Sweden, in the western part of Sweden
- Welsh Development Agency, in the UK

Local investment agencies:

- Economic Development Agency for the Province of Liège, in Belgium
- Manchester Economic Development Office, in the UK
- Czech Technology Park in Brno, in the Czech Republic

It is important for placemarketing to understand how business firms make investment and location decisions. As a rule, business firms rate places as potential sites after considering various factors that constitute in total the overall *local business climate* of any given place. These factors – so called *attraction factors* – can be divided into two basic categories: hard and soft (see Table 3.3). The *hard* factors are those that can be measured in more-or-less objective terms. *Soft* factors are not easily measured and represent more subjective characteristics of a given place.

Placemarketers can use these factors as guides in trying to improve their attractiveness to a target market. Since not all factors can be maximised, it is critical to develop a unique combination. Exhibit 3.2 describes the aggressive marketing mix of Hannover.

Table 3.3 ◆ Hard and soft attraction factors

Hard factors	*Soft factors*
◆ Economic stability	◆ Niche development
◆ Productivity	◆ Quality of life
◆ Costs	◆ Professional and workforce competences
◆ Property concept	◆ Culture
◆ Local support services and networks	◆ Personnel
◆ Communication infrastructure	◆ Management
◆ Strategic location	◆ Flexibility and dynamism
◆ Incentive schemes and programmes	◆ Professionalism in contact with the market
	◆ Entrepreneurship
	◆ Unexpected relevances[a]

[a] *Unexpected* connections or events sometimes influence investment decisions in very subjective ways. A personal connection (common friend), shared interest (art, sport, nature, wine, etc.) of unusual importance to one party may be discovered to be shared with equal passion by the other party. This sometimes forms the basis of trust building or relationship building, which ultimately becomes *relevant* for the overall decision. Surprisingly, investments have often been influenced by unexpected but relevant factors.

Hannover – a central position in Europe: target marketing for a competitive edge

EXHIBIT 3.2

Hannover has developed a value-added marketing process that focuses on its strategic location in Europe with appealing offers to *specific* target groups. Target marketing concentrates on mounting congresses and conventions for various businesses. Since Hannover enjoys a central position in Europe, where road and rail routes converge from Copenhagen and Rome, Paris and Moscow, the city aggressively markets its location. Even travelling times from Hannover by intercity train are part of the marketing strategy: Hannover to Berlin, 1 hour 40 minutes; Hannover to Hamburg, 1 hour.

Hannover's strategic marketing slogan is heard everywhere in Europe: Hannover – '*The City of International Fairs*'. The list of major shows reinforces its slogan. Two of the biggest events take place every year: the Hannover Fair Industry and the CeBIT (Information and Communications Technology). Other events include EuroTier (International Exhibition for Livestock Production and Management) and Euro-BLECH (International Sheet Metal Working Technology Exhibition).

However, placemarketers in Hannover feel that this is not enough. In anticipation of the millennium, Hannover wanted to augment its marketing positions. Hannover, in terms of hall-space, is currently the world's largest fairground, with Milan and Frankfurt in pursuit. The world competition is heating up with Munich spending DM2.3 billion to become a leading site, and countries such as France, Italy and the USA rapidly building new exhibition space.[1] While Hannover is still a dominant player, the city needed a bold move to augment its marketing position.

After extensive planning and marketing, Hannover won the rights to host World Exposition 2000. Building on the foundation of the trade fairs, the theme for Expo 2000 is '*Mankind–Nature–Technology*'. Planners are committed to expanding airport facilities, building a massive train station capable of handling as many as 2,000 trains a day, and hosting 40 million people in 153 days. ▶

► Seeing Expo 2000 as an opportunity to open up networks with business and industry from around the world, Hannover established a strategy to exploit the infrastructure that will remain after hosting Expo 2000: 'Intelligent and ecological planning that looks beyond the short-term effect towards long-term utilisation – this is not merely a coincidence but the fundamental idea behind Expo 2000 Hannover.'[2]

The commitment is evident and concrete in all endeavours. For example, in order to show the serious concern of Hannover in relation to intelligent and ecological planning, the city has decided on a Climate Protection Strategy. The city council decided in 1992 to reduce carbon dioxide emissions by 25 per cent by 2005. All areas of the city are actually covered by the plan: energy supply, transportation systems, land use planning, housing development and waste management. The city argues that 'the strategy is valuable not only to protect the climate but also to save scarce resources, to support local economy, and to improve the quality of life in our city.'[3] The high ambitions of Hannover to use its own case as a state-of-the-art example for the rest of Europe is reflected in the following statement: 'We hope that our strategy will give a further incentive to state and federal governments, the European Community, and international organisations and decision-makers on other levels to act accordingly to accomplish an effective reduction of carbon dioxide.'[4] The ecological and marketing strategy of Hannover, a city focusing on international expos, is clearly outlined and focused on actions.
Hannover is using the Expo as a launching pad to maintain its dominance as the fair centre of Europe. The key issue here is positioning Hannover as the centre of global solutions for the twenty-first century.

Sources:

1. Ira Schaible, 'The German fair and exhibition market more crowded', *Deutsche-Agentur*, 28 August 1996 (Lexis Nexis).
2. Expo 2000, The World Exposition sales guide 1997/1998, pp. 12–13.
3. Internet: http://iclei,org/aplans/hannsap.htm.
4. *ibid.*

A place can maintain and strengthen its economic base in four ways. *First*, the place must retain its current businesses or at least the desirable ones. This is all the more important in a world with increasingly 'rootless' enterprises in the European market. Every day we can see how businesses leave or threaten to leave one place for another. Cross-border migrations are increasing. For the Hoover Company, it was profitable to move from Dijon, France, to Glasgow, Scotland. A financial package was offered reaching – at least officially – about ECU 10 million. Additional factors were involved which concerned the freezing of salaries and other working conditions. In spite of hard efforts, Dijon failed to dissuade Hoover from moving.

To successfully retain its businesses, a place and its businesses must invest in a regular dialogue. Local decision-makers must understand how their place compares with other places with respect to its advantages and disadvantages. For the first time, many representatives in the public sector will be encountering the importance of evaluating world-wide competition.

Second, the place must devise plans and services to help existing businesses expand. When these businesses sell more products and services to more distant markets, they produce more income and jobs within the local economy. To a large extent the city can identify hard and soft factors that it can influence, and on that basis it can begin to develop carefully-tailored offers. This is the core of the value-added process. The following two cases illustrate what can be achieved.

In southern Sweden lie a number of competing, fine glass manufacturers. Some have well recognised global brand names, such as Orrefors and Kosta Boda. To further strengthen their prominence, in the 1980s a new concept was created, *The Kingdom of Crystal*. The glassworks involved promoted the message to increase the number of visitors to the fine glass manufacturers. Today, over 1 million tourists and shoppers visit The Kingdom of Crystal on an annual basis. The concept has worked, and given the fine glass communities an important advantage in an internationally competitive market. Thus, one plus one has become three. By providing the customer an attractive destination and not just a visit to a factory, businesses in the region have mutually created a brand or trademark with which to compete aggressively.

Limerick, Ireland, has chiselled out a compelling position as a place of '*language excellence*'. The five-line verse called a limerick has put Limerick on the global map. Today Limerick is nurturing its language theme. Famous authors such as W.B. Yeats, James Joyce, Samuel Beckett, Oscar Wilde, Oliver Goldsmith and Seamus Heaney are associated with the region. Several language companies have established themselves in Limerick. Europeans and others travel to the region to take part in intensive language learning courses. Without the local co-operation between the public and private sectors, Limerick's placemarketing would not have occurred. The value-added process in Limerick is illustrated in Figure 3.5.

Third, the place must make it easier for entrepreneurs to start new businesses. The SME (small and medium-sized enterprises) programmes are numerous and often backed by the EU. During the 1990s representatives of many nations, regions and even communities in Europe visited US cities to get practical guidance on how to improve the business climate for entrepreneurs. The European job crisis stimulated European planners to travel to the USA to observe entrepreneurial support programmes.

As a result, today there are growing numbers of examples in Europe of places introducing aggressive entrepreneurial support programmes. These include developing local SME agencies to train and advise entrepreneurs, encouraging local banks to get involved in helping start-up businesses, providing loans, bringing together venture capitalists and entrepreneurs, promoting research parks or technopols (in France), helping secure government contracts, and using various incentives to aid business starts-ups. Exhibit 3.3 illustrates one of the best European examples of combined efforts to improve the local climate for entrepreneurs.

Fourth, a place must try to attract strategically relevant development projects. Such projects often create valuable 'side contacts' with commercial consequences. The region of Wales is a good example of how an aggressive marketing strategy can attract both investors and productive projects, often with an EU connection. As an indication of its ambition to draw special projects to Wales, the region publishes a project catalogue that also describes new EU-sponsored programmes in which Wales could fill a role.

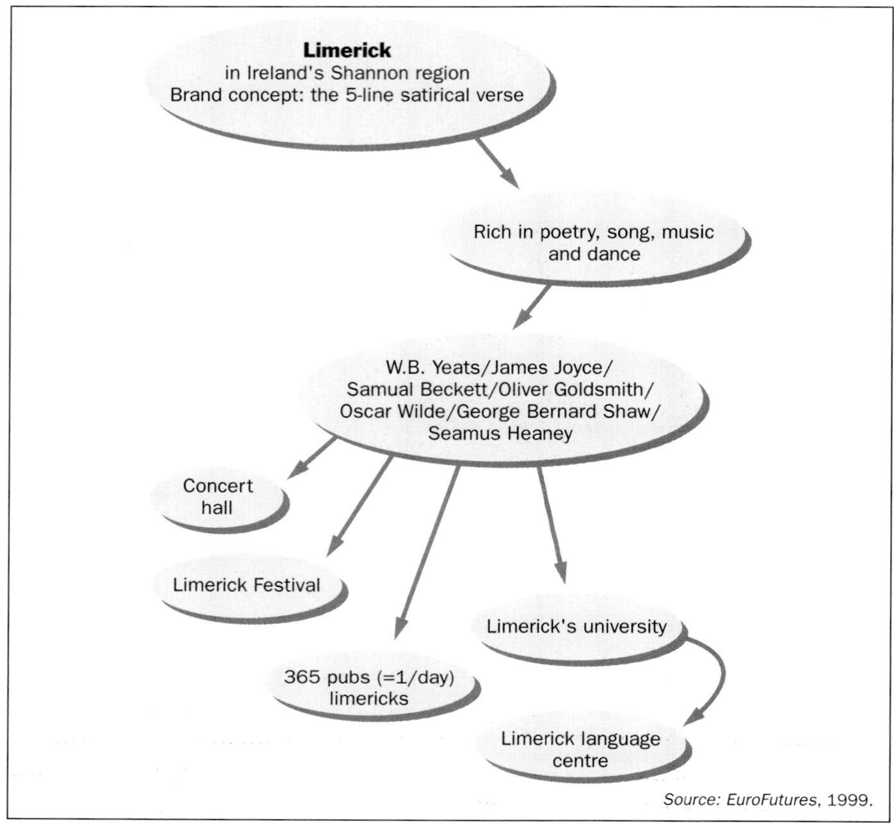

Source: EuroFutures, 1999.

Fig 3.5 ◆ The value-added process

Cambridge: an entrepreneurial umbrella

EXHIBIT 3.3

Entrepreneurship flourishes in Cambridge, making it the envy of most communities in Europe. In 1996, the Cambridge city council estimated that local research and development in the technology sector produced 19,000 jobs in 600 firms. Thus, the average firm size is not more than about 31 jobs. But what actually generated all these start-up companies in Cambridge? Why is the 'Cambridge phenomenon' such a powerful story in Europe? There are five concrete factors:

1. Cambridge spawns specialised technical knowledge from its world-class educational institutions. The start-up companies are often based on cutting-edge scientific research that has not been replicated elsewhere.
2. Cambridge has concentrated on two growth niches: computers/telecommunications (especially during the 1970s and 1980s) and bio-technology (1990s). As a result, Cambridge has the highest concentration of emerging biotech companies in Europe.
3. Meeting places have been created where different disciplines and talents can gather. There is a 'brain centre' in Cambridge Science Park (see Figure 3.6, p. 48).

4. There are several venture capital firms in the region. They supply capital and stimulate critical market-thinking among entrepreneurs (see Figure 3.7).
5. There is active co-operation between private firms and city officials in Cambridge.

These five factors combine to create a value-added process in Cambridge. A scientist living and working in Cambridge said: 'We all know each other fairly well and tend to network fairly easily. It is a group of people who came together in the last 20 or 30 years and who have this kind of why-shouldn't-we-do-this-attitude.'[1]

Cambridge is now trying to strengthen that partnership in larger regions surrounding the area. Guy Mills, an economic development officer at Cambridge County Council explains: 'We are getting to the stage where we feel there needs to be a more formal umbrella organisation to co-ordinate various activities in the public and private sectors.'[2] A regional investment agency has been established, thereby effectively strengthening the regional aspect of the effort. If Cambridge can successfully clone its formula to a country-wide region, it will make more competitors envious; but the strategies of capitalising on strengths and synergies are available to all place-marketers.

Sources:

1. Jane Martinson, 'Huge network of friends', Survey–Cambridge, *Financial Times*, 12 December 1996, p. 2.
2. Richard Adams, 'A second phenomenon in Fenland', Survey–Cambridge, *Financial Times*, 12 December 1996, p.1.

In today's Europe, most nations and regions have launched placemarketing programmes. Some rely on government employees distributing brochures, while others have developed more sophisticated and innovative programmes that incorporate all four previously described strategies. To slide into a market strategy in a laissez-faire manner will bring success only as an exception. Generally it is a clear, comprehensive strategy that creates fertile results.

Export market

A fourth target market is export expansion – the ability of a city or a region to produce more goods and services that other places, people, and business firms are willing to purchase. Consider the small city of Boskoop in the Netherlands that today successfully exports its well-known garden plants and flowers to the whole of Europe. Boskoop's successful exports sprang from a little gathering of 'marketwise' actors – a critical mass of 700 garden masters who know what Europeans want to buy. Consequently, they have learned both to 'garden' and to 'market' what they grow.

As another example, the many watch firms in Switzerland have created a strong image of 'Swiss Made' high-quality watches. The Swiss brand name is carefully exploited worldwide. In 1997, Omega expressed it this way: '*Omega – Swiss Made Since 1848*'. To further underscore its excellent quality positioning, the company chose to link itself to a familiar face: '*Omega – The Sign of Excellence. Cindy Crawford's Choice in Switzerland*'. In Switzerland, especially in Bern and Geneva, the Swiss brand name is marketed globally and protected very closely in order to prevent any fraudulent copies from damaging its superior image.

Source: Financial Times, 12 December 1996.

Fig 3.6 ◆ 'In 1970 Trinity College created The Cambridge Science Park'

Cambridge Research and Innovation Ltd

CRIL is a seed fund with an established base in Cambridge. We invest in early stage high technology ventures. CRIL has developed a specialist investment approach to these potential star performers. We invest in ventures based on technologies protected by intellectual property rights, where these technologies have large markets. We act as a corporate business angel, supporting those businesses we invest in with management input whilst they become established.

13 Station Road, Cambridge CB1 2JB Tel: 01223 312856

Source: Financial Times, 12 December 1996.

Fig 3.7 ◆ Cambridge Research and Innovation Ltd. (CRIL) is a seed fund

Other European places have also developed a strong export image. Milan and its famous fashion firms are known the world over. The region of Bayern and Munich, well known for quality car manufacturers including Audi and BMW, underscored this quality with the phrase: '*The Quality Edge of the New Europe*'. Audi is an example of a carmaker with a strong export strategy, Exhibit 3.4.

Audi rises from unintended acceleration

EXHIBIT 3.4

A place's image is irrevocably tied to the products that it exports. In 1986, Audi sales in the USA plummeted with the news of a charge of a major safety defect. The car was implicated as allegedly suffering from unintended acceleration, and accident cases were reported of cars suddenly taking off and crashing into garage doors. To compound the problem, Audi representatives appeared on the television news show *Sixty Minutes* and seemed as baffled as the interviewers as to why the car seemed to have a mind of its own. The situation contradicted the high-quality image of Germany's standards for automobile manufacturing and threatened the future security of Audi.

In the weeks following the television show, new car sales stopped and resale values crashed. However, the company was exonerated later as it was determined that because of the closer and unfamiliar European-style configuration, drivers were hitting the accelerator and not the brakes. Driver error defined the problem. ▶

▶ To compound the situation, the Japanese introduced the Legend, the Lexus and the Infiniti – all cars aimed squarely at the high-end European market. These cars were European-style luxurious, but were less expensive and had softer rides and plusher interiors that appealed to US consumers who wanted it all. Moreover, the cars were more reliable than European models. The very image of European superiority at making high-end, expensive automobiles was threatened by the Japanese strategy. The situation looked hopeless, and many car analysts were predicting that Audi, Saab and Volvo would join Renault, Peugeot, Rover, Fiat and Alfa Romeo as US export failures.

The Audi response was classic export strategy. They lowered the price, increased the content, offered no-maintenance agreements and, most importantly, used style as a marketing device. The Audi's body design was on the cutting edge. It simply looked better than everyone else's car. As a result, with the introduction of the A4 model in 1995, Audi became one of the most sought after imported car lines in America. Audi succeeded because it looked carefully at its competitors, judged accurately its own strengths, and then applied a consistent and focused campaign to rebuild its market share. And by focusing its export mission Audi not only saved itself, but enhanced the collective image of the region, country and even Europe.

On the other hand, regions must avoid producing substandard products. The Italian automobile industry, specifically Fiat and Alfa Romeo, has been hurt in their global expansion plans by the reputation – perhaps ill-deserved – of producing poor quality products.

Thus Boskoop, Milan and Munich illustrate the growing importance of regions and enterprises joining forces in order to add unique value to their own place products or services. This is clear in the case of the tourist industry where regions develop a unique character, such as gastronomy (the Provence kitchen); sunny beaches and other environments (the sunny image of the Canary Islands); relaxing café culture (the Vienna tradition). Knowledge collected from destination development efforts in the tourist industry is diffusing to other product and service areas.

To further its exports a place can use a number of tools:

1. Public and private sector actors can co-operate to develop a place positioning that strengthens local business on the export market (co-branding).
2. The local government can establish export advisory offices.
3. The local government can provide financial incentives to stimulate export-oriented actions, for example participation in trade shows.
4. The local government can assist export interested businesses in recruiting personnel with relevant experience. Training in intercultural relations and languages are two increasingly important attributes.

How do placemarketers market their place?

A place faces a number of important choices when it begins the task of placemarketing. These are four broad strategies for attracting visitors, residents and employees, business and industry, and increasing exports. These strategies are:

1. Image marketing
2. Attraction marketing
3. Infrastructure marketing
4. People marketing

Image marketing

Europe consists of over 100,000 competing communities that need to attract potential place-buyers by projecting a strong and relevant image. Without a unique and distinguishing image, a potentially attractive place may go unnoticed in the midst of the vast European placemarket. One of the goals in image marketing is to develop a clever slogan that is believable and demonstrable. For example, Ireland uses the slogan '*Ireland – The Celtic Tiger of Europe*'. This slogan is not without foundation: a small country on the periphery of Europe, Ireland has attracted one-quarter of all available US manufacturing investments in Europe although it accounts for just 1 per cent of the European population. Over the past two decades, more than one thousand overseas companies have chosen a base in Ireland.[12]

Ireland also uses other messages. For example, when arriving in Ireland the first message one sees at the Dublin airport is: '*Ireland – The Call Centre Country of Europe*'. Here, too, there are hard facts: Ireland provides professional staff with multilingual ability, low telecommunications tariffs, low taxes, and a one-stop shopping concept. Not surprisingly, not only has Ireland managed to attract numerous international call centres, but the small island country has also become a European leader in this business.

However, not all slogans work. Europe is saturated with many unfocused and easily copied slogans. While they may be catchy, slogans cannot do the job of image marketing alone, especially if they are not part of a larger marketing strategy. A place's image must be valid and communicated in many ways and through many channels if it is to take root and succeed.

A place may find itself in one of five image situations.

1. Overly attractive image

Some places suffer from having too attractive an image. Those who have visited the French Riviera in the summer have experienced traffic jams, noise, long queues, large numbers of people, and high prices everywhere. Such a place needs little marketing and might even consider undertaking some demarketing.

A similar situation marred Mallorca, which also suffered from a highly attractive image. But Mallorca finally decided to go after quality, not quantity. Instead of building more hotels, the authorities decided to demolish some of the least desirable ones. Mallorca is now pursuing a strategy of *sustainable tourism* based on a more targeted approach.

Several EU reports such as *Competitiveness and Cohesion: Trends in the Regions, Fifth Periodic Report on the Social and Economic Situation and Development of the Regions in the Community*[13] and *Europe 2000: Outlook for the Development of the Community's Territory*,[14] point out the need to direct expansion, investment and population development to the peripheral European areas. This shift in emphasis would have the favourable effect of reducing the problems of highly attractive areas and stimulating the growth of peripheral areas.

2. Positive image

Hannover, Frankfurt, Venice, Geneva, Salzburg, Prague and Stockholm have positive images. Although these cities do not require an image change, the challenge is to amplify the positives and deliver them more effectively to desired target groups.

Businesses like to take advantage of places that are viewed positively: perfume-makers exploit their connection with Paris; clothing companies emphasise their Milan connection, and diamond companies do the same with Antwerp. Ironically, as the world market becomes more global, businesses increasingly want to identify with a positively viewed local place.

A sophisticated example of a business associating itself with cities that have positive images is the '*Absolut Cities of Europe*' campaign. Absolut vodka chose to associate itself with a host of highly visible European cities. The image is reflected in both text and visual form. Figure 3.8 shows two examples.

3. Weak image

Many places have a weak image. They lack a marketing strategy with a clear message and leadership. A weak image can also result from the place having a small population, being located in a peripheral area, lacking resources, and so on. These places have to be especially skilful in changing their weak image. They may have attractive features but fail to turn them into competitive advantages. Without effective images these places will remain anonymous. Many small places in the Alps have simply disappeared behind the megastars such as Chamonix, Alberville and Davos. In spite of impressive facilities their weak image has not brought them up to the European winter-sports standard. Kirchberg in Austria near the famous Kitzbühel in Switzerland and Maribor and Bohinj in the shadow of Kranjska Gora (all of Slovenia) need to address their problem of low visibility. Some places are just awakening to their obscurity (see Exhibit 3.5).

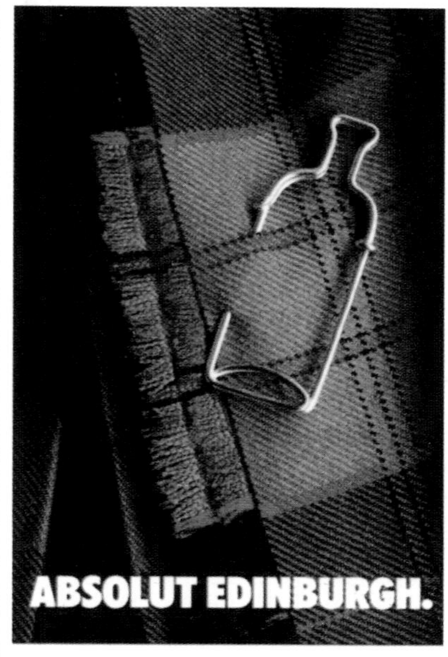

The classic Scottish tartan is cleverly pinned with the Absolut bottle.

The famous watchmaking image of Geneva is reflected in the ad with the discreet Absolut bottle inside the watch.

Source: 'The story', Marketing material from the Absolut Company, Stockholm, 1997.

Fig 3.8 ◆ Absolut advertising campaign

Utsira wants you!

EXHIBIT 3.5

Utsira is one of the smallest and most isolated communities in Europe. Located on the Norwegian west coast of the Atlantic, it has only 200 residents and is a ninety minute ferry-ride from the mainland. The island can be characterised as having an extremely peripheral location and a unique position with its minimal size. The island wishes to raise its visibility and attract business and tourists. What are the possibilities?

On the business side there are opportunities for back-office services because they can be anywhere and the residents are highly skilled. This desire demands the creation of a business attraction strategy and a marketing team. In the tourist area the attraction should appeal to adventure seekers, campers and other nature lovers. While the ambience is not surf and sand, it is in the category of peaceful, natural and relatively untouched. The place will have to make its market niche in tourism fairly narrow and intense. A good start would be a detailed inventory of assets, a public relations campaign to attract free media on the big plans of a small place, and the creation of a Website. While some major places may scoff, they might try to match Utsira's 1997 resident attraction rate of 6 per cent. That equals thirteen new citizens and the potential for a story line – 'Lilliputian town slays city giants!'

Source: Interview with project leader Marit Cecilie Farsund, in Utsira, 11 June 1998.

4. Contradictory image

Many places have contradictory images because people hold opposite views about some features of the place. Brussels is perceived on the one hand as a hypermodern, administrative, international city which works well, while others see Brussels as sterile, congested and costly, with a sharp division between Flemish and French-speaking people. Zurich, Switzerland, also conveys contradictions. While to some Zurich is seen as a modern, well-developed place with many company headquarters, much of Europe has seen TV programmes describing the public park outside the Zurich railway station as being filled with drug abusers. City planners closed the public park in an effort to ease the controversy and strengthen the positive image.

Many places in Eastern Europe also carry contradictory images. However great these cities may have been in pre-communist times, in the post-communist era the belief persists that these cities lack work ethics, quality consciousness and business/entrepreneurship.

The strategic challenge is to accentuate the positive image while simultaneously trying to change the realities that give rise to negative images. Image reversals are hard to accomplish. One reason is that first impressions can be long-lasting. Another is that media, especially local media, tend to accentuate the negative aspects of their place by prominent reporting of crime and corruption.

5. Negative image

Many places are stuck with a negative image. On the placemarket, regions south of Rome are often referred to with negative characteristics. This is how *Corporate Location* presents the region: 'They [the regions south of Rome] are collectively known as the Mezzogiorno [translated as half day], so sleepy is their performance. They rely on tourism and agriculture, the infrastructure is poor and the people lack skills.'[15]

In the south of Italy on the island of Sicily is the city of Corleone that has a world-wide reputation for its Mafia. Entrenched in public memory are the Mafia films such as *The Godfather* which portray Corleone as the seedbed of US crime. This depressed image is something that is felt throughout the whole region of Mezzogiorno. According to a survey carried out by an Italian management magazine, 56 per cent of 200 managers rejected the idea of investing in the deep south (Sicily, Calabria, Campania, Basilicata and Apulia). The Mafia image was cited by 34.5 per cent of respondents, while 30 per cent said poor infrastructure was paramount.[16]

There are other places in Europe that suffer from image problems. Charleroi in the old Belgian coal district has high unemployment and a run-down image; recently it has also picked up a paedophile image owing to a local scandal. The media, by zeroing in on a place, can hurt its image; for example, the little community of Pieksämäki, north of Helsinki, was identified in 1995 as 'Finland's most boring city'.

Places like this actually need less attention and some time to work out a new strategy for a more positive profile. In the case of Corleone, the community is eager to change its image. Guiseppe Cipriani, the 35-year-old mayor of Corleone, has commissioned the marketing strategist Oliviera Toscanis, who conceptualised the international profile of Benetton clothes, to highlight positive features of Corleone. Likewise, Pieksämäki residents have observed that the negative publicity surrounding 'Finland's most boring city' has stimulated activity within the community itself to launch a 'Happy Days' campaign with activities including steam engine tours, writers' seminars, and a late night market.

Yet images are not easy to develop or change. Image marketing is no quick-fix. It can take years to create or transplant a new image effectively. Many political mandates are for only three or four years, making a substantial image change difficult. Image marketing requires research into how residents, visitors, and external and internal businesses currently perceive a place. Many places have no experience in initiating market analysis of this kind. Nor is it easy to get various individuals and groups to decide on the new image, let alone make the investments required to validate the image.

Attraction marketing

Improving an image is not sufficient to increase a place's fundamental attractiveness. Places also need to invest in specific attractions.

Some places are fortunate to have natural attractions. One such place is Venice, often called 'The Jewel in Italy's Crown'. The remarkable canals make it unlike any city in the world. In Venice, boats, not cars, prevail. These unusual conditions have a particular attractiveness to tourists, residents and even businesses. Stockholm, too, makes much of its own island and water, calling itself '*Beauty on Water*', or the '*Venice of the North*'. Stockholm has also managed to keep its water so clean that fishing and swimming in the middle of the city is a way of life in the summer. This attraction is strengthened by a yearly '*Stockholm Water Festival*', a week-long celebration of Stockholm water life.

The same water theme, '*Venice of the North*', is turning up in Norway's Aalesund. The city of Colmar, in French Alsace, calls itself '*La Petite Venice*', shyly promoting its small cluster of canals and bridges. The two Belgian cities of Ghent and Bruges are surrounded with picturesque waterways which are deliberately exploited to attract visitors. Ghent, for example, with a population of only 250,000, has over 350 restaurants. As a thriving business centre and port in Belgium's East Flanders, Ghent has managed to put itself on the European map.

Other places benefit from a remarkable legacy of historical buildings, such as Athens with its Parthenon, the Moorish palace of the Alhambra overlooking the sleepy Spanish town of Granada, or the Hermitage with its 1057 rooms in St Petersburg. Krakow is another unique European place that embraces at its centre 8,000 historical buildings. The city markets itself as '*One of the Most Beautiful Cities in Europe*'.

Other fortunate places are home to world-renowned edifices, such as Paris's Eiffel Tower and Arc de Triomphe. London is the site of Big Ben, the world's most famous timepiece, 98 metres high and with thirteen bells that mark the hour. Marketers call this type of attraction a *Guinness attraction*. It must be the biggest, highest, longest or best in its class in some dimension.

Some places benefit from having beautiful landscaping or gardening. Tim Wilson, who runs a British company which promotes national heritage, estimates that a historically recognised garden can increase the price demanded for a property by 30 per cent or more.[17] Selected trips are frequently organised for gardeners to see historic European gardens such as the rose garden of Westbroekpark in The Hague, Parque del Oeste in Madrid, or the Westfalenpark in Dortmund.

One very common strategy to enhance a place's attractiveness is to build giant convention and exhibition centres. The huge exhibition centre called Fiera Milano or 'The Heart of Milan' is today generating 40–50 per cent of all hotel bookings in the city. The general secretary of Fiera Milano, Professor Marcello Marin, argues that 'Fiera Milano is an asset to the city, and the city is an asset to Fiera Milano.'[18] In 1995, the centre attracted 2.9 million visitors and over 27,000 exhibitors. It also hosted 866 conferences with 105,000 delegates. The centre was extended from 380,000 square metres to 486,000 square metres in 1997. Marin emphasises that Milan is associated mainly with fashion, furniture and machine tools, which are precisely the industries served by Fiera Milano's most important trade exhibitions. The role of the exhibition centre in the attraction process is obvious from this example. Exhibit 3.6 illustrates the increasing stakes for success in the exhibition market.

Trade fair wars in Germany

EXHIBIT 3.6

The history of trade fairs in the eastern German city of Leipzig is distinguished. As far back as the medieval period, the city thrived when the entire downtown was a series of tunnels and alleyways hosting the best of Europe's wares. Following the Second World War, as Leipzig became the trade fair capital of the Eastern Bloc, the trade fair was moved to a large site out of the downtown area. In 1996, after much promotion and money (over DM 2.6 billion) the battle was on in Central Europe for trade fair dominance. Leipzig built a third site, a five-hall, 102,500 square metre trade mecca that was promoted as the principle exhibition hall between Eastern and Western Europe.

In spite of this strong market position, Leipzig's competitive situation is marked by a number of factors that create a mixed image. Leipzig has lingering infrastructure problems such as deteriorating waterpipes and service problems that revolve around training an inexperienced workforce. Still, Leipzig has revamped its railway station into a modern terminal with a spectacular shopping mall and has made major improvements in air quality and other quality of life issues. The success or failure of the supermodern trade fair is viewed as a predictor of the city's future.

Now, the test. The competition has a head start in the race for customers. In the marketplace, Berlin has made a major effort to dominate the trade fair business and has increased business nearly fivefold. Frankfurt has a monopoly on the book market fairs once dominated by Leipzig. It is imperative that Leipzig offer more quality, better service and lower prices to win back its position from the competition.

Source: Clive Freeman. 'Leipzig's new trade fair pavilions and Congress Centre inaugurated', *Deutsche Press – Agentur*, 12 April 1996 (Lexis Nexis).

Among other types of attraction is the conversion of a downtown area into a pedestrian mall. Places of all sizes can conceptualise their own main street. The walkway Strøget in Copenhagen has proved to be a remarkable artery for many visitors. Dublin's Grafton Street and the Temple Bar area are today highly attractive walking streets. Businesspeople enjoy a mental lift when the rush of automobile traffic is replaced by more casual pedestrian traffic.

A number of cities have capitalised on their major business streets. For example, Berlin's Kurfürstendamm (Ku'damm) and Unter den Linden are today the heart of the unified city. In St Petersburg the principal business street is Nevsky Prospekt, which functions as a four kilometre long shopping window to the west. Moscow has its own version of Nevsky Prospekt – the 'Perestroika-street' Arbat. The majority of cosmopolitan people understand exactly what the Avenue des Champs-Elysées in Paris symbolises in terms of attraction power. Bond Street and Oxford Street in London's West End are important elements in supporting the city's image as a leading shopping mecca. In Oslo we find the well-known 'Karl Johan'. In Birmingham, England, lies Colmore Row, which is its 'Wall Street'.

Infrastructure marketing

Clearly, neither image nor attractions can provide the complete answer to a place's development. An effective infrastructure is required at the base. In almost all placemarketing the infrastructure plays an important role and throughout Europe investments in infrastructure now play a more central role. Not only are infrastructure investments desirable in themselves but they also help to ease unemployment. Such investments have the strong support of the EU in Brussels and the European Investment Bank with a special infrastructure department in Luxembourg.

Streets and highways, railways, airports and telecommunication networks are the most frequent infrastructure improvements. Businesses and organisations in Western Europe spent ECU 315 billion on them alone in 1996. Placemarketers are trying to differentiate their standings in IT. *First*, some places try to communicate that they offer excellent IT knowledge and resources (for example Telecom Valley in southern France). *Second*, some places claim to have outstanding application experience (for example Ireland –'*The Call Centre Country of Europe*', Luxembourg with its '*Mediaport Europe*', or '*TelecomCity*' in the Swedish city of Karlskrona). *Third*, some places are claiming a niche application position (for example '*Landesinitiative Media for Online Services*' in Dortmund and the region of North Rhine–Westphalia). And *fourth*, some places are marketing their low telecommunications tariffs (for example Sweden and Finland).

Railways have also experienced a renaissance in Europe. According to current EU plans Europe will be covered with a network of high-speed trains reaching a speed of 300–350 kilometres per hour. By 2010 this state-of-the-art system will span 29,0000 km, out of which 12,500 km will be newly constructed high-speed track. Investments in this huge upgrading in infrastructure, including trains, is calculated to cost ECU250 billion.

These investment plans will cause European places to compete for designation as highly attractive high-speed European station stops. For example, the little place of Saint-Cyr-sur-Loire lies south west of Paris, close to the city of Tours. The railway has opened up new market opportunities for this place. Equatop, a new place created in direct connection to the railway, claims: 'Every day 15 high-speed trains stop in Equatop from Paris. Travel time: less than one hour.' As a result, Saint-Cyr-sur-Loire is able to market itself for suburban living and shopping. In other words, the primary investment in infrastructure breeds *secondary investments* that are marketed in their turn.

The same phenomenon can be seen in Ashford, UK. Ashford, which lies south east of London, found itself in a new position after the opening of the Channel Tunnel in 1994. A primary investment was the International Station, which Ashford inaugurated in 1996. Eight Eurostar departures are offered each weekday to Paris and Brest. As a secondary investment, Ashford established Eureka Science Park, which is completely accessible from the International Station. The park is an infrastructure investment to create a 'Silicon Valley' in that part of the country.

Science parks have appeared in many parts of Europe. Most of them specialise in some niche: for example, the San Raffaele Biomedical Science Park in Italy, the Business and Science Park Enschede in Holland, the Science Park Ulm in Germany, the Science Park Odense in Denmark, the AREA Science Park in Italy and the Cambridge Science Park in the UK. Science parks will certainly remain an important infrastructure factor, as they provide a natural tie between business and research institutions. In some cases these science parks have developed into huge conglomerates that incorporate many of the characteristics of a city. For example, Kista, originally a science park outside Stockholm, has developed retail stores, residential areas, recreational facilities and other city features.

Other worthwhile infrastructure investments include harbours, electricity and heating generation and distribution, facilities for water supply, availability of land, and housing and office space. Figure 3.9 shows a typical attraction message that emphasises infrastructure.

People marketing

The fourth marketing strategy is for a place to market its people. As far back as the sixteenth century, Niccolò Machiavelli concluded that the success or failure of an independent republic depended on the character of its citizens, the civic virtues they possess. The character theme has not lost impact, as it is a major focus in many place campaigns. A typical placemarket example is Ireland, whose message exclaims: '*People are to Ireland as Champagne is to France*'.

National differences in Europe have been captured in an ironic way on a popular postcard (see Figure 3.10). Behind such national stereotypes might be some grains of truth.

People marketing may take on at least five forms, described below.

1. Famous persons

Europe is crowded with famous persons participating in placemarketing promotions. Connecting a famous face with a place offers a fast and effective means for creating a positive association. Antwerp calls itself '*Rubens' Own City*'. Rovaniemi in northern Finland positions itself as '*Santa Claus's Home*'. During the Christmas season, Rovaniemi arranges international Santa Claus tours including one of its Arctic Centre which has received a three-star rating (the highest) from the Michelin Guide. Prague markets itself as '*Franz Kafka's Hometown*'. Liverpool reminds visitors that it is '*The Birthplace of the Beatles*'. Genoa markets the name, memory and glory of Christopher Columbus.

Individual athletes and teams also give identity to many places in Europe. Naples has its Napoli, Madrid its Real Madrid, Milan its AC and Inter Milan, and Manchester its Manchester United. The leader of Manchester's city council, Richard Leese, said of the connection: 'Football gives the city an identity. It offers an important life content for many. It gives the city a sense of self-confidence that we very much need. United is Manchester's most world famous company!'[19]

Some places are advertising their scientific rather than athletic heritage. The Vienna Business Promotion Fund markets its famous scientists internationally to help position the city as a modern meeting-place for top intellectual endeavours (Figure 3.11).

2. Enthusiastic local leaders

Renown can spread fast for those places that have skilful business and politi-

Invest in France Agency

Excellent Infrastructures

France has one of the most extensive road networks in Europe including 9 000 km of motorways and an additional 3 000 km under construction

12 000 km motorways toward the year 2 000

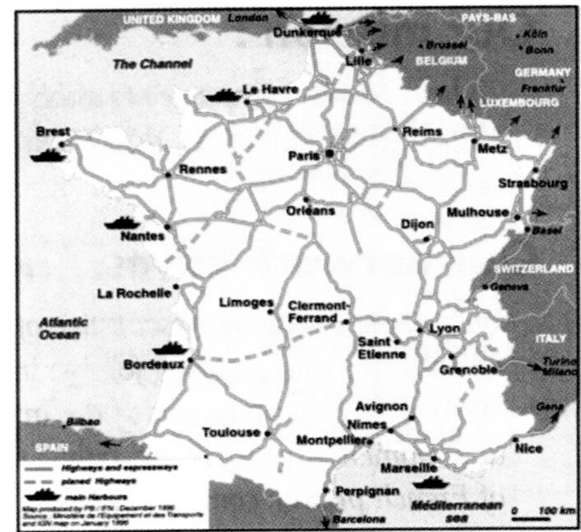

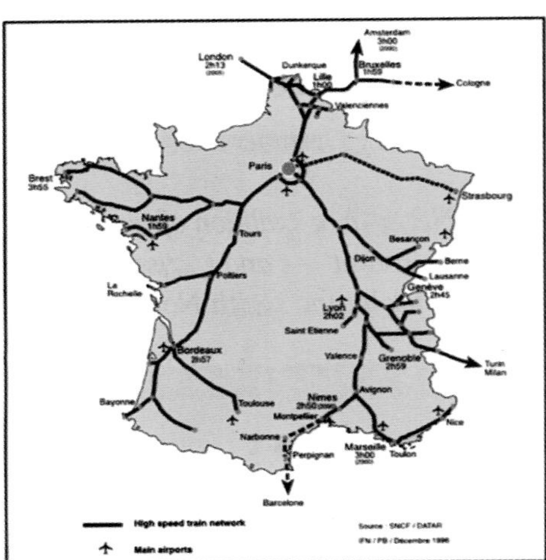

Travelling time from Paris airport by TGV high speed train

With the TGV high speed train you reach several large cities in Western Europe in only a few hours.

France offers you access to ISDN in the whole country and decreasing telecommunications rates of up to 40% until 1998

Cost of a 3-minute call to New York (USD)

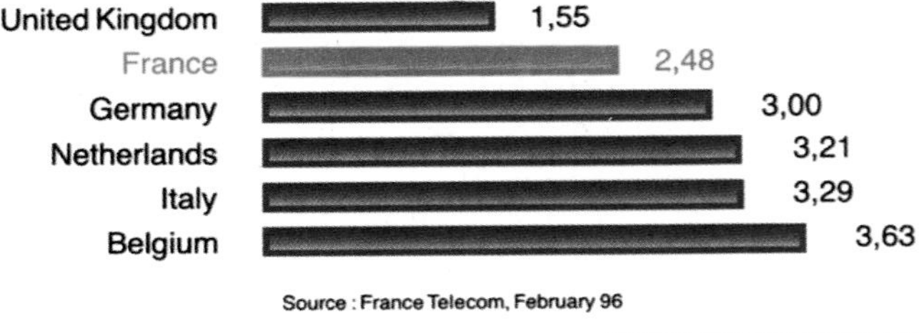

Source: 'Invest in France,' Newsletter, January 1997.

Fig 3.9 ◆ 'Excellent Infrastructures'

Fig 3.10 ◆ 'The perfect European should be ...'

Source: Postcard, Euroline, Brussels 1995.

cal leaders. In a climate of high unemployment and low investments, it can be rewarding for leaders to step forward with professional enthusiasm and optimism. This approach is more visible in the USA than in Europe. In North Carolina, when Jim Hunt took office as governor, the message stated: '*Our New Governor Means Business!*' Hunt appeared in photographs on construction sites wearing a confident smile and a yellow construction helmet. Frank McKenna, former premier of the Canadian province of New Brunswick, believed that his mandate was first and foremost to develop the region. *Financial Times* coined McKenna's methods with the headline 'A politician you can do business with'. He proclaimed to future clients, 'We have embarked on a major initiative in service quality. It allows us to provide better service to our customers. We intend to be quality-driven. If we're not – tell us. You are the client.'[20] Already some forty call-centre companies have moved into New Brunswick and have created more than three thousand jobs.

In Europe we find noticeably fewer examples of how different regions have marketed their local leaders. But the number is growing. In the one-million-population-city of Nizjnij Novgorod in Russia, the young governor became recognized for the '*Nizjnij model*'. A physicist by training, Governor Boris Jefimovitj Nemtsov opened his city to the outside world and ushered

Source: *EuroBusiness*, September, 1994.

Fig 3.11 ◆ Vienna positions itself on the international placemarket

in market economy reforms and innovative projects. He created new life in the region's administration and earned respect even in the West from potential place-buyers. Unfortunately for Nizjnij Novgorod, his skills led him to Moscow for a post as vice prime minister to Boris Yeltsin until he was suddenly replaced in the summer of 1998.

Ricardo Illy, the popular mayor of the Italian city of Trieste, has a vision for his city and its 224,000 citizens. 'Trieste can be a driving force to develop the economic and cultural exchanges between the Western and Central/Eastern European countries. We want to open the city in all directions, attracting citizens from all over the world. We will be recognized as the city able to support western companies wanting to sell into the east.' Business mayor Illy sees 'Trieste in a role to Eastern Europe as Singapore is to China'[21] – the intellectual, cultural, financial centre of the region. At the same time there are several places in Europe lining up for the same position as a gateway between West and East. However, Illy's leadership style is one that can communicate a vision and combine it with effective implementation. The East–West gateway role has created 400 import/export companies. Trieste has developed a research park where 800 world-class scientists and engineers have settled. The Elettra Laboratory in the research park produces soft X-rays of high quality, which enable metal, chemical reactions and pharmaceutical products to be studied. Only Grenoble and Berkeley have comparable facilities. The port of Trieste provides another unique position in Europe as it offers a special tax treatment for imports, which allows payment of duties and VAT to be suspended until six months after import. The common theme in Trieste's strategy is to offer something sophisticated which does not simply stop with a catchy slogan.

With equal strategic ability, Raymond Barre, mayor of Lyon, and former French prime minister, is trying to outline a new market position for Lyon with his concept of a '*Latin Arc*' which will encompass cities such as Barcelona, Lyon, Geneva and Genoa. This '*Latin Arc*' can, according to Mayor Barre, act as a 'counterweight to the rapid development of Central and Northern Europe'.[22]

3. Competent people

Local access to competent people is a strong attraction factor in European placemarketing. When a place decides on its industry mix, it must attract the necessary competent people. With a population of only 15 million, the Netherlands has attracted over 6,300 foreign companies. Jochem Hanse, commissioner of the Netherlands Foreign Investment Agency, attributes these results partly to a well-educated labour force. A *Newsweek* story entitled 'Europe's New Leader in Education',[23] describes how the Netherlands plays host to a multicultural student community: 'The Dutch are providing quality schooling from primary through university level and beyond. The Dutch education system produces an exceptionally well qualified labor force widely cited by foreign companies as one of the Netherland's biggest assets.' John

Holloway, a manager in a newly established UK company, claims: 'What stands out particularly is their [the Dutch] very high level of computer literacy and language ability.' Target groups such as French expatriates can choose to send their children to the Lycée Français in The Hague, Americans to the American School of Hague, and Britons to the British School of Amsterdam.

The Dutch also offer broad programmes on the university level. Webster University maintains one of its four European campuses in the city of Leiden where it offers American-style undergraduate programmes and postgraduate MBA options in finance, international business, management and marketing. Other distinguished institutions are the Maastricht School of Management and the Rotterdam School of Management – Erasmus Graduate School of Business.

One of the most aggressive countries in training is Ireland, with its unusually young population – 50 per cent are under 30 years old. Ireland has set the highest priority on developing competence. Its message '*Dublin, Europe's New Financial Centre. Powered by People*', targets companies seeking skilled workers (see Figure 3.12).

As quickly as the Industrial Development Administration (IDA) gets a signal that a certain type of specialised competence is needed among its customers and prospects, they initiate contacts with those who can provide or develop such education and training. This type of feedback from the market is crucial.

4. People with an entrepreneurial profile

Entrepreneurial traditions vary quite a bit over the European landscape. In a region such as Emilia-Romagna in northern Italy, one finds a clear entrepreneurial tradition. The business climate is influenced by the dense network of small and medium-sized firms. Although there are only 4 million inhabitants, the business climate of the region has generated 90,000 small enterprises.[24] Consequently, the unemployment rate in Emilia-Romagna is one of the lowest in Italy. Emilia-Romagna actively uses its entrepreneurial character in its placemarketing.

A place's entrepreneurial profile can be supported in many ways: sponsoring special educational programmes for entrepreneurs, stimulating new entrepreneurial networks and actively marketing the place's entrepreneurial profile. Such marketing can strengthen a region's *internal* self-identity and simultaneously attract entrepreneurs and their companies.

5. People who have moved to the place

An approach that can best be described as the 'follow-me phenomenon' is used in many cases. Profiling persons who have moved into a certain place can create appeal. We see at least three different profiling approaches. *First*, we can tell the story of an entire family that moved to the new place. The family members describe their experiences in their new hometown, and the message

DUBLIN,
EUROPE'S NEW FINANCIAL
SERVICES CENTRE.

POWERED BY PEOPLE.

Irish people, educated, flexible, skilled, the main attraction for companies operating from Dublin's new International Financial Services Centre.
Ireland with half its population under 28 is rich in the resource that matters most in business today – skilled people.
Furthermore, 55% of students in third level education choose engineering, science or business studies. Add the most advanced digital telecommunications system in Europe and you will understand why the Dublin International Financial Services Centre has already attracted more than 230 of the world's leading financial companies.
Companies like: Dresdner Bank A.G., Eagle Star, Sumitomo, American International Group, Württembergische Feuerversicherung A.G., National Westminister Bank plc, Kredietbank N.V.

For information about business opportunities in Ireland contact IDA Ireland at: LONDON Ireland House, 150 New Bond St., London W1Y 9FE. Tel. (071) 6295941, AMSTERDAM (20) 679 8666, DUSSELDORF (211) 4360200, STUTTGART (711) 221468, NEW YORK (212) 750 4300, TOKYO (3) 32627621 Head Office Wilton Park House, Wilton Place, Dublin 2, Ireland Tel (01) 6686633

Source: IDA, Ireland Industrial Development Agency, *EuroBusiness*, November, 1994.

Fig 3.12 ◆ 'Powered by people'

often revolves around a heightened quality of life. The *second* approach is to focus on a special expert, scientist or businessperson who has chosen to move to a given place. These people are usually quoted, and a number of centrally attractive attributes are named. *Third*, personal statistics from an opinion survey can be presented regarding how people feel about living and working in the place. The attributes they most appreciate are then summarised.

A special case of 'people who have moved to a place' is when a business owner provides a personal view of investing in a given place. Such a testimonial humanises and puts a recognisable face on the place-choosing process. Consider the following example:

> Forty years ago Thomas Watson Jr, the Scottish-born president of IBM, met a Scottish member of parliament at the UN in New York who convinced Watson to consider Scottish sites for an IBM typewriter plant. After seeing a number of unsatisfactory places, Watson looked at the Spango valley behind Greenock. At that moment, Watson, not unlike Moses in the film *The Ten Commandments*, declared it the spot. An IBM plant would be built there, and the valley would be renamed '*The Valley of Opportunity*'.[25] This decision changed the destiny of the valley. Today, Silicon Glen leads Europe in PC production. Among other place-buyers who followed IBM to Silicon Glen are National Cash Register, AT&T, Compaq, Digital, Honeywell, Hewlett-Packard, Motorola, National Semiconductor, Sun Microsystems and Tandem. In hindsight we can say that Thomas Watson's highly personal decision ignited the interest in that corner of the world.

Beyond marketing specific people, a place must encourage its citizens to be more friendly and considerate towards visitors and new residents. Places must raise the level of their citizens' skills and attitudes so that they can meet the needs of the target markets. As an example, the mayor of Aberdeen, Scotland, was dissatisfied with the way the city's taxi drivers handled visitors. The mayor and the city council made a decision to provide a day's training session to improve the drivers' manner of relating to visitors. Both customers and taxi drivers reacted positively to this initiative, a necessary step in living up to Aberdeen's claim to being an 'International City'.

Who are the major placemarketers?

The marketers of a place can sometimes be difficult to identify. Placemarketing is a continuous process that involves all citizens. However, the groups listed in Table 3.4 constitute the most active placemarketers.

Table 3.4 ◆ Major actors in placemarketing

Local actors	*Public sector actors* Mayor and/or city manager Business development department in the community Urban planning department of the community (transport, education, sanitation, etc.) Tourist bureau Conventions bureau Public information bureau
	Private sector actors Individual citizens Leading enterprises Real estate developers and agents Financial institutions (banks and insurance companies) Electricity and gas utilities, telecommunications companies Chamber of commerce and other local business organisations Hospitality and retail industries (hotels, restaurants, department stores, other retailers, exhibition and conventions centres) Travel agencies Labour market organisations Architects Transport companies (taxi, railway, airline) Media (newspaper, radio, TV)
Regional actors	Regional economic development agencies Local and state government Regional tourist boards
National actors	Political heads of government Inward investment agencies National tourist boards
International actors	Embassies and consulates Inward investment agencies Economic development agencies with a specific link to a region or a city International enterprises with a place-bound link

We will focus on the local-level actors. Placemarketing strategy frequently emerges as a process in which the local actors provide the driving force. One could say, 'Think globally with your placemarketing strategy – but work it out locally.'

Public sector actors

In a Europe where unemployment and weak economic dynamism are perceived as primary problems, citizens often expect that the elected officials should manage to improve the climate for local growth. Unfortunately, public sector actors often do not know what to do when taking office, in spite of their electioneering promises. They have a long tradition of focusing resources on *distributing* wealth. They often lack competence in *generating* wealth. Europe's public sector enjoys a proud tradition of 'social engineering', rather than 'growth engineering'. However, the economic crises of the 1990s now act as a strong force driving public sector actors to deal with growth engineering. Consider the new policy of the British Labour Party, now called 'New Labour'. Upon winning the general election in May 1997, New Labour's main message was '*Labour Is Good For Business*'. Such a political slogan would not have been possible twenty or thirty years ago. At that time, public officials focused completely on social welfare and struggled to keep public companies publicly owned and to protect union rights. As a consequence of Tony Blair's political re-engineering, more social democratic parties in Europe are reconsidering their traditional positions. The impact on Europe could be great since the majority of EU countries placed Social Democrats in power during the late 1990s.

A similar driving force is evident also on the local level. Political leaders such as mayors and party members as well as individual citizens are pressing for a new approach. They have witnessed how new strategies implemented in other regions and communities have produced results. European media now widely distribute cross-border success stories. There is a *European benchmarking* of local strategies for growth. The members of one community will visit successful communities to learn how they did it. When a sufficient number of local public sector actors adopt a growth orientation, a climate for change is felt nationally.

But the climate for change is not driven forward by itself. Leadership, talent and a capacity to work out long-term strategies are necessary characteristics of the effective public sector actors. A city mayor, a city manager and other public executives can act as important catalysts for creating a new local business climate.

Private sector actors

Without the consent and active participation of individual citizens, not much growth engineering will be possible. In Warsaw after the Second World War, the old and unique inner city was reconstructed. The city architect said afterwards: 'Among us there are a million city planners with practical construction experience. Almost all have worked, if not laying bricks then at least cleaning, digging, and planting trees. We are, naturally, very proud of our city'[26]

This type of collective effort is based on local pride. '*Pride-building*' is a primary element in a placemarketing strategy and it can apply to community involvement behind large events like the Olympic Games, world championships, a city or regional celebration, a festival or an international exhibition. Those visiting Salzburg in the summer or Edinburgh International Festival in

August understand what pride-building means in practice. Today, Europe is crowded with places where mega-events have unleashed collective energy.

But general pride among community members must go beyond the occasional mega-event. Pride must extend to a school with a unique profile, a science park with associated entrepreneurial companies, a new railway with an attractive high-speed connection, a profitable leading business with an exciting success story, or even to low prices, tele-tariffs, housing costs and lower income tax. We can say this in a more fundamental way: the place's marketable value proposition and theme must be widely known and accepted by its citizens.

A place-bound pride is something that visitors quickly discover. Go to Krakow and you will notice the place-bound pride that is associated with the old inner city. Or go to Cambridge and discuss the 'Cambridge phenomenon'. In both cases, citizens have a fundamental knowledge about the uniqueness of the place and they act consciously or unconsciously as placemarketers.

The second important type of private sector placemarketer is *leading enterprises*. These enterprises recognise the advantage they will accrue by helping to improve the place's image. The enhanced image should create a valuable identity that can be used in the international arena. It could be Diesel Jeans and Workwear from the small village of Molvena in north east Italy, or the national confectionery company Toblerone closely associated with Switzerland, or even the 'Spectacle Valley' and its famous Italian eyeglass frame industry in and around the small community of Agordo.

Banks, insurance companies, telecommunication companies, electricity utilities, and real estate agencies in particular recognise the need for local identification as important for their future business growth. Even the most global of companies are considering their accountability to their places. ABB, headquartered in Zurich, participates actively in various placemarket programmes for the so-called Greater Zurich Area. McDonald's is systematically making efforts to be integrated in the development of its places. The good citizen efforts of these organisations have contributed to improving goodwill with their communities and consumers.

European real estate developers and agents have played less critical roles than their American counterparts. American real estate agents and developers are very active in economic development efforts and one can anticipate that their European counterparts will play an increasing role in the future as place competition accelerates. We see today an increasing number of examples of how real estate developers and agents not only sell and develop property but also participate in larger efforts to rehabilitate an entire city. Real estate developers often have a good understanding of how potential place-buyers make their decisions based on the attractiveness of a given place.

European financial institutions (banks and insurance companies) also tend to participate less actively than US financial institutions in local and regional economic development. However, this is beginning to change, especially on the local level where financial institutions are expected to serve the market for a long period of time. If these companies are to grow, the local market must grow as well. Therefore, an active presence becomes a natural aspect of business strategy for banks and insurance companies.

Telecommunication companies and electric and gas utilities are normally as locally rooted as the financial institutions. Owing to the deregulation of the European market, many of these infrastructure companies must for the first time compete with more subtle weapons than under previous monopoly conditions. Consequently their interest and investment in placemarketing is growing. A number of these companies such as Midland Electricity in the UK have set up special economic development departments or business location teams specifically to assist in placemarketing efforts.

European chambers of commerce and other local business organisations vary greatly in quality of skills and level of involvement. The French system with its strong chamber of commerce and almost public duty orientation is unique in Europe. These types of organisation offer considerable potential. Their influence depends on their vision and leadership. As a result of the European employment crisis during the 1990s, there has been increased interest in the public sector to establish dialogue and partnership with local business organisations.

Hospitality and retail industries (hotels, restaurants, department stores, other retailers, exhibition and convention centres) are beginning to recognise that in many ways their success rests on the local image. A convention centre may have excellent facilities, but if it is in an area with a bad image, it is seriously handicapped. There is increasing co-operation among convention centres and hospitality and retail enterprises in placemarketing and destination development. Often, the personnel working in the hospitality and retail enterprises provide visitors with the first and last impressions of the place, and therefore their possessing good communication skills and a friendly attitude is essential.

Travel agencies fill a natural role in distributing information about a place. Their job is to make the place as attractive as possible without overstating and then disappointing. Many visitors are looking for something unusual, and travel agents must be increasingly prepared to respond with more specialised packages. One European travel agency has even called its company 'Select Travels'.

Labour market organisations have a potentially high impact on a place's attractiveness. There are individual cases where local and regional labour organisations have played a constructive role. Often this follows a crisis threatening the closing of a manufacturing plant or business. Only recently have local labour organisations started to understand the wisdom of co-operating in building a pro-place alliance. Individual labour leader circles have taken active roles in Scotland, Wales, northern Italy and several places in Germany. But generally speaking, labour market organisations need to play a broader and more constructive role in placemarketing strategies.

Architects can also help to create and promote a sense of place. Style and design reflect prevailing attitudes of a place. The skyscraper architecture of early twentieth-century New York communicated much of the attitude of New York: powerful, ultramodern and dominant in industrial and financial aspirations. Also during the twentieth century, architects in Europe created a number of trends that spread to many places. *Art Nouveau* was a romantic and decorative movement that swept through Europe between 1890 and 1910. A reaction to Art Nouveau emerged in Vienna and German Darmstadt. The decorative approach was replaced by a more functional style. Between the two world wars the International Style flourished with architects such as Le Corbusier and Gropius. Le Corbusier was also involved in city planning. The League of Nations Building in Geneva, designed by Le Corbusier, is today part of Geneva's placemarketing as an international meeting point. After the Second World War there was a reaction against the International Style. The post-war period is characterised by standardised construction, inspired partly by a Scandinavian style. Now, though, the pendulum has swung back. The international market is moving away from mass standardised construction towards more place-bound architecture that conveys a sense of the location and people.

Standardised construction is being replaced by styles that emphasise *diversity* and *uniqueness*. Architects are filling a role as interpreters of the special character of a place. They are involved in city planning, introducing pedestrian malls, redesigning marketplaces and returning parks to their original glory. The common theme is that architecture and design should reflect the soul or heart of a place.

Transport companies (airline, taxi and railway) play an important role as placemarketers. A nation's airlines are flying advertisements for nations: Alitalia, Scandinavian Airlines System (SAS), Air France, Austrian Airlines, British Airways and SwissAir. Upwards of 50 per cent of the articles in flight magazines are special-interest pieces intended to sell a destination. The place-bound theme also emerges in airline meals by presenting local, regional and national cuisine. In Figure 3.13, potential customers sample Vienna and its 'highest café'.

Flying different airlines provides an unavoidable international comparison of service orientations and intercultural personnel competence. For many travellers, the first encounter with a nation/place begins with the airline that hosts their travel. The airport can also be used as an important gateway for placemarketing.

Taxi trips, too, influence one's impression of a place. The demeanour of taxi drivers often colours how visitors feel about a place. An aggressive place-marketing strategy should include training taxi drivers to be knowledgeable and good hosts. For example, London taxi drivers are carefully trained and often make a good impression. Other cities in Europe could spend more time training taxicab drivers in courtesy, knowledge, and safe driving.

Railways too can play an important role in placemarketing. For example,

An invitation to Austria's

highest café

Even at 10,000 metres you can enjoy the traditional hospitality of a Viennese café.

Let Austrian Airlines spoil you with coffee, Austrian cakes, pastries and liqueurs on selected flights in Grand Class Europe.

Savour the famous atmosphere of the Viennese café while relaxing in the extra-wide Grand Class Europe - Seats.

A reservation with Austrian Airlines is your ticket not only to the best connections but also to traditional Austrian hospitality.

Visit us at the Internet:
http://www.aua.com

Welcome to
The Friendly
Airline

Welcome to our

Grand Class Europe

AUSTRIAN AIRLINES

Source: Business Week, 16 June 1997

Fig 3.13 ◆ 'An invitation to Austria's highest café'

the high-speed train between Madrid and Seville features TV monitors positioned above the passengers to provide information. The spark in this case was the World Expo in Seville when all of Spain was enthusiastic about presenting its most attractive face to the tourist market.

Media (newspaper, radio, TV) in the 1990s developed a more local and regional focus. Local newspaper, radio and TV stations are bringing more local news, articles and analyses of local development. Media, of course, can help or hurt. If they focus on negative stories – crime, poor schools or pollution – they hurt a place's image. Therefore placemarketers must work closely with their local media to communicate their placemarketing strategy. In successful places, a regular dialogue takes place between the placemarketers and the key journalists because they both have much to gain if the local area becomes more attractive.

Conclusions

In this chapter we have identified four broad strategies to attract the target markets: image marketing, attraction marketing, infrastructure marketing and people marketing. Today, European places are engaging more actively in these types of placemarketing strategies. However, the approaches vary in professionalism and sophistication. Often, difficulties arise because decision-makers lack a useful structure for organising placemarketing strategy and action. Another difficulty is a failure to understand how the target market – the potential buyers – really makes its choices. In the next chapter, we focus on these problems.

4

How place-buyers make their choices

Place-buyers always have a number of high priorities influencing their choices. These priorities and criteria are complex with many factors influencing their evaluations of places. Furthermore, a place-buyer is often represented by more than one person, each with her or his own personal criteria. Some of these criteria are not expressed directly.

These unspoken criteria may be very private and yet of the highest priority. For example, a personal desire to guarantee continued good education for one's family may be critical in a place-buyer's decision; or local access to language training can be important. Such criteria can weigh more heavily in a place-buyer's choice than more formal criteria. A skilful place-seller appreciates, imagines, understands and can in essence put his or herself in the mindset of the place-buyer.

The absence of professional placemarketing strategies in Europe has led naturally to an almost random handling of place-buyers, and, consequently, almost random results. Few places in Europe actually anticipate a place-buyer's priorities and understand the resulting decision processes.

This chapter addresses three questions:

1. What are the main steps and factors influencing place-buyer decisions and steps in the decision process?
2. What additional factors influence place decision-making?
3. How influential are published ratings of places in the place-buying process?

Steps in the place-buying process

Place-buyers always go through a decision process irrespective of whether they are a company planning an investment, a family making a moving decision or visitors planning a vacation. First we will examine the geographical dimension of the decision process and then the administrative dimension.

Geographical dimension

Consider a company going through a site selection process. The potential steps in choosing a site are illustrated in Figure 4.1.

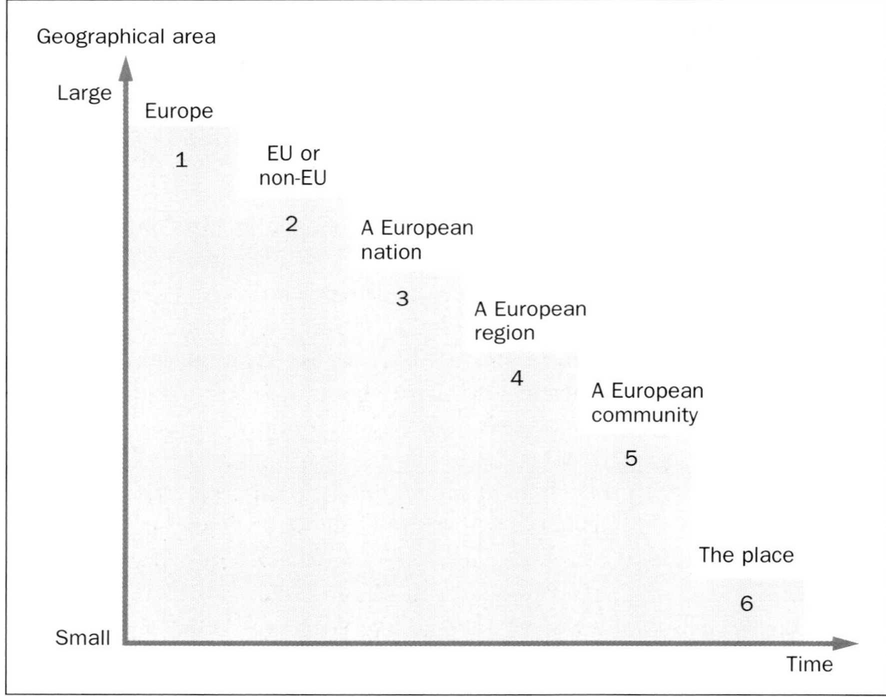

Fig 4.1 ◆ Place-buyers' steps in the European site selection process

The *first step* addresses the question: Europe or not Europe? Considering that 800 million inhabitants make Europe the biggest market in the world in terms of purchasing power, most place-buyers cannot afford to stay outside Europe. Hundreds of places use 'Europeanised' messages in order to boost buyer interest.

In the *second step*, place-buyers are seldom interested in claims such as 'Best in the EU' and instead respond to a more functional argument that the place-buyer will have access to the internal European market. A post-Berlin-Wall theme, especially used in border areas between EU and non-EU, is '*We Provide a Gateway between East and West*'.

In the *third step*, place-buyers throughout Europe face a whole basket of national offerings. Since all European countries today have established national agencies for inward investments and tourism promotion, this third step is crowded with offerings, some unique and many not. Place-buyers will normally inform a number of European nations that a site selection process has started with the obvious intent to boost place-sellers' competition. The paradox, however, is that in a Europe where harmonisation is the core intention behind the internal market, place-buyers receive increasingly differentiated offerings.

The *fourth step*, which concentrates on European regions, is often the most competitive part of the selection process. Only 10–15 years ago, because international competition was not as strong as it is today, regional platforms for business and tourism promotion were few and co-operation was uncommon. Today's Europe is witnessing an enormous upheaval in regionally based activities to meet place-buyer expectations. One example is the establishment of new regional offices in Brussels during the past decade. Today, their number exceeds 160. Place-buyers become quickly spoiled by the service they receive at the regional level. In this fourth step, place-buyers get concrete answers to their concrete questions.

In the *fifth step* the complete basket of attraction factors is made visible when the buyer encounters the potential of the 100,000 communities in Europe. Here the place-buyer meets the decision-makers. Precise hard and soft factors are evaluated. Many soft factors become highly relevant. Place-buyers quickly discover if place-sellers are living up to initial marketing messages and promises, and whether local representatives are acting in a professional manner. If the place-buyer is from a foreign country, it helps if place-sellers are able to communicate in the place-buyer's first or second language. Basic intercultural differences should be known and understood in advance.

The *sixth and last step* is the place itself, where the buyer must choose from among the various 'hot districts' within a specific place. Owing to the decentralised structure of places, new place-sellers sometimes seem to emerge from nowhere. Contradictory and internally competing solutions can be suddenly presented. A climate of local confusion often surfaces at the eleventh hour. Here it is necessary to keep the one-stop shopping model intact. Steps five and six should therefore be co-ordinated to the fullest possible extent.

The knowledge that a place-buyer has made a choice spreads fast among competing places. So does the place's reputation for being a good or bad partner. Places are wise to demonstrate aftercare for their new arrivals to make sure that a good reputation is spread to others. Exhibit 4.1 discusses the roles of information exchange.

Everyone's a seller – exchanging information

EXHIBIT 4.1

For most places, information exchange is crucial to influencing a buyer. Once the company or locators have decided on places to consider for investment, the process of information-gathering begins. It is crucial that everyone in a place be trained as a potential seller. That includes not only the usual suspects – water and traffic experts, human resource specialists – but also the university president and the taxi driver. The intelligent buyer will seek out all sources that forecast place support and quality of life.

What should a place do to prepare itself to become a good seller?

1. *The place needs accurate and thorough information.* A place should routinely examine key areas such as schools, wages, transportation and labour pools for *accuracy*, and have up-to-date information and responses immediately available. These requests can be anticipated and should be ready for sending on demand. Many places fail at this level and eliminate themselves from competition.
2. *The seller should convey the material in a clear, concise and audience-centred manner.* In interviews, all sellers should be well armed with information and be capable of answering questions. Training is essential and can range from a comprehensive videotaped simulation of an important interview to a one-day training session for all service employees.
3. *Information needs to be returned quickly.* Places need to see the search for information as a tight, competitive race. Information is usually sent via fax or email. If a place is decisive and immediate, the buyer will feel that future developments will go smoothly as well.

Most of this information advice is good communication practice – thorough, clear and quick. An effective place-seller will set high standards and follow through on every detail.

Source: Interview with Bob Ady, managing partner of World Business Chicago, 31 August 1998.

Administrative dimension

When an organisation finds itself with a place problem, need or opportunity, it must find a mechanism to retrieve information in order to make a decision. A company may feel that its present location is no longer favourable (a problem); a recruiter may attempt to interest a potential place-buyer in seeing the advantage of a move (a need); or a visitor may be seeking a destination (an opportunity).

Although one may play a variety of roles as place-buyer, the person who has the problem or need or is exploring an opportunity may not be the one who will make the ultimate decision. We can distinguish six place-buyer roles:

1. *Initiator:* The process may be initiated by a person who has the responsibility to investigate the business climate of different markets and places. The impetus might be, for example, 'Europe is one of the world's largest markets. We ought to consider entering the European market'.
2. *Influencer:* Influencers could be colleagues of the initiator. They may provide support, reflection or ideas. It is important to be cognisant of who

influences decision-makers. A wise strategy in a large investment project is to make an effort to identify and influence the influencers.

3. *Decision-maker:* Here we meet the persons who have the formal authority to make decisions. Lots of unnecessary work – and wishful thinking – can be avoided if the place-seller tries to ascertain the real intentions of the decision-maker. To understand this, one has to be sensitive to intercultural differences. For example, a refusal to say 'no' may not mean an eventual 'yes'.
4. *Approver:* This is a person or persons who can approve or reverse a decision. It can be, for example, members of a supervisory board. These people must be convinced that the decision is based on hard evidence in order to avoid backpedalling or backlashes later in the process. For example, a specific investment project backed by financial incentives from a place can experience problems afterwards if doubtful payments are discovered.
5. *Buyer:* The place-buyer is the person who implements the final decision. This person, or in many cases a team, has an important role because he or she will share with others the experiences from the implementation. If the buyer becomes dissatisfied with the implementation, the place risks getting a negative image. Potential buyers will ask colleagues about the outcome. Negatively reported experiences are dangerous for the reputation of a place.
6. *User:* The end-users of the place-buying process include employees, investors, visitors, delegates to conventions or exhibitions, experts, and families moving to the new place. These users are undoubtedly the best placemarketing ambassadors for a place.

To illustrate, imagine that a Boston-based software company selling Internet packages wants to enter the growing European market. The process started after a European conference on teleworking in Vienna in 1995. One of the Boston company's employees participated in the Global Village Conference and she was so inspired by some of the seminars and forecasts that, on her way back to Boston, she wrote a memo to her colleagues (role: *initiator*). The marketing manager was interested and started to gather some general information on European market developments and the location of the desirable places (role: *influencer*). The marketing manager prepared for the CEO a list of potential places: Seville, Milan, Vienna, Hannover, Rotterdam, Milton Keynes, Cambridge, Riga and Stockholm. The CEO, together with the marketing manager, decided to conduct a fact-finding mission. They travelled to three of the places: Vienna, Hannover and Cambridge (role: *decision-maker*). Returning to Boston, the CEO presented to the board of directors a plan for establishing the company's first European office in Vienna. The board approved the plan (role: *approver*). To facilitate the implementation in Vienna, the CEO hired a well-known Austrian who was given complete responsibility to establish the Vienna office (role: *buyer*). After six months, the original initiator moved to

Vienna, took over as business manager and hired six additional employees (role: *user*).

In this place-buying process, different people played different buyer roles. In simpler cases, one or two persons can play all six roles. For example, a person considering travelling to Europe for business purposes can complete the process after a ten minute dialogue with his or her travel agent. At the other extreme, a Korean electronics giant may spend three years involving hundreds of persons in different place-buying roles before deciding where to locate.

Placemarketers need to understand the structure of the buyer's decision process. By understanding the different roles played by different people, placemarketers can implement a proactive strategy instead of following a reactive response. In summary, a place-seller must consider the following:

1. Which persons are involved in the place-buying decision and what are their buyer roles?
2. What specific factors, hard and soft, are used by the various decision-makers?
3. What are the typical patterns of various target market decisions in the place-buying process?

The answers to these basic questions help placemarketers choose effective messages, media, and consultants to make the right decisions at the right time.

Additional factors influencing place decision-making

Information search

Place-buyers often look for different levels of information.

Minimal information search implies that the buyer already highly favours a place and needs confirmation. Basically, the buyer wants to make the best possible deal with the place and may talk about alternative places in order to improve the negotiating position. The actual information search goes quickly and could even be a sideshow. The place-seller's art entails finding out what type of information search is actually taking place in each particular case.

Medium information search indicates a limited number of place options on the buyer's shopping list. An authentic choice situation exists. The place-buyer needs information to acquire an understanding of available opportunities and may already have a basic knowledge of the places being considered.

Maximum information search is characterised by the fact that a total scan of potential places is required. If the project is a large one, consultants are often invited to conduct the information search. With the increasing number of European places competing and at the same time frequently sharing similar offerings, the need for maximum information search exists.

Of key interest to the placemarketer are the major sources of information that the place-buyer consults and the relative influence each has on the subsequent place decision. Buyer information sources fall into four categories:

1. *Personal sources:* family, friends, neighbours, acquaintances, work colleagues.
2. *Commercial sources:* advertising, placemarketing material, data bases, place-sellers, experts, travel agents.
3. *Public sources:* mass media, place-ratings, public reports.
4. *Experiential sources:* visits to places.

The importance of these sources varies with the decision situation. Figure 4.2, describes the steps that a place-buyer goes through in making a choice. In the *first* step, *the total set*, the place-buyer recognises that many eligible places may exist, many of which he may not be aware. In the *second* step, *the awareness set*, having viewed public and commercial sources of information the place-buyer becomes aware of certain potential information. In the *third* step, further search narrows the set to a *consideration set* based on certain important criteria influenced by more personal and experiential sources of information. In the *fourth* step, the *choice set*, only the main competitors remain. Experiential sources now become crucial. The *final choice set* is often formed after intensive negotiations and is more-or-less guided by the exact fulfilment of the search criteria.

In the *total set* and the *awareness set*, various European place-ratings may provide an initial picture of a place's business environment. The Michelin Guide with its popular ratings of various European attractions is an example. Later in the choice process the value of various place-rating guides decreases and more specific factors, hard and soft, become important.

The real value for the place-seller comes from understanding which stage a place-buyer is in. Knowing this, the place-seller can undertake appropriate measures to meet the place-buyer's needs. Then, once a decision is made, a place-seller can obtain more information by following up with questions about why and how the choice was made. This feedback process rarely is exploited even though it is essential that a place should understand its market, its competitors and how potential place-buyers make their choices. Then the place can adapt its strategy to the current placemarket environment. Exhibit 4.2 examines how the site selector gathers information.

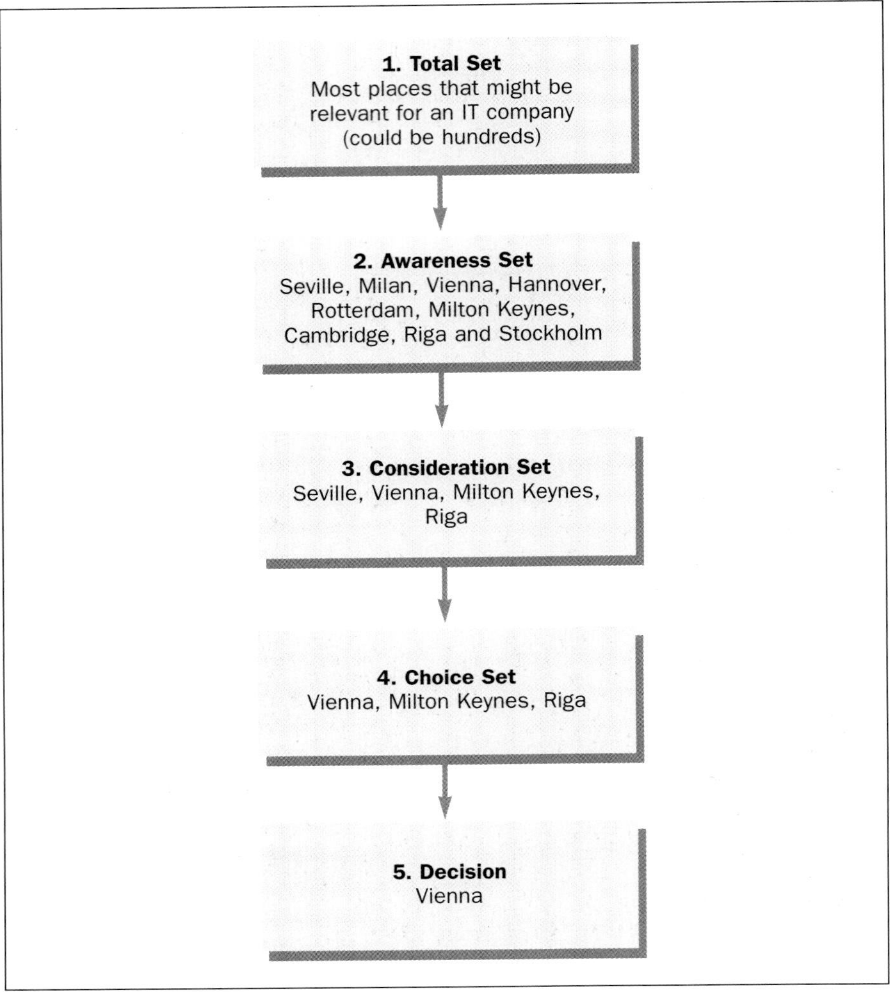

Fig 4.2 ◆ Successive sets involved in place-buyer decision-making

How site selectors buy

EXHIBIT 4.2

The decision to select a site has traditionally been surrounded by mystery and speculation and it is not unlike the selection of the pope or the next site for the summer Olympics. Andrew Levine of Development Counselors International polled 1,000 US companies in an attempt to get into the site selector's head. The results are surprising and demonstrate that place-sellers make investments that buyers consider low priority.

1. The prime source of site selector information was the *corporate grapevine* (informal communication), followed by *new stories* and *corporate travel.*
2. Seen as less valuable were *direct mail,* meetings with *economic development agencies*, and *print advertising.*
3. Site selectors found that the most important place activities were specific and not general. For example, help in

getting permits, *relocating information* and *accessing training programmes* was rated high. Also important was the *speed of response*.

4. Less important to site selectors were general site information, non-requested mailings, phone calls and lavish parties.
5. The solutions suggested by Levine are important: listen carefully to what the client wants; be precise in answering requests; improve the place actors' communication skills to recognise needs; communicate clearly and effectively; and try not to confuse or dazzle the client.

While Levine surveyed only US companies, these results have implications for buying practices in Europe.

Source: Andrew T. Levine, 'Getting inside the site selector's brain', *Commentary*, Fall 1997, pp. 20–26.

Evaluation of alternatives

Place alternatives are evaluated by combining subjective (soft) and objective (hard) factors. The role of subjective factors should not be underestimated, as shown by the examples in Exhibit 4.3.

Subjective evaluation

EXHIBIT 4.3

Example 1

During the 1980s, many individuals and companies invested heavily in apartments located throughout Brussels and London. However, failure to thoroughly analyse the real estate market before investing resulted in poor investment choices. Many people purchased real estate as a reaction to the increasing demand for such property. Some even bought property over the telephone without seeing it, fearing that if they did not invest immediately, the property's value would grow sky-high. The bubble burst in the beginning of the 1990s when the real estate market collapsed with property values plummeting as much as 50 per cent.[1]

Example 2

When a place makes a massive investment in a poorly researched project that is driven by subjective factors, the effects are often costly. In the late 1970s, Britain invested US$121 million in a Belfast plant to build John DeLorean's gull-winged, fibreglass sportscar. The desire to build the plant was, in the words of then Northern Ireland secretary Roy Mason, 'of the utmost political, social, and psychological importance ... and was designed to deal a hammer-blow to the IRA'.[2] However, a week prior to his dramatic announcement, Mason was clearly put on notice by the management consultants, McKinsey and Co. who admonished: 'The chances of the project succeeding as planned are remote'.[3] After four years of lawsuits and bitter acrimony, the project failed. The loss of money and jobs was detrimental, but even more telling was the Industrial Management Board of Belfast's inability to recover, as new projects continue to miss job targets.[4]

Sources:
1. 'I own, I owe, so off to work I go', *The Economist*, 26 December 1992, p. 95.
2. 'Britain saw DeLorean plant as weapon against IRA', Reuters World Service, 16 August 1996 (Lexis Nexis).
3. Reuters.
4. Frank Fitzgibbon, 'North finds little southern comfort', *Sunday Times*, 1 November 1998 (Lexis Nexis).

In spite of subjective considerations, certain basic concepts can help us to understand a place-buyer's evaluation processes.

First, the buyer sees a given place as a bundle of particular attraction factors. Such factors vary with the type of decision. For example:

1. *Vacation sites*: unique attractions, recreation, climate, nature, cost.
2. *Places to live*: job opportunities for both family members, educational system, cost of living, quality of life.
3. *Production sites*: relevant labour skills, labour relations, taxes, land costs, energy.
4. *Service sites*: purchasing power on the local and regional market, relevant labour skills, IT-standards, network of available competences.
5. *Convention sites*: service facilities, capacity, accessibility, service, costs.

Second, place-buyers vary in which attractions they find salient and important. Some attractions are salient because the place-buyer has recently been exposed to a message of high relevance, placing these attraction factors at the 'front of the mind'. The buyer then decides which attraction factors are really important and attaches *importance weights* to the relevant factors.

Third, the place-buyer is likely to develop a set of *beliefs* about where each place stands on each attraction factor. The total set of beliefs that the place-buyer holds about a particular place forms his or her image of the place. There may be a discrepancy between the image and the true standings of the place. The negative image of Croatia – as part of the Balkan crisis – does not necessarily reflect the true situation of investors in, or visitors to, that country.[1] Competition on the placemarket is often a competition between perceptions and images.

Fourth, the place-buyer is assumed to have a utility function for each attribute. The utility function describes how the place-buyer expects value or satisfaction to vary with different levels of each attraction factor. Place-sellers need to estimate the utility function of place-buyers in order to adapt to their offerings and arguments.

Fifth, the place-buyer arrives at attitudes and judgements of place alternatives through some *evaluation procedure*. Buyers may apply different evaluation procedures to make a choice among alternatives. For example, suppose that the Boston-based software company has narrowed the consideration choice set to Vienna, Milton Keynes and Riga. Assume that the company is primarily interested in four attributes: professional competences, strategic location, productivity and costs. Table 4.1 shows how each city rates on the four attributes as judged by the company.

The question is, which city is the Boston place-buyer most likely to favour? If one city dominates the other on all criteria, we would predict that the planners would choose it (such a case is most uncommon). But the choice set consists of cities that vary in their appeal. If the planners rate costs above

Table 4.1 ◆ Place-buyer's rating of three sites

Each attribute is rated from 1 to 10, with 10 representing the highest level for that attribute. Thus, Vienna is rated as having the best strategic location and Riga the best cost profile.

	Attributes			
	Professional competence	*Strategic location*	*Productivity*	*Costs*
Vienna	9	10	9	6
Milton Keynes	10	9	7	7
Riga	7	5	7	10

everything, Riga is the preferred choice; if the planners rate strategic location, above everything, Vienna is the choice. For place-buyers who care about only one attribute, we can easily predict their choices.

In the real evaluation process, place-buyers consider several attributes and assign different weights. If the place-sellers knew the weights that the Boston planners assigned to the four attributes, then they could more reliably predict the preferred city.

Suppose the planners assigned 40 per cent of the importance to competence, 30 per cent to strategic location, 20 per cent to productivity, and 10 per cent to costs. To find the planners' preference for each city, the weights are multiplied by beliefs about each city. This leads to the perceived values set out in Table 4.2.

Table 4.2 ◆ Perceived values of three sites

	Professional competence	*Strategic location*	*Productivity*	*Costs*	***Total***
Vienna	0.4 (9)	0.3 (10)	0.2 (9)	0.1 (6)	**9.0**
Milton Keynes	0.4 (10)	0.3 (9)	0.2 (7)	0.1 (7)	**8.8**
Riga	0.4 (7)	0.3 (5)	0.2 (7)	0.1 (10)	**6.7**

We would predict that in this case the planners, given the weights, will favour Vienna. However, when differences are so small as between Vienna and Milton Keynes, one should be careful about the outcome. An efficient place-seller will add some other factors to the evaluation process.

This model, called the *expectancy value model* of buyer choice, is one of several possible models describing how buyers in practice go about evaluating alternatives. Place-sellers understanding this expectancy value model have great opportunities to intervene. For example, Riga's placemarketers could improve Riga's chances in six ways:

1. *Improve the relevant attributes:* Riga could invest in improving professional competence in the field of software knowledge and Internet and electronic commerce. Riga may already have a fairly strong position, as in theoretical software knowledge, but what Riga needs is practical knowledge of western-style commercial software development. A plan to do this will result in *real repositioning*.
2. *Alter beliefs about attributes:* Because it is generally underestimated it is important that Riga's actual competence in the area of software development should become better known. Attempting to alter beliefs about a place calls for *psychological repositioning*.
3. *Alter beliefs about competitors' standings:* Place-sellers could try to change place-buyer's beliefs about where competitive cities stand on each attribute. This makes sense when buyers mistakenly believe that a competing place has more quality than it actually has. Such *competitive depositioning* could be relevant where a 'new' place like Riga has emerged on the placemarket. Riga should distribute well-targeted, comparative information to potential decision-makers.
4. *Alter the importance weights:* Place-sellers could try to persuade place-buyers to attach more importance to the attributes that the place possesses. Riga, for example, might emphasise the importance of low costs for the Boston-buyer. Productivity figures could also be addressed.
5. *Call attention to neglected attributes:* Riga could draw the buyer's attention to neglected attributes. The good reputation of the huge Riga Technical University can be highlighted. The place-buyer could be invited to meet board members of the university and faculty members with similar research interests. The fact that IBM has established a software team in Riga is another attribute.
6. *Shift the place-buyer's ideals:* Riga can attempt to influence the Boston company's basic priorities, and could point out that its strategic location would permit better entry into the East European marketplace of 50 million people. By attempting to 'reset' the place-buyer's priorities, Riga potentially creates a new set of criteria to be weighed by the place-buyer.

Purchase decision

In the evaluation stage, the place-buyer forms preferences among the places in the choice set and begins to lean towards a particular place. However, at least four factors can intervene between purchase intention and purchase decision.

One factor is the *attitudes of others*. Suppose that the CEO of the Boston company meets a colleague in Boston who warns the CEO about Vienna's relatively high costs. Such attitudes can influence the ultimate purchase decision.

The second factor concerns the place-buyer's *perception of the credibility* of persons involved in the purchase process. A place-buyer's preference increases if he greatly respects the other person's opinion, so it is important for the place-sellers to build credibility.

A third factor influencing a purchaser's intentions is *unanticipated situational factors* that can emerge and alter the buyer's perception of cost and benefits. If the Boston company's CEO learns from the latest edition of the *World Competitiveness Yearbook* that Austria is falling in international ranking in the labour costs category as well as in overall performance, then his/her assessment of Vienna could change. This is especially the case when the evaluations of one or more cities are very close.

A fourth factor is that of *perceived risk*. Purchases, especially costly ones, involve risk-taking. Place-buyers cannot be certain about the purchase outcome. This often produces anxiety and delay. The amount of perceived risk varies with the amount of money at stake, the amount of choice ambivalence, and the amount of buyer self-confidence. Different place-buyers develop different routines for reducing risk, such as postponing decision, further information-gathering, and establishing preference for safe situations. Place-sellers must understand the factors that create a feeling of risk and provide information and support to counter them. Being interested in Riga, our Boston company might feel uncertainty about future relations between the Baltic countries and Russia. At the same time, place-sellers in Riga are probably aware of this objection and must be prepared to soften these concerns.

Place-buyers throughout Europe may face uncertainties owing to political union turbulence. There can suddenly occur a new tax situation in Austria, labour market disputes in France, or overnight withdrawals of incentive packages in any country. Consider the shake-up in investor confidence following the economic transition in Central Europe. Jan Bielecki, director in the European Bank for Reconstruction and Development (EBRD), with a responsibility for Poland, Bulgaria and Albania, described the risk environment: 'Transition countries from the Czech Republic to Albania face serious problems cleaning up their act in politics and business. These countries need to restore – and in some cases create – public confidence in the new system fast, or face consequences ranging from chronic financial scandals to all-out economic collapse'.[2] Most place-buyers approach such turbulence with caution, and place-sellers need to be realistic in countering the problems with real fixes and timely and clear arguments.

In general, there are five types of place-buyer who are frequently encountered in Europe (see Exhibit 4.4).

Who's the buyer?

EXHIBIT 4.4

Place-buyers appear in many guises. The place-marketer's challenge is to identify, as early as possible, which of five types of place-buyer he or she is meeting.

1. The Shopper
A typical shopper from outside Europe, eager to enter the European market, asks many general questions in an attempt to narrow options. The shopper wants to have a general taste of Europe. In this case, the placemarketer should help the buyer structure the decision alternatives and create trust in the place-seller's judgement and helpfulness.

2. The Pawn
The pawn is someone who represents the place-buyer whose identity might be open or hidden. The place-seller should try to identify the real buyer and his or her true options and preferences.

3. The Quick-decider
Like General Patton, a quick-decider is keen to make a decision. Such an approach should be met with the same place-selling attitude and decisive behaviour.

4. The Detailer
This person needs to collect large quantities of detailed information prior to making a decision. Even if some of the details could be questioned, the place-seller must be prepared to deliver specific data.

5. The Grinder
This place-buyer focuses on costs and incentives. The grinder, in the role of a visitor, wants to pay almost nothing while at the same time discover half of Europe. The grinder, in the capacity of an investor, is sensitive towards precise economic bargaining results. The place-seller should be prepared to quantify the economic benefits and avoid vagueness.

By distinguishing these different types of place-buyer through systematic questioning, the place-seller can increase his or her marketing effectiveness.

Post-purchase behaviour

After purchasing and operating in the chosen place, the place-buyer will experience some level of satisfaction or dissatisfaction. The place-seller's job, therefore, does not end when the purchase is made but continues into the post-purchase period. This phase can be called the aftercare period. Indeed, in some European regions such aftercare has been used as one of the main attraction factors to the region.

Post-purchase satisfaction

What determines whether the place-buyer is highly satisfied, somewhat satisfied, or dissatisfied with a purchase? The place-buyer's satisfaction is greatly influenced by how closely the place's perceived performance matches the buyer's prior expectations. Place-buyers form their expectations on the basis of information received from the seller, colleagues, friends and other sources. If the seller exaggerates attraction factors, the buyer will experience *unconfirmed expectations*, leading to dissatisfaction. The larger the gap between expectations and performance, the greater the buyer's dissatisfaction. This suggests that the place-seller must make claims that faithfully represent the place's likely performance levels so buyers are satisfied. A few place-sellers might even understate performance so that buyers experience higher-than-expected satisfaction with the place.

The result of the increased place competition is generally to overstate performance. Instead of giving in to this temptation, the place-seller should stress what is unique about the place rather than exaggerate common factors. Furthermore, the seller should manage a strong aftercare programme. In too many cases there is no marketing follow-through strategy behind advertised messages. This gap between messages and actual place performance should be avoided.

Post-purchase actions

The place-buyer's level of satisfaction or dissatisfaction will influence his or her subsequent behaviour. A satisfied place-buyer has a higher probability of saying good things about the place to others. Many places actively use their satisfied place-buyers as ambassadors. The Alava province, for example, in the southern part of the Basque region, is heavily promoting its satisfied buyers (Figure 4.3).

Dissatisfied customers may resort to one or two courses of action. They may try to reduce dissonance by asking for some sort of compensation, or they may do the opposite and seek information that might confirm the place's high value in spite of their experience. Between these two extremes, the place-seller can act in several ways in order to minimise post-purchase dissatisfaction. In redressing customer grievances the main requirement is to listen and to respond quickly. Responsive place-sellers welcome feedback as a way to improve their performance, and more and more European communities use opinion polls and focused enquiries to gather such feedback information.

Understanding buyer needs and buying processes is essential to building effective marketing strategies. By understanding how buyers go through the process of need recognition, information search, evaluation of alternatives, the purchase decision and post-purchase behaviour, placemarketers can continuously improve their effectiveness.

Influence of place-rating information

Place-buyers typically search for comparative data on the attractiveness of different places. In the case of nations, the data usually include gross domestic product (GDP) per capita, adjusted to purchasing power parity (PPP), annual rate of inflation, interest rates, unemployment level, and other factors. During the 1990s many new indicators have emerged leaving almost no aspect of a nation, region or community untouched.

Place ratings, which have played an active role in the USA, have now

Discover

In Alava your business will have the following advantages:

- A strategic location
- 3 million m² of fully-developed ready-to-use land
- A well-established industrial network
- An intercontinental goods transport logistics centre
- Telecommunications
- Tax incentives for investment
- Highly-skilled labour force
- High quality of life
- Advanced health and social services

Multinational Companies Based in Alava

Company	Country
BAUMANN	CH
BAKELITE AG	D
BAYER	D
DEGUSSA	D
DLW	D
FUCHS	D
MERCEDES BENZ	D
PFERD RUGGEBERG	D
ALCATEL GROUP	F
MICHELIN	F
USINOR SACILOR	F
Giovanni BOZZETO	I
NAKAGAWA DENKI	J
OMROM	J
SMC Corp.	J
DAEWOO	K
QUINTON HAZELL	UK
SAUNIER DUVAL	UK
AMERICAN AIR FILTER	USA
DHL	USA
GUARDIAN INDUSTRIES Corp.	USA
HOME FITTINGS	USA
IBM	USA
PEPSICO	USA
SCOTT	USA
TNT	USA
U.S. PLAYING CARD Corp.	USA

ALAVA+active

ALAVA DEVELOPMENT AGENCY

Landázuri, 15. 01008 Vitoria-Gasteiz (Alava) SPAIN
Tel.: +34 45 15 80 70 Fax: +34 45 15 80 71

CIRCLE 223

Source: 'Basque country Spain', Investment opportunity report, *Site Selection*, June/July, 1997.

Fig 4.3 ◆ Multinational place-buyers already established in Alava

become a common tool in Europe as a result of the intensified competition between places.

Consider the following examples of place-ratings covering European places.

Empirica

The German institute Empirica provides place-buyers and place-sellers with European ranking covering 267 European regions. It points out where the most attractive regions are to be found. The indicators in this case are based on about thirty criteria which include growth dynamics, access to markets, available skills, costs and quality of life. The twenty winning regions – called 'Europe's top 20 regions 1998' – are listed in Table 4.3.

Table 4.3 ◆ Europe's top 20 regions 1998

Rank		*Region*
1	Upper Bavaria	Germany
2	Hannover	Germany
3	Oxfordshire	UK
4	Utrecht	Netherlands
5	Cologne	Germany
6	Paris	France
7	Braunschweig	Germany
8	Gelderland	Netherlands
9	Vienna	Austria
10	Alsace	France
11	Darmstadt	Germany
12	Karlsruhe	Germany
13	Haute Normandie	France
14	Luxembourg	
15	Basel	Switzerland
16	Salzburg	Austria
17	Hamburg	Germany
18	South Holland	Netherlands
19	Tübingen	Germany
20	Zürich	Switzerland

Source: 1998 Investors Guide to Western Europe, Empirica, 1998.

Immediately after these results are published the winners usually exploit their positions in their placemarketing promotions. For example, in 1992 the rating result gave a positive boost to the small and peripheral Swedish region of Jamtland, where place-sellers initiated an international marketing campaign in which the results from Empirica played an integral part.

The growing influence of Eastern Europe is beginning to put pressure on the traditional rankings. Empirica director Wolfgang Steinle observes: 'With more and more members from Eastern Europe joining the union, the centre is walking twenty miles to the east each year'.[3] In the years to come, Eastern Europe is certain to have a greater impact on the rankings.

The World Competitiveness Yearbook

The World Competitiveness Yearbook, produced by the IMD in Lausanne, Switzerland, has an impact that is difficult to overestimate. The yearbook analyses 46 countries that are 'all key nations on a world scale'.

Each year, judgements of nation-attractiveness are announced. Some places welcome the judgements, while others try to forget or disparage the results. The media like to play up these results. Figure 4.4 shows the 1997 results.

As can be seen in Figure 4.4, Northern Europe shows excellent results, especially from a growth point of view. This will certainly be used by various place-sellers in the region. Positive IMD results tend to stimulate a nation to improve its performance. Finnish place-sellers now have a strong argument as

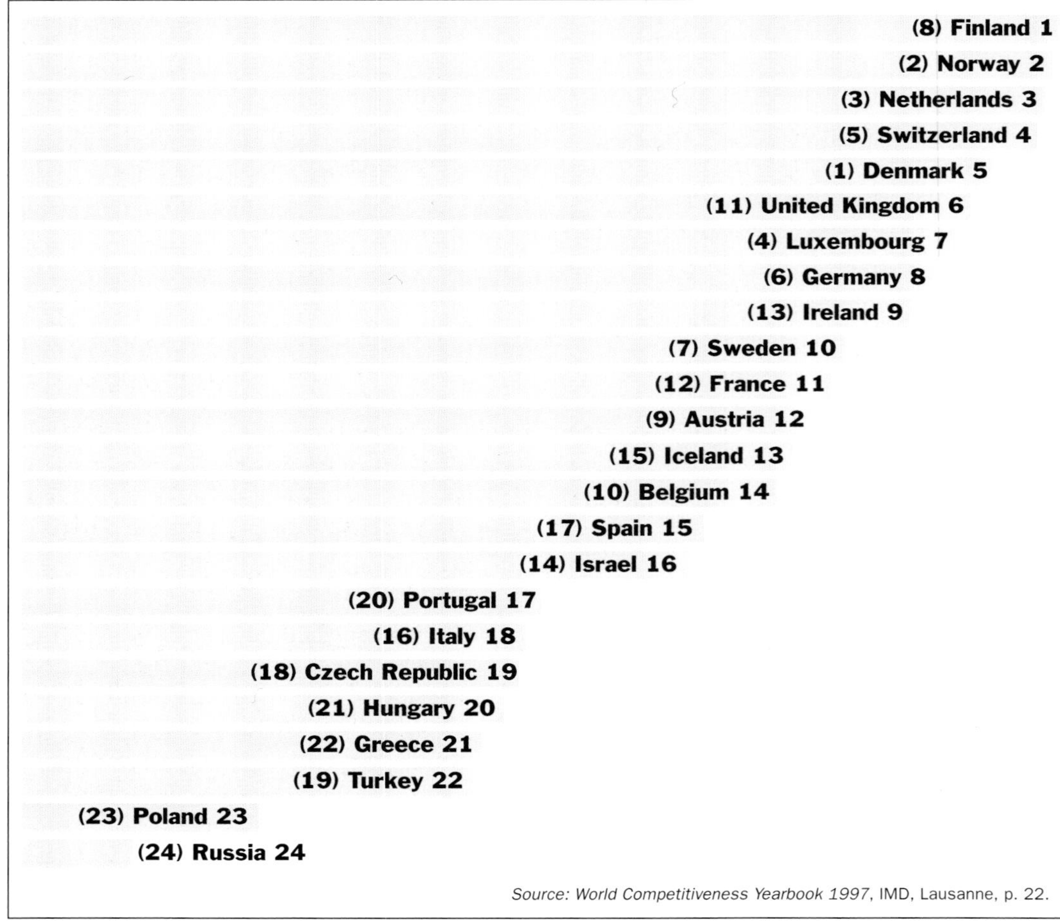

Fig 4.4 ◆ The European scoreboard. Twenty-four European nations are covered (note that Israel is included even though this is not the normal definition of Europe). 1996 rankings are in brackets

to who is the overall winner in Europe after a very severe recession. Among the winning Finnish attractiveness factors are: growth in domestic savings, access to foreign capital markets, connections to the Internet, new information technology, technological co-operation, financial resources, relocation of R&D, and basic research.

Michelin Guide – a readable rating for visitors

In sharp contrast to the hard statistical facts furnished by the *World Competitiveness Yearbook* and *Empirica*, the famous *Michelin Guide* emphasises soft factors. In a new series called the *Michelin Green Guide*, regional ratings from all over Europe are presented. The guide indicates whether a specific region is worth a journey. Regions are classified according to a three-star rating system. One star means that the region is 'interesting', two stars indicate 'worth a detour', and three stars indicate to place-buyers that the region is 'worth a journey'. For example, Denmark has only one place, Copenhagen, qualifying for three stars. Copenhagen is described in three sentences with many soft factors:

> Copenhagen conquers most visitors at first sight and makes them feel at home in no time. This instant appeal is due to a subtle blend of contradictions: there are no grand vistas, yet the large squares, wide avenues, vast green open spaces and lakes create a definite impression of spaciousness. Moreover, the contrasting architectural styles, illustrated by the colourful 18th century houses crowded on both sides of the old harbour, the austere late 19th century town hall, or the ultra-modern shopping arcades welcoming the northern light through their huge glass panels, in no way break up the overall unity, emphasised by the numerous red-brick buildings, green copper roofs, and tall spires punctuating the skyline, but the greatest contradiction of all lies in the unique atmosphere of the place, at once conducive to relaxation and arousing a feeling of feverish excitement, which could explain why so many people are fascinated by the lonely figure of the Little Mermaid gazing out to sea at the entrance to one of northern Europe's busiest harbours. Copenhagen could thus be described in a nutshell as a charming provincial town with the lively atmosphere of a capital city![4]

Of course, Danish place-sellers can exploit these soft and positive evaluations in their marketing strategies.

Since many regions receive no star at all, the implication is that *Michelin Guide* has not found anything of interest there. An obvious marketing goal, therefore, for an excluded region is to put more effort into a value-added process to emerge with more attractions and receive better attention in subsequent editions of the Michelin Guide.

Portrait of the Regions

Another source of information is the *Portrait of the Regions*, which presents each region of Europe one-by-one, in an identical format via maps, diagrams, statistical tables and textual commentaries on regional strengths and weaknesses, population patterns and trends, employment, the economic fabric and the environment.[5] The identical format helps place-buyers to compare places and regions in a practical way. Data for the research have been produced by the European Commission in Brussels in co-operation with Eurostat (Statistical Office of the European Communities) and the member states' statistical institutions.

Other ratings

Various consulting companies in Europe produce ratings covering different aspects of business and placemarkets. For example, the Monks Partnership specialises in rating senior management pay and benefits across Europe. In its *European Real Estate Monitor*, the company Healey & Baker rates quality of life in European cities. The Euromoney publication, *Corporate Location*, rates the placemarket share of various nations. This rating, based on a sample of 500 companies – 100 from each industry sector – reports where each place-buyer has located in the last three years and where it intends to set up over the next three years. Table 4.4 presents a glimpse of this type of placemarketing results.

Table 4.4 ◆ Top five locations in Europe: computing and semiconductors

Country	*Regional ranking*	*Number of plants*	*Regional share*	*World share*	*World ranking*
UK	1	23	13.9%	6.7%	1
Germany	2	20	12.1%	5.8%	2
Ireland	3	18	10.8%	5.2%	4
France	4	13	7.8%	3.8%	7
Hungary	5	9	5.4%	2.6%	13

Total projects: 345.

Source: Philip Swinden, 'A Conservative Victory', *Corporate Location*, May/June, 1997, pp. 8–12.

How are place-ratings compiled?

To understand how ratings may be compiled we illustrate the IMD method of determining the most competitive nations. IMD defines eight different factors broken down into 244 criteria, which aggregate 40,000 data points over a five-year period. Less tangible aspects are measured via a worldwide survey of more than 2,500 leaders. The eight factors which make up the competitive environment are presented in Table 4.5.

Table 4.5 ◆ Factors of competitiveness

Factor	*Description*
1. Domestic economy:	Macro-economic evaluation of the domestic economy (GDP, investments, savings, consumption, production, cost of living, and forecast indicators). Overall 28 criteria
2. Internationalisation:	Extent to which the country participates in international trade and investment flows (balance of trade, exports, imports, exchange rates, foreign investments, protectionism, openness). Overall 40 criteria
3. Government:	Extent to which government policies are conducive to competitiveness (national debt, expenditures, fiscal policies, state involvement and efficiency, justice and security). Overall 39 criteria
4. Finance:	Performance of capital markets and quality of financial services (cost and availability of capital, stock markets dynamism, banking sector efficiency). Overall 20 criteria
5. Infrastructure:	Extent to which resources and systems are adequate to serve the basic needs of business (basic and technological infrastructure, energy self-sufficiency, environmental constraints). Overall 30 criteria
6. Management:	Extent to which enterprises are managed in an innovative, profitable and responsible manner (productivity, labour costs, corporate performance, management efficiency). Overall 27 criteria
7. Science and technology:	Scientific and technological capacity (R&D resources, technology management, scientific environment, intellectual property). Overall 20 criteria.
8. People:	Availability and qualifications of human resources (population and labour force characteristics, unemployment, education, quality of life, attitudes, and values). Overall 40 criteria

Source: The World Competitive Yearbook 1997, IMD, Lausanne, Switzerland, p. 40.

Most of the criteria listed in Table 4.5 can be measured by hard data supplied by various statistical sources. Other criteria of high relevance which are more qualitative are gathered by an annual survey sent to executives in top and middle management positions in all the countries covered by the yearbook. The panel of experts includes 2,515 executives. Each respondent rates only the country he or she is working in to ensure that they possess a deep knowledge of the business environment of a particular place. The overall results are published in the annual yearbooks, which are sold and intensively quoted in the countries covered.

How reliable are place-ratings?

Place-ratings are seen to have at least three questionable characteristics. *First*, different ratings services often produce inconsistent rankings for the same community, region or nation. Confusion may occur when a city receives the highest rating in one survey but then, a month later, another rating using similar criteria reveals that the same city has fallen into third position.

The *second* problem is that the same rating service can change the place's position owing to new definitions and methods of collecting data. This can generate frustration and, if methods are profoundly changed, even undermine general trust in the rating.

The *third* problem is the difficulty of rating over one hundred thousand communities and hundreds of officially recognised regions in Europe. So much data are available that place-buyers have difficulty extracting meaningful information. Two Eurostat sourcebooks, *Europe in Figures* (425 pages) and *Portrait of the Regions* (three volumes) are examples of abundance in statistics and comparisons.

How useful are place-ratings to buyers and sellers?

In a world with so many new and competing 'hot spots', place-ratings can offer a quick and convenient picture. They require little effort to understand. Place-sellers can easily exploit the results, especially in relation to media looking for quick and convenient headlines. A placemarketer can use positive ratings in advertising activities as well. On the other hand, negative ratings stimulate a place to strengthen its efforts to improve.

For a place-buyer, ratings should basically be seen as a scanning tool supplying initial data. It would be foolish to rely only on these. The place-buyer needs additional facts and needs to put personal weights on these attributes.

Conclusions

This chapter has described the steps in the place-buyer's evaluation process. With more than one hundred thousand European communities and hundreds of regions, place-buyers have much to consider. Many new and unknown places are emerging in the placemarket, creating new opportunities for place-buyers. As a consequence, the place evaluation process is becoming increasingly complex. In order to discover desirable locations, place-buyers are forced to be more systematic.

The model helps placemarketers to organise their understanding of what many place-buyers go through in making a place decision. While being useful, the model may provide an overly rational explanation of how place decisions are made. Many place-buyers shortcut the decision-making process for a variety of reasons. Effective place-sellers must continuously improve their understanding of what place-buyers think and do in making their place choices.

5

Place auditing and strategic market planning

European media are reflecting the plight of many cities, communities, regions, and nations. A sampling of headlines includes:

- '*Saab to shift convertible production to Austria*':[1] The annual production of 20,000 Saab convertibles in Finland (Valmet) will be reduced.
- '*Money and jobs flowing out of Germany*':[2] Foreign investment has sunk to a new low, while German firms are moving out.
- '*Electrolux hit by $113m loss in wake of shake-up*':[3] Electrolux, the world's biggest supplier of household appliances, is planning to shut 25 plants and 50 warehouses.

Why are places in such predicaments? Are they victims of powerful global and European forces that no amount of planning could have averted? Or have these places failed to plan a better future?

The fact is that most troubled places are both victims and contributors to their downfall. Seismic changes are occurring in the location and investment patterns of the world's major industries. When automobile production moved into Eastern and Central Europe in the 1990s, traditional auto production places could do little to prevent this out-migration.

But places themselves share some of the blame. Many fail to anticipate changes, and many simply resist change (see Exhibit 5.1). They drift until shaken by some great crisis that causes a loss of companies, residents and visitors. Faced with an upheaval, concerned public officials and some business leaders hastily form commissions charged with saving their place. When the early warnings in the automobile industry are heard in many Western European places, it is puzzling to observe that so little is done to make a place more attractive to these companies.

Smoke rings in Spain

EXHIBIT 5.1

World consumption of tobacco is falling. At the same time, the European Community is annually subsidising European tobacco production with ECU1 billion. One centre of production is the area that surrounds the Spanish village Talayuela in the Estremadura region. Here, about 170 kilometres south west of Madrid, tobacco production is a key industry. The region produces 85 per cent of the 42,000 tons of Spanish tobacco. The region employs 16,000 workers in full-time jobs while the country grapples with 22 per cent unemployment. More than 80 per cent of what farmers receive per kilo is based on subsidies from Brussels. Most people understand that this subsidy, at least in the long run, is unsupportable. In spite of this, the region devotes its resources to defending the high level of subsidies. A new place development strategy is not high on the agenda. Yet place sellers from the region are only marking time, as one day the subsidy will end and 16,000 jobs will disappear.

Source: Tove Nandorf, 'Without EU subsidies there is no hope', *Dagens Nyheter*, 14 July 1997, p. 4.

Usually there is a local or community-level organisation in charge of economic development. Too often, officials at this level do not do their job. There may be at least five reasons behind this problem:

1. Rethinking incentives happens too infrequently. Officials may think that some governmental agency will provide a rescue package.
2. There might be a lack of expertise concerning the ability to prepare and comprehend forecasts.
3. Often, no dialogue takes place between the leading enterprises and the public officials of a place. No early warnings are communicated and discussed.
4. Weak local leadership can undermine even the best attempts of forecasting and problem solving.
5. Plans are carefully constructed and hopes are high for completion. But no one is able to implement action and the plans collect dust.

Places often have access to some apparatus – an economic commission, a development agency, a community business unit, a chamber of commerce – that is supposed to take responsibility for forecasting and planning the future of the place. Here we will address two questions that define the place issues:

1. What planning approaches are places using today to guide their development?
2. How can strategic market planning help places to improve planning results?

Four approaches to place development

There are four basic approaches to place development:

1. Community service development
2. Urban redesign and planning
3. Economic development
4. Strategic market planning

While each approach follows a different philosophy for creating and maintaining viable communities, combinations among the different approaches are most common. We describe each approach below.

Community service development

The basic idea behind community service development is to create a quality environment for two target markets: (1) citizens currently living and working in the community, and (2) potential citizens (external place-buyers).

Community service development experts support good schools, adequate health facilities, daycare service, accessible bureaucracy, and so on. All of this contributes to the quality of life in the community. At the same time, the cost aspects are of a definite concern for citizens and place-buyers. A balance must be struck between adequate and attractive community services and the costs associated with supplying them.

Communities should search for innovative methods to provide good public services at a reasonable cost. Europe is full of community experiments in this area. For example, a clear trend is the increased use of information technology and intercommunity service co-operation to cut costs and increase communication feedback. The small communities of Naestved in Denmark and Ennis in Ireland have developed a new dimension to community services by using IT on a broad scale. Naestved participates in a pan-European project called 'Infoville' aiming for improved community service by using information technology. Other demonstration sites are Torino, Valencia, Meissen in Germany and Hampshire County Council in the UK.

Urban redesign and planning

Urban redesign and planning focuses on enhancing the design qualities of a place, that is, its architecture, open spaces, land use, street layout, pedestrian areas, cleanliness, and environmental quality. Larger European cities have during the past two decades invested huge resources in local redesign with both large and small projects. In London, for example, large investments are being made in the London Docklands, while considerably smaller investments also occur, such as in the newly dedicated Globe Theatre that provides the atmosphere of a living Shakespearean theatre. In Paris – 'the Mega-project Mecca of Europe' – we find the Pompidou Centre, the impressive La Grand Arche in La Défense resembling the famous Arc de Triomphe, and the new library Bibliothèque François Mitterand. Almost all large European cities today are carrying on redesign programmes to make their place more attractive in the placemarket.

Smaller cities and communities have also been turning to urban redesign projects, often using a 'back to our roots' theme. The city of Dubrovnik in Croatia – with a population of 70,000 – rebuilt its medieval city after the Serb bombardment. Its citizens are committed to keeping their ancient roots alive and to communicate their heritage to the world market of visitors.

These projects can often create a new sense of pride in local traditions. The successful urban designer should have the capacity to express the historical tradition and heritage of a place within a modern context. The presumption is that the urban redesign programme is part of a well-thought-out and long-term strategic marketing plan.

Urban designers have begun incorporating greater ecological/environmental considerations into their planning. They are assessing the ecological consequences of greater population density, high-rise living, traffic and parking congestion, air pollution, city spaces, and so forth. Quality of life is interdependent with ecological concerns and has become a common driving force behind much redesign and planning. During the 1990s most communities in Europe have worked out some basic ecological plans. These efforts are often being marketed.

Economic development

Poor growth performance in many European places has pushed communities to improve their economic development services. Economic development professionals focus largely on helping a place to enhance its competitiveness. They analyse a place's strengths and weaknesses, opportunities and threats. On this basis, they then propose various projects.

Many cities, communities and regions have established economic business development units or agencies. These are normally separate from urban community planning units, which focus on infrastructure. There are at least three different ways of organising economic development activities.

First, there is the *in-house model* that is completely under public control. The leading politicians and public officials are the decision-makers, while the actual day-to-day work is carried out by the unit's head and staff. The problem in this case is that the unit will have to listen to people from different parts of the community 'who speak different languages' and have different agendas. The unit has to decide whose opinions they should give the most weight to.

Given its interest in potential votes, the unit may not always pursue the most rational course of action.

Second, there may be a *mixed model* where responsibility is shared between the public and private sectors (often the leading local companies). The advantage here is that the business community shares responsibility and may also share the financial burden. The disadvantage is that division of work-sharing and responsibilities between the parties can be unclear.

Third, some communities and regions have chosen an *outsourcing model*. It can be in the form of a company with shares being bought by various local actors (for example 50 per cent by the community and the rest from leading companies and perhaps even local institutions). Another outsourcing model is to buy all placemarketing planning and services from a specific consulting company.

Of these three models, the second is most common in Europe. And frequently, the co-owned community-company (mixed model) outsources some placemarketing activity to existing consultants as in the third model.

Strategic market planning

More and more communities have adopted a strategic market planning approach in contrast to places doing *ad hoc* planning. Strategic market planning, in the context of places, has passed through three generations (see Table 5.1).

The *first generation* consisted largely of smokestack chasing, which has a long history and is still far from over. Generous incentive packages, especially concentrating on manufacturing industries – 'the real jobs' – and low operating costs, are some of the key ingredients in these place-selling messages. Cheap labour and land, combined with certain tax offerings, make up the more attractive local business climate. Many Eastern and Central European communities are now using these arguments.

In the 1970s and 1980s, places moved slowly to the *second generation* of strategic marketing planning. This generation is marked by the emergence of a number of new target groups in the planning efforts. Instead of a single goal, such as luring manufacturing jobs from other places, multiple goals appeared such as retention, start-ups, tourism, export, promotion and inward investment. Places changed from using a *hit-or-miss* approach and quick fixes to more refined strategies based on competitive analysis and market positioning. Some places have started to segment markets and identify various types of place-buyer. These places moved from *mass marketing* of diffuse products (typically financial incentives and pure subsidies) to *specialised marketing* emphasising the place's unique products that are tailored to specific customer needs. Parallel to this, places put more emphasis on maintaining internal markets and resources: existing businesses, industries, entrepreneurs, products and services,

Table 5.1 ◆ Three generations of strategic market planning

Generation	*Objectives*	*Methodology*	*Underlying marketing rationale*
First generation Smokestack chasing	• Manufacturing jobs	• Luring facilities from other locations	• Low operating costs • Government subsidies
Second generation Target marketing	• Manufacturing and service jobs in target industries now enjoying profitable growth • Improving physical infrastructure	• Luring facilities from other locations • Retention and expansion of existing firms • Improving vocational training • Public/private partnerships	• Competitive operating costs • Suitability of community for target industries • Good quality of life (emphasis on recreation and climate)
Third generation Competitive niche thinking	• Preparing the community for the jobs beyond 2,000 • Manufacturing and high-quality service jobs in target industries expected to enjoy continuing growth into the future • Selectivity and sophistication are key objectives	• Retention and expansion of existing firms • Spurring local entrepreneurship and investment • Cluster building • Selective recruiting of facilities from other locations • More intense public/private partnership • Developing technology resources • Improving commercial and technical education	• Prepared for growth in the contemporary world-wide economy • Competitive operating costs • Human and intellectual resources adaptable to to future change • Good quality of life (emphasis on cultural and intellectual development)

Source: Adapted from John T. Bailey, *Marketing Cities in the 1980s and Beyond*, American Economic Development Council, Chicago, 1989. Used with permission of American Economic Development Council.

and collective resources such as universities, research parks and financial institutions.

During this generation, more public/private partnerships grew. This was especially the case where some leading companies in the local context were willing to participate actively in the process. However, a truly broad spread of such partnerships did not occur in Europe during the second generation. Many European approaches remained quite centralised.

In the 1990s, with increased unemployment rates, European places began moving into the *third generation* of product development and competitive niche thinking. In the global economy it is crucial to develop competitive positions that stand out in the marketplace. Places are seeking to define themselves as distinctive places with specific advantages for target industries. Niche products based on unique combinations are offered to the selected target markets. Local clusters of related industries are being stimulated. Each place wants to combine its clusters with training facilities and infrastructures of railways, roads, telecommunications, and airports. Quality of life is now interpreted more broadly than in the second generation. The intellectual climate, openness of the place and entrepreneurial encouragement are now important attraction factors.

In recent years, place-bound identity has become increasingly effective and prevalent in business positioning strategy. Companies are therefore more open to different types of local/regional co-operation. This is seen increasingly among banks, insurance companies, power utilities, telephone companies and hauliers. These companies, in particular, have in common the simple fact that it is not easy to move away from the home market. One consequence is that a more intense public/private partnership is occurring in Europe.

These facts reflect the growth, development and sophistication of place competition in a changing world economy. Many places have become more *businesslike* and market-oriented in their economic development activities as a result of intensified competition. Residents themselves have come to notice the lack of long-term and sustainable results of the first- and second-generation's approach. What once was a question of lowering costs and attracting subsidies has today become a much more professional and sophisticated value-adding planning process. These processes are anchored in long-term strategic plans.

The economic downturns in Europe of the 1990s have strengthened the third generation diffusion. The old '*state–national model*' maintained by large subsidies to local and regional levels has been questioned, or more accurately stated, has failed. The old approaches are replaced by a strong decentralisation where places themselves take the initiative. In such a decentralised world a strategy best described as 'in search of excellence' emerges. This provides the nucleus or key for a more dynamic and developing Europe.

The strategic market planning process

Places must begin to do what business organisations have been doing for decades, namely *strategic market planning*. By strategic market planning we do not mean *budgeting* as when a community estimates annually its expected revenues and costs in order to achieve an appropriate balance. Nor do we mean *project planning* as when a place decides to build a stadium, a new town hall or waterfront. Nor do we mean *short-range planning* as when a place makes some decisions about finances, taxes and investments for the next year or two. Nor do we mean *long-range planning* which consists of extrapolating the place's future population and resources and developing suitable infrastructure expansion as may be found in capital budgets.

Strategic market planning starts from the assumption that the future is largely uncertain, but on the other hand, the future of a place can be influenced by strategic actions and plans. The community's challenge is to design itself as a flexible system that can absorb shocks and adapt quickly and effectively to new developments and opportunities. This means that the community must establish *information, planning, implementation* and *control systems* that enable it to monitor the changing environment and respond constructively to *changing opportunities* and threats. The aim is to prepare plans and actions that integrate *objectives* and *resources* with the changing opportunities of the place. Through the strategic planning process, places can create a unique selling proposition. Certain attraction factors are encouraged while other factors may be de-emphasised.

Managing strategic market planning is more difficult for communities and regions than for individual companies. Companies typically have a clear line of authority and hierarchy as well as a balance sheet and a profit-and-loss statement to measure yearly progress. Communities, on the other hand, are chronic battlegrounds where interest groups battle for power and push their competing agendas and strategies. Whereas the private sector company pursues the unifying goal of profit, community economic development runs the risk of being compromised by multiple interest groups and periodic elections. Where institutional arrangements fail to reconcile conflict and leadership fails to emerge, communities typically fail or stagnate. Strategic market planning is highly unlikely to succeed in sharply divided communities where consensus-building mechanisms fail to work. However, European practice shows that the strategic market planning process can work in most communities where leadership, institutions and procedures exist that favour structured decision-making about the future of a place. Placemarketers can talk in terms of a high intellectual capital in these places.

But one should not underestimate a place's opportunity, just like that of business, to find objective and measurable performance criteria. For a community, success can be measured in terms of a strengthened tax base, solidity, business start-ups, new residents, and so on. These measures already exist. It simply means putting them in a development context.

The strategic market planning process moves through five stages that answer the following questions:

1. *Place audit:* What is the community like today in a comparative perspective? What are the community's major strengths/weaknesses, opportunities/threats (called SWOT)?
2. *Vision and goals:* What do the community's businesses and residents want the community to be?
3. *Strategy formulation:* What broad strategies will help the community reach its goals?
4. *Action plan:* What specific actions must the community undertake to carry out its strategies?
5. *Implementation and control:* What must the community do to ensure successful implementation?

The following discussion describes the major concepts and tools used at each stage of the strategic market planning process.

Conducting the place audit

The first task facing a team responsible for charting a community's future course is to understand accurately what the community is like and why. The tool for doing this systematically is called a *place audit*. Hard and soft attraction factors must be scrutinised in a comparative context. The team must make an attempt to sort these factors into competitive strengths and weaknesses, and then follow up with an effort to relate them to opportunities and threats, thus providing the basis for visions and goals. An example of how a place audit can serve as a launching pad for success is Sophia Antipolis, Exhibit 5.2.

Sophia Antipolis invents itself

EXHIBIT 5.2

In 1960, Pierre Lafitte, then deputy director of the Ecole des Mines de Paris, formed a vision of 'An international city of wisdom, science and technology'. In a climate where big companies did not share information or work together, this city would be a break from the European norm. The park would combine industry, education, research, lifestyle, commerce and culture into a positive and fertile work and living environment. In 1972, Sophia Antipolis was launched at a location 18 kilometres outside Nice.

To turn this vision into reality, planners established an operative platform. Sophia Antipolis SAEM was co-founded by the Alpes–Maritimes District Council and the Nice–Côte d'Azur Chamber of Commerce and Industry. A number of small communities ▶

in the area such as Mougins, Biot and Valbonne also understood and supported the vision. With the co-operation of these local community leaders and the execution of basic marketing strategy, the operative organisation developed Sophia Antipolis.

Before the project was begun, the organisers conducted a self-audit to best identify the strengths, weaknesses, opportunities and threats of Sophia Antipolis. The goal was to create a 'cradle of creativity' by bringing science and technology together with business and art so as to afford the most productive and interactive environment. The result was an outline of a twenty-year strategic plan.

In order to realise these goals and make Sophia Antipolis a success, the choice of a location was critical; the proximity of France's second largest airport, the French Riviera and Monaco all added to the marketing power of Sophia Antipolis. Equally important were the park's landscaping and zoning, which were carefully planned to encourage the development of residential areas (only 10 per cent of the park's 5,750 acres are paved or built on).

Several important lessons can be learned from Sophia Antipolis. *First*, the importance of co-operative, goal-oriented planning cannot be stressed enough. It is owing to the hard work and committed interest of a diverse range of community and business leaders that Sophia Antipolis is able to use so many existing resources to attract potential investors. *Second* is the necessity of a long-term strategy. Sophia Antipolis could not have succeeded as a creative centre without the plans for a long period of development. Quick-fix solutions are seldom successful. *Third* is the success of a focused design. Sophia Antipolis built itself around growing technology, arts and culture, and a positive living environment. These factors were instrumental not only to the realisation of the park's twenty-year plan, but they also offered buyers a clear set of benefits to boost the park's marketing potential.

Forty years later, Lafitte's vision is a thriving success. Sophia Antipolis spans a space equivalent to a quarter of the surface area of Paris and is home to 1,050 companies, 17,000 engineers and technicians, and 5,000 researchers. An excellent example of co-operative, proactive success, Sophia Antipolis has transformed a once tourist-dependent region into a thriving centre of creative achievement and prosperity.

Sources: Sophia Antipolis, Internet: http://www.saem-sophia-antipolis.f...polis/sophia/gen_info/gen-info.htm; interview with Alain André, CICA, Sophia Antipolis, 20 August and 29 October 1998; interview with Christian Cabrol, Marketing Manager, Sophia Antipolis, 31 October 1998.

Establishing the place's attraction factors

A place audit must start with relevant information about its attraction factors. Of course, economic and demographic features are basic. Every community must assess its population; purchasing power; competence; housing market; industry structure and labour market characteristics; health profile; natural resources; transportation facilities; quality of life; and education and research institutions. This type of basic data is published annually by many European communities.

Unfortunately, simple existing data are not enough. New combinations of data are part of a winning market planning effort. The team must therefore initiate *fact-finding missions* with an innovative ambition. If, for example, data show that senior city residents are seeking quieter, more affordable places to live, a small town may find it advantageous to package tranquil virtues and market them to this target audience. Suddenly this prospect reveals a whole new set of opportunities. The art is to find the winning combination.

Identifying the place's main competitors

A place must do more than simply establish that it provides a good fit to the target market's needs. Every place needs to identify its competition. Thus London, Paris and Frankfurt are competing for the same concept of the 'European financial centre'. On a much smaller scale, numerous wine producing regions and places in Europe are competing with each other over which has the best brands, vineyards and production resources.

A place needs to identify its main competitors in each specific niche or arena. This identification process extends beyond even European borders. For example, Malta with its place-selling message '*We've Created a World-class Climate*' competes with Singapore and Miami in the niche of financial services. In some areas there is the possibility that competitors could also be future partners. The concept of *twin cities* is becoming more popular in Europe because partnerships can provide new resources in the global placemarket.

Relative to other places, a place can be one of the following: a superior competitor, a poor competitor or a weak competitor.

1. *A superior competitor:* A place that is a superior competitor must protect its position. If it is excessively attractive, it might experience too much growth. This can result in traffic congestion, rising rents and labour costs, and damage to the infrastructure. The place must also worry about the possible emergence of new competition. The decision to build the Oresund Bridge between Copenhagen and Malmö – one of the biggest European infrastructure investments in the 1990s – has pushed the two nearby communities of Helsingør on the Danish side and Helsingborg on the Swedish side to join forces in order to compete more effectively against potentially superior competitors.
2. *A peer competitor:* Here, two competing places might be equally attractive. Intense competition can stimulate each to develop better strategy. Co-operation is also an alternative. Consider the co-operative telecommunication agreements between some places, such as the agreement between '*Telecom Valley*' in southern France and '*Telecom City*' of Karlskrona, Sweden. Such cross-border agreements between places that can work together as peers can offer new stimulation to the local business climates.
3. *A weak competitor:* When a place is a weak competitor, quick fixes won't really solve its problem. The only solution is to make extraordinary efforts in the field of strategic market planning. Europe has already seen many examples of how such repositioning is possible, even in places with a smokestack image such as in the Ruhr area, Belgian Wallonia, the industrial rust belt in England, and in a number of places in the Czech Republic and Poland.

The first challenge is to learn from good competitors what they have done to be successful. Second, the place must learn how to do it better.

Identifying the major trends and developments

Since strategic market planning is a long-term process, it is vital to anticipate main trends and developments likely to affect places. These trends should be discussed not only on individual levels, but also more collectively within all kinds of community organisations in the search for new ideas.

Communities need to pay special attention to the following trends:

- In spite of current generous national and EU funding for regional and community programmes, European communities in the future will have to rely more on their own capabilities to generate a dynamic local climate.
- Places will be impacted increasingly by European and global developments and changes. Therefore, they must actively monitor and even anticipate developments in other parts of the world. So far, too few European communities appreciate the impact of globalisation on their future.
- Places are often stuck in a dilemma. They are caught between the need to support public services, owing partly to high unemployment, and service decline owing to tax-resistant voters. As a result, these places will need to make the most of diminishing financial resources. This means different and more innovative approaches to service delivery. European taxpayers in many countries are on the verge of a tax revolt.
- Places will need to be more attentive to environmental forces and regulations in planning their future. A current European battle concerns which places are environmental leaders. Stronger places can use this as part of their strategic market planning; Geneva, for example, proclaims itself to be the '*Cleanest City in the World*'.
- Places are also competing to be leaders in the growing area of information technology. Many communities see the advantage of becoming a pilot community for new IT applications, often with the support of an EU programme.

These and additional macrodevelopments (for example lifestyle changes, the growing number of the elderly, decentralisation from national to local levels, integration between Western and Eastern Europe) must be identified. The community must assess the impact of these developments and take steps to respond in a proactive way.

On a less macro level, there are vital trends and developments influencing the business environment in specific industry sectors. Here are examples:

- With threats surrounding the long-term future of Airbus, German places have been confronted with the question of what to do without Airbus production. Places such as Hamburg, site of the Airbus GmbH management headquarters, Bremen, the second development centre after Hamburg, and Dresden, Laupheim, Stade and Varel are all integrated into the Airbus system.

- What are some of the main issues brought about by the restructuring of Contract Electronics Manufacturers (CEM)? Electronics companies, as well as others, are now systematically outsourcing production to the best possible enterprises/places. In the electronics industry this means that only clusters of absolute global excellence in Europe have a chance to compete. The CEM megawave, while a threat to many places, is an opportunity for others. The electronics industrial cluster in Irvine, outside Glasgow in Scotland, could be a winner owing to its tight concentration and cost structure. The main challenge for the threatened places with electronics industrial clusters is to identify how to outperform Glasgow or perhaps to join forces.
- If car manufacturers with production plants in Central and Eastern Europe achieve higher productivity and better quality than those in Western Europe, the latter will have to respond. But it will not be easy. A maintenance engineer earns the equivalent of about DM 650 a month at Audi's engine plant in western Hungary; the same engineer in a German Audi plant earns eight times as much.[4] The German location will have to mount an aggressive value-added process to compete.

Analysing the place's strengths and weaknesses

It is one thing to catalogue the characteristics of a place and another to classify them into major *strengths* and *weaknesses*, as well as *opportunities* and *threats* (SWOT analysis). Unfortunately, many communities publish great volumes of facts and figures without classifying their impact. The potential place-buyer is left with the burden of sorting out the trees from the forest. The relevant message and the unique attraction factors are hidden in endless and meaningless data. In contrast, the Swiss city of Lausanne markets itself with a clear focus supported by *relevant* data. The focus is captured in the slogan: '*Lausanne – Olympic Capital*'. Lausanne has taken a unique position as the seat of the International Olympic Committee and several international sports federations. This fact is further reinforced by a long list of supporting activities: international sports events, Lausanne's Olympic Museum, one of Europe's foremost congress towns, host of several multinational headquarters, and international training facilities. Thus, the strategic market position of the city includes a sharply-drawn focus and related attributes which are packaged and delivered to the place-buyer.

A place needs to take an outside-in approach and identify which of its characteristics represent a major strength, minor strength, neutral factor, minor weakness, or major weakness in terms of what specific place-buyers are seeking. A place's competitive position reflects two sets of conditions: (1) outside forces that are generally beyond local/regional influence, and (2) location characteristics which specific location actions might influence. What is needed is a clear and sufficient long-term strategy where major strengths are levered to a maximum and where there is time enough to improve certain weaknesses.

Consider a hypothetical community that conducts an analysis on its strengths and weaknesses. The strategic market team assesses the eighteen attraction factors discussed in Chapter 3, and the results are shown in Table 5.2.

Table 5.2 ◆ Strengths and weaknesses

	Major strength	*Minor strength*	*Neutral*	*Minor weakness*	*Major weakness*
Hard factors					
Econonomic stability		x			
Productivity				x	
Costs	x				
Property concept					x
Local support services and networks				x	
Communication infrastructure		x			
Strategic location	x				
Incentive schemes	x				
Soft factors					
Niche-development		x			
Quality of life			x		
Professional and workforce competences			x		
Culture		x			
Personnel		x			
Management				x	
Flexibility and dynamism			x		
Professionalism in market contacts					x
Entrepreneurship				x	
The unexpected relevancies			x		

Of course, all the attraction factors are not equally meaningful to different target groups. It is necessary to choose the factors of importance to each target group and assign importance weights to these individual factors. When combining performance ratings and importance levels, four possibilities emerge (see Figure 5.1).

Cell A importance factors indicate that the place rates poorly and that critical improvements are needed, hence 'concentrate here'. In cell B the impor-

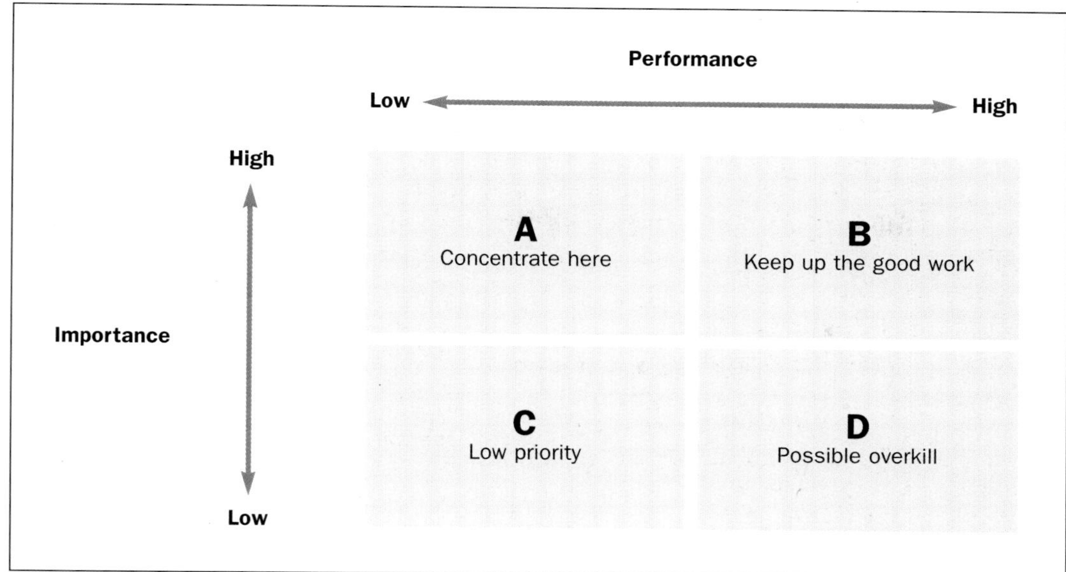

Fig 5.1 ◆ Performance/importance matrix

tance factors show that the place is already strong, hence 'keep up the good work' and continue the value adding process. In cell C, low-importance factors indicate that the place is performing poorly; these factors consequently are of 'low priority'. Into cell D fall unimportant factors where the place is performing strongly; perhaps it is 'overkill' or overinvesting in these factors.

Even the concept of a strength must be interpreted carefully. Although a place may have a major strength, that strength does not necessarily constitute a competitive advantage to the selected target market. Competitors may have the same strength level on that factor. What becomes important, then, is for the place to have greater relative strength on factors important to the selected target group. Thus, two competing places may both enjoy low manufacturing costs; but the one with the lower cost has a net competitive advantage. The other place may have to provide some extra inducements to compensate. In practice it is often difficult to compare two places on cost, especially when the places are in different countries and a cross-border comparison must be made. On the other hand, the single currency in Europe will facilitate such comparisons.

Thus, a place does not have to correct all its weaknesses or promote all its strengths because factors vary in their importance to different target markets. The place must probe deeply into which strengths and weaknesses most affect the perceptions and behaviour of target markets. The resulting analysis becomes a major basis for laying placemarketing plans.

Exhibit 5.3 describes how Estonia executed a plan to change its image.

Tallinn as a Hong Kong on the Baltic

EXHIBIT 5.3

The task was great from the outset. Since regaining independence in 1991, Estonians have aimed to restore their image as a free market power. Just six years later, Estonia was progressing smoothly towards its goal of being accepted by the European Commission as a possible member state (together with the Czech Republic, Hungary, Poland, Slovenia and Cyprus).

Estonia's efforts focused on aggressive economic reforms including rapid liberalisation of prices, tariff-free and open trade policies, privatisation, and the introduction of a stable and fully convertible national currency. The government made these moves despite intense internal pressure to go more slowly so as not to create job and personal dislocation for workers and institutions. As a result, 65 per cent of Estonia's GDP (1996) came from the private sector – one of the highest levels in Central and Eastern Europe. Estonia signed a free trade treaty with the European Union in 1994. The economic opinion leaders, World Bank and IMF, see the strong focus on economic reforms as the desirable strategy that other European countries ought to pursue.

Estonia provides a good example of what can be done according to the performance/importance matrix in Figure 5.1. The Estonian government, all of its political parties and most Estonian citizens focused on cell A in the matrix. The Estonian Investment Agency argues that Estonia may be a small country, but it has a great deal to offer the inward investor:

- A central location with a market of 70 million
- Fastest growing economy in the region
- A pro-Western, free-market economy based on minimal state interference
- Inexpensive labour costs and low-cost raw materials equaling high-quality goods at attractive prices
- Highest rate of inward investment per person in Central and Eastern Europe

Estonia has won the respect of the European Commission. The country has systematically and relentlessly taken advantage of diplomatic relationships in all European countries to market Estonia's attraction factors. The concept of '*Tallinn as a Hong Kong on the Baltic*', may well become a reality.

Sources: Jüri Sakkeus, Director General, 'Invest in Estonia at the heart of Northern Europe', Estonian Investment Agency, April 1996; Mert Kubu, 'Estonia convinces the EU', *Dagens Nyheter*, 16 July 1997, p. 3.

Identifying the place's opportunities and threats

The next step is to identify the opportunities and threats facing the particular place. We define a place opportunity as follows. A place opportunity is an arena for action in which a place has a fairly good chance to achieve a competitive advantage.

Consider the city of Antwerp in Belgium, which has the opportunity to become the second largest port in Europe. Through a coordinated strategy, Antwerp could create a competitive advantage. For Antwerp, a port in *itself* is perhaps not the most inspiring driving force for business, visitors and residents. Therefore, Antwerp has to identify opportunities that combine the port with a number of additional attractions. Today, the chosen combination integrates *port – gateway – history – trade – openness* in one total concept. This combination takes a number of forms which are described in a promotional package that emphasises modern port facilities for potential place buyers.'The Port Route itself is 65 or 40 km long depending on your choice and takes you through 1,000 years of port history: from the medieval Steen through the nineteenth-century port to the most modern plants in Europe's largest port for fruit, paper and timber products, iron, and steel'. The *gateway* element places the port in perspective:'Those who have seen the port understand why the delightful city of Antwerp has been called a metropolis for centuries'.The *historical* element claims: 'Antwerp is Rubens, Van Dyck, Jordaens, Bruegel, Plantijn, but also a thousand years of architecture, five centuries of music and artistic and decorative crafts'. The *trade* element is marketed as:'A brilliant city and the world diamond centre. The [diamond[sector has an annual turnover in excess of 17 billion dollars. Today the sector employs some 30,000 people either directly or indirectly'. The *openness* element is reflected via a reference to the *Financial Times*: 'According to the *Financial Times*, Antwerp, that little piece of the globe, is home to the highest percentage of quadrilingual people. The native language of the people of Antwerp is Dutch, but most have few problems with French, English and German'.[5]

Antwerp has managed to define itself as a highly desirable opportunity for certain target groups.

In addition to opportunities, every place faces threats or challenges posed by an unfavourable trend or development in the environment that would lead, in the absence of purposeful action, to the erosion of the condition of the place. Planning teams need to identify various threats that can be classified according to their seriousness and probability of occurrence. *Major threats* are those that can seriously hurt the place and have a high probability of occurring. The place needs to prepare a contingency plan that spells out what steps to take before, during or after the occurrence of a major threat. If the European Airbus project is running into big financial and other problems, the question is, what will happen to the main production sites? This could well be defined as a major threat. *Minor threats* are those with a low probability of occurring that would not hurt the place badly; they can be ignored. *Moderate threats* are those with either high potential to harm the place or high occurrence probability but not both; they must be watched.

By assembling a picture of the major threats and opportunities facing a specific place, it is possible to characterise the overall attractiveness of the place. An *ideal place* is one that is high in major opportunities and low in major threats. A *speculative place* is high in both major opportunities and threats. A *mature place* is low in major opportunities and threats. Finally, a *troubled place* is low in opportunities and high in threats.

Establishing the main issues

There might be as many opinions as there are citizens on the point of what constitutes a main issue. Every place must try to identify the main issues that it must address. Too common a response when establishing the main issues is to omit the most troublesome ones in order to avoid conflict even though they may be crucial.

Another problem is created when the community treats all issues as equally important. We see many places in Europe that work on all fronts at once. All target groups and all market niches are treated equally. For example, Hamburg makes broad offers to all markets and niches. Under the umbrella of 'Eurogate', it markets to everyone. The question is, what are the priorities? Without making choices, a community has no way to choose between potential value-added investments.

Liechtenstein is another place that must carefully replan its future. The image of the country suggests that it provides high bank secrecy and exploits loopholes in European tax regulations, but those loopholes are disappearing. Facing a Europe where tax advantages are less marketable, Liechtenstein has to establish new main priorities.

Setting the vision and objectives

As a result of carrying out a SWOT and issue analysis, strategic planners form a comprehensive picture of the community's situation. But it is not easy to choose among the many value-added projects that can be imagined. Divergent projects may not add up to coherent development plans and visions. Without a coherent vision, it is difficult to prioritise the various projects.

Vision development calls for planners to solicit input from the citizens as to what they want their community to be like ten or even twenty years from now. One helpful tactic is circulating two to four scenarios for comments. Since each place is a complex environment, the scenarios become tools for stimulating deeper thoughts about possible futures for the place.

Consider, for example, the Spanish island Mallorca and its very attractive image. What are the possible scenarios for Mallorca twenty years down the road? At least four scenarios can be distinguished:

1. *Uncurbed growth:* In this scenario, Mallorca encourages free and open growth. A 5 per cent increase per year of sun-and-play activity occurs. Congestion and pollution may well follow. The image erodes as premium buyers search for higher quality and more attractive environments.
2. *Managed quality growth*: In this scenario, Mallorca's decision-makers choose to invest systematically in the development of more sophisticated services. Conferences with high-quality services become a niche. Total annual visits increase at the rate of 1 per cent. More of the visitors come for business purposes. Business travellers spend more money and generate several new and unexpected networks of other investments for Mallorca. A more diversified Mallorca grows. The early years of this development are not without conflict. Tensions arise in those who wish that development would follow its traditional freebooting path.

3. *Zero or even minus growth:* Here Mallorca takes steps to reduce mass tourism. Environment and quality become the guiding criteria for local planning. The number of visitors decreases, and the proportion of business visitors grows. Mallorca commits to being a place of year-round activity. The new and complementing niches become banking, insurance and telemarketing. Mallorca nurtures the language skills of its residents and its intercultural experiences gained from decades of success in tourism.
4. *A passive approach:* The fourth choice is to drift along rather than to adopt any vision at all. Most places cannot agree on any scenario, and there is consequently no resulting vision. The leaders tend to believe that a vision limits their freedom to manoeuvre. There could also be a lack of knowledge regarding what strategies other successful places have used to develop a long-term vision. The vision step is critical because places without one are usually without direction and motivation. Exhibit 5.4 describes what a vision can do in practice.

Grenoble's vision on how to exploit synergies

EXHIBIT 5.4

The French city of Grenoble in the region of Rhône-Alpes has systematically followed a vision which aims to offer new, commercially important, knowledge synergies to its place-buyers. This vision is spread not only within the community but also among different R&D institutions and businesses. Grenoble has a tradition of several decades of active industrial and economic planning. For eighteen years (until 1983), the mayor, Hubert Dubedout, a former nuclear scientist, used his local government resources to help put Grenoble on the map. His most important policy was to encourage links between scientific research and industry. Dubedout's successor at the town hall, Alain Carignon, continued the process. Under his tenure, the city funded university chairs – normally the domain of the central government in France – and merged the area's disparate economic development organisations into a single powerful body, Grenoble Isère Développement.

Historically, Grenoble has been a centre for waterpower technology. Investment in power technology has gone hand-in-hand with knowledge development in mathematics and physics. The Institut Joseph Fourier, the mathematics department of Grenoble University, has a worldwide reputation. Today the city has four universities and 250 laboratories. A natural part of the vision was a decision of the French state to establish a nuclear research centre in Grenoble. Currently in the city the Atomic Energy Commission (CEA) employs as many as 2,600 people. Grenoble has also made great strides in the information technology area as the city hosts the Institut National de Recherche Informatique et Automatique (INRIA). The synergy outcome is equally impressive, as almost 10,000 processing specialists are located in the Grenoble area. Furthermore, many of the 140 foreign companies in Grenoble are electronics specialists, many of which are American, such as Sun Micro Systems and SCI Systems. Investments in the public research infrastructure have created an estimated 15,000 jobs in electronics and computer software and hardware.

In this case, Grenoble based its vision on creating synergies and used its strategic ability and implementation ability to accomplish successful international placemarketing.

Sources: 'Success in Rhône-Alpes', Marketing material from Entreprise Rhône-Alpes International (ERAI), 1996; Andrew Jack, 'Change of style and substance', Survey – Rhône-Alpes, *Financial Times*, 19 February 1993, p. 3; William Dawkins, 'Innovating is a tradition', Survey – Rhône-Alpes, *Financial Times*, 18 April 1996, p. 2.

Developing visions goes further than simply distinguishing among potential growth paths. A vision should take a stand on such issues as:

1. Which unique combinations of attraction factors should the community concentrate on?
2. Which are the target markets of the community?
3. Which are the long-term and short-term goals?
4. Which are the operative prerequisites for the vision?

Given that a community can prepare different scenarios, how might it work out clear choices and a final vision? One can draw certain observations. *First*, the main actor is normally and formally the community. However, informally one can always trace some leading person either employed by the community or with some tight relation to the community. This leading person acts as a catalyst.

Second, a vision is normally born in a complex process involving citizens and relevant interest groups. One problem in Europe has been that in many cases the public sector is over-represented and favours short-term activities without future revenue-generating potential. Today, as opposed to just a few years ago, it is recognised that a successful vision must be created in a joint effort between the public and the private commercial sectors.

Third, it is not unusual for a community to seek external inspiration in developing future visions from different resource persons and consultants. Although external inspiration and perspectives are valuable, it is necessary that the primary motivations and actions are the responsibility of persons who have roots in the community. A vision needs a motor and this motor cannot – at least in the long run – be the consultant.

Fourth, the vision often spans a period of five to ten years. Only a few years ago conventional wisdom was to 'set the sights' on the turn of the century. Now that we are there, the focus instead is on the years 2005–2010. Some European communities have taken a much longer-term perspective and focus on 2025.

Fifth, the community council or its equivalent normally decides on the acceptance of the vision. A vision needs authoritative approval for credibility.

Once the community agrees on a vision, it is essential that it set specific *objectives* and *goals*. Objectives are clear statements about what a place wants to achieve; goals add specific magnitudes and timing to these objectives. For example, if a community vision states an objective to increase the number of jobs over the next several years, the vision can be more operational if the objective is turned into the following goal: Before the year 2005, at least seven new enterprises should be established which should create 400 jobs and bring in 800 new residents. Such goal statements make it easier to allocate the resources necessary to accomplish the goal and assign responsibilities. The EU has encouraged goal-setting by making it a prerequisite for receiving certain regional support.

Formulating the strategy

Once the community planning team has defined the vision, goals and objectives, they can move into identifying and choosing strategies for accomplishing the goals. For example, the Flemish regional government laid down its vision in a document called *Vlaanderen-Europa 2002* at the beginning of the 1990s. The vision is to make Flanders into a 'Star Region in Europe'. The basic strategy as described by Luc Van den Brande, Minister-President of the Government of Flanders, is to attract inward investments. 'The services we offer to companies and to private individuals are organised according to the "one desk per project" principle. This formula is especially appreciated by foreign investors as one department handles the entire project from start to finish, and advises them on the procedure to follow'.[6] The strategy emphasises Flanders' international advantages: international airport, the densest rail networks in Europe, four modern and international sea ports, toll-free motorways, highest per capita exports in the world, ideal test market for Europe, highest number of quadrilingual speakers, and offices in Singapore, two in the USA, and in Stockholm.[7]

For each potential strategy, the planning team must ask the following two questions:

1. *What advantages do we possess that suggest that we can succeed with that strategy?* In the Flanders case the international advantages form the basis of its strategy.
2. *Do we have the resources required for a successful implementation of that strategy?* The long-term strategy approach in Flanders made it easier to attract new resources.

Even communities lacking sufficient resources can sometimes develop a creative strategy solution. After the Second World War, the French city Grenoble, discussed earlier, was one of those anonymous small industrial towns with no obvious future strengths. Now, fifty years later, Grenoble is the largest research centre outside Paris. Two other cases where no strengths were initially obvious are illustrated in Exhibit 5.5.

How Pamplona and Holstebro developed tourist attractions

EXHIBIT 5.5

What happens when a community lacks an obvious hook upon which to build a strategy? The community may be small, isolated or unattractive. The answer may be to promote an event that is not widely known or to create some attraction that has media appeal. Pamplona and Holstebro are examples of how to generate a market.

Pamplona

Every summer the quiet little Spanish town of Pamplona becomes an international destination. There are many similar places competing for tourists, but Pamplona has managed to create a distinctive marketing position with global recognition. The town discovered that many tourists were looking for the famed Spanish ▶

bull culture and was able to transform a fourteenth century tradition into a twentieth century blockbuster. Pamplona stands out in the global market for the unique running of the bulls during the Festival of San Fermin in the first two weeks of July. The sleepy town is transformed overnight into a non-stop party with bulls and sangria. The images of Pablo Picasso and Ernest Hemingway are also used to emphasise Pamplona's marketing advantage, the *bull event*. Hemingway has become the patron saint of promotion for Pamplona as the author of *The Sun Also Rises*, immortalising the town's festival. A street is named in Hemingway's honour, and a bust stands before the venerable bullring symbolising the drinking, madness and danger of the eight-day adventure. This mega-event is now being used as a central destination in order to market many under-promoted attractions in the city and the region.

Holstebro

The small Danish town of Holstebro lying ten kilometres from the coast in north west Jytland with its surrounding old farmlands has no natural attractions. Nevertheless, an aggressive focus by the community leaders on culture in all forms has succeeded in placing Holstebro on the European map. Facing serious economic decline, Holstebro's town council decided to make a serious investment in a cultural strategy. According to the then chairman of the town council's culture committee, the strategy was 'to improve the environment and facilities and to attract people from a higher educational background'.[1] The strategy began in the 1960s when the community leaders travelled to Paris and purchased a renowned sculpture 'Woman on Cart' by the world famous artist Alberto Giacometti. The price, astonishing for that time, was DKr210,000. Today the sculpture is valued at DKr17 million. This purchase made a powerful statement throughout Europe, as Holstebro continued making cultural investments. Since then the town has added important artworks, Odin Theatre (a travelling theatre company), and a music school. As an example of their risk-taking and commitment to long-range planning, they provided a home for controversial dance director Peter Schaufuss and his ballet company. The community is now noted in national and international circles for its artistic image – an international art community in a small town. That image has appreciated over time, and negative local economic development trends have been reversed as housing has been built for new residents moving in to take advantage of Holstebro's lifestyle and jobs. The key positioning here is *culture*.

These two places do not have the attraction packages which Paris, Frankfurt, or London can market. On the other hand, they illustrate that even a small place without obvious strengths can capture attention in the global placemarket.

Sources: 1. David Ward, 'The town that wears art on its sleeve', *Manchester Guardian Weekly*, 11 September 1983, p. 19 (Lexis Nexis).
Lena Blomquist, 'Expensive art – an improvement for a poor city', *Svenska Dagbladet*, 17 November 1996, pp. 10–11; Jeremy Kingston, 'Reason takes a holiday', *The Times*, 20 March 1998 (Lexis Nexis).

Developing the action plan

In order to be meaningful, strategy must be elaborated into an action plan. This is especially important in complex communities and regions where much strategic thinking runs the risk of falling through the cracks. Many of the positive results achieved by small communities derive from the fact that it is easier for them to assign responsibility and create simpler and quicker decision processes than it is for larger, more complex communities.

An action plan should list each action and next to it four additional components:

1. Who is responsible.
2. How the action is to be implemented.
3. How much the action will cost.
4. The expected completion date.

This level of detail provides several advantages. *First*, everyone involved in the action plan knows what he or she must accomplish. *Second*, the place-marketer can easily discern whether the various actions are being satisfactorily implemented. *Third*, the action detail permits cancelling specific actions and their subsequent costs if towards the end of the period costs exceed the budget.

Some European communities have created long checklists of short- and long-term projects. These checklists are used also as a marketing tool. The detailed lists are published in order to make clear the degree of implementation and, in some cases, to attract potential place-buyers.

As European communities develop their local marketing strategies, it is critical to spell out concrete action plans identifying the actions of participants. A lack of clear goal-setting and detailed action planning is one of the most serious threats to successful community development.

Implementing and controlling the market plan

Visions, strategies and plans are useless until they are effectively implemented. The planning team needs to convene at regular intervals to review the community's progress towards its goals.

Most communities prepare some sort of annual summary which reflects hard facts such as number of citizens, economic results, jobs, income, taxes, and so on. We believe that facts and figures should be presented in relation to the vision, goals and strategies. Successes as well as failures and concerns should be included. We call this, the *place's annual report*, which is an integral part of strategic market planning.

The community's annual report should receive broad public distribution; it could, for example, be included as an insert in the major local newspapers. Many communities have their own place magazine that is sent directly to every household once or twice per year. During the past few years, more European communities have been using the Internet to show citizens – as well as the general placemarket – what they have accomplished. Their wish to reach the international placemarket is evidenced by offering to Internet users a choice of languages in which they receive messages and information. For example, Figure 5.2 depicts Hamburg's introductory pages on the Internet.

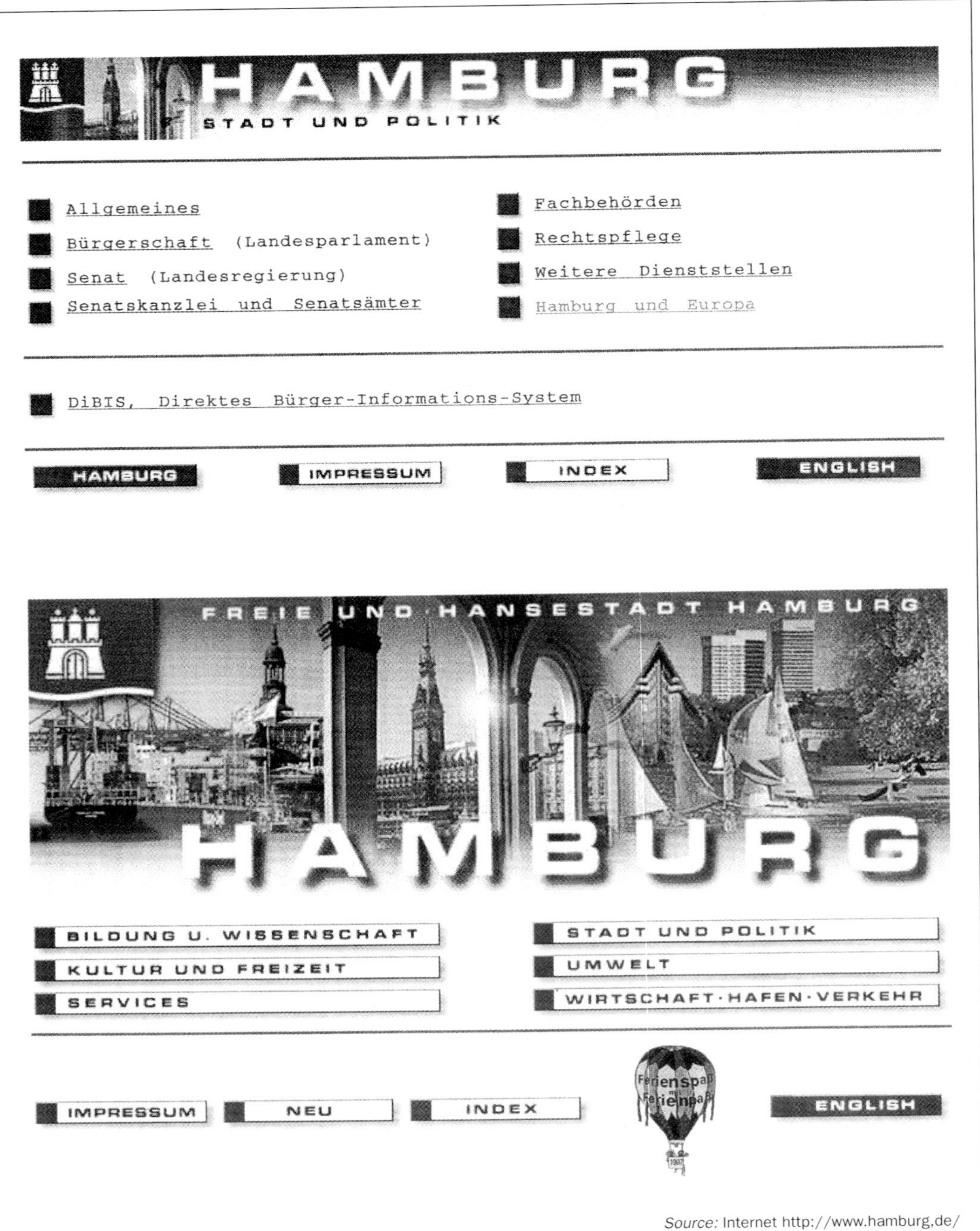

Source: Internet http://www.hamburg.de/

Fig 5.2 ◆ A new way of distributing community performance

If you click on 'Index' in the menu you will find facts on everything from A to Z concerning Hamburg's policies and offerings. Most relevant factors are broken down in a systematic and readable way. It is easy to see how this medium can communicate with citizens as well as the placemarket.

The two abilities: strategy and implementation

Every community in need of a real change and a positive spiral must develop its ability in two basic dimensions: *strategy* and *implementation*. Unfortunately, these two dimensions are seldom developed under the same leadership in the same place. Therefore it is useful to differentiate between at least four basic environments in which strategy and implementation can take place. These environments are presented in Figure 5.3.

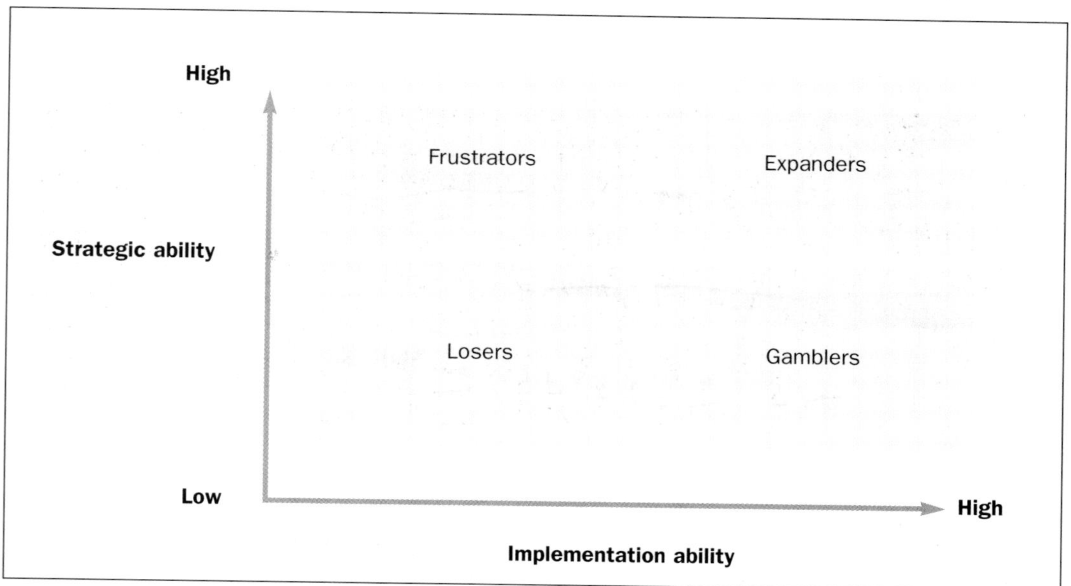

Fig 5.3 ◆ The four place abilities

Losers include those communities and places that have no capacity to take actions along either dimension. Unfortunately, many communities fall into this category. Under crisis, they seek and demand heavy investments, subsidies or other compensatory actions. They argue on the basis of 'justice' or 'need'.

Frustrators have the ability to think strategically but a weakness in implementation. After some time the planners become frustrated and then give up and quit the organisation, or even leave the place.

Gamblers have a well-developed ability for implementation but their strategic ability is lacking. With luck and extremely hard work, gamblers may experience some success, at least in the short-term. In time, the amount of extremely hard work required to succeed without effective strategic planning can lead to personnel burnout and turnover. Gamblers tend to work on all possible fronts, and target marketing and focusing rarely occur.

Expanders are communities that are good at strategy and implementation. In almost all cases, there is leadership that is prepared to defend a long-term strategy and simultaneously stimulate concrete substrategies and action plans. In this book we have mentioned several examples of the best practice communities.

Conclusions

Too many places fail to recognise threats before they become overwhelming, if not irreversible, and they consequently react rather than proact. But such passivity is not inevitable. Some European places have responded with active approaches such as community development, urban design, urban planning, and economic development. Strategic market planning represents an approach by which a place can design a better future. It calls for profiling the situation of the place: identifying the strengths/weaknesses, opportunities/threats, and main issues; setting a vision, objectives and goals; defining effective strategies for accomplishing these goals; developing appropriate actions; and implementing and controlling the plan.

In this process, even places with no obvious strengths can redefine their situation and find new combinations of attraction factors that should offer a unique value in the placemarket.

Although this version of strategic planning oversimplifies many of the problems of managing complex entities such as cities, communities and regions, it represents a more promising approach than any other alternative, including a trial and error approach with its risk of haphazard changes. Many European communities have already put into practice important elements of strategic market planning. The next chapter addresses the importance of evaluating and improving the assets of a place.

6

Strategies for place improvement

Many place improvers believe that *marketing a place* means *promoting a place.* Promotion is, ironically, one of the least important marketing tasks. Promotion alone does not help a troubled place. In fact it only helps place-buyers to discover early how troubled the place really is, see Exhibit 6.1.

Calling Athena

EXHIBIT 6.1

Consider that the Greek National Tourist Organisation marketed the country internationally in the early 1990s as a divine place for tourism under the slogan '*Greece – Chosen by the Gods*'.[1] Unfortunately, what the arriving tourist discovered was anything but divine. Visitors were instead confronted with inadequate facilities at airports, low standards of service, old hotels in urgent need of refurbishing, and beaches cluttered with garbage. Disappointed visitors often cut their visit short, leaving after all expectations had been shattered. The potential long-term effect of Greece's promotion campaign was an unshakable negative image promoted by disillusioned visitors. Such disappointments lead to counterproductive word-of-mouth communications that affect future tourism potential. However, with the selection of Greece for the 2004 Summer Olympic Games, the country has a significant opportunity to enact viable marketing plans rather than unfocused promotion campaigns.

Source: 1. *The Economist*, 3 July 1993, p. 20.

Placemarketing means designing a place to satisfy the needs of its target markets. It succeeds when citizens and businesses are pleased with their communities, and the expectations of visitors and investors are met.

In this chapter, we examine various investments a place can make to improve livability, investibility and visitability. We see this as a process made up of four components. As we shall demonstrate, these components are not mutually exclusive.

1. *Place as character:* A place needs a sound design that enhances its attractiveness and more fully develops its aesthetic qualities and values. There is a specific sense of the place.
2. *Place as a fixed environment:* Places need to develop and maintain a basic infrastructure that is compatible with the natural environment.
3. *Place as service provider:* A place must provide basic services of quality that meet business and public needs.
4. *Places as entertainment and recreation:* Places need a range of attractions for their own citizens and visitors.

While we cover more generic strategies for place improvement in later chapters, these place improvement strategies – design, infrastructure, services and attractions – can be viewed as the building blocks for specific competitive strategies. Careful attention to these features and factors will create the foundation for setting a strong place strategy.

These components are often assumed to be a given in place competition. For the most part, attention to them is well within the range of a place's collective endeavours. They are preconditions that set the stage for often riskier and more opportunistic efforts to compete for economic advantages. They also lie squarely within the purview of legitimate public responsibility and provide real value for existing residents and business enterprise.

Place as character – aesthetic urban design

Place-buyers often refer to '*the sense of the place*' or its specific character. Urban design reveals a great deal about the character of a place and redefines how that character is transmitted from one generation to the next. Interweaving a diverse array of physical structures into an overall place fabric is an art. Urban design makes a statement about a place because it reflects how values and decision-making combine on issues that affect development.

Historically, places have formed around natural harbours, near river confluences, and along canals, followed by railroads that often paralleled water routes. Dirt paths turned to horse and wagon routes that later accommodated trams and automobiles. Transportation patterns shaped the contours of place development by connecting commercial, industrial and patterned residential growth internally, and markets for raw materials and finished goods externally.

Older European cities followed a concentric form of expansion, pushing outward from a hub business district along the nexus of key transportation routes that separated labourers, middle-class and more affluent residents. As manufacturing situated itself along transportation grids, concentricity gave way to more sectored forms of development in which industrial, commercial and residential areas took on more random patterns pushing out from the central city to the urban fringe and beyond. Within this patterned development, some cities formed a gridlock geometric pattern of streets with rectangular blocks, as in London, Moscow, Berlin and Vienna. Others, like Paris and Brussels, followed a wheel-and-spoke pattern where roads radiated from the centre. A third, more random pattern combined several design formats, specifically in places of irregular terrain and village annexation, such as Rome and Milan.

Mary Hollingworth's book on *Architecture of the 20th Century*[1] analyses the relationship between urban design and planning as it reflects geography and culture of places in Europe. The post-war period in Europe saw a great demand for new housing spawned by the birth of numerous urban design ideas and projects. Hollingworth observed that in 1946 the British Parliament passed the New Towns Act for the state financing of twelve new towns. She notes that among these new towns constructed as satellites to metropolitan areas were Hatfield, Basildon, Bracknell around London, Peterlee in County Durham, and Cwmbran in South Wales. According to theories from Le Corbusier, they were to be surrounded by green belts, an idea born in the famous English garden cities of the late nineteenth and early twentieth centuries.

As for much of strategic market planning in general, urban master plans have emerged from strong and visionary leadership. Paris, Venice, Florence and St Petersburg are examples: see Exhibit 6.2.

Four Crown Jewels

EXHIBIT 6.2

The redevelopment of *Paris* began in 1853 when Napoleon III selected Georges-Eugène Haussmann to conceive and implement a plan to completely renew the central section of Paris. Baron Haussmann worked for seventeen years to actualise a plan that blended order, variety, convenience and grandeur. Haussmann fathered many monuments, the wide boulevards, the famous Opéra, and Les Halles, the central marketplace of Paris.

One of the most famous urban design places in Europe today is *Venice* with its Piazza San Marco. The history of the Piazza began early in the ninth century when the Venetians chose the site for the seat of their government. Under the rule of Doge Sebastiano Ziani (r.1172–1178), it was extended to its present size. Today, the piazza is a popular attraction always crowded with tourists from all over the world.

Florence, the capital of Tuscany, has an urban design that ranks it as one of Europe's most atmospheric cities. The small, late-medieval centre stems back to the influence of the Medici family's interests in banking, trade and art. Owing to the Medici's extensive patronage of the arts, Florence has long been characterised by its culture. This general image remains intact as Florence manages to attract the highest quality in art exhibitions as well as modern fashion.

It has been said by a visitor to *St Petersburg*, 'It is as though they took all the palaces in the world and put them in St Petersburg!' The outstanding city design that can cause such a visitor's comment originates from Tsar Peter the Great (1672–1725). The city had such glory that it was proclaimed capital of Russia between 1709 and 1918. In the 1990s its urban design is being exploited again as St Petersburg ▶

markets itself as a re-emerging glorious city.

The business street Nevsky Prospekt functions as a window or a gateway between East and West, and the aesthetic qualities of the place are enhanced in, for example, the Winter Palace, the Hermitage Art Museum and the Mariinsky Theatre.

These four places – Paris, Venice, Florence and St Petersburg – represent four master plans formed by visionary leaders. Today, they are still models of global attractiveness. But most places historically have never had the benefit of any visionary leaders who could create an attractive aesthetic and translate it into physical structures. The usual approach is that new transport technologies, economic changes and new consumer behaviour slowly, step-by-step, push urban design in one direction or another. This has resulted in urban decline, crime, vacant buildings, traffic congestion and loss of attractiveness in many European cities. A lack of local leadership and strategic thinking has led to a 'more of the same' approach to development. Innovative solutions are lacking, as illustrated by the universal answer to traffic problems in the 1980s: building more roads.

During the 1990s a noticeable change has occurred regarding strategies to market places. Urban planning increasingly is incorporating a place-selling theme. Quality of life and environment are frequently emphasised as attraction factors. Tough competition between European places in conjunction with the economic downturn of the late 1980s has encouraged the start of quality thinking in urban planning. The underlying motivation is the need for places to offer a unique and exciting quality of life and an environment that is anchored in the history and traditions of a place. The new and the old are consciously combined in Exhibit 6.3.

'Kop van Zuid, City of the Future'

EXHIBIT 6.3

How do we want to live? Thinking into the future, a place should include the key concepts of quality, synergy between old and new, and integration between residents and working facilities. A place that is at the forefront of the new model of integrated urban living is the new city centre Kop van Zuid in Rotterdam.

The urban design project of Kop van Zuid is marketed as a premier location for housing, working facilities and recreation. It was designed to be internationally attractive and a showpiece for Rotterdam's economic future.

A major strategy was to mix business, facilities, housing and recreation to create a complete urban community. The 100 year old dock area is conceptualised as a 24 hour city that will be full of activity for all its workers and residents.

This project, started in 1990, is expected to be complete by 2010. It involves the redevelopment of 125 hectares of a former rail and dock site into a high quality residential, business and recreational location. For example, the former head office of the Holland America Line now houses the popular hotel and trendy restaurant called New York, which serves as a symbolic centrepiece for the restoration of the formerly rundown docks. Nicknamed 'Manhattan on the Maas' by Rotterdam's municipal authority, the finished project will add to Rotterdam's city centre more than 5,300 homes, 400,000 m^2 of office space, 35,000 m^2 of commercial space, 45,000 m^2 of educational facilities, and 30,000 m^2 of recreational and other facilities. The mayor of Rotterdam, Dr Braun Peper, says of the new direction, 'Under the slogan "The New Rotterdam," the city made a radical shift from problem registering to problem solving, to innovation, and to the seizing of opportunities. These ground-breaking principles and schemes have led to major changes in both the architectural and cultural skylines of the city. But we're not finished yet. Building on the success of the concept ten years ago, Rotterdam has now analysed the threats and opportunities for the city: New Rotterdam, target 2005.'[1]

As the highlight of a street party in the neighbourhood of Kop van Zuid in May of 1997, US President Bill Clinton unveiled a brass plaque of George Marshall, the US Secretary of State who initiated over US$12 billion in aid to war-torn Europe in 1947. Speaking to thousands of Dutch and Americans, including the Dutch cabinet and royal family, Clinton said, 'Our purpose must be to summon the spirit of the Marshall generation to create a structure of opportunity, freedom and security for the next 50 years and beyond.'[2] It seems fitting to choose the city of the future to commemorate a plan that represented an investment in the future of Europe. With the long-term support of city leaders combined with an overall vision and strategy, Kop van Zuid has become the symbol of urban renewal.

Sources: 1. Rotterdam City Development Corporation, *AI Magazine*, March 1997, pp. 8–9.
2. Lien van der Leij, 'Rotterdam street fest pays tribute to Marshall aid', Reuters World Service, 28 May 1997 (Lexis Nexis).

Urban design is an important issue not only in big cities of Europe but also in small towns that are witnessing a renewed interest in small-scale urban design. The more clearly defined underlying force here is to go back to old values/attractions and to nurture them and then to present them as a contrast to the problems of the larger placemarkets.

The small Norwegian town of Aalesund – 36,000 citizens – is marketing itself as '*The Art Nouveau Town*.' The redesign process started in 1904 when a fire destroyed the town centre and left ten thousand people homeless. Help came from many countries. The German emperor Wilhelm II was particularly generous. A new master plan was worked out and within three years a new urban design was implemented. The redesigned Aalesund was completely characterised by the art nouveau style, which at that time was the fashion. Today, Aalesund markets itself as the town with the most and best-preserved art nouveau architecture in Western Europe. The Michelin Guide says: 'Today Aalesund is a tasteful blend of modern architecture and of a unique heritage from the turn of the century.'[2] The value of this positioning on the placemarket is not difficult to calculate as tourists from Europe and elsewhere are lining up to admire Aalesund.

A growing number of small towns such as Sopron in Hungary are marketing their architecture with great confidence. The curved, narrow streets and the trademark red roofs define this medieval town. The town protects its heritage with laws that prohibit companies from building factories that pollute the environment. Its message is even more convincing since Sopron was awarded the European Prize for the Protection of Monuments. Its slogan, '*We know how to preserve this beauty*', is also a summing up of its position. In Austria, places like Salzburg, Innsbruck, Murau and Zell am See are all trying to stick to a specific architectural style and urban planning. Place-buyers still recall the sense of such places from the film *The Sound of Music* which was produced partly in Salzburg and served to help brand the old-world-style buildings, streets and intimacy of the region to the rest of the world.

Another growing European trend in urban design is the building of 'greenfield' sites in the countryside. This is in contrast to inner city urban 'brownfield' projects. Small communities within a convenient commuting distance from a big city tend to use various 'greenfield' approaches. Such examples can be seen in areas around Paris, London and Copenhagen.

The common thread in these cases is the effort to use urban design in place competition. Current approaches to urban design emphasise what is environmentally compatible with physical, local, regional and national features along with ways to resurrect the older character and history of places. Such thinking also requires vision, blending old with new, and an appreciation that place character is a valuable asset in retaining place-buyers.

Infrastructure improvement

Where urban design gives character to a place, infrastructure makes the design possible. How magnificent would Paris' spacious boulevards be if they were riddled with potholes? What would Leipzig or Seville be without their convenient railway access? How could Dublin compete internationally for back-office services without its high telecommunications standards? Countless examples illustrate the basic fact that much of a place's advantage stems from the infrastructure that either supports or detracts from its attractions.

While excellent and well maintained infrastructure cannot guarantee a community's growth, its absence is a serious liability. To sustain quality of life and to support economic productivity, a place – no less than a nation – requires that infrastructure be developed and maintained. This challenge is exemplified by Russia and Eastern Europe, which aspire to the transition to market economies but with vastly under-developed infrastructures that inhibit the movement of people, goods and information. These countries' prior underinvestment now requires governments, businesses, the World Bank, the European Bank for Reconstruction and Development, and the European Union to invest heavily in order to facilitate future growth.

Far too often, residents take infrastructure for granted on the principle that out of sight is out of mind. What one generation put in place with great difficulty may be lost to the following generation that assumes that the water and sewer systems, bridges and tunnels, roads and waterways never need replacement. For older, more developed places, their in-place infrastructure can confer unique advantages in competition with new places that have to build from scratch entirely new systems just to accommodate growth. However, as many older places have allowed their infrastructures to deteriorate, they face the ever-growing liability of replacing and renewing their capital stock.

Every community must provide some basic standard of services to attract and retain people, businesses and visitors. Admittedly, no uniform standards exist except where set by law and health and safety regulations. The issues of who pays, who administers and who delivers services are vastly blurred by complex systems of national governments, regional public organisations and communities. Thus, all places are subject to varying degrees of responsibility for transportation, roads, water and energy supply, and meeting environmental standards.

Throughout Europe, places gradually have awakened to their infrastructure problems. It has been said that the 1980s were a decade of renewed European interest in infrastructure. The climate was influenced by the following four trends.

1. *Higher unemployment rates* pushed politicians to improve competitiveness. Infrastructure-projects became one answer in the battle to improve European competitiveness.
2. *Traffic congestion* reached unacceptable levels throughout European cities. The European Commission expressed the competitive problem: 'Traffic jams are not only exasperating, they also cost Europe dearly in terms of productivity: bottlenecks and missing links in the infrastructure fabric; lack of interoperability between modes and systems; non-communication between too many closed and scattered telecommunications circuits. Networks are the arteries of the single market. They are the lifeblood of competitiveness, and their malfunction is reflected in lost opportunities to create new markets and hence in a level of job creation that falls short of our potential.'[3]
3. *Cross-European infrastructure projects* were supported by governments and the EU.
4. *A more critical environmental debate* acted as a catalyst for a number of infrastructure projects.

Needs assessment

All places require a needs assessment of their capital facilities by age, condition and scheduled repairs as well as related five-to-twenty year plans for rehabilitation and replacement. Years ago, city engineers and architects possessed a fairly good inventory of the relative condition, costs and schedules for maintenance of a place's infrastructure. In many cases that institutional knowledge and capacity has been lost because of shifting public and political responsibilities, the growth of separate authorities, or systematic neglect. In other cases, places have been so committed to growth or development that they have underestimated or simply failed to anticipate the related infrastructure requirements and costs that accompany growth.

Many places in Europe have failed to catch up with their declining infrastructure. One example is Spain where its isolated position during the Franco period contributed to a declining standard. In contrast, the past twenty years have brought huge infrastructure investments to Spain. The national plan for 1993–2007 calls for investments totalling US$133 billion.[4] Spain has managed to receive a high proportion of its infrastructure investments from the EU's structural funds. It can be seen as European champion in this field. Topping the list of projects are intercity transport, urban transport, water works and environmental projects. Today, Spain often promotes its infrastructure standard in its placemarketing.

Furthermore, during the past decades Eastern and Central Europe have systematically neglected their infrastructure. The new trade patterns of Europe require as much as US$200 billion to revitalise and upgrade deteriorating rail links and roads.[5] In the case of Poland, it is estimated that US$50 billion of investment is needed to bring the transportation infrastructure up to the required level.[6] Even in these contexts, place-sellers in Eastern and Central Europe are frequently marketing their new infrastructure visions and projects.

While the exact costs of deterioration and neglect can only be estimated, various studies have documented losses to governments, businesses and people that stem from infrastructure underinvestment. Poor road conditions add considerably to the cost of operating motor vehicles. Bad communication links between Eastern and Western Europe slow down growth. The lack of efficient rail connections from the natural resources in the Barents region in Northern Europe creates a serious bottleneck for the region and thus for international investors. Deficient water and sewer systems impede residential development and detract from business investment. Traffic congestion in the big European cities increases commuting time and consequent loss of employee productivity. Lack of energy availability and unreliability of services constitute a greater competitive disadvantage in the information age than high-energy costs. When housing stock is allowed to deteriorate beyond a certain point, replacement costs greatly exceed the expenses of rehabilitation. Today the lack of housing maintenance in St Petersburg and Moscow generates enormous residential costs (in the same range as in Tokyo or Hong Kong). Places learn the hard way that maintenance, repair and rehabilitation pay for themselves.

Infrastructure management

A good assessment of infrastructure needs, periodically updated and systematically tracked, is essential for performance management – a new approach to infrastructure required by resource and environmental constraints. The mobility of jobs and people from cities to suburbs to exurbia has created its own paradoxes. Cities have built costly new infrastructures on the expanding urban fringe while abandoning the already built, fixed urban environment in central cities and places. Simply building more and better roads to accommodate an expanding demand for auto transportation in many cases increases traffic congestion. The old idea of adding greater capacity to roads to handle more vehicles has gradually given way to the notion of moving more people with less fuel to generate less air pollution and less traffic congestion. Most European communities argue that they have elaborate air pollution programmes. Almost as many argue that they are an eco-community.

Thus, needs assessment and the management of infrastructure are linked by new emphasis on performance, not simply construction. Places cannot replace everything. Formerly, capital budgeting and planning took on the character of wish lists, that is, everything a place would like to build, rehabilitate or replace should unlimited resources become available. However, resource constraints have compelled places and infrastructure authorities to think through various options that improve system-wide performance, provide the greatest return on investment and balance multiple needs. In spite of the many new European infrastructure projects under way, the majority of European local leaders would agree with Bruce McDowell that, 'The future is more likely to focus on maintaining and getting the most out of existing facilities, keeping costs down, making public facilities fit more comfortably into the natural environment, and being more ingenious in meeting needs in the most efficient ways that science can devise.'[7] Logically, the concept of 'smart cities' or 'smart regions' has become more common.

Each stage of the infrastructure management process introduces new opportunities for doing things differently. Design now involves better materials, technologies and design techniques. Construction is enhanced through improved materials and quality control. Operations and maintenance draw on new material, techniques, scheduling methods, and management tools. Monitoring incorporates newer needs assessment methods, better management systems, and improved ways of estimating demand. Finally, in this integrated and multistage process, planning and programming use better forecasting, budgeting and project development techniques.

Intergovernmental planning

In the best traditions of architecture and engineering, everything is connected to everything else when it comes to infrastructure planning. Whether for historical reasons or owing to financing requirements, infrastructure systems and responsibilities are dispersed horizontally across separate public and sometimes private actors and are vertically regulated, funded or operated by several public levels.

In bygone eras, when each community was responsible for its own city or village dump, places did not have to think about co-operating on non-polluting landfills, building expensive solid waste incinerators, disposing of hazardous waste materials or developing waste reduction recycling programmes. They do now. Not co-operating horizontally as well as vertically puts communities in great peril.

Separate public policies once governed environmental, transportation and energy conservation programmes. Gradually these programmes are becoming linked in novel ways. Increasingly, they affect everything that places do in the name of place development including housing, zoning, land use, public health and education. Consequently, places may find themselves suffering from system overload – contrary and contradictory regulations imposed by higher government levels that can result in operating paralysis. Regulators and consumers now require utilities to scale back new construction and embrace conservation. NIMBYs ('not in my backyarders') and environmental groups have stymied the siting of new landfills and expansion of existing ones. Anti-noise citizen groups and environmentalists have organised to block new airport construction and expansion of existing facilities. All of this has contributed to urban sprawl by forcing the outward push of development. As both populations and economic activity disperse throughout metropolitan areas, public transport systems experience declining use and taxpayer resistance to subsidising transport at the expense of personal auto use and more roads.

Thinking across systems requires that places learn from one another through new technologies, innovations and experiments. For example, the TGV trains in France started the European infrastructure programme in high-speed trains. Two decades later, high-speed trains are part of the normal planning from northerly to southerly Europe. The new high-speed link between Oslo and Gardermo International Airport is the first example in Norway. Another high-speed train runs between Madrid and Seville. The European learning process can go quickly.

As Europe becomes more interdependent, vast opportunities exist for infrastructure strategies that cross geopolitical boundaries and involve intergovernmental co-operation.

The environmental imperative

'Think environmentally' is not simply a good maxim but an operating imperative of many places. California's automobile pollution measures have inspired many national and regional decision-makers in Europe. The long-term effect in Europe of the California automobile policy cannot be overestimated.

Most cities in Europe are adopting ambitious systems for recycling and composting waste. New energy efficiency technologies are underway such as combined heat-and-power systems and heat pumps.

But the obstacles are enormous. In the Netherlands, where major cities can no longer bear the traffic loads, congested roadways are the cause of 50 per cent of the environmental pollution. 'London, for instance, currently requires 20 million barrels of oil equivalent per year, or two super-tankers a week, and discharges some 60 million tonnes of carbon dioxide a year. Its per capita energy consumption is amongst the highest in Europe, yet the know-how exists to bring down these figures by 30 to 50 per cent without affecting living standards and creating tens of thousands of jobs in the process.'[8] In spite of current know-how, little is done in practice. One has to conclude that there are weaknesses in the strategic planning process in London. To think environmentally is one thing; to act environmentally is another.

Most large cities and their immediate suburbs suffer from major traffic congestion. Transportation choices and travel times affect people's decisions on where to live relative to work and schools, where they shop and dine, and where vacationers visit and stay. Millions of hours a year are lost as commuters find travel times – suburb-to-city or suburb-to-suburb – increasing because of constantly clogged roads. Obviously this growing problem detracts from worker productivity and quality of life.

Some places experiencing this phenomenon have employed different solutions to ease the problem. A *first option* is to use new information technology. One such example is the intelligent vehicle highway systems (IVHS) – radar, sensors, smart cars and satellite-linked electronic navigation system – which offer prospects for moving urban traffic more efficiently and safely. In Europe one can already observe how certain places in Germany, for example, are using such traffic projects in their placemarketing. However, while new technologies may improve the flow of people and goods, they alone are unlikely to solve the people-moving problem.

A *second line* of defence that many places employ is to discourage auto use by limiting parking options and increasing the costs of auto use. Places may raise fees for motor vehicle registration and licences, increase parking meter fees and fines, and stiffen penalties for minor traffic offences. The war on the automobile extends to special permits for neighbourhood residents and various restrictions on downtown parking. All European countries use petrol taxes as a means of discouraging auto use and for developing viable mass transport alternatives. Florence, Italy, like several other European cities, has built large parking facilities at the city's rim and has banned private cars from driving to the city centre. Athens admits cars into the city based on the number of their licence plate, which means only half of the region's cars can enter the city on a particular day. In Oslo, cars are automatically registered and invoiced when entering the inner city. Such initiatives are frequently emerging in placemarketing. They can be seen in the mega-placemarketing of the Olympic Games in 2004 where the competing candidates used the ecological aspects frequently as an argument for their selection.

A *third option* is to improve collective transport systems. During the 1990s Europe witnessed a revival of transport systems in central cities. Old European inner cities have damaged their 'sense of the place' because of unrestrained automobile expansion. In an era where unique and attractive cities are favoured more than ever, the pressure for collective transport systems is growing. Architect Walter Bor on rethinking the future of Prague criticised the traffic patterns: 'Vehicles are invited not just right into the city, but right through the city. I've always been shocked when coming here by car from Austria that you're brought in or out of here by a pincer movement around the National Museum and right across the top of Wenceslas Square. This was a huge mistake. It ruined the very fine city park up there and a couple of very nice streets, too.'[9] Such observations, common as they are, act as driving forces for the rethinking of inner city transport systems. Along such lines the European Commission has set up an initiative known as Car Free Cities. A number of cities have decided to reject the car-free city concept and instead improve cycling routes and public transportation, clean up vehicle emissions, and implement other stop-gap measures. It is all enacted under the umbrella of 'sustainable mobility'.

When places seek to demarket automobile use in central cities, a corresponding pressure builds for them to improve their mass transport systems. Metro areas experiencing no growth or even modest growth in population, however, face passenger losses with little adjustment in the supply of transport services. To operate effectively, mass transport requires certain population densities and levels of demand which are undermined by continuing population sprawl and make transport service less efficient to provide. Still, public demand for inter-suburban van service has increased with the result that both public and private providers now offer this service.

A *fourth option* is to enforce auto emission standards to discourage the purchase of larger cars. The European car industry is trying to adapt to such standards. In September, 1997, the 'Smart City Compact' was introduced by Swatch–Daimler Benz in Frankfurt. This diminutive smart car with extremely low gas consumption could well represent a new approach to the environmental challenges in European inner cities.

Synchronising place development needs with infrastructure development

Infrastructure development must meet multiple needs, but none is more important than adjusting to overall place development priorities. Just as waging war may be too important to leave to generals, so infrastructure is too important to be left simply to engineers, architects, and the narrow confines of single-purpose infrastructure authorities (for example a tollway authority). Various constituencies must be tapped so that public works are synchronised with broader place development goals.

A new example of how planners are rethinking the interconnections of infrastructure systems, environmental imperatives and multipurpose inner city design is found in Manchester, UK. After experiencing a devastating IRA bombing attack on the centre, the city embarked on a £500 million rebuilding project and, over a four year period, created a Millennium Centre inspired by the Pompidou complex in Paris. The cross-European learning is obvious here again. Sir Alan Cockshaw, chairman of Manchester's urban redesign judging panel, said: 'We want to create the very best centre in the whole of Europe, fit for the 21st century, and one which the people of Manchester can be very proud of.'[10] The Millennium Centre, with an appealing city centre and a tram system project feeding it, is a good example of a multipurpose project, typical of current European interconnective planning.

In many cases, infrastructure investments, whether in getting more out of existing facilities or in making new investments that meet multiple needs and priorities, may be the most critical decision that places make in improving their competitive position. Strategic market planning must deal intelligently and creatively with the choice of various infrastructure proposals.

Basic service provider: protection of people and property, social security and education

Like place design and infrastructure, successful places also demand good public services. Poor public services, especially of education and police protection, can create substantial place liability. Quality public services, on the other hand, can be marketed as a place's primary attraction and product.

Consider the following questions for your place. Do tourists or visitors worry about their personal safety when coming to your community? How far from work must employees and executives live to obtain either the public services or the environment they desire? Are you pleased with sending your children to the local schools?

The ability of a place to attract and retain business activity is vastly diminished when its reputation for high crime or poor schools is paramount in people's minds. In bygone eras, business often gravitated to places that had low taxes but few services. Now, with offshore locations providing such advantages, business is drawn to places that offer high-quality services that contribute to improved productivity and quality. Visitors increasingly factor security and safety considerations into their travel decisions. Parents' decisions on where to live and work often turn on the location of the best educational opportunities for their children. The practice of ranking the best schools and colleges in the USA has been introduced in Europe.

All places should be concerned about their core public services: *protection of people and property, basic social security and education*. In Europe, these basic, visible and high-citizen-contact services are often locally financed, administered and controlled. The overall decentralisation in Europe has put more of these responsibilities into the hands of the communities. Local place-sellers have the power to intervene and make the core public services more attractive.

Yet all places face resource constraints. Resources are constrained by a place's fiscal capacity, tax limits and public willingness to spend. Much public debate surrounds the relationship between spending and outcomes. The quality of a place's public services depends on the level of resources and the degree to which they are used efficiently. Even with limited resources, places will realise some gains by using a different mix or allocation of resources.

Programmes for improving security

The task of protecting people and property can be a formidable undertaking for a place. In Germany, 'nearly 40 per cent of the population said in a recent survey by the Emnid Research Institute that domestic security was Germany's biggest political problem at present.'[11] In Hamburg, one of the richest cities in Europe, the once attractive squares encircling the central station are avoided by citizens, as safety has become a top concern. These squares are the province of the city's unemployed (13 per cent),[12] and a combination of drug and prostitution rings. Paul Grimm, chief executive of the Deutsche Polizeigewerkschaft, the German police trade union, says, 'The police force is no longer capable of guaranteeing people's safety.'[13] This startling admission is even more ominous since there is little money to hire additional police officers. The answer for many citizens is to hire private security forces and auxiliary police officers or to recruit vigilance committees.

In a climate of this type, places often put a higher priority on security than on other public sector services. But new solutions are needed. Moving from a bureaucratic top-down approach to greater citizen involvement can deter certain types of criminal activity and behaviour. This change can have a positive impact on how the public perceives police services.

Programmes for improving education

Place-sellers in Europe are competing today with claims of having a highly qualified workforce. This depends in turn on how much the place invests in its educational system. Before place-buyers make a location decision, they must be convinced that a suitable workforce really exists.

According to a study by Ernst & Young on place location selection, companies often move to the wrong place.[14] A number of electronics companies attracted by low-wage locations have located in Southern Europe only to find out that they cannot recruit staff with the right skills. These companies, according to Ernst & Young, have been forced either to employ staff from other countries or bring in trainers from the parent company to teach new recruits.

A place's response to educational needs requires three approaches: (1) local support of the educational sector; (2) action plans for improvement, and (3) integrated approaches to education.

Local support of the educational sector goes far beyond how parents and others rate the quality of their schools. The issue here is to what extent parents, public leaders, local and regional businesses, and other organised interests are openly and actively involved in a place's educational system. The decentralisation trend in Europe has pushed responsibilities down to the individual school. Local groups that capitalise on the opportunity to develop a unique school offering will have a distinct marketing advantage. For example, the international image of Geneva is enhanced by education: 'The canton's cosmopolitan character will make it easy for your family and your employees' families, to integrate swiftly and smoothly into their new environment. Most of the programmes offered in international schools are taught in French and foreign languages. Your children will benefit from a wide choice of education offered by Geneva's public and private schools, as well as its universities.'[15]

Action plans for improvement of the local educational systems are more common today now that the whole issue of education has been linked to the attractiveness of the place. This new focus coincided with the rise of youth unemployment in Europe during the 1980s. The public response, irrespective of party politics, was to present action plans, often with a local and regional profile, which aimed at improving the educational system. In the 1990s, with the even higher unemployment figures, such action plans are emerging everywhere throughout Europe.

Integrated approaches to education link together community colleges, local and regional businesses, research parks and other centres, and state universities. The motive, again, is to foster local economic improvement in some type of cluster. In many places the integration approach is inspired by science parks. From these concentrations of qualified personnel, often with a specific knowledge-image, integrational inspiration is diffused. Often it is called bridge-building. From Cambridge to Aberdeen in the UK there are more than fifty science parks, and in France the many science parks have organised themselves into the Club des Technopoles. The integration of these parks has been compared to the medieval pattern in which each industry was concentrated in a single street within the town: clothiers, leatherworkers, goldsmiths and other artisans. The benefit is that specific education and training can be supported by many different local partners.

Attractions

There is a difference between saying that a certain place works and saying that it is attractive. We use the term 'attractions' to cover physical features and events that appeal to citizens, new residents, visitors, businesses and investors.

Places can be graded according to whether they have no attractions, a single attraction, a few attractions, or many attractions. Many cities and communities fall into the first group; they lack any self-evident attractions that might draw new residents, visitors or businesses. Driving through Europe on the main motorways, one encounters city after city of 'lookalikes'. The residents may love their city, but to the traveller there is nothing noteworthy or unique. As these cities evolve, they increasingly resemble each other in featuring many of the same fast-food outlets, hotel chains and national merchandisers. They take on a quality of 'placelessness'; travellers feel they have been there before, even though it is their first visit. The place has no sense of being different or special.

Even though a small city or community may lack attractions, it is possible to begin a value-added process. Our experience tells us that the process can be even easier in smaller cities owing to closer human contact between local interest groups. This implies that a 'no attraction-place' usually can develop a new attraction. Driving on the motorways through France one frequently passes the brown signs announcing a special place attraction. Suddenly, even the smallest place can make itself visible on the market (Figure 6.1).

Source: Author's photo, 1997.

Figure 6.1 ◆ Even the smallest place can be visible. A motorway sign in France

Some cities and communities feature a few attractions, enough to entice visitors from reasonable distances to visit them but not enough to hold them more than a day or two. Many of these places try to add new attractions in order to create a more competitive value package. For instance, in the city of Bilbao, in the Basque province, the US$100 million Guggenheim museum was inaugurated in October 1997. According to the newspaper *The European*, Bilbao welcomed this world-class attraction, especially since it was experiencing a dying industrial economy.[16] It was fortunate that Thomas Krens, the director of the Guggenheim Foundation, spoke the same economists' language as the local politicians: 'They did not buy it as a cultural venture. For them, it is a high-risk cure for the city's economic and social recovery.'[17] There are many cases of such recovery initiatives in modern-day Europe. The risks are high, but local and regional decision-makers are nevertheless prepared to invest in visionary attraction-building.

A number of European places possess a great number of attractions: Paris, Vienna, Prague, London, Berlin. These places are not compelled to invent new attractions to add to their place appeal. Their basic problem is maintaining the infrastructure and services to support the huge numbers of tourists and business visitors who continuously descend on them to enjoy their treasures. However, in practice, these large, world-class cities continue to develop new attractions.

Laying aside world-class cities, let us focus on those places that need to create more attractions. A place cannot alter its climate, natural terrain or geographical position, but it can add new attractions. Places can consider ten major types of attractions:

1. Natural beauty and features
2. History and famous personages
3. Shopping places
4. Cultural attractions
5. Recreation and entertainment
6. Sports arenas
7. Festivals and occasions
8. Buildings, monuments and sculptures
9. Museums
10. Other attractions

1. Natural beauty and features

Natural beauty, in the minds of most people, consists of mountains, valleys, lakes, oceans and forests. A place with a spectacular sight or world-class wonder such as some of the small villages in the Alps or the Stockholm archipelago (with its 24,000 islands) or Lake Garda in Italy (often called '*The King of the Italian Lakes*') has a competitive edge. Places resting on picturesque terrain and enjoying splendid vistas can capitalise on these features if they conscientiously protect and develop them.

Older European places have opportunities to make their cities more environmentally, physically and aesthetically attractive. Long-term urban redesign focusing on aesthetic values can enhance the natural attractions.

2. History and famous personages

Many places in Europe identify and promote themselves via an historical and famous person. The region Sachsen-Anhalt in Germany now markets itself as '*Luther's Land*'. With a target market of at least of 70 million believers within the Lutheran church and on all five continents, the region has recognised the potential market involved (Figure 6.2).

Places that were the scene of historical events or retain the flavour of bygone periods are potential magnets on the placemarket. An old battlefield is one such example. (see Exhibit 6.4).

Source: Sachsen-Anhalt placemarketing material, 1997.

Figure 6.2 ◆ 'Luther's Land', historical roots in Sachsen-Anhalt

'Waterloo – finally facing my Waterloo'

EXHIBIT 6.4

The history of Europe was altered drastically at Waterloo. This suburb outside Brussels is synonymous with the battle of 18 June 1815, in which Allied forces commanded by Wellington defeated the French army of Emperor Napoleon. Four days later Napoleon abdicated for the second and final time. This historic event has served as the premise for Waterloo to package its historical past with an energetic pursuit of popular culture and the attraction of new residents.

Waterloo is unusual in that it is a stand-alone destination with few other attractions in the immediate surroundings. Today, the whole battle event is vividly commemorated for visitors on the Waterloo tour. The magnet of Waterloo is exploited via the Internet where the potential visitor is invited for a four-day trip to Waterloo. The booking for 'Historic 1815 Tour' can be made on the Internet.

Itinerary

Day 1: Depart London 08.45. Dover–Calais 12.00 ferry. To Charleroi. Dinner.

Day 2: Breakfast. The Battle of Quatre Bras. Napoleon's HQ and viewpoint at Belle Alliance. The 'Battle of Waterloo' including the Panorama, Mercer's Battery and Hougoumont Farm. Dinner. Talk with Colonel Desmet.

Day 3: Breakfast. Napoleon versus Blücher at Ligny. Retreat to Wavre. The actions at Plancenoit. Wellington's HQ at Waterloo. To Brussels. Dinner.

Day 4: Breakfast. Visit Waterloo Monument at Evere Cemetery and Museum complex including Military Museum. Shopping time and lunch break. Calais–Dover 1815 ferry. Arrive London 20.45.

This relatively long weekend tour is packed with monuments, dramatic battle re-creations and military celebrities. Waterloo becomes a complete and fully satisfying tourist destination.

Waterloo's image has also been enhanced by becoming prominent in the music market. Waterloo's name surfaced with Abba's winning entry 'Waterloo' in the Eurovision Song Contest of 1974. Much of Europe was singing.

'Waterloo – I was defeated, you won the war
Waterloo – Promise to love you for ever more
Waterloo – Couldn't escape if I wanted to
Waterloo – Knowing my fate is to be with you
Waterloo – Finally facing my Waterloo.'

Pop culture channels brought a unique place-message in a seductive package, a song, to the world. Teenagers everywhere were reminded of Waterloo's historical background, and repeated plays on radio and TV drummed in the lyrics and beat.

The effect of Waterloo's singular focus on the past has delivered a steady stream of visitors and a bonus of attracting new residents. Many places have historical attractions that could be similarly levered with energy and focus. Waterloo recognises the battle's marketing value and relentlessly promotes it.

Source: Holts Tours Ltd, Golden Key Building, 15 Market Street, London; 'Waterloo' permission granted by Polygram International, London.

Malaga on the Spanish Costa del Sol is a place trying to enhance its value via a famous person: *Pablo Picasso*. Since Malaga is competing with so many other tourist destinations providing perfect temperature, sunny beaches and natural beauty, it is important to add celebrity value. The mayor of Malaga, Don Pedro Aparicio, has understood this value and has created the Pablo Picasso Foundation. The work of the foundation falls into three categories: a perpetual tribute to avant-garde artists including Picasso; the creation and maintenance of a centre of documents relating to Picasso; and the encouragement and promotion of the world of art in general. Exhibitions, lectures, reproductions of his works, student grants, a museum, a specialised library, a projection room, a reading room, an exhibition hall and a laboratory are all examples of this value-added packaging in Malaga.[18] Malaga continues to develop new associations to the Picasso brand name and in doing so enlarges its market.

A small Swedish community, Kristinehamn, has also understood the Picasso value. Upon entering the city, one is greeted by the message: '*Picasso chose Kristinehamn. Welcome to you too!*' Kristinehamn managed to acquire one of the most famous works of Picasso and used the association as a surefire attention-getter. While Kristinehamn's association with Picasso is marginal compared with Malaga, it does illustrate the power of names to draw visitors (Figure 6.3).

The city of Ülm in Baden-Württemberg is also marketing one of the twentieth century's most famous persons: *Albert Einstein*. The birthplace of the great scientist, the city not surprisingly has built a science park close to the university. The Ülm Science Park is the largest of Baden-Württemberg's 36 science parks, which collectively give the state the highest ratio of scientists per head in Europe.[19]

Another world-famous person is marketed by the small city of Arles (35,000

Source: Author's photo, 1997.

Figure 6.3 ◆ 'Picasso chose Kristinehamn. Welcome to you too!' Sign on entering Kristinehamn

inhabitants) in Provence. The artist Vincent Van Gogh lived here at the end of the nineteenth century. Memories from this time are now treasured as crown jewels. For decades the legacy of the artist was ignored by the Arlesians and landmarks related to him were neglected or destroyed. Today, however, people from all over the world go to Arles to experience what drew Van Gogh to this place. The revival of Van Gogh's image has encouraged Arles to accommodate art lovers with attractions such as guided tours, themed restaurants and other authentic or recreated places of interest. The celebrity place market is one of the fastest growing tourist attractions in Europe, and communities with undervalued assets need to rediscover and repackage their stars.

3. Shopping places

Every community has one or more shopping areas where people buy their food, clothing, appliances, furnishings, and hundreds of other objects. Streets like Kurfürstendamm and Unter den Linden in Berlin, via Monte Napoleone in Milan, or Oxford Street in London are all famous examples of shopping places with a global appeal. However, on a micro level most cities have natural marketplaces that can be improved in various ways.

Today, many street-oriented shopping areas, whether main street or neighbourhood retailers, are fighting for survival against the growing appeal of regional and local shopping centres. Large shopping centres contain major department stores, dozens of franchised stores, medical and health services, and often cinemas and other entertainment. They offer easy parking, concentrated and easily accessible stores, and, when enclosed, air conditioning and protection against bad weather. Yet even these centres now suffer in many cases from overbuilding and intense competition, which leads to various adaptive reuses of once prosperous malls.

In such a hotly competitive environment, comprehensive downtown development projects have been one answer to the decline. Collective traffic is improved, residential houses and apartments are built in the inner cities, footpaths are improved and trees are planted. Many larger street-oriented shopping areas have created a new attractiveness by opening the area for pedestrians only. Copenhagen's famous walking street *Strøget* is attracting visitors in search of a special shopping experience. Venice itself is one giant walking area since motor traffic is non-existent.

Active communities throughout Europe are trying to improve the attractiveness of their natural marketplaces. Redesign programmes are common. One can call this a *catch-up move* after decades of public neglect. Berlin is probably the most far-reaching example. Of course, the building blitz in the inner city increased substantially after the decision to make Berlin the capital of a united Germany. New shopping areas are being built as well as hotels (10,000 hotel rooms will be added within the next few years). To enhance attractiveness, the Berlin marketplace aggressively pursues festivals and events, and special outdoor markets are organised all year round. The strategy here is to encourage citizens to move into the downtown area, and attractive city apartment buildings are being built to convert the new urban dwellers to permanent residents. Such *multipurpose marketplaces* are also being created in many smaller communities throughout Europe as cities and towns are reverting to an age-old strategy: recreating the town centre as the focus of commerce, entertainment and social life.

4. Cultural attractions

Many communities are now sponsoring cultural programmes in order to add new value to their place. European decentralisation from national levels to various place levels accelerates the interest in local community culture.

In 1983, Melina Mercouri, at that time minister of culture in Greece, supported by Jack Lang, the French minister of culture, proposed that each year Europe should appoint a '*cultural capital*'. The ministers of culture within the EU endorsed the idea, and the Council of Ministers adopted it in 1985. The first cultural capital was Athens. After that have followed Florence, Amsterdam, Berlin, Paris, Glasgow, Dublin, Madrid, Antwerp, Lisbon, Luxembourg City, Copenhagen, Thessaloniki, Stockholm and Weimar. The year 2000 honours nine cities: Avignon, Bologna, Prague, Helsinki, Bergen, Brussels, Reykjavik, Santiago de Compostela and Krakow.

The various cultural capitals have leveraged this honour in different ways. Paris did not do much, arguing that 'Paris is a cultural capital *every* year!' On the other hand, Glasgow, with a deep need for industrial restructuring, seized the opportunity. The community developed an ambitious urban redesign programme, far beyond what is traditionally defined as cultural initiatives. In general, many of the cultural capitals were able to increase the number of visitors by 10 per cent.

Cultural programmes, however, are not important to all groups. The OECD asked high-tech industries what they rank as important factors when making a place-buying decision.[20] The cultural factor ranked number ten on the list. Higher rankings were given to hard factors such as access to qualified workforce, tax levels, cost of living.

5. Recreation and entertainment

Every place needs to provide its citizens with areas for recreation and amusement. The traditional institutions serving this function are the local restaurants, bars, cafés, clubs, discos, parks, community centres, performing arts companies, zoos and sports arenas. More complex attractions and combinations of attractions are now emerging.

One example is the emergence of various theme parks. There are some giant examples: *EuroParis* outside Paris, the *Warner Brothers Movie World* in Bottrop-Kirchhellen in the Ruhr region, and *Legoland* in Danish Billund. Investors (place-buyers) are attracted by the strong potential of a successful theme park. Place-sellers are eagerly looking for an opportunity to put their place on the European place-map and a theme park offers investment and visibility.

In the case of Warner Brothers Movie World, the investment cost US$250 million. The park covers 450,000 square metres. This huge investment was made possible by a joint effort among Warner Brothers, the German company Nixdorf Computers, and the state of Nordrhein Westfalen. Place-buyers and place-sellers chose to locate in Bottrop-Kirchhellen, a place known for heavy industry which needed to expand its service sector.

Europe has become dotted with theme parks in a relatively short time. For example, another large-scale theme park is *Port Aventura* operated by the Tussauds Group. It is situated outside Barcelona along the Catalan coast and is the first theme park in the south of Europe. In the north of Europe we find *Legoland*, a land made up of toy bricks, which started thirty years ago. It has spread its specific theme to the UK where the Lego Company chose Windsor, just outside London, for its £80 million investment. With a strategy of opening a new theme park every three years the company has established *Europa-Park* outside the city of Rust/Baden in Germany, where the European dimension is focused on sixty attractions from various European countries.

In Figure 6.4, the top twenty European theme parks, ranked by attendance, are indicated on the map.

Smaller theme and amusement parks have appeared throughout Europe. In southern England alone, the following examples can be pointed out: Alton Towers (Staffordshire); American Adventure (Ilkeston); Brean Leisure Park (Burnham On Sea); Butlin's Somerwest World (Minehead); Chessington World of Adventures (Chessington); Dreamland (Margate); Flambard's Village Theme Park (Helston); Great Yarmouth Pleasure Beach (Great Yarmouth); Smarts Amusement Park (Littlehampton). To help families identify theme parks, a new service has been set up via the Internet: *Theme Parks Interest Group* at *http://pages.prodigy.com/alpha/themecoi.htm*.

Some places integrate entertainment and theme parks as their main industry. Brighton is one good example. However, the best European model is probably Monte Carlo. With its world renowned casino, its outstanding plays, operas and concerts, and its annual Formula One Grand Prix motor race, the tiny principality has become a theme park for Europe's prosperous citizens. (See Chapter 7, Exhibit 7.1, 'Monte Carlo: wheel of fortune'.)

Source: The European, 6–11 November 1997.

Figure 6.4 ◆ Top twenty European theme parks

6. Sports arenas

Almost all places feature some sport where there is a strong local tradition. A winning team or an individual sports star can build civic pride and enthusiasm for a place. A major sports team can put a city's name on the map. *Manchester United* is much more than a winning football team for Manchester. It provides a common theme of identification among the 100,000 members and 200 branches of the worldwide supporters club. European football plays this role for many places: Milan (AC and Inter), Moscow (Spartak Moscow), Munich (Bayern Munich), Madrid (Real Madrid) and Lisbon (Sporting Lisbon). The San Siro stadium in Milan is the real symbol of the city. It is the stage of memorable matches between the city's two famous clubs. A sports arena of course requires a serious investment. Consider the massive investment of FFr3 billion in the new football arena, Stade de France, in suburban Paris. The prized return is when a place's sport and facility becomes a premier brand.

Many sports have a clear place-bound connection: Le Mans, Monza, Silverstone, Spa Francorchamps (motor racing); St Andrews in Scotland, 'the birthplace of golf'; Wimbledon (the mecca of tennis); Athens (the first Olympic Games and now the place for the games in 2004); Colosseum in Rome (the first gladiators); Garmisch Partenkirchen (skijumping).

In most of these places, one can identify alliances between the community, some leading businesses and the local sports association. The aim of the alliance can be to improve or open a new sports arena, promote the sport, organise sports events or attract new players.

Owing to a constant expansion of pan-European broadcasting and other cross-border news coverage, places will invest even more in the sports arenas in the future. The name of the place can easily be integrated into the local teams and hence distributed by the media, free of charge. Daily newspaper sports recaps and live television reports and summaries give cities and towns constant exposure and, in the case of winning teams, even more promotion benefits.

7. Festivals and occasions

Most places sponsor public events to celebrate occasions and anniversaries. Perhaps the prototype of these events is the annual festival. Local festivals have always existed, but the new trend is that Europe, reflecting the interest in local specialities, has spawned a decade of *festival innovation*. The smallest city or community today organises its own festival to celebrate its specific character.

One popular theme is to commemorate a celebrated person born in the city. Genoa has put much effort into remembering its great son *Christopher Columbus*. *Mozart* is the focus during the annual music festival in Salzburg. Gérard Mortier, responsible for the festival explains: 'You can't go back to being a touristic festival, because there are hundreds like that today – Salzburg would find the competition too great. The key to the festival is what you put in the programme, not the number of stars you engage. Only by doing things that can't be seen elsewhere will Salzburg stay on top.'[21] Salzburg is clear about the need to present something unique.

Besides famous people, the theme can also be classical music (Flanders International Festival); theatre/dance (Lille Festival); or movies (Nice, Cannes, Venice). Products with a place-bound link can be another theme with high commercial value. In this category we frequently find wine celebrations. Thousands of small cities and communities in France, Germany, Italy, Spain and Portugal have their local festivals related to wine production.

Among the unique festival themes is Norway's Bergen *Rain Festival* inspired by the rainy climate of Bergen. Another opportunity for celebration was the new *millennium*. Many places organised huge millennium projects. For example, in the UK a special commission invested more than US$2 billion from the National Lottery to erect a huge dome for the year 2000 (Exhibit 6.5) .

Attraction chasing

EXHIBIT 6.5

It has become a mantra among tourism planners that adding attractions is a key to place-marketing success. Worldwide there has been a race to build the tallest building, largest indoor garden or biggest ice hotel. In the London suburb of Greenwich, the government built a monument to the year 2000 called the Millennium Dome. It is the largest structure of its kind in the world, and it celebrates the location of Greenwich as the place time began. Does attraction chasing such as Greenwich makes sense for places?

The answer is not always clear. In the case of the Millennium Dome it is projected that 12 million people will visit in the year 2000 and produce benefits ranging from hosting large numbers of visitors to increased hotel and restaurant business throughout London. After 2000, the Dome has an uncertain future, perhaps turning into a film production site or a sports arena. The financial numbers are less than compelling, and yet places continue to find obscure reasons to build extravagant new structures.

Most attractions can be evaluated on two criteria. Will they pay for themselves? What will they do for our image? In many cases such as professional sports franchises and one-time attractions such as the Dome, the value of the payout is hard to determine. Any place considering such an investment needs to conduct a careful cost analysis of benefits. In many cases the hard factors (building revenues) are insufficient, but the so-called slippery spin-offs (hotel, restaurant, visitor sales) tip the scales. However, attractions are often about image-making and self-esteem – the so-called soft factors. In studies of the impact of attractions, it is clear that residents of places with attractions feel better about their place. The residents and city officials also feel that the attraction can bestow a big-league reputation to a city. And there is often a silver lining in even the gloomiest financial forecast. If the Dome can still be used to celebrate the year 2100, the $1 billion price tag may well seem like a bargain.

Sources: Ray Mosely, 'Huge dome project inspires criticism', *Chicago Tribune*, 25 February 1998, p. 6; David Swindell and Mark Rosentraub, 'Who benefits from the presence of professional sports teams', *Public Administration Review*, January/February 1998, vol. 58, pp. 11–20.

The expo-trend in Europe is also being exploited by many places. The World Expo in Seville and its continuation in the World Expo in Lisbon (1998) are two giant examples. Lisbon was marketed as the '*Last World Exposition of the 20th Century*'. The expo theme in Lisbon was directed towards the exploration of the oceans with special 'guest appearances' by Vasco da Gama, Bartolomeu Diaz, and Ferdinand Magellan. Thus even the most giant expo has to focus on certain unique themes and target groups. As Lisbon was the last expo in the twentieth century, plans for the first world expo in the next century, as earlier discussed, were already underway in Hannover.

Underneath such mega-expos, European cities and communities are generating thousands of expos on all possible themes and target groups. Places today are thinking creatively about developing events that, on a one-time or permanent basis, can bring higher visibility to a community.

8. Buildings, monuments, and sculptures

Another pathway to place distinction is to add or preserve interesting local buildings monuments, and sculptures. A European 'Attraction Map' can easily be drawn on the basis of unique and *world-class buildings*, monuments and sculptures. Such a map could start in Athens with its Parthenon – 2,500 years old – and end in modern London with its Docklands or the new National Library in Paris. In between one finds important draws such as the Leaning Tower in Pisa, or Villa Savoy in Poissy, south of Paris, where Le Corbusier captured the essence and beauty of modernistic architecture (1933). Everywhere on the map we find places where efforts have been made to use building attractions for placemarketing.

Because there are so many world-class monuments, a special European 'Attraction Map' would be comprehensive and useful. One of the most famous monuments in Europe is the *Brandenburg Gate*, built in 1791. Since the fall of the Berlin Wall, the Gate has become the symbol of national unity. Thus a monument can be interpreted in various ways according to changing historical events and values in the market. *Big Ben* in London is another example of a world-class monument so universally recognised that it frequently serves as a symbol of the city. The *Astronomical Clock* in Prague (1410) in the high tower of the Old Town Hall shows the movement of the sun and moon through the zodiac and indicates the months of the year. Every hour, a crowd of tourists gathers to watch the statues of the twelve apostles appear in procession.

Statues and sculptures can develop into effective place-symbols. The statue of the small boy *Manneken Pis* in Brussels, close to the famous Grand Place, is doing what his name suggests. The unique Manneken is Brussels' unofficial symbol, one so powerful that over the past hundred years various groups have contributed clothes for the beloved little boy, which are on display at the Maison du Roi. The statue is so valuable to Brussels that it is carefully attended

365 days of the year, and the likeness is recreated on everything from plates to keyrings.

9. Museums

Never before in European history have so many museums been inaugurated as during the past two decades. We can talk in terms of the '*Museum mega-wave*'. This phenomenon is a direct result of place competition and the determination to improve attractions. It is not surprising that the Council of Europe annually awards the *Museum Prize* to the best European museum. The prize was introduced in 1977 and goes to a museum which has made an original contribution to protecting the European cultural heritage.

Today, Europe can provide the market with a museum for every taste and target group – even the most exclusive connoisseurs have something to explore. There is everything available from the *British Lawnmower Museum* to the *Vatican Museum* in Rome. The Vatican was one of the first (1506) museums. Another early museum was the *Louvre Museum* (1793). Covering an area of 40 hectares on the right bank of the Seine in the middle of Paris, the Louvre offers today almost 60,000 square metres of exhibition rooms dedicated to preserving items representing 11 millennia of civilisation and culture. In order to add to the image, the Sino-American architect I. M. Pei was asked to participate in the modernisation of the Louvre. The result was the famous and controversial huge glass pyramid.

A place without a museum is like a place without a festival or a sports team. A museum conveys a place's sense of culture and history and adds to its stature in the placemarket.

10. Other attractions

There are many other types of attraction. Take, for example, the attraction potentials of a concept such as '*Top of Europe*' which communicates adventure, natural beauty, contrasting colours and climate. The combination of attractions is actually the attraction.

Cape Canaveral, Florida, where the public can watch NASA lift-offs, represents a type of attraction that exists in the form of *sites hosting modern and industrial activities*. It can be the launching site of rockets or manufacturing plants producing cars, trains, steel, glass, fibreoptics, watches or nutritional products. Such living sites can have an immediate attraction when they carefully recreate the enterprise. The paradox is that in Europe such sites are often playing a role only when production has stopped. Then, the usual approach is to transform the place into some nostalgic industrial museum. In contrast, the Cadbury chocolate factory in England now gives tours which enable visitors to observe production and sample the products.

Attractions can also be connected to *infrastructural systems* and sites. It can be the Channel Tunnel, the TGV trains in France, the meeting point of a huge airport (for example Charles de Gaulle Airport), a subway (for example Moscow), a TV/radio tower (for example Berlin), or even an impressive bridge (for example Pont de Normandie in northern France). One can easily foresee the attraction potential of the planned Messina bridge that will link Sicily to the Italian mainland. This bridge, 376 metres above the Mediterranean, will be the world's longest single-span suspension bridge.

People

A place can possess a fine infrastructure and many attractions and yet be unsuccessful because of the way visitors perceive its people. The hospitality of the residents of a place can affect the place's attractiveness in a number of ways.

Outsiders often carry an image of the people who live in a particular place. Some places inherit an unfortunate and often undeserved image that is hard to shake. Such an image may have a strong effect on whether outsiders will deal with the community. Here are some widely shared images of the people living in certain places:

- Sicily – dangerous, criminal traditions
- France – snobbery, rudeness, language problems
- Finland – silent and reserved, depression, alcoholism

Communities whose inhabitants are unfriendly to visitors spoil what might otherwise be a positive experience. Many tourists who visited Paris in the 1950s and 1960s admired the marvellous character of the city but left complaining about the shopkeepers. The shopkeepers were haughty, especially to Americans. In the mid-1970s the French government started a campaign to recultivate French attitudes towards foreigners. Eventually the attitude and demeanour of French shopkeepers and citizens improved considerably.

The behaviour of a place's citizens is always a critical ingredient in its image. Visitors to Rome complain about the aggressiveness of the motorists and the difficulty of getting help on the street when lost or looking for an address. One can contrast this to the service-oriented attitudes often reported from England. Probably no European country invests more in customer service from cabs to hotels than England. Many places are finding an invaluable resource in using retired older citizens as paid service agents and unpaid volunteers in place promotion. Thus, places seeking to expand their tourist and attraction markets must invest in customer services from points of entry at airports or other transit facilities to points of delivery at hotels, restaurants and other attractions. To the extent that communities seek tourist and hospitality business, they must promote public understanding regarding the multiple jobs, spending and related opportunities that flow from satisfied visitors and investors.

Conclusions

Few places have or even can have it all: character, infrastructure, services and attractions. Great character in design and history may support tourism and visitors but may lose other vital or new business opportunities unconcerned with nostalgia and aesthetics. A city with top-flight attractions may be inundated with crime, pollution and poor public services. Great infrastructure without sufficient business investment will deteriorate. Clean air, friendly people and an attractive environmental setting may not help a place that lacks transportation, access to major markets and key attractions.

In focusing on four aspects of place development – urban design, infrastructure, basic services and attractions – we have presented readers with a series of options, namely a practical appraisal concerning what improvements may be necessary and how such improvements can respond to more than one need (for example infrastructure and the environment). We have offered illustrations and examples to emphasise the range of possibilities and opportunities. Table 6.1 offers an audit instrument that a place can use to assess its infrastructure, attractions and people.

Table 6.1 ◆ Audit instrument for infrastructure, attractions and people

CURRENT STATUS

	Poor	*Fair*	*Good*	*Excellent*
Infrastructure				
Housing				
Roads and transportation				
Water supply				
Power supply				
Environmental quality				
Basic social security				
Education				
Lodging and restaurant facilities				
Convention facilities				
Visitors service				

	Poor	*Fair*	*Good*	*Excellent*
Attractions				
Natural beauty and features				
History and famous persons				
Shopping places				
Cultural attractions				
Recreation and entertainment				
Sports arenas				
Festivals and occasions				
Buildings, monuments and sculptures				
Museums				
Other attractions				
People				
Friendly and helpful				
Skilled				
Civic				

POTENTIAL IMPROVEMENT

	None	*Modest*	*Major*
Infrastructure			
Housing			
Roads and transportation			
Water supply			
Power supply			
Environmental quality			
Basic social security			
Education			
Lodging and restaurant facilities			
Convention facilities			
Visitors service			
Attractions			
Natural beauty and features			
History and famous persons			
Shopping places			
Cultural attractions			
Recreation and entertainment			

►

	None	*Modest*	*Major*
Sports arenas			
Festivals and occasions			
Buildings, monuments and sculptures			
Museums			
Other attractions			
People			
Friendly and helpful			
Skilled			
Civic			

IMPACT POTENTIAL

	None	*Modest*	*Major*
Infrastructure			
Housing			
Roads and transportation			
Water supply			
Power supply			
Environmental quality			
Basic social security			
Education			
Lodging and restaurant facilities			
Convention facilities			
Visitors service			
Attractions			
Natural beauty and features			
History and famous persons			
Shopping places			
Cultural attractions			
Recreation and entertainment			
Sports arenas			
Festivals and occasions			
Buildings, monuments and sculptures			
Museums			
Other attractions			

	None	*Modest*	*Major*
People			
Friendly and helpful			
Skilled			
Civic			

7

Designing the place's image

What comes to mind when you hear the name *Budapest*? The capital of Hungary has a dramatic history that was by necessity reborn after the Second World War when Budapest was a city in ruins and a city without bridges. After the war, a dismal communist period brought civil strife and invasion. Budapest developed a negative image as the city was engulfed in pollution, poorly designed buildings covered the landscape, and priceless old buildings collected grime. Budapest, once considered the '*Paris of the East*,' appeared beaten and tired.

Now, as we move into the twenty-first century, the city is striving to develop a new and positive image. As the city consists of two different parts – Buda and Pest – there are today two distinct images linked to Budapest. Separated by the Danube, Buda is a hilly, medieval and historic enclave; in contrast, Pest is industrial, with wide boulevards, and a hustling urban aura. In order to design a new image, the city planners are building mental bridges to Budapest's romantic and colourful pre-communist heritage. Attractions built in the nineteenth century are rediscovered on famed Andrassy Boulevard: the Hungarian State Opera (built 1857–1884) where Mahler was the artistic director is a focal point; many of the 1870s mansions are rehabilitated, and the continent's first metro is restored to its late nineteenth century charm. The international market is also courted by two dozen hot water baths, including Gellert Thermal Bath, which is one of the most beautiful in the world. Such unique and historical attractions are used to design the new image of Budapest, but it will take time before the positive image has overcome the negative one completely.

What comes to mind when you hear the name of the country Turkey? For those who have seen the film *Midnight Express*, Turkey's image is of a country that violates human rights and where social injustices are part of daily life. Today, the Council of Europe as well as the European Parliament has criticised Turkey for its human rights violations. The image is not improved by the Kurdish struggle, tensions over Cyprus, and big city slums.

Turkey has taken a proactive stance on repositioning its troubled image. In a 1994 report, the Press and Information Office of the Turkish government cited negative journalistic reporting as the culprit and withheld work permits of offending reporters.[1] A more productive approach was hiring a public relations firm to manage Turkey's image. Turkey's message, according to Edward Bickham, public affairs head of Hill and Knowlton (UK), is to position Turkey as 'fascinating and challenging because Turkey is a major democracy and a Western ally operating in a difficult part of the world, but which gets a much worse press than it deserves.'[2] Moreover, there is a huge potential in a number of Turkish vacation destinations with a spectacular combination of good weather and historical sites. Tourism in Turkey is the largest foreign exchange earner at US$8.1 billion (1997), and the government is promoting a large-scale international image campaign which encourages local regions, hotels and travel agents to participate.[3] However, a traveller looking for sun and antiquities is still more likely to think first of Greece, which has branded these attributes. The image of Turkey remains out of focus and under stress.

Budapest and Turkey are examples of places where efforts are being made to reposition their images in the effort to attract new industry and to create ways to compete for tourists.

The image of a place is a critical determinant of the way citizens and businesses respond to that place. Therefore, a place must try to manage its image. Strategic image management (SIM) requires examining the following five issues:

1. What determines a place's image?
2. How can a place's image be measured?
3. What are the guidelines for designing a place's image?
4. What tools are available for communicating an image?
5. How can a place correct a negative image?

What determines a place's image?

We define a place's image as the sum of beliefs, ideas and impressions that people have of that place. Images represent a simplification of a large number of associations and pieces of information connected with the place. They are a product of the mind trying to process and pick out essential information from huge amounts of data about a place.

An image is more than a simple belief. The belief that Sicily is an island of Mafia gangsters would be only one element of a larger image of Sicily; other elements would include that it is a picturesque island, it is warm most of the year, and it has a unique culinary tradition. An image implies a whole set of beliefs about a place.

On the other hand, people's perceptions of a place do not necessarily reveal their attitudes towards that place. Two persons may hold the same image of Sicily's warm climate and yet have different feelings about it because they have different attitudes towards warm climates.

How does an image differ from a stereotype? A stereotype suggests a widely held image that is highly distorted and simplistic and that carries a favourable or unfavourable bias. For instance, the European continent, Poland, Bavaria or the city of Belgrade, all generate a number of well known stereotypes. An image, on the other hand, is a more personal perception of a place that can vary from person to person.

Different people can hold quite different images of the same place. One person may see a particular city as a childhood hometown while others may see it as a bustling city, an urban jungle, or a great weekend getaway destination. Therefore, a place wanting to build an attractive image should help place-buyers to discover this image. It is like the answers of the three stonecutters, who were asked what they were doing:

The first replied: '*I am cutting this stone into blocks.*'
The second replied: '*I am on a team that is building a cathedral.*'
The third replied: '*I am honouring God.*'

Thus, a place should have a strategy and the capacity to make the 'cathedral' – and not only the blocks – visible to place-sellers as well as place-buyers.

Image has always been of great interest and concern to marketers. What is our brand image? How do consumers perceive our product relative to the competition's product? How can we identify, measure and control our product's image to attract consumers and build market share? All these questions must also be of concern to the placemarketer. Today's placemarketer must consider a place's image as a major influence on a buyer's choice. After all, once a place-buyer locates in a given place, that place becomes part of the place-buyer's image to its customers. For example, Rolex of Geneva and Chanel of Paris are inseparable in the public's mind.

Likewise, a vacation place-buyer will more likely choose Greece instead of Turkey if the image of Greece is more familiar and positive. The fact that Greece will host the 2004 Olympic Games has the potential to improve Greece's image. At the same time, the winning position is in itself a good illustration of what a world-class strategic image management effort can achieve.

Strategic image management (SIM) is the ongoing process of researching a place's image among its various audiences, segmenting and targeting its specific audiences, positioning the place's attractions to support its desired image, and communicating those attractions to the target groups. The underlying premise of SIM is that because place images are identifiable and change over time, the placemarketer must be able to track and influence the image held by different target groups. Normally, an image sticks in the public's mind for a long time, even after it loses its validity. Some people still think of Cardiff in Wales as a coal district with huge structural problems, even though today's Cardiff is very different. At other times, a place's image may change more rapidly as media and word-of-mouth spread vital news stories about a place. Yugoslavia was once seen as an unorthodox part of Europe with an image of locally 'self-governed' enterprises with its socialist Tito-approach. In a short period this image disappeared as Tito died and new forces entered the arena. Now, Croatia – previously a part of Yugoslavia – is doing its best to create a new image. The city of Moscow is another place where image changes have moved quickly. Just a decade ago Moscow had a very negative image: queues and communist decadence everywhere. When, in 1997, Moscow celebrated its 850th birthday, the emerging image was that of a freewheeling, entrepreneurial city and a leader in Russia's attempt for economic rebirth. There is a danger that Russia's ongoing economic problems will again change Moscow's image.

Image management is an ongoing process of researching image changes and trying to understand their dynamics.

How can a place's image be measured?

Planners follow a two-step process to assess a place image. *First*, they select a target audience. The target audience must be easily characterised by common traits, interests or perceptions. The *second* step requires planners to measure the target audience's perceptions along relevant attributes. We now examine these two steps.

Selecting an audience

The first step in assessing a place's image is to select the audience segment whose perceptions are of interest. Seven broad audiences might be interested in living, visiting, working or investing in a place, and they may hold different images of it. They are:

1. *Residents:* Most places want to attract new residents who can improve the tax base of the community. To understand how potential residents are thinking is strategic information in placemarketing.
2. *Visitors:* Only a few over-attractive places do not want to increase the number of visitors. Places need to know visitors' images of the specific place.
3. *Managements:* Places want to know what the prospective management target groups know and think about the place.
4. *Investors:* Places may want to attract investors such as real estate developers and other financiers who show confidence in the place's future by making generous loans and investments.

5. *Entrepreneurs:* Small businesses and entrepreneurs are important and places need to know how the prospects view the place as a community in which to live and work.
6. *Foreign purchasers:* Products and services – even on the global market – can be linked to a specific place. The image of this place can add value for foreign purchasers.
7. *Location specialists:* Various location specialists have important roles in the place-buying and place-selling process. A place must know what opinions these specialists currently hold.

Even within each broad audience, a large variation in the image of a place often exists. Tourists' perceptions differ depending on whether the tourists are 'sunlusters' or 'wanderlusters'; the perception of managements differ depending on whether they are heavy-duty industrial or 'software' developers.

There are numerous ways of splitting a market into smaller segments (see Exhibit 7.1). Researchers should identify characteristics that maximise discrimination among groups holding different images. The characteristics include simple objective measures (demographics, geographical), complex objective measures (social class, family lifecycle), behavioural measures (lifestyle, buying occasion, usage rate), or inferred measures (personality, needs, sought benefits).

Monte Carlo: wheel of fortune

EXHIBIT 7.1

One of the most well-defined places in Europe is Monte Carlo. The target group is narrowed to rich people who are choosing a place where taxes are low or non-existent, where banking confidentiality is high, and where entertainment is streamlined to their target group. While focusing primarily on upper-class and higher-income earners, Monte Carlo directs its most strategic marketing appeals to a well-defined population. Marketing an image of luxury along with an environment of privacy and relaxation allows Monte Carlo to target a specific audience and cater to its needs.

Assertions from the glamorous tourist guide of Monaco illustrate their focus:

- 'Monte Carlo evokes a different, more magical world, a world of glamour and dreams.'
- 'No other place in the world can match the glamour and splendour of Monaco's hotels.'
- 'No experience of Monaco is complete without a visit to the most famous casino in the world...'
- 'In Monte Carlo, companies can find not only the luxury and variety for unforgettable incentives but unrivalled venues for meetings as well.'[1]

A long-standing reputation for affluence and confidentiality enables Monte Carlo to cater exclusively to those who are wealthy and value their privacy. Social class, lifestyle, buying behaviour, personal needs are all evident in products and services offered in Monte Carlo. The highly controlled principality is not unlike a film set with civic workers dressed in pink overalls brushing up the scant debris, immaculate gardens with non-wilting flowers, and shops and cars that signal exotic and expensive. In a principality filled with rich people, an efficient banking industry is an invaluable asset. In this well defined place, ▶

1,400 of its 30,000 citizens work for banks.

'According to unofficial estimates, the average bank balance in Monaco is $58,000.'[2] It is no surprise that this protected, tax-free place has attracted so many famous personalities from all over Europe, including Bjorn Borg, the tennis player from Sweden, and Mika Hakkinen, the Formula One motor racing driver from Finland. Film and business celebrities are also moving there, attracted by Monte Carlo's well-maintained, discrete and exclusive reputation.

However, being able to continue a development of offerings to attract a more demanding market is a challenge for Monte Carlo. A key issue that must be countered is the increasing number of casinos throughout Europe. Jacques Dubost, currently based in Monte Carlo and a former director of casinos in Dieppe and Cannes, states, 'Twenty-five years ago there were 500 casinos in Europe, now there are 10,000.'[3] Monte Carlo, recognising its vulnerability and defending its market position, has added and upgraded new facilities in response to such challenges. For instance, Monte Carlo has decided to develop its telecoms sector and is constructing a new luxury conference centre and a top-class business centre. Consistency being the key, Monte Carlo needs to monitor its competitive positions and keep pace with the changing needs of the target market.

Sources:

1. 'Monte Carlo', Direction du Tourisme et des Congrés de la Principauté de Monaco, 1997.
2. Charles Jacoby, 'Full monte for the seriously rich', *The European*, 25-31 May 1998, p. 3.
3. David Buchan, 'A sting in the fairy tale', *Financial Times*, 7 January 1997, p. 4.

The segments are most useful when they have six characteristics:

1. *Mutually exclusive:* The various identified segments should not overlap.
2. *Exhaustive:* Every potential target member should be included in some segment.
3. *Measurable:* The size, purchasing power and profile of the resulting segments can be readily measured.
4. *Accessible:* The resulting segments can be effectively reached and served.
5. *Substantial:* The resulting segments are large enough to be worth pursuing.
6. *Differentially responsive:* The segment is useful only if it responds differently from the other segments to various amounts, types and timing of marketing strategy.

To illustrate these criteria, suppose that some golf clubs in the Malaga/Gibraltar corridor, together with real estate developers, want to advertise their offerings via direct mail to high-potential prospects for visits and even investment. They would need to characterise the people who would be interested in golf, know that they have the discretionary income to respond positively, access their addresses and languages, ascertain that many of them exist, and project that a sufficient number of them will open their mail and respond positively.

Once the overall audience is segmented by relevant criteria and groups of interest selected, the key task is to identify the attributes a particular target audience uses to evaluate a place. Only in a few cases has such segmentation has been done by European places.

Measuring the audience's image

Many methods have been proposed for measuring images. We describe three approaches.

Familiarity–favourability measurement

The first step is to establish how familiar the target audience is with the place and how favourable members feel towards it. To establish familiarity, respondents are asked to tick one of the following:

1. Never heard of
2. Heard of a little bit
3. Know a little amount
4. Know a fair amount
5. Know very well

The results indicate the audience's awareness of the place. If most of the respondents tick the first two or three categories, the place has an awareness problem.

The respondents who have some familiarity with the place are then asked to describe how favourably they feel towards it by ticking one of the following:

1. Very unfavourable
2. Somewhat unfavourable
3. Indifferent
4. Somewhat favourable
5. Very favourable

If most of the respondents tick the first two categories, the place has a serious image problem.

Semantic differential

The placemarketers must go further and research the content of the place's image. One of the most popular tools for measuring images is the semantic differential, which involves the following steps:

1. *Developing a set of relevant dimensions:* The researcher asks people to identify the dimensions they would use in thinking about the place. People could be asked: What things do you think of when you consider a vacation? They might reply: weather, recreational opportunities, historical interest and

cost. Each of these would be turned into a bipolar scale with adjectival extremes at each end. The scales can be rendered as five- or seven-point scales.

2. *Reducing the set of relevant dimensions:* The number of dimensions should be kept small to avoid respondent fatigue in having to rate several vacation sites. The researcher should remove redundant scales that add little information.
3. *Administering the instrument to a sample of respondents:* The respondents are asked to rate one place at a time. The bipolar adjectives should be arranged so as not to load all the negative adjectives on one side. After the results are in, the scales can be rearranged to display all the positive adjectives on one side for convenience of interpretation.
4. *Averaging the results:* The respondents' perceptions are averaged on each scale. When the averages are connected, they represent the average image that the audience has of the place.
5. *Checking on the image variance:* Because each image profile is a line of means, it does not reveal how variable the image actually is. If the variance is large, the image does not mean much and further audience segmentation is necessary.

Table 7.1 shows a set of bipolar scales used to measure the tourist image of Copenhagen. The line connecting the means shows the image that a particular group of respondents had of Copenhagen. In this case the respondents consisted of middle-aged persons living outside Denmark with good incomes and grown-up children; the eight respondents had a deep personal knowledge of the city.

Table 7.1 ◆ The image of Copenhagen

	1	2	3	4	5	6	7	
Innocent						x		Sinful
Feminine				x				Masculine
Friendly	x							Cold
Romantic		x						Boring
Old		x						New
Safe			x					Unsafe
Clean				x				Dirty
Interesting	x							Boring
Vibrant	x							Stagnant
Pretty		x						Ugly
Sophisticated				x				Simple
Natural				x				Artificial
Harmonious					x			Conflictual

Evaluative maps

One measure of how citizens view a place is to make an inventory of their visual impressions. This technique involves interviewing a city's residents and collecting their impressions and feelings about different areas of the city. Afterwards, words and responses are structured in a geographical dimension. Each part of the city, community, region, or even a nation is given certain characteristics, for example most liked to least liked.

Another way of gathering data, impressions and feelings about a place is to interview a panel of experts with a deep knowledge of the place. Figure 7.1 shows one such example: an evaluative map of European regions.

What are the guidelines for designing a place's image?

Once planners understand the place's current image, they can deliberate on what image they can build. One challenge in doing this is to create an effective image for each target group. For an image to be effective, it must meet the following five criteria:

1. *It must be valid:* If a place promotes an image too far from reality, the chance of success is minimal. When the promotion agency of Marseilles is marketing the city as '*A Setting for Every Project*', the image is stretched too far.
2. *It must believable:* Even if the proposed image is valid, it may not be readily believable. When the Flanders Foreign Investment Office markets Flanders as '*Europe's Best Business Location*', this may be true. However, the problem is that place-buyers might not be ready to believe it. Overselling is dangerous in the long run.
3. *It must be simple:* If the place disseminates too many images of itself, there will be confusion. Since most places have not worked out any strategy, they often disseminate any image that seems vaguely positive. In this scenario there are no priorities and everything ends up being promoted. The result is confusion, at best.
4. *It must have appeal:* The image must suggest why people would want to live, invest, work in or visit the place. The link between Salzburg and Mozart is promoted in many different contexts that give Salzburg a compelling, permanent appeal.
5. *It must be distinctive:* The image works best when it is different from other common themes. There is overuse of the phrases '*A Friendly Place*', or '*In the Middle of Europe*' (probably the most common approach for the moment) or '*Best Business Climate*'. European cities and communities can find plenty of innovative ideas to exploit real and distinctive approaches.

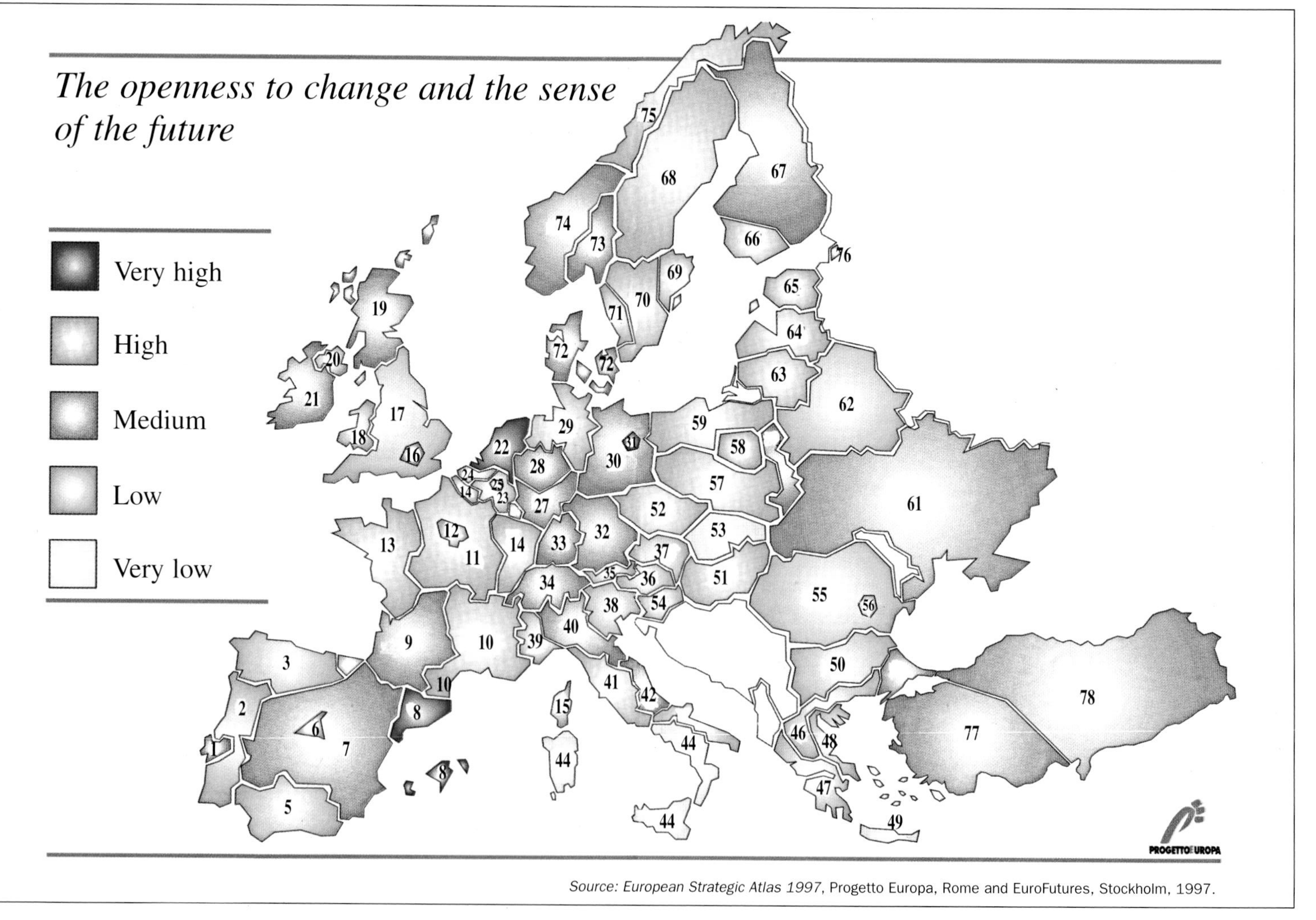

Figure 7.1 ◆ The evaluative map of European regions: the openness to change and the sense of the future

However, sometimes the very name of a place may be in dispute (Exhibit 7.2).

What's in a name?

EXHIBIT 7.2

The Czech Republic has a name problem. A clumsy title crafted as a compromise in the early 1990s is under continual pressure by critics to find something more suitable. The problem according to Jiri Felix, a language professor at Charles University, Prague, 'is a question of international prestige for our country. Who says, "I'm going to vacation in the Kingdom of Spain"?'[1] Some places inherited great names. A name that is exciting (Milan), romantic (Navarre), or stately (Geneva) has an advantage in our image-conscious global economy. Others like the Czech Republic are the victims of regional battles or ethnic controversies and end up with names that satisfy very few.

The leading possibilities for a name change point to 'Cesko' or 'Czechia' as translated in English. The shorter name has the advantage of being more suitable to maps. Other names such as 'Czechland', 'Czeckovia', or the beer-suggesting 'Lagerlandia' are seen as outside possibilities.

In the entertainment business actors routinely change their names for a number of audience-related reasons, and, unlike places, there is no need for a consensus. Places that do not like their name and feel the need for an image change have many possibilities: Spain to Bull Land, France to Wineovia, Portugal to Magellen, or Frankfurt to Hot Dog. If it seems ridiculous, consider that in the USA the state of North Dakota considered dropping the word North because it sounded so cold. What a place calls itself is often determined by history, political pressures, products or leaders' names. When the communist era in East Germany ended, the city of Karl Marx-Stadt became Chemnitz. In the new age of unions, crowded maps and the search for distinction, names will undergo surgery. The semantically cool place will want to protect a name like Paris, but barter to avoid 'Czechomorania.' In reality, nations are most unlikely to replace their brand names, but emerging regions, on the basis of cross-border relationships, new product development or tourism, are candidates for change. In these cases, accuracy, attraction potential and differentiation concepts are all crucial.

Sources:

1. David Rocks, 'After years, Czech Republic still searching for a short name', *Chicago Tribune*, 10 May 1998 (Lexis Nexis); RJC, 'Country's academic launch "Cesko" campaign', *Czech News Agency*, 23 March 1998 (Lexis Nexis).

What tools are available for communicating an image?

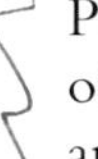

Place image-makers can draw on three tools to implement an effective image of a place: (1) slogans, themes and positions; (2) visual symbols, and (3) events and deeds. Each medium has its own rules and possibilities.

Slogans, themes, and positions

Typically, image-makers develop a slogan to unify a specific campaign and the slogan, if successful, is carried through many campaigns. A slogan is a short catchall phrase that embodies an overall vision of the place. Table 7.2 lists place slogans. When integrated into a strategic marketing plan, slogans can be useful in generating enthusiasm, momentum, and fresh ideas.

Table 7.2 ◆ Place campaign slogans

Place	*Slogan*
Spain	Everything Under the Sun
Amsterdam	Capital of Inspiration
St Petersburg	The White Nights City
Copenhagen	Wonderful Copenhagen
Scotland	Silicon Glen
Budapest	A City with a Thousand Faces
Hannover	The City of International Fairs
Switzerland	Incredible Swiss. Incredible International

A good slogan provides a *platform* from which the place's image can be further amplified. Thus, a slogan such as Spain's '*Everything Under the Sun*' is a short, clear and encompassing image of a warm place; it is also broad enough to be used by government and business organisations in their marketing.

A variation from using a catchall slogan is to spell out *themes* to drive specific marketing programmes addressed to defined target groups. The most effective themes are versatile and flexible yet grounded in reality. The Estonian Investment Agency has developed a platform from the theme '*Leading the Way in Reform*'. The country has backed the theme with real performance as the government quickly moved to reduce trade barriers, end artificially fixed prices and encourage private control of business. The theme in this case is the underlying assumption for all action and change.

Another tool is *image positioning* where the place positions itself in regional, national and international terms as the place for a certain type of activity or as a viable alternative location or attraction to another place that may have a stronger or more well-established position. The challenge of image positioning is to develop an image that communicates benefits and unique attributes that make the place stand out among other places. A number of image positioning statements with a clear European dimension are:

Berlin	*Capital of the New Europe*
Flanders	*Europe's Best Business Location*
St Petersburg	*Gateway to the West / Gateway to the East*
Munich	*Insurance City Number One in Europe*
Glasgow	*An Arts Capital of Europe*
Luxembourg	*Mediaport Europe*
Slovenia	*The Best Kept Secret in Europe*

Visual symbols

Visual symbols have figured prominently in placemarketing. Many landmark sites of places are permanently etched in the public's mind:

Red Square	Moscow
Big Ben	London
Brandenburg Gate	Berlin
European Parliament Buildings	Brussels/Strasbourg
The Viking Ship	Oslo

When used in a systematic way, these visual symbols appear on official stationery, brochures, billboards, videos, pins and dozens of other places.

To be successful, a visual image needs to reinforce an image argument. If the visual is inconsistent with the slogan, theme or position, it undermines the place's credibility. Such inconsistent situations are common because of a non-existent or incoherent placemarketing strategy. This is a big challenge, particularly for small places where a focused approach is even more necessary in order to reach the market.

Here are four commonly used visual image strategies:

1. *The diverse visual:* In the diverse strategy, viewers are treated to a wide range of visual images about the place. The aim is to dispel the notion that the place has a single character. Many big European cities have a diverse strategy. On the other hand, even here there are different levels of visual images. Two or three world-class images usually have a top priority. These are supplemented by a whole range of 'minor' images building up the complete and diverse image. Iceland is marketing itself as a place with a mystical atmosphere where sagas still can be told. Throughout their marketing material is a huge number of diverse saga attractions, museums, music and cultural sites, and mystical geological phenomena. The overall visual effect is one of versatility and completeness.[4]
2. *The consistent visual:* This is the opposite of the diverse visual. When a place possesses a clear and positive image, it is easier to assemble a consistent visual. On the other hand, problems may occur if quite different target groups are approached with one and the same consistent visual. One visual, 'the sacher torte' of Vienna, may be of little relevance for certain target groups such as international businesses.
3. *The humorous visual:* In the humorous strategy, the visual treats the place in a witty style. This is especially useful when dealing with a negative aspect of the place. When Bradford, UK, was trying to combat its negative image as a sooty, industrialised relic, the city introduced its first-tourist-to-Bradford campaign. After touting the city's newly revived central city, cleaning the buildings, and promoting historical and literary stars, they produced a memorable shot. They filmed 'the first tourist' alighting from the train

amidst bands, hoopla and political proclamations. It worked! The visual told the entire story: Bradford is redeveloping, it is a short-trip destination, and it is a city that trusts itself enough to self-parody.

4. *The denying visual:* Another way to handle a negative image about a place is to overwhelm the target audience with positive images, some of which subtly deny the negative aspects. Many places use a denying visual, but there are risks. The denied negative aspects may turn up when visitors confront the realities. The message of the visual image may be that of a romantic and picturesque inner city with medieval traditions, but in reality it is a place with modern traffic congestion and without any urban planning to support the visual image. Many visitors to Brussels complain about traffic congestion and a lack of urban planning. A typical question is, how can the 'Capital of Europe' be destroyed like this? At the same time the city of Brussels continues to market the picturesque inner-city image, with the Grand Place as a world-class icon where cars are excluded. This denying visual can cause frustration among visitors.

Events and deeds

Most image campaigns take the form of catchy slogans, advertisements, brochures, pamphlets and videos. But images can also be communicated through events and deeds. A successful effort can brand a place and its image permanently. The events can be bold, or they can be on the quiet side, subtly influencing an audience over time. For years, the former Soviet Union and East Germany were showcasing their gymnasts and various cultural professionals to other countries. The aim was to build up a quality image abroad and at home. Many places are of course still doing this for various reasons. The difference is that the Soviet Union and East Germany systematically used it as a national tool for political and economic reasons.

The fair and festival business is a constant in historical Europe. Such established festivals as Glastonbury in the UK and Roskilde in Denmark are sell-outs every year. When the leaders of Leipzig decided to make their city a destination, they began from scratch a summer festival devoted to native son Johann Sebastian Bach. And, a town like Aix-en-Provence in France, by re-establishing quality and innovation to its festival, can reap enormous favourable publicity.

How can a place correct a negative image?

Many external forces beyond the place's control shape a place's image. When Italy suffers an earthquake, or England experiences an oil spill, or Bilbao is victim to another act of terrorism, there can be a tremendous wave of negative publicity. This can also happen as a consequence of a chronically poor economy and bad local leadership. Under such circumstances the place has to address the problem of its negative image. Exhibit 7.3 discusses the strategies of reversing an image of violence.

Beating an image

EXHIBIT 7.3

A real threat to a country's image is the threat of violence. The reputation of the English hooligans at soccer matches has forced a re-evaluation of how England is viewed worldwide. A not untypical observation is from an article entitled ominously, 'The shame of the game: hooligans' and cites the mayhem in Marseilles during the 1998 World Cup, 'shopkeepers and other citizens were terrified … men and women trembled and cried.'[1] The stories of looting, drugs and beatings were lead headlines all over the world. The damage to a place's image can be swift, and controlling the problem is essential.

The English hooligan issue has revolved around soccer matches since 39 people died before a 1985 European Cup final between Liverpool and Juventus. Since that time England has put into place a number of crowd control mechanisms aimed to stem the tide of rioting. The measures include major police supervision at the stadiums, targeting ringleaders, and on-site cameras for surveillance. The results were evident as the 1996 European Cup was a model of decorum. The problem re-emerged when the hooligans travelled to France and the same supervision was not in place. During the 1998 World Cup, German hooligans also trashed the city of Lens causing former German chancellor Helmut Kohl to deplore the attack, 'This is a disgrace, really a disgrace for our country.'[2] The potential damage to an image is clear, but what is the solution?

The rules of response to an image attack should be automatic for places:

1. A clear, early and forceful verbal or written response to the attack is often effective. Kohl's remarks were strong and added that he endorsed swift prosecution.
2. Any confusion in the media regarding events or remedies should be addressed whenever possible.
3. Any advertisements or announcements that promote the negative image should be withheld until resolution.
4. A set of solutions should be offered as quickly as possible. Whenever the remedies are in place, the promotion should be thorough and evident on all the channels of communication – TV, radio, print, Internet.

The English hooligan problem is usually cyclical and not as persistent a problem as inner-city crime or longstanding environmental image issues. However, a relatively minor image problem can imply lack of control, deep-seated hostility or cracks in the EU. In the competitive place wars, travel agents may redirect their clients and companies and seek more peaceful and reliable locations.

Sources:

1. William Gildea, 'The shame of the game: hooligans', *Washington Post*, 1998 (Lexis Nexis).
2. *Deutsche Presse-Agentur*, 22 June 1998 (Lexis Nexis).

Making a positive out of a negative

One obvious option is to admit to the problem and turn the negative into a positive. For years, many places in the north of Europe have been complaining about the lack of tourist potential in the dark and cold climate which starts in October and persists until April. This extreme climate is now used as an opportunity and aggressively promoted. Northern Norway, Sweden, Finland, and now also Russia are trying to turn negative elements into positive images. The slogan '*Top of Europe*' indicates not only a geographical position but also top performance in many other dimensions. Hence, the various countries are increasingly using the climate as a positive argument in relation to various target groups. The city of *Kiruna* in Sweden hosts an annual snow festival where visitors can admire the results of the snow sculpture competition. In wintertime, the darkness is illuminated by the Northern Lights and tourists are awakened in the middle of the night in order to view brilliant stars. This improbable attraction is marketed all over the world, especially in Japan. Together all these northern examples show how a region, in an international economy, can change a number of traditionally interpreted weaknesses into world-class opportunities.

Another image-building technique is to transform a place that was originally negative into something positive. The Second World War has given several hard-hit places a special position on the tourist map: *Dunkirk*, the French harbour from which 338,000 Allied soldiers made their retreat to England in May 1940; the *Ardennes*, sometimes called the *'Forest of France, Belgium, and Luxembourg'*, witnessed in December 1944 the Ardennes Offensive; in February 1945, allied bombs hit *Dresden* and left the city in ruins, and destroyed the Church of Our Lady (*Die Frauenkirche*), which has been described as 'one of the worst architectural losses of the Second World War'. Such negative events have put the places in a highly visible historical perspective, and Europeans easily recognise them as significant to the past. Museums and other monuments, which have been built in order to keep history living for new generations, attract large numbers of visitors. In many cases, companies are involved in restoration and other activities to make history more vivid. For instance, in the case of Dresden, IBM is marketing its assistance in helping to 'raise the Church of Our Lady from the ashes of the World War II'.

Marketing icons

Another strategy for correcting a negative image is icon marketing. Consider the image of the former Soviet Union which until recently struck visitors as a vast, closed country – a prison. The image evoked pictures of Siberian forced-labour camps; grim shortages of food and products; citizens living in stark apartments; repression of Jewish citizens; clunky Russian cars based on a thirty-five year old design; and taciturn, secretive Soviet leaders. The overall impression was one of darkness and control, a place that few people wanted to visit.

Enter Mikhail Gorbachev, then Soviet premier and new-style international icon. In a winning demonstration of impression management, Gorbachev used his own 'warm personality' to help reshape the public's image of his country. Together with his witty wife Raisa, Gorbachev introduced a new openness, *glasnost*, which gave the country a new image. Slowly, the fabled iron curtain lifted, revealing a new, co-operative partner. His successor Boris Yeltsin, as well as a number of new local leaders, can also be seen as important icons. See Exhibit 7.4 regarding a current Moscow icon.

A Moscow icon

EXHIBIT 7.4

The popular mayor of Moscow Yuri Luzhkov, a tough political boss with an engineering background, is a living icon who symbolises the vast improvements in Moscow. Luzhkov became mayor of Moscow in 1992 when the city was a dimly lit, unpainted financial wreck. He adopted the style and image of a non-stop doer – building on a gigantic scale, investing government money and power in private enterprise, and muscling private companies into co-operation. He accomplished all of this in an aggressive style, while impressing and intimidating his opponents.

The style of Luzhkov is best expressed in two ambitious projects: the rebuilding of the massive Cathedral of Christ our Saviour torn down by Stalin in 1931 and his decision to make the down-at-heel automobile manufacturer ZIL a viable company. The rebuilding of the church was supervised personally by the mayor for the 850th anniversary of Moscow. It stands as a monument to the mayor's determination and belief in the restoration of the city. In the case of ZIL, he forced his government agencies to buy their products instead of more reliable and sophisticated Western vehicles. His long-term goal is to be the rebuilder of Russia's future, and his energetic style gets him and his city major news coverage.

In his 1996 campaign for a return to office, Luzhkov received 90 per cent of the vote. He has managed, despite criticism of strong-arming, alleged dealing with the Russian mafia, and a major economic crisis, to position himself as a living symbol for the restoration of Moscow.

Sources: Inga Saffron, 'Moscow mayor painting the town red', *Philadelphia Inquirer*, 31 August 1997 (Lexis Nexis); Valerie Korchagina, 'Luzhkov orders city to buy ZIL's woes', Internet: http://www.spb.vu/times/203-204@bc2.html.

Removing the negative

Image improvement, rather than real improvement, is too often used as a panacea or a quick-fix for a place's problems. Place-leaders besieged by failing businesses or a drop in tourism are usually quick to demand a new image. Yet in most instances, it does not work if the place has not started to correct its deep-rooted problems.

Consider the case of Glasgow, Scotland. When Europeans prepared a list of deeply troubled urban cities, the city of Glasgow would inevitably be included. A place with an unemployment rate of more than 21 per cent, high crime rates, and buildings blackened by coal dust, Glasgow had earned its reputation. One of Glasgow's politicians described the city as 'a hellish mixture of poverty, drink and violence.'[5]

Yet today, Glasgow, while not without problems, is an improving city that is considered an '*Arts Capital of Europe*'. What steps did it take? *First*, the city attracted government grants from London, Edinburgh and its own city council to rehabilitate tenements and rebuild public spaces. One project was to repair the Burrell Museum, now considered one of Britain's most significant art galleries. Various political forces co-operated for the first time to improve the city's condition. One city official saw the starting point as 'a change of attitude in the people that ran the city.'[6] When Glasgow citizens began to witness the cleaning up of their city and the new jobs created, their attitude started to improve. They began to police themselves, encourage innovation and change, and monitor their own political, economic and educational institutions.

Second, the city image-makers began to tie together the changing reality of Glasgow. They adopted the slogan, '*Glasgow's Miles Better*'. They produced glossy brochures demonstrating the city's transformation visually and in words. Articles began appearing in newspapers and magazines heralding the arrival of a new giant in the arts. Image met reality in Glasgow. A visitor to the city saw the changes and experienced the arts revival. Glasgow truly was 'miles better.'

Conclusions

The creation of a powerful image is part of the entire marketing process. It demands a good strategic marketing audit, determined improvement of the product, and creative invention of the symbols. Once the place has taken these steps, its next task is to disseminate its new image to its target groups.

The next chapter examines how place messages and images can be efficiently distributed.

8

Distributing the place's image and messages

Every place needs to develop a story about itself and to tell it consistently and well. Yet, the sheer number of markets and media channels indicates a high risk of sending contrary and confusing messages. If the tourist commission in the Malaga/Gibraltar corridor promotes the booming tourism sector and the chamber of commerce promotes the same area as a site for production companies, confusion could easily arise.

This chapter examines the challenges involved in distributing a *strong and coherent* image of a place. Those in charge of distributing the place's image must address the following questions:

1. Who is the target audience?
2. What broad influence tools are available?
3. What major advertising media channels are available and what are their respective characteristics?
4. What criteria should be used in choosing specific advertising media vehicles?
5. How should the advertising messages be timed?
6. How can the media mix be developed?
7. How can the communication results be evaluated?
8. How can conflicting media sources and messages be handled?

Clarifying the target audience and desired behaviour

The *first step* before choosing messages and media is to clarify the target audience. For example, how should the Navarre region, one of the smallest autonomous regions in Spain, clarify its target audiences with so many diverse attractions? Navarre's romantic past has inspired Shakespeare – '*Navarre shall be the wonder of the world*' – and, as noted earlier, Ernest Hemingway, in his book *The Sun Also Rises*, describes in detail Pamplona's (one of the cities in Navarre) annual bull-running ritual. This historical past, geographical gateway location, and shared border with France give rise to many tourist target audiences. But at the same time, Navarre is in the middle of Spain's greatest industrial activity, the Madrid–Barcelona–Bilbao triangle. This fact, along with the tourist profile, makes it difficult to clarify and prioritise target audiences. Each potential target market calls for different messages and media. Should the Navarre Development Agency rely on advertisements or feature articles? Should it place messages in *Le Soir* or in Iberia's in-flight magazine?

A *second step* calls for visualising the target behaviour that the placemarketers want to elicit from the target audience. That behaviour may be to spend three days in the mountains, to buy a holiday apartment, or to visit in the summer rather than in the winter.

Beyond these steps, it is necessary to determine the *target buyer's stage of readiness to undertake the target behaviour*. A tourist seeking a romantic vacation in Pamplona may hold one of several mindsets regarding Pamplona as a destination: *knows nothing* about Pamplona and the Navarre region, *has some awareness* of Pamplona, *knows a lot* about Pamplona, *would like to go* to Pamplona, *intends to go* to Pamplona. A media strategy for those who *want to go* might be to mail them discount coupons to provide an incentive to act. Another strategy is to communicate some additional information on 'unknown' attractions. In this case it could be an invitation to taste some of the prized wines from the ninety wine producers.

The same issue of the buyer's readiness arises with business targets. In marketing a factory site, place-sellers need to distinguish between *suspects*, *prospects*, *hot prospects* and *customers* (see Chapter 4, Exhibit 4.4, 'Who's the buyer?'). Each buyer group warrants a different media mix strategy. Advertisements in trade journals offering a free booklet describing the factory site and its advantages might ferret out suspects. Prospects might receive phone calls followed by sales calls. Hot prospects might be personally invited and driven to the site, and introduced to the community leaders and some relevant businesses.

Choosing the broad influence tools

Place-sellers can use several broad influence tools to promote their place to target groups. The major promotional tools are advertising, direct marketing, sales promotion, public relations and personal selling. Descriptions of their characteristics, effectiveness, use and costs follow.

Advertising

Advertising is the use of any paid form of non-personal presentation and promotion of ideas, goods or services by an identified sponsor. Thus, the purchase by a community, region or nation – or even an individual company promoting its place – of printed space (magazines, newspapers, billboards) or broadcast time (television, radio, Internet) constitutes advertising.

Because of the many forms and uses of advertising, it is difficult to generalise about its distinctive qualities as a component of the promotional mix. Yet the following qualities can be noted:

1. *Public:* Advertising is a highly public mode of communication. Its public nature confers a kind of legitimacy on the place and its products and also suggests a standardised offering. Because many persons receive the same message, place-buyers know that their motives for purchasing the product will be publicly understood. Thus, if a person vacations in Pamplona, he or she will expect others to interpret Pamplona in the same romantic way that the travel ads present it.
2. *Pervasive:* Advertising is a pervasive medium that permits the place-seller multiple repetitions of a message. It also allows the place-buyer to receive and compare the messages of various European places. A seller's large-scale advertising suggests at least that the place has certain resources behind it.
3. *Dramatic:* Advertising provides opportunities for dramatising the place and its products through the artful use of print, sound and colour. However, sometimes the tool's very success at expressiveness may dilute or detract from the message.
4. *Impersonal:* Advertising is often less compelling than personal presentation. The target group feels no obligation to pay attention or respond. Advertising is able to carry on only a monologue, not a dialogue, with the audience.[1]

Advertising can be used to build up a long-term image for a place or, on the other hand, to trigger quick sales, such as an advertisement offering a special low-price airfare to Cyprus. Advertising is an efficient way to reach numerous geographically dispersed buyers at a low cost per exposure. Certain forms of advertising, such as television and video productions, require a large budget, while other forms can be done on a smaller budget.

During the past two decades, European newspapers have witnessed a sharp increase in the scope of placemarketing advertisements. A borderless Europe has helped to grow the market. When analysing the European placemarketing advertisements, one can draw three conclusions:

1. A lack of uniqueness in the advertisements.
2. The European dimension is turning up in 80–90 per cent of all the ads.
3. The more compelling and innovative messages often emanate from communities or cities and not nations or regions.

Direct marketing

Direct marketing encompasses the use of communication media to reach individuals in the audience where the effect is measurable. The two traditional tools of direct marketing are direct mail and the telephone. Individuals in the places database can be sent appropriate newsletters, brochures, postcards or videos about the place. Lately it has become popular even to send Christmas cards to potential place-buyers.

The direct marketer is able to measure the response rate of direct mail in terms of enquiries, intentions-to-buy or sales. This feature contrasts with advertising, which usually does not contain any response mechanism such as a mail-back coupon or a sponsor's telephone number. Although direct marketing advertising costs more per person reached, its superior targeting and response features often more than make up for the extra cost.

Direct marketing media have taken on new forms in recent years, including direct response radio and television where a product is offered and the customer can immediately call a freephone number to place an order using a credit card. Logically, the personal sales call also is an example of direct marketing since the salesperson knows the response at the end of the visit. However, we treat personal selling later as a separate influence channel.

Direct marketing has a number of distinctive characteristics:

1. *Targeting efficiency:* The marketer can be selective as to who should receive the message.
2. *Message customisation:* The marketer can customise the message for each prospect, based on what is known about that prospect.
3. *Interactive quality:* The prospect or customer who receives the message can interact and communicate with the marketer with questions, suggestions, complaints and orders.
4. *Response measurement:* The marketer can measure response rate to evaluate the success of the marketing programme.
5. *Relationship-building:* The marketer can build and enhance the relationship with a particular prospect through sending thoughtful messages on special occasions (for example birthdays and anniversaries) or giving patronage awards.

These characteristics of direct marketing offer placemarketers a variety of interesting possibilities. Direct marketing is an efficient way to acquire leads on prospective enterprises, potential residents, vacation seekers and other place-buyers. Once the leads are collected, direct marketing can further present offers, test interest and measure readiness to buy. For these reasons, we expect direct marketing to occupy a growing part of the placemarketer's budgets in the coming years.

An example of direct mail dialogue is in Figure 8.1. Note that the place-

Your Ref
Our Ref AW
Please ask for Mrs. Angela Whittaker
Direct Line/Ext 0115 977 2052
Date 8th May, 1997

Nottinghamshire County Council
Planning & Economic Development
Director **H Jackson**

Economic Development
Head of Economic Development **B Holdsworth**
Centenary House, 1 Wilford Lane, West Bridgford
Nottingham NG2 7QZ
Tel (0115) 982 3823 **Fax** (0115) 977 2431

Ron Jones
Pearson Education Limited
128 Long Acre
London WC2E 9AN, UK

Dr Mr Jones

INVEST IN NORTH NOTTINGHAMSHIRE

Many thanks for returning our response form and for your interest in North Nottinghamshire.

As requested I have pleasure in enclosing your English copy of our new "Invest in North Nottinghamshire" information pack

Please do not hesitate to contact me if we can help with:-

* **Further information about investment in North Nottinghamshire.**
* **A briefing tailored to your Company's or client's particular requirements.**
* **A visit to you by North Nottinghamshire representatives.**
* **A visit by you to North Nottinghamshire.**

Looking forward to hearing from you.

Yours sincerely

ANGELA WHITTAKER
Marketing Executive Inward Investment

North Nottinghamshire - In Partnership
Ashfield District Council Bassetlaw District Council
Mansfield District Council Newark & Sherwood District Council
North Nottinghamshire Training & Enterprise Council
Nottinghamshire County Council

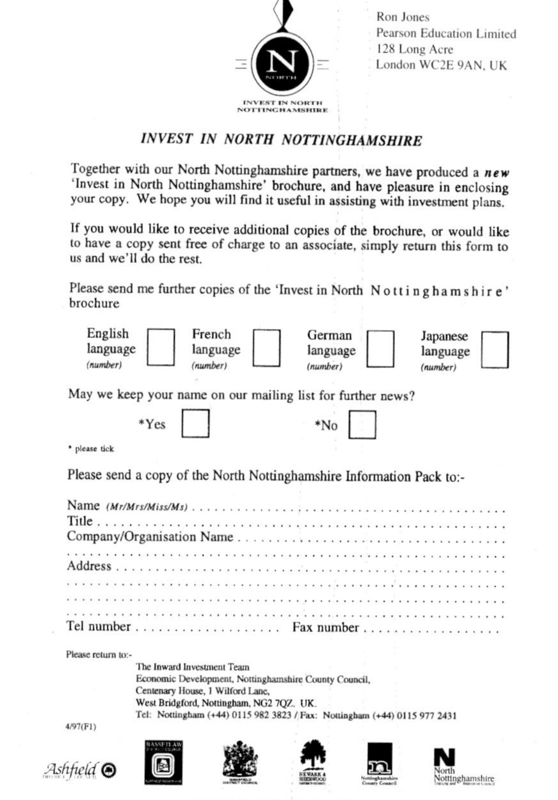

INVEST IN NORTH NOTTINGHAMSHIRE

Ron Jones
Pearson Education Limited
128 Long Acre
London WC2E 9AN, UK

INVEST IN NORTH NOTTINGHAMSHIRE

Together with our North Nottinghamshire partners, we have produced a ***new*** 'Invest in North Nottinghamshire' brochure, and have pleasure in enclosing your copy. We hope you will find it useful in assisting with investment plans.

If you would like to receive additional copies of the brochure, or would like to have a copy sent free of charge to an associate, simply return this form to us and we'll do the rest.

Please send me further copies of the 'Invest in North Nottinghamshire' brochure

English language *(number)* ☐ French language *(number)* ☐ German language *(number)* ☐ Japanese language *(number)* ☐

May we keep your name on our mailing list for further news?

*Yes ☐ *No ☐

* please tick

Please send a copy of the North Nottinghamshire Information Pack to:-

Name *(Mr/Mrs/Miss/Ms)* . . . .
Title . . . .
Company/Organisation Name . . . .
. . . .
Address . . . .
. . . .
. . . .
. . . .
Tel number . . . . Fax number . . . .

Please return to:-
The Inward Investment Team
Economic Development, Nottinghamshire County Council,
Centenary House, 1 Wilford Lane,
West Bridgford, Nottingham, NG2 7QZ. UK.
Tel: Nottingham (+44) 0115 982 3823 / Fax: Nottingham (+44) 0115 977 2431

4/97(F1)

WORKING IN PARTNERSHIP

Fig 8.1 ◆ Direct mail dialogue in practice

Source: Nottinghamshire County Council, Planning and Economic Development, 1997.

seller, in this case Nottinghamshire County Council, personalised by Angela Whittaker, is outlining a number of tools for the place-buyer to use, and encouraging the receiver to send in for even more information.

Sales promotion

Sales promotion encompasses the use of short-term incentives to encourage buyers to purchase a product or service. Whereas advertising offers a *reason* to buy, sales promotion offers an *incentive* to buy. Not surprisingly, sales promotion yields faster purchase response than does advertising.

Sales promotion includes such devices as free samples, coupons, cash refunds, discounts, premiums, prizes, patronage rewards, free trials, warranties, demonstrations and contests. Place-sellers have developed a whole set of such tools in their bidding wars for corporate and factory relocation: inducements include tax concessions, subsidised housing and job retraining, special financing, infrastructure improvements and cheap land. Sales promotion of this kind has increased in Europe during the past decade.

Although sales promotion tools – coupons, contests, premiums, and the like – are highly diverse, they have three distinctive characteristics:

1. *Communication:* They gain attention and usually provide information that may lead the target audience to show more interest in the place.
2. *Incentive:* They incorporate some concession, inducement or contribution that gives specific target packages to the audiences.
3. *Invitation:* They include a distinct invitation to engage in an immediate transaction.

Sales promotion tools create a stronger and quicker response than any other influence channel. Sales promotion can dramatise product offers and boost sagging sales. Promotion effects, however, are usually short term and do not build lasting place preferences.

Public relations

Public relations is the effort to build good relations with an organisation's publics by obtaining favourable publicity, building up a good public image, and handling or heading off unfavourable rumours, stories and events. Major public relations tools include press relations, event publicity and lobbying. The appeal of public relations is based on its three distinctive qualities:

1. *Highly credible:* News stories and features written by independent journalists seem more authentic and credible than ads.
2. *Indirect:* Public relations can reach many prospects who might avoid salespeople and advertisements. The message gets to the place-buyers as news rather than as a sales-directed communication.

3. *Dramatic:* Public relations has, like advertising, a potential for dramatising a place.

Marketers tend to under-use public relations or use it as an afterthought. Yet a well-thought-out public relations programme co-ordinated with other promotion-mix elements can be extremely effective. Within the EU countries, the number of public relations companies may be more than five thousand.[2]

The craft of public relations is segmented and specialised. Areas of speciality in public relations include financial, employee, product and government, among others. The branch we are interested in is marketing public relations (MPR).[3] In the hands of a placemarketer, MPR can contribute to the following tasks:

1. *Assist in the launch of new products:* Each time McDonald's establishes a new place, a public relations campaign targets the local market with special events, press releases and other media-focused activities.
2. *Assist in repositioning a mature product:* The whole Ruhr region in Germany, with its mature industrial image, is ambitiously using public relations to reposition the place. The long-term goal is to build up and enhance the service sector.
3. *Create interest in a product category:* The European shipbuilding industry – and now also shipping companies – have struggled for years to survive in a highly competitive global market. Shipbuilding companies and corporate headquarters of shipping companies have sponsored public relations campaigns in conjunction with places to attract attention to this industry.
4. *Influence specific target groups:* Greece, in its efforts to build up more tourism, implements special campaigns directed towards Greek communities in the US. Oberammergau in Bavaria enacts the Passion of Christ every ten years, which attracts an international religious audience.
5. *Defend places that have encountered public problems:* Hundreds of European places with a military installation are now threatened with shut-downs. These places are initiating public relations programmes aimed at convincing governments and other public groups to keep their military unit. An obvious target for a campaign is the challenge to convince the EU to earmark Konver-programme money to a place.
6. *Build the place image in a way that reflects favourably on its products:* The reorientation in the Ruhr region towards the service sector creates a climate for new place image initiatives. For example, the city of Essen organised a garden festival to make its new green image more vivid. Even more ambitiously, Essen targeted the conference market by hosting such significant events as the Ruhr summit in 1994. The carefully crafted invitation reflected the image: '*Welcome to the Meeting Point of Europe's Future* ... A region with 5.5 million people working together to build an economic powerhouse of European proportions. Restructuring traditional industries

into new centres of excellence in research and production. Creating an extraordinary, new quality of life. Signposting Europe's future. When will you join us?'[4]

As the power of mass advertising weakens owing to rising media costs, increasing clutter and fragmented audiences, marketing managers are turning more to public relations. Often, public relations can create a memorable impact on public awareness at a fraction of the cost of advertising. The place-seller does not pay for the space or time obtained in the media. Instead, it pays for a staff to develop and place stories and to manage certain events. Sometimes the community pays the public relations company only when a story is actually accepted in a newspaper. If the place develops a story with an interesting angle, it could be picked up by all the news media and be worth millions of ECU in equivalent advertising. Furthermore, it would have more credibility than advertising. Some experts say that an audience is five times more likely to be influenced by editorial copy than by advertising.

Personal selling

Personal selling is the most effective tool at certain stages of the place-buying process, particularly in building up a buyer's preference and conviction towards an action. The reason is that personal selling, when compared with advertising, has three distinctive advantages:

1. *Personal confrontation:* Personal selling involves a live, immediate and interactive relationship between two or more persons. Each party is able to observe the other's needs and characteristics firsthand and make immediate adjustments.
2. *Cultivation:* Personal selling permits all kinds of relationships to spring up, ranging from a matter-of-fact selling relationship to a deep personal friendship. Effective sales representatives keep their customers' interests at heart if they want long-term relationships.
3. *Response:* Personal selling makes the buyer feel under some obligation to respond after having listened to the sales talk. The buyer feels a responsibility to be attentive and to respond, even if only with a polite thank you.

These advantages come at a cost. A salesforce represents a fixed financial commitment. Advertising can be turned on and off, but the size of a salesforce is more difficult to alter.

Other tools

Additional image and promotion tools – not all under a place's control – can help or hurt a place. Included are television, song, sports and various novelty icons. Here are some examples.

Television

Television broadcasting has at least two routes that can influence the place-marketing context. *First*, a place can suddenly be hot in the European or world arena owing to a television appearance. For example, the long-running German television programme *The Clinic*, filmed in a romantic part of Schwartzwald, made the whole area well known to a broad international audience. *Second*, there is often a place battle when a broadcasting company is announcing its plan to open for a new TV studio/TV team. Place-sellers know from experience that close connections to such a media centre – irrespective of its size – makes the place much more visible.

Song

Marketing places through music can help brand a place's image. *Riverdance*, the show built around Irish music, song, and dance, gives sound and visual appeal to Ireland and its traditions. The songs *A Foggy Day in London Town* and *I Love Paris* pay tribute to two legendary places. And who visits Hungary without listening to gypsy music or frequents night-clubs in Portugal without hearing Fado? And the European Union has adopted the theme of 'Ode to Joy', the fourth movement of Beethoven's Ninth Symphony as an anthem.

The annual *Eurovision Song Contest* opens image-creating opportunities for placemarketers. There is a pan-European marketing opportunity for the place holding the event as well as for the participating countries. When Birmingham landed Eurovision in 1998, it felt that it had achieved world-class status as a destination.[5] Each country is invited to market itself before the performance of its song. When the song's theme reflects the place's image, there is an added marketing bonus. Moreover, when the Beatles created a new rock sound in Liverpool, the image of the industrial port began to be redefined. Other art forms can also affect public perception of a place (Exhibit 8.1).

Getting the big picture

EXHIBIT 8.1

In the film *Ronin* three spectacular car chases took place in Paris, Arles, and Côte d'Azur. The location shots were so alluring that the places received what amounts to a free promotional package. A film can reach millions of people and has the potential to celebrate, define or even vilify a place. Places that are looking for a marketing edge might find the practice of encouraging local filmmakers and enticing film companies to shoot in their communities to be a visibility builder.

The movie-making business and cinema attendance is on the rise in Europe. EU member states out-produced the USA in film production in 1996: 669 to 421. European cinema admissions rose 18 per cent between 1990 and 1996,[1] indicating a dramatically increased interest in film.

While US blockbusters still dominate the industry, Europe is finding ways to stimulate the film market. In many countries, such as Italy, state loans are encouraging film production. There is also an increase in the number of large-scale, multiscreen cinemas that can show a wider variety of films. Films such as *Cinema Paradiso, Four Weddings and a Funeral, Il Postino* ▶

and *The General* are not only winning awards, but are also making significant inroads into the worldwide market.

Still, Europe can do more for promoting its film-producing image. The major US film studios outspend European producers in promotion and marketing at the rate of 20 to 1.[2] Also affecting distribution is the continuing practice of using subtitles, which limits a worldwide market. Despite these reservations, European-based films are going to grow and places that are eager to accommodate high-speed car chases and to cut red tape are most likely to find their place marketed to millions, almost free of charge.

Sources: 1. 'Film industry: cinema-going making a comeback in the EU', *European Report*, 1 April 1998 (Lexis Nexis).
2. Monica Larner, 'What brought Italian films "Out of a Coma"', *Business Week*, 17 November 1997 (Lexis Nexis).

Sports

Places often compete to host sporting events because of their placemarketing appeal. A championship season is often the catalyst to launch effective place distribution campaigns. A downhill skiing event in the smallest Alpine-village can quickly spread the in-place image to the mass-sports market. The famous '*Tour de France*' cycle race is actually a place tour, and a town will make huge financial commitments to host a stage start, such is the value of the extra business and publicity generated by the race. And sports teams can encompass all the dimensions of a place's ambitions and image. When Sheffield landed the UK Institute of Sport housing five British sports and three organisations, it was transformed from the city of steel to the city of sport.

Novelty icons

The media occasionally shines a sudden spotlight on an icon that causes tourists to become determined to visit the place. One such example is the *Loch Ness Monster*, or simply Nessie, in the highlands of Scotland. Millions of people have made the pilgrimage to Scotland to search Loch Ness in hopes of a Nessie sighting. This unlikely icon has created a tourist industry which features attractions such as submarine rides and a multimedia tourist centre that disseminates the latest news on the slippery creature.

Even an individual church or a castle can be refocused via a literary icon. Based on Victor Hugo's classic figure Quasimodo who lives alone in the bell-tower of the Cathedral of Notre Dame in Paris, a number of films have managed to shape the image of that church. A recent example, Disney's worldwide release of *The Hunchback of Notre Dame* has implanted the image of the church in the minds of many children. The haunted castle, Kronborg, outside Helsingør, is closely linked to Shakespeare's *Hamlet*. The tormented Hamlet can still attract tourists who in turn buy postcards and souvenirs, eat meals and shore up the local economy.

Selecting advertising media channels

The selection of effective media channels and vehicles is a formidable task. Choices are more complex than ever. For instance, Europe has witnessed an explosion in the number of TV channels during the past ten years. There were four times more channels in 1993 than in 1981.[6] Today, there are 'generalist' channels, for example the BBC (UK), RA1 and Canale 5 (Italy), TF 1 and FR 23 (France) – and at the same time so called 'thematic' channels, for example Eurosport and Discovery.

The *first step* in selection calls for allocating the advertising budget to the major advertising media channels. These channels must be examined for their capacity to deliver reach, frequency and impact and include: television, radio, Internet, telephone, newspapers, magazines, newsletters, brochures, direct mail and billboards. Table 8.1 summarises the advantages and limitations of these media.

Table 8.1 ◆ Profiles of major media types

Medium	*Advantages*	*Limitations*
1. Television	Combines sight, sound and motion; appealing to the senses; high attention; high reach	High absolute cost; high clutter; fleeting exposure; less audience selectivity
2. Radio	Mass use; high geographic and demographic selectivity; low cost	Lower attention than television; non-standardised rate structures; fleeting exposure
3. Internet	High selectivity; interactive possibilities; relatively low cost	A relatively new medium with a low number of users in some countries
4. Telephone	Many users; opportunity to give a personal touch	Too little local co-ordination in tele services
5. Newspapers	Flexibility; timeliness; good local market coverage; broad acceptance	Short life; poor reproduction quality
6. Magazines	High geographic and demographic selectivity; credibility and prestige	Long ad purchase leadtime; some waste circulation
7. Newsletters	Very high selectivity; full control; interactive opportunities; relatively low costs	Costs could run away
8. Brochures	Flexibility; full control; can dramatise messages	Brochure production can be a goal in itself; costs could run away
9. Direct mail	Very high selectivity; measurable	Relatively high costs; 'junk mail' image
10. Billboards	Flexibility; high repeat exposure; low cost; low competition	No audience selectivity

Television

Television is the most effective medium for dramatising the look and sound of a place. Television placement can range from some 15 to 60 second network commercials to full programmes produced in co-operation between a place and the broadcasting company. Various place themes are common and popular and are often integrated in news programmes. Compared with the situation in the USA, placemarketing in television commercials is not yet common in Europe. On the other hand, air travellers – and now also train travellers – are more often confronted with placemarketing messages which are distributed within a terminal, an aircraft, a railway station, or even onboard some European trains.

Radio

Radio can be used in a number of ways to promote a place. Spot radio ads can advertise vacations, land availability or job availability. Different radio stations deliver different audiences and, therefore, must be selected carefully.

Radio stations can also serve as effective channels to build up a local identity. A feeling of belonging and expression of the 'sense of the place' are common goals of local radio stations. Thus, the local radio station can play a key role in the place-selling strategy.

Internet

The Internet is an increasingly important place-selling tool. Even the smallest European place has a Website that can be accessed from anywhere in the world.

The Internet is so new that placemarketers are just beginning to exploit its vast marketing potential. As a consequence, a major problem is that placemarketing via the Internet is usually generic. Why not use this potentially strong selective medium in a much more precise manner? Places need to craft more carefully the messages they send to the global marketplace. Upon surfing the Internet in search of European places, one is struck by the following observations:

1. Form and content of messages often take the same form irrespective of the character of the place.
2. One gets the impression that places on the Internet are lacking a placemarketing strategy. In the absence of a strategy, most messages enumerate many descriptive details instead of promoting a selective theme.
3. Target marketing and specific packages aimed at selected audiences are lacking.
4. The interactive potential of the Internet has not yet been fully exploited.

Yet in the future, the Internet may become the most important channel to advertise to and to communicate with place-buyers. For such potentially broad market coverage, initial costs are relatively low. On the other hand, there are long-term costs involved in keeping the Website current and appealing to viewers. Obsolete information can be a negative image factor for a place that is unwilling to support reinvestment in the site.

Telephone

Telemarketing is a fast-growing sales tool. It has all the virtues of direct mail plus the ability to add a personal touch. The telephone can be used to gather leads, qualify them, sell to the leads and arrange personal meetings.

A major problem for many places, communities and regions is co-ordinating the rapid proliferation of their telephone services. New technologies are now opening for places to provide placemarkets with excellent day and night call-centre service. Ireland and Sweden are leading Europe in this respect. Some communities have expanded their tourist service by employing free-phone numbers and offering potential visitors a professional information and reservation service in relevant languages day and night. This is certainly only the beginning, as in the future buyers will call one number and basically book reservations and meet all their travel needs with a one-call service.

Newspapers

Newspapers offer a quick way to communicate messages about a place, such as news about festivals, exhibitions and various new projects. The weekly travel section of newspapers provides an opportunity to promote editorial material as well as place advertisements. Stories and ads about business opportunities can be placed in the business sections of newspapers. Newspapers do not provide the same quality of artwork as magazines can, but they are able to offer lower costs to reach selective geographical audiences. An additional advantage of newspapers over magazines is that they can reach audiences in a more timely manner.

A placemarketer must also establish a strong relationship with key editors. Many mayors and civic leaders complain bitterly about the lack of understanding by local journalists and the problems of their place, but when officials are asked what they have done to improve the place's economic climate, an all too common answer is: 'Nothing concrete'. Keeping the reporting community well informed with prompt and accurate information is a key link in the placemarketing process.

Magazines

The virtue of magazines is that so many are available that the advertiser can reach almost any target group by knowing that group's reading habits. Public relations people often attempt to place favourable stories about a place in magazines such as *Bild Zeitung*, *Business Week*, *EuroBusiness*, *Site Selection* and *Corporate Location*. In-flight magazines are also a popular channel to spread placemarketing messages.

A place advertisement must be credible if it is to be effective. For instance, if the place-selling message focuses on tax incentives and various subsidies the place runs the risk of implying that financial incentives are offered as a compensation for negative factors. Such risks are apparent in the case of Schleswig-Holstein in Figure 8.2. Among the *five hard facts* being marketed, the first three have a clear compensatory dimension: low labour costs, low rates of trade tax assessment, and favourably priced industrial and commercial space.

Newsletters

One way of building up long-term relations is to send highly selective newsletters to potential place-buyers. This tool has grown in usage during recent years. The newsletters often have a simple layout. Yet they can have impact because they provide industry-specific news that cannot be found elsewhere. Furthermore, the information is very specialised and concentrates on narrow audiences.

Newsletters also have the advantage of focus and low cost. The Internet has emerged as a means of publishing newsletters electronically, for example, online journals, leaving the cost of printing them to the reader. Whether distributed in print or via the Internet, newsletters should be produced on a regular basis to encourage a strong customer relationship.

Brochures

The advantages of brochures are their low cost, flexibility and portability. Place-sellers can use brochures to tell the story of a place in a complete and sometimes dramatic manner. In tourism, brochures are staples, as the many outlets in hotels, shops and restaurants can easily feature them in small but highly visible stands. A tourist who is looking for information or something to do for a one-day or weekend visit often finds the brochure to be the clearest and most timely of sources. Yet managers in charge of site selection often complain about the massive number of placemarketing brochures which come from various parts of Europe and the stereotypical impression they give. Brochures are often distributed without any target strategy and therefore entail much waste. If so, this part of the whole marketing project could be considered superfluous.

Some positive facts on Germany

as a Business Location

5 hard facts out of 10 that speak for your investment in Schleswig-Holstein.

1. An advantage in labour costs of up to 16%.
2. Low rates of trade tax assessment.
3. Favourably-priced industrial and commercial space.
4. Exemplary technological sponsorship of innovative employers and company-founders.
5. Highest expenditure on research and training* (per student).

It is not without reason that Schleswig-Holstein, in 1995, had the fastest economic growth of all the West German states. Interested in more positive facts? Then send for our detailed file.

* In comparison with the old German federal states, excluding Berlin.

Use this advertisement to reply by fax, or send it to us along with your visiting card:

Business Development Corp. of Schleswig-Holstein
Lorentzendamm 43 · D-24103 Kiel · Germany
Phone ++49-431-5 93 39 31 · Fax ++49-431-55 51 78

Name ....

Company ....

Street ....

Post Code, City ....

Tel., Fax ....

(97CL)

**Business Development Corp.
of Schleswig-Holstein**

we promote business

Source: *Corporate Location*, July/August, 1997.

Fig 8.2 ◆ To compensate for what?

Direct mail

Direct mail has the capacity to reach a highly focused target audience. The message can be standard or completely customised for each recipient. Direct mail can describe an offer, serve as a reminder, make a suggestion or issue a request. It can consist of a long letter with personal greetings or it can include four-colour graphics to jump-start interest in a place. The medium permits experimentation with different headlines, copy, envelopes, offers or prices in order to produce the most effective advertisement. Also, direct mail, in contrast to mass advertising, is a measurable response medium.

Billboards

Billboards represent a geographically fixed medium seen only by those who drive or walk past them. Like brochures, billboards can not only create a long-term impression but also encourage people to make spontaneous decisions, prompting them to visit the advertised location. Billboards are also used in air terminals, railway stations and other public meeting places to greet visitors to the specific place. Increasingly, the billboard message is much more than a simple '*Welcome!*' A higher value is communicated if the billboard is more specific, like '*Welcome to the Call Centre Country of Europe*', which greet travellers arriving at Dublin Airport. Unfortunately, the main airport messages in Europe cover 'standardised' international products such as Diners Card, EuroCard, Motorola, Ford, and other high profile advertisers. The traveller could be anywhere in the world and not know it from the signage.

Alternative media

The media planner needs to consider an additional range of less conventional media channels, such as audiotapes, videotapes, faxes, trade missions, CDs, postcards, welcome centres, consulates and sponsoring.

Here are examples of how less conventional media channels have been used to promote a place:

- An *audiotape* with typical local music or a famous local artist is sometimes given as a gift to the guest of the community.
- *Videotapes* are conventional tools today. Moreover, the content of the tape can be flexible and effective as a placemarketing vehicle. In many ways the videotape is the most vivid and dramatic tool in the placemarketing arsenal.
- *Faxes* are used as an *ad hoc* tool to communicate to specific audiences.
- Only a couple of years ago, *place-bound CDs* were rare. Today, the standard content must be of absolute top quality to imply a positive image of a place.

- The international *postcard* war is an important battle. Unconventional layouts have not been explored, which implies that there is much room for creative expression.
- *Welcome centres, consulates* and *embassies* are meeting places where media impact can be achieved (see Exhibit 8.2).
- *Sponsoring* of stickers on cars and elsewhere is potentially effective. Total design programmes for a place are sometimes worked out. A snowball effect can start in connection with a world expo or the Olympic Games. Barcelona is a good example of such a programme.

There is also huge potential for a place to integrate its marketing efforts with a company to exploit a place-bound relationship. Unconventional and creative ideas can originate from such a joint effort as company products, trade shows, and advertising can help promote the place.

Call the consul: is anyone home?

EXHIBIT 8.2

A good test for a place's ability to handle enquiries is its consul. At 3.45pm, 14 July 1998, the Chicago consuls of the following countries were called on the subject of locating a business in their country. The results:

- *Germany and Poland*: No answer or phone message. Given that there are more Poles in Chicago than any city other than Warsaw, the apparent lack of support is surprising.
- *France and Spain*: Closed. Phone messages stated hours for France from 9 to 1 and Spain from 9 to 2. Could make out little else. It was Bastille Day, a fact that the caller learned from the local paper – not the consul.
- *Ukraine*: Leave message after the beep. Voice spoke so fast that it was unintelligible.
- *Hungary*: Message announcing closing and moving to New York as of 1 April.
- *Britain*: Reached a person. She transferred call to a representative from Invest in Britain. Caller was given a complete overview of their marketing pro-gramme, and promised more inform-ation on sector and region material, and factsheets on taxes and employment. A personalised follow-up packet of this material was received in two days.

Consuls, besides answering enquiries about tourism and business, serve as the natural communication link between local people from their country. If a country has a number in the telephone directory, it should make sure the message meets the expectations of people who need their questions answered. The answering machine message should be clear, audible and informative. Hours should reflect the culture of the country. Nine-to-one office hours suggests a four-hour work ethic. A live person is best, one who is well trained, has good communication skills, and has the support and material to follow a precious lead.

Choosing among advertising media categories

Marketers choose among these several media channels by considering the following variables:

1. *Target audience media habits:* For example, direct mail and telemarketing are among the most effective media for reaching location decision-makers.
2. *Product or service:* Media categories have different potentials for demonstration, visualisation, explanation, believability and colour. Television, for example, is the most effective medium for describing a place or for creating an emotional effect, while magazines are ideal for presenting a single four-colour image of a place.
3. *Message:* A message containing a great deal of technical data might require specialised magazines, the Internet or direct mailings.
4. *Cost:* Television is very expensive, newspaper advertising is comparatively inexpensive. What often counts is the cost per thousand quality exposures rather than the total cost.

Many place-sellers employ a variety of media because they recognise that different audiences pay attention to different media. Using several media extends the message's reach and re-emphasises the content but may run the risk of repeating the message to the same audience. It is a difficult task to choose the right media mix since the product, that is, a specific place, has so many complex offerings and thereby possible target groups. The best way to leverage the options is to base the media mix on a systematic marketing strategy in which basic offerings and target groups are well defined. Much remains to be done in Europe on this point.

Selecting the specific media vehicles

The planner's *second step* is to choose the specific media vehicles within each media category that would produce the desired response in the most cost-effective way. A major marketing decision is how and why places mix costs and choose products (see Exhibit 8.3).

Croatia targets two audiences

EXHIBIT 8.3

Croatia, determined to throw off the image of its socialist past, decided to advertise its new image for place-buyers of two types: investors and visitors. For the investors, they chose to promote the new image and a number of investment offerings in the special survey of the *Financial Times*.[1] The issue included a number of editorial articles on Croatia together with ads from Croatian Airlines, Zagreb Bank, an electric power company and a number of consulting companies. A special event for the target group was also announced: 'International Conference on Doing Business in Croatia' at the Sheraton Hotel in Zagreb.

At the same time, Croatia marketed itself to European tourists. Croatia advertised its historical links with the rest of Europe to the European audiences via four-colour brochures. The main message emphasised its cultural heritage: 'Many European kings and emperors, heirs, dukes and famous artists came here to conduct their affairs – of state or otherwise. Or to seek inspiration'.[2] As a supplementary channel, Croatia place-sellers participate in European tourist exhibitions. Each of these communication vehicles, which form a critical part of the Croatia media mix, has a targeted audience and specific channel characteristics.

Sources: 1 Survey – Croatia, *Financial Times*, 28 May 1997, pp. I–VI.
2 *Croatia: Small country for a great holiday*, Croatian National Tourism Office, Zagreb, 1997, p. 5.

To co-ordinate marketing efforts similar to Croatia's, media planners utilise data published by *Standard Rate and Data* that provide circulation and cost information for different ad sizes, colour options, ad positions and quantities of insertions. Beyond this, the media planner evaluates the different magazines on qualitative characteristics such as credibility, prestige, availability of geographical or occupational editions, reproduction quality, editorial climate, leadtime and psychological impact.

The media planner makes a final judgement as to which specific vehicles will deliver the best reach, frequency and impact for the money. The first variable, *reach*, is a measure of how many people are normally exposed to a single message carried by that medium. When the objective is to deliver the message to a large audience, mass media, particularly national television, are recommended.

Some messages are effective only if they result in multiple exposures to the same individuals: this second variable is *frequency*. Some frequency of exposure is necessary if places are to avoid fading into oblivion. One or two Ingmar Bergman films shot on the island of Gotland in the Baltic Sea do not guarantee any lasting impression of the place. Follow-up support is necessary in order to provide frequency.

The third variable, *impact*, describes how effective a particular medium is with the type of message and the target audience. Thus, *The Economist* would have more impact carrying the new Croatian image than the magazine *Elle*; the latter reaches the wrong audience. Usually, media that customise the message (such as direct mail and newsletters) or allow personal contact (such as conventions, exhibitions, trade missions and personal selling) achieve greater impact.

Media planners normally calculate the cost per thousand persons that a particular vehicle reaches. Suppose that Berlin wants to market its new capital image to the London area and is considering advertising in either the *Evening Standard Magazine* or in the weekend *Guardian*. In 1997 a one-page four-colour ad in *Evening Standard Magazine* cost £12,000 and it has 1,527,000 readers. Weekend Guardian cost £11,550 and it has 1,275,000 readers. Thus, the cost per reader in *Evening Standard Magazine* is £7.85 per thousand readers and for weekend *Guardian* £9.05. These figures suggest that the *Evening*

Standard would be the best buy. On the other hand, this cost advantage must be evaluated by considering the different profiles of the readers. For instance, weekend *Guardian* readers tend to travel more and be interested in new and cultural destinations.[7] Costs for other potential vehicles, including television and radio, can be calculated and compared in the same way.

Communication objectives and costs guide what planners want to do, but budget determines realistically what they can do. Budget heavily shapes media choices. Many methods have been proposed for setting communication budgets. The budget can be set by arbitrarily allocating a certain amount of money or percentage of sales to be spent, deciding what the place can afford, basing the decision on previous experience, establishing a percentage of the financial return expected to result from the campaign, or observing what competitors have done.

The budget is also influenced by the amount of information and persuasion that is necessary to market the place. How much should a place spend to attract visitors? Paris, Nice and Barcelona are international destinations and are included in tourist itineraries. However, if the Norwegian city of Tromsø in the Barents region wants to attract tourists, it needs to launch a wide range of promotional tools to persuade prospects. A budget for Tromsø has to be large enough to overcome its off-the-beaten-track image. To have a chance, the city of Tromsø must also find new and innovative resources through regional placemarketing co-operation.

Finally, planners should know that communication investments and returns are not necessarily linear. To invest too little money can be worse than investing no money. A certain minimum level of investment is required to create initial interest in a place. Higher levels of investment produce higher levels of audience response. However, above a certain level, further investment may not be cost effective. In fact, if the message is seen too frequently, many people stop noticing it or become irritated.

Deciding on media timing

The *third step* in media selection is timing. It breaks down into a macro-problem and a micro-problem. The macro-problem is that of cyclical or seasonal timing. Audience size and interest in a place vary at different times of the year. Most marketers do not advertise when there is little interest but spend the bulk of their advertising budgets when natural interest in a place increases and peaks. Counterseasonal or countercyclical advertising is rare. On the other hand, to market, for instance, the Alps on the off-season can be of great economic value. However, the attraction must have real value to be effective; it cannot simply offer less expensive incentives to visit a place in the off-season. The Alps could be marketed as being more beautiful and less crowded during the off-season. Visitors are offered more space, a peaceful setting and different activities such as hiking.

A micro-problem is of the short-run timing of advertising. How should advertising be spaced during a short period of, say, one week? Consider three contrasting patterns:

1. The first is *burst advertising* and consists of concentrating all the exposures in a very short period of time, such as all in one day. Presumably, this burst will attract maximum attention and interest and, if recall is good, the effect may last for a while.
2. The second pattern is *continuous advertising*, in which the exposures appear evenly throughout the period. This pattern may be most effective when the audience buys or uses the product frequently and needs to be continuously reminded.
3. The third pattern is *intermittent advertising*, in which intermittent small bursts of advertising appear with no advertising between. This pattern creates somewhat more attention than continuous advertising and also has some of its reminder advantage.

Timing decisions should take three factors into consideration:

1. *Audience turnover* is the rate at which the target audience changes between two periods. The greater the turnover, the more continuous the advertising should be.
2. *Behaviour frequency* is the number of times during the year that the target audience makes the decision, one that the placemarketer is trying to influence. The more frequent the behaviour, the more advertising should be continuous.
3. The *forgetting rate* is the rate at which a given message is forgotten or a given behaviour change extinguished. Again, the shorter the audience's memory, the more continuous the advertising should be.

Evaluating media results

Measuring the results of media campaigns is not an easy task. To measure placemarketing results is even more difficult since there are so many interconnecting variables.

Nevertheless, evaluation research helps media planners to locate possible weaknesses in the communication or implementation process. Did the place message reach the right people? Did they understand the message and find it credible and persuasive? Did it reach them frequently enough and at the right times? Should more have been spent? The placemarketer should regularly evaluate the communication effects and sales effects of advertising.

Measuring the communication effect tells whether an ad is communicating well. *Copy testing* can be done before or after an ad is printed or broadcast.

There are three major methods of advertising pre-testing. The first is through *direct rating*, in which the advertiser exposes a consumer panel to different ads and asks the panel members to rate the ads. These direct ratings are meant to indicate how well the ads attract attention and how they affect consumers. Although an imperfect measure of an ad's actual impact, a high rating indicates a potentially more effective ad. In *portfolio tests*, consumers, taking as much time as they need, view or listen to a portfolio of advertisements. Then, aided or unaided by the interviewer, they are asked to recall all the ads and their content. Their recall level indicates the ability of an ad to stand out and its message to be understood and remembered. *Laboratory tests* use equipment to measure consumers' physiological reactions to an ad – heartrate, blood pressure, pupil dilation and perspiration. These tests measure an ad's attention-getting power but reveal little about its impact on beliefs, attitudes or intentions.

There are three popular methods of post-testing ads. Using a *recall test*, the advertiser asks people who have been exposed to magazines or television programmes to recall everything they can about the advertising message. Recall scores indicate the ad's power to be noticed and retained. In *recognition tests*, the researcher asks readers of a given issue of a magazine to point out what they recognise from before. Recognition scores can be used to assess the ad's impact in different market segments and to compare the company's ads with competitors' ads. In *persuasion tests*, persons are asked whether the ad has caused them to be more favourably disposed towards a place and by how much.

The sales effect of advertising is often harder to measure than the communication effect. Many factors besides advertising affect sales, such as place features, price and availability. One way to measure the sales effect of advertising is to compare past sales with past advertising expenditures. Another way is through experiments where similar territories receive different advertising intensities to see whether this leads to different sales levels.

Advertising's communication impact is most easily measured where direct response measurements can be obtained. Mail or phone orders, requests for catalogues, or sales calls all help the marketer to measure response. They allow the placemarketer to determine how many enquiries the mail pieces generated and how many purchases came from the enquiries.

In general, measurement efforts are designed to answer three basic questions: (1) What was the response obtained? (2) Were the objectives met? (3) What changes are recommended? A well-designed set of evaluation procedures enables the message and the media to be constantly improved.

Managing conflicting media sources and messages

A place can spend millions of ECU advertising for visitors, residents or investors only to find uncontrolled communications overwhelming the formal messages. For example, uncontrolled international attention caused by the paedophile cases in Charleroi, Belgium, is an illustrative case. This negative communication contrasts sharply with the formal messages about Charleroi's attraction for investors, visitors and residents. Many places have discovered such conflicting attention from media: drug problems in Amsterdam, terrorist attacks in Bilbao, high unemployment in southern Italy, or charges against a mayor using his community credit card at a night-club in Brussels. Long and serious image efforts could quickly be destroyed in a world with global news coverage.

The best of all possible worlds occurs when informal and formal impressions merge to reinforce the image. Such good fortune occurred when the Irish rock band U2 performed its famous concert before all three of Bosnia's battling enemies in Sarajevo in the autumn of 1997. The message was for reconciliation, which is the same message as the city leaders of Sarajevo try to communicate. Bono, the lead singer of U2, said of the widely praised event: 'There were 1,000 people from Republika Serpska there and they didn't have Kalashnikovs but U2 tickets in their hands'.[8]

Ideally, a place would like to showcase only its positive features. It would like to hide from view the slums, homeless people, indelicate treatment of minorities, unemployment and other unflattering impressions. However, this degree of media control is impossible. More typically, a place finds itself driven by unplanned and often unwelcome events.

What should places do about such negative impressions? There are three possibilities. The first is to *ignore them*. The thinking is, 'act as if it doesn't exist and it will go away'. The second is to *counterattack* by swiftly sending out a countermessage. The third is to *solve the problem* that gives rise to the negative impressions.

None of these responses is the best under all circumstances. Much depends on how serious the negative impression is, how widespread it is, and how easy it is to remedy. If the damage is not serious, if public knowledge is very limited and if it is easily remedied, it is best to ignore the negative impression. If the damage is not serious but is widely known and easily remedied, it may pay to counterattack. If the situation is very serious and widely known and not easily remedied, it is best to work towards a long-term response rather than ignoring the situation or counterattacking.

The case of the A-series Mercedes-Benz is an expensive example of a serious negative situation that was at first ignored, then counter-attacked, and ultimately addressed with an approach to 'solve' the problem. The small car, upon testing, was labelled as having a dangerous rollover problem. The consequences for the Mercedes-Benz image go far beyond the costs for 'solving the problem with the automobile'. The impression of incompetence implied a lack of skill on the part of the entire German automobile industry. All the manufacturers are heavily invested in German quality, and the little car rolling over was a threat to an image developed painstakingly over most of the twentieth century. The threats were multiplied when the company failed to assess the situation accurately which allowed media to set the agenda. Mercedes finally solved the problem with an expensive fix. Parallel cases can be traced in European cities where apparent drug abuse problems have been consistently ignored and even denied. Such situations could quickly develop into negative images that not only relate to the original abuse problem, but may also create distrust of the place itself and its civic decision-making processes.

Conclusions

The number of places that compete for the attention of place-buyers is overwhelming. A casual reading of Europe's major city Sunday travel sections reveals ads for every place on the globe. Trade journals for business sites are full of promises of co-operation and offers of brochures, videotapes, newsletters and other inducements to begin a relationship.

In this competitive environment placemarketing has the best chance for success when the message is matched to the media, all players are pushing in the same direction, and informal impressions reinforce the paid efforts.

In the next three chapters we apply marketing thinking to the four major sources of place enrichment: tourism and business hospitality, business attraction and development, export promotion and new residents.

9

Attracting tourism and hospitality business markets

Travel writer Nicholas Woodsworth[1] presented a list of top ten destinations for tourists. The first three were the following:

1. *Istanbul:* 'About the most exotic and atmospheric place you can reach from London on a short city break'.
2. *Corsica:* 'Has an off-putting reputation for terrorism, which has left the island one of the friendliest, most beautiful and best preserved areas in the Mediterranean'.
3. *Lake Lucerne:* 'Switzerland: astonishing mountain beauty and bourgeois self-assurance'.

Notice how each destination is distinctly described and promises something real and different. And each is accessible; for example you can reach Istanbul from London '*on a short city break*'. Even the smallest and most specialised place can compete on the tourist and hospitality market as long as it offers something attractive and remains accessible.

This chapter presents an analysis of two markets: tourism and the hospitality business (conventions, trade shows and business meetings). Although the two overlap somewhat, they are distinctive enough in markets, needs, facilities and competition to warrant separate treatment.

Tourism market

European Tourism Year 1990 marked a recognition of the importance of tourism within the European Union. Tourism that year accounted for 7 per cent of total employment, or over 9 million people, and 6 per cent of GDP.[2] Since that year the European interest in tourism has grown substantially. This attraction is not surprising at a time when 18 million people are unemployed within the EU and when public leaders know that tourism can be increased more rapidly than other areas of the economy.

In marketing tourism we will want to consider the following questions:

1. How important is tourism to a place's economy?
2. How can the tourist market be segmented and monitored for shifting trends, lifestyles, needs and preferences?
3. What kinds of strategies and investments must places and businesses make to be competitive in the tourist industry?
4. How can a place establish a niche in the tourist business, and what are the risks and opportunities?
5. What kinds of message and media are effective in attracting and retaining tourists?
6. How should a place's tourism activities be organised and managed?

How important is tourism?

Most European communities and places are actively seeking to increase their share in the tourism industry. Tourism not only produces jobs and income but also more subtly generates spin-off decisions regarding business locations or new residents. Such secondary effects are often underestimated and seldom calculated when tourism is discussed.

Prague, already one of the major tourist destinations in Europe, has an enormous potential to develop additional placeselling programmes and offerings to business, investors and potential residents. Prague's real estate market has exploded in the past few years. *Munich's Oktoberfest*, with 5 million litres of beer and tourists from all over the world, is developing into a strong competitor for business meetings: Italians, Australians, New Zealanders, Japanese and Americans are among the most enthusiastic visitors.[3] Munich manages to deliver a sense that it is one of the world's most important destinations. The feeling of place authenticity is enhanced when the Bavarians dress in their lederhosen, worn with fancy white shirts, knitted jackets, thick socks and boots, and hats with tufts of chamois hair. This communicates that Munich residents are Bavarians first and Germans second.

The Prague and Munich examples illustrate the direct and indirect importance of tourism. The complex links to other target groups illustrate the difficulties in calculating the exact value of tourism. The various place-sellers and place-buyers are so closely interlinked that tourism and business are two sides of one product. Exhibit 9.1 demonstrates how two cities leveraged a once-in-a-lifetime opportunity.

After the dance: Barcelona and Seville

EXHIBIT 9.1

Playing host to an international event is a coup for any city. The potential gain from infrastructure investment and a surge in tourism can help turn around even the most beleaguered city economy. However, playing host to such an event is no guarantee for success, as the stories of Barcelona and Seville demonstrate.

The year 1992 was to be a big one for Spain. Seeking to turn around depressed economies and lacklustre tourism, both Barcelona and Seville were planning to host major international events: the Olympics in Barcelona and the world's fair Expo '92 in Seville. Both cities made considerable investments in facilities and both received a large influx of tourism and media coverage; yet nearly a decade and one global recession later, Barcelona is booming while Seville is floundering. What accounts for this disparity?

Barcelona's mayor at the time of the Olympics, Pasqual Maragall, sought to place Barcelona, formerly known for little more than being the metropolitan centre of Spain's coastal Catalan region, firmly on the international map by promoting the city as the site for the 1992 Olympic Games. While tourists were attracted to the Catalan coast, most neglected to spend time or money in and around the city of Barcelona. Making the Games the centrepiece for his platform of change, the pragmatic and progressive Maragall produced a rapid and lasting change for his city by focusing on 'personalised leadership, ambitious planning, and a strong reliance on municipal power as an agent of change'.[1] Sprucing up the municipal infrastructure was the first step. When Barcelona's Olympic visitors arrived, they were greeted by a new airport, new trains, new highways, new hotels, new museums and a renovated waterfront. In addition, both the city's transportation system and telecommunications system were overhauled for the event.

But Maragall's efforts did not end with the games. In the following year he launched the Foundation for the International Promotion of Barcelona which was conceived as a total programme for tourism. Focusing on Barcelona's 'distinctive culture and its appeal as an incentive destination',[2] Barcelona's leaders have effectively positioned their city as the key Spanish tourist destination, offering a wide array of activities in a relatively small area. In 1995, boasting a 75 per cent return rate, the Catalan region welcomed over 16 million tourists – almost one-third of Spain's total tourism.

Maragall continued his strategy by making Barcelona a strong economic centre as well as strong tourist destination. Half of Spain's inward foreign investment is generated by Catalonia, host to numerous conventions, congresses and trade fairs, thus proving that tourism can indeed help bring about a strong economic recovery when channelled towards the improvement of the city itself.

Unlike Barcelona, Seville has seen little improvement since Expo '92. Intended to forge a new era for Seville as a thriving 'technopolis of scientific research and development that would modernise the city',[3] Seville remains plagued by one of Europe's highest unemployment rates (39.6 per cent in 1997), water shortages and poor housing.

While the Seville Expo began auspiciously with the construction of 100 fair pavilions and an attendance well above the expected 18 million, the city's leaders failed to capitalise on the opportunity to improve key municipal infrastructure. Instead of working to improve public works and help 'develop the small and medium-sized technologically underdeveloped, under-skilled companies that dominate the local economy',[4] great amounts of money were spent on constructing facilities for a research park and a bullet train connection from Madrid to Seville. Unfortunately the site that cost £750 million of public and private expenditure to develop employs a mere 1,000 people through just over 30 companies. The major investors failed to appear and the Expo site remains a dilapidated embarrassment still plagued by unreliable sewers.

►

▶ The difference between Barcelona and Seville was neatly summed up by Barcelona's deputy mayor (and successor to Maragall), Joan Clos, who, regarding his city's resurgence, said, 'Everyone understood from the first that the Games were the excuse, not the aim'.[5] Seville's Expo '92 acts as a classic case of misguided intentions that yielded unfulfilled results. Instead of focusing investments on Seville's problem areas, city leaders squandered their resources on impractical solutions.

Sources: 1. Simon Kuper and Andrew Adonis, 'Mr Barcelona on a winning ticket', *Financial Times*, 12 June 1995, p. 19 (Lexis Nexis).
2. Maria Lisella, 'Olympian efforts to woo tourists are paying off for Barcelona', *Travel Agent*, 11 March 1996, p. S9 (Lexis Nexis).
3. Elizabeth Nash, 'Will substance follow the show?' *The Independent*, 22 September 1996, p. 13.
4. Anne Johnstone, 'Dream that turned into a nightmare', *The Herald* (Glasgow), 10 November 1995, p. 14.
5. Kuper and Adonis, *op. cit.* p. 19.

Although Europe still leads the rest of the world in international tourism (see Figure 9.1), Europe's share of world tourism is now slightly decreasing. The Pacific Rim experienced a growth rate up almost 10 per cent compared with Europe's 3 per cent in 1997. The current solid European position must therefore be defended as competing destinations will continue to mount challenges. One way of consolidating is through improvement of local and regional placemarketing strategies. Another important factor is the opening up of Eastern Europe – which will draw increased tourism to Europe.

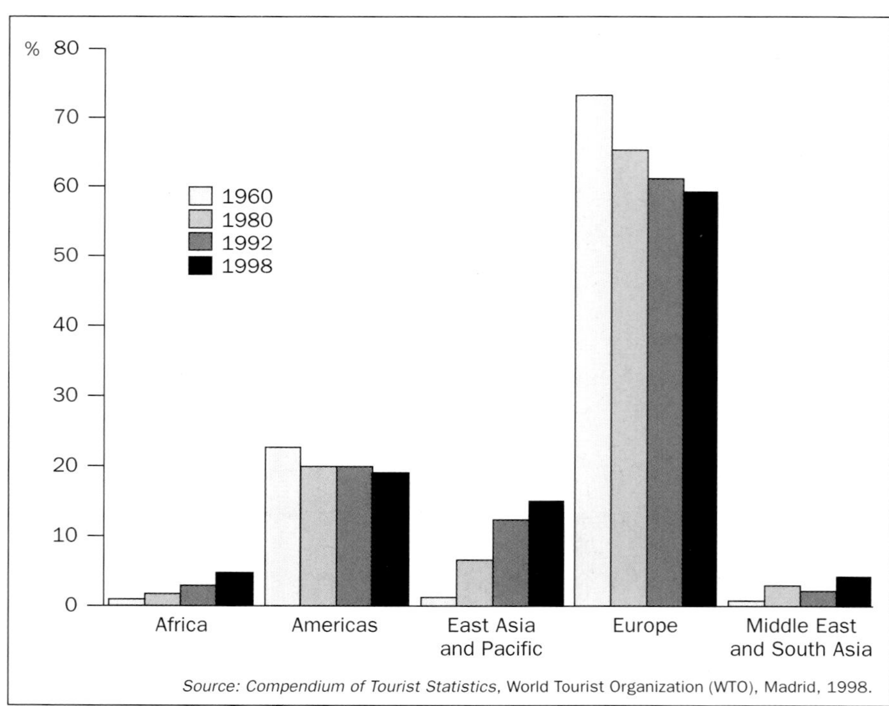

Source: Compendium of Tourist Statistics, World Tourist Organization (WTO), Madrid, 1998.

Fig 9.1 ◆ International tourism, selected years 1960 to 1998

Segmenting the tourism market

Places must decide not only how many tourists they want and how to balance tourism with other industries but also *what kinds* of tourists they want. Of course, choices will be constrained by the place's climate, natural topography and resources, history, culture and facilities. As in any other business, tourist marketers must distinguish between the actual and potential customers, know their needs and wants, determine which target markets to serve, and decide on appropriate products, services and programmes to serve these markets.

Since not every tourist will be interested in a particular place, a place would waste its money trying to attract everyone who travels. Instead of a scattergun approach, a place must take a rifle approach and sharply define its target groups. Exhibit 9.2 explains how modern technology helps tourists to find the markets they seek.

Electronic buying

EXHIBIT 9.2

The experienced travel agents of yesterday are rapidly dying out. The new travel agents often have less firsthand knowledge and tend to leave the place-buyer frustrated over trying to figure out how to plan a trip. The travel industry is now in a major transition, trying to develop solutions to this problem.

There are three main avenues that represent the wave of the future for travel agencies. The *first* is better training of current agents. In this regard, countries like Austria and Ireland are offering discounted tours to agents who may become experts on what their country has to offer. The *second* is using the Internet to link customers to animated and interactive sites as well as fares and hotels. In some Northern European countries, this is already a widespread way of finding the right tourist offerings. *Third*, there is a major move towards sophisticated customer profiling that promises an extensive customer database. A visitor may well expect his or her most exotic wishes anticipated by the service provider, such as pre-ordered concert tickets or an individualised tour of modern art galleries. These innovations come in the face of increased competition from many companies seeking the visitor's patronage.

Who are the leading players in the travel market business? The results are mixed. There is increasing use of the Internet by travellers who are seeking place awareness and deals. The frequency and execution of purchasing a trip varies greatly from country to country. In Germany, for example, individually owned travel agencies reported that for April 1998, business declined 10.7 per cent from one year earlier.[1] Much of this decline is related to increased Internet bookings. The increased competition is beneficial to the customer and means that places will have to be increasingly proactive to gain the attention of the travel industry.

To be effective, place-sellers need to encourage travel agencies to package their destination competitively and in a way that stands out amidst the cyberspace glut. Moreover, place-sellers will find it necessary to co-brand their festivals and events with travel agencies for maximum impact. It will be advantageous for the principle players to market a complete and identifiable image that is constant and that has a broad appeal.

Source: 1. Wolf Achim Wiegand and Jay Dougherty, 'Book it from home: the travel market conquers the Net', *Deutsche Presse-Agentur*, 28 June 1998 (Lexis Nexis).

Placemarketing can use two methods to identify natural target groups. The *first approach* is to collect information about current tourists. Where do they come from? Why do they come to this place? What are their demographic characteristics? How satisfied are they? How many are repeat tourists? How much do they spend? By examining these and other questions, the place can determine which tourists are worth attracting.

The *second approach* is to audit the place's attractions and conjecture about the types of tourist who would have a natural interest in these attractions. The aim is to identify new sources of tourists. One cannot assume that the current tourists reflect all the potentially interested target groups. For example, if the Italian Dolomites promoted only skiing, the region would miss other target groups interested in summer hiking and living in genuine farmhouses.

Different tourists are attracted by different place features. The local tourist board or other units must ask questions keyed to the segmentation variables in Table 9.1. These variables – attractions sought, market areas or locations, customer characteristics and/or benefits sought – can help to define the best tourist prospects to attract.

Table 9.1 ◆ Segmentation variables for the tourist market

Attractions sought	*Market areas/ locations*	*Customer characteristics*	*Benefits*
• Sea, sun, ski • Natural beauty/ wilderness • Recreation • Gaming • Culture/history • Events/sports • Theme parks • Facilities/hotels/ restaurants • Unique products: wine, beer, perfume, clothes, watches	• Non-European • European • Domestic • Regional • Local • Seasonal/ year around • Language	• Age • Income • Family • Singles • Professionals • Lifestyles • Ethnic/religious	• Price • Convenience • Quality • Food • Service • Facilities • Transportation

After a place identifies a natural target market, the tourist board must research where these potential tourists are found. Which countries, non-European and European, contain a large number of citizens who have the means and motivation to enjoy the particular place? For example, religious tourism involves the movement of about 100 million people per year (1991). In Europe, Italy (Rome) leads in this target market, ahead of France, Germany, Poland and Spain.[4] It is important to know where the various target markets are for Judaism, Christianity and Islam.

An analysis can uncover too many or too few potential target markets. If too many are identified, the tourist board must calculate the potential profit from attracting each segment. The potential profit of a target tourist segment is the difference between the amount that the tourist segment would spend and the cost of attracting and serving this segment. The attraction cost depends on the marketing plan. The serving cost depends on the infrastructure requirements. Ultimately, the tourist board ranks the potential tourist segments in order of their profitability and concentrates on attracting those segments highest on its list (see Exhibit 9.3).

Norway identifies the Swedish winter market

EXHIBIT 9.3

Norway launched a number of ambitious marketing campaigns following its successful 1992 Winter Olympics in Lillehammer. A provocative effort was launched in the autumn of 1997 as the Swedish market was inundated with a Norwegian campaign to attract Swedish skiers. Owing to the proximity to their neighbour – combined with the Swedish interest in winter sports – it was logical that the Norwegian Tourist Board, Nortra, should target this market. The theme of the campaign was '*Hogrefjall*' – *Higher Mountains* in Norway than in Sweden. The key message compared facilities: 'We have 18 ski resorts with a height of over 500 metres. In Sweden there are only three.' This type of appeal flourished with tag lines exclaiming 'More options', 'Bigger adventures', and 'Better skiing'. Swedish ski resorts attempted a counterattack but only caused the Norwegian campaign to be quoted and republished in many articles and media.

Source: 'Winter campaign 1997/98', Nortra, National Norwegian Tourist Council, Oslo.

If the analysis identifies too few natural tourist segments, the tourist board must undertake *investment marketing*. A natural market is attracted by the existing features of the place; an investment market is attracted by new features that might be added to a place. Investment marketing consists of allocating money towards infrastructure improvements (hotels, transportation, and roads) and attractions that can potentially attract new types of tourists. The payoff from investment marketing comes some years later, but this investment is necessary if the place cannot identify a sufficient number of natural tourist segments. Exhibit 9.4 illustrates how a new attraction can broaden the appeal of a mature market.

Donald Duck meets Baudelaire: culture blinks

EXHIBIT 9.4

When Disneyland Paris celebrated its fifth anniversary in April 1997, the theme park's owners had much to celebrate. Once accused of being a plague on French culture by Gallic intellectuals, 'a cultural Chernobyl', Disneyland Paris has seen considerable improvement since 1994 when the park posted a loss of $366 million[1] and was in danger of closing its gates for ever. However, following a financial restructuring and a retooling of the park's ▶

image and marketing strategies, Disneyland Paris saw a record attendance of 12.6 million visitors in 1997 alone,[2] making it Europe's top theme park and one of the continent's most popular attractions.

Despite early attempts to 'Frenchify' the park, pressure from visitors forced the management to implement a traditional Disney-style image. For example, food service was changed back from table service to self-serve, and retail stores were transformed from a low-key to more aggressive sales approach. Changing the park's name from the original 'EuroDisney', to Disneyland Paris, helped to 'strengthen the park's identity',[3] but the most significant change was the reduction in ticket and hotel prices. Making a visit to the park more affordable helped to increase attendance as well.

The growing success of Disneyland Paris can also be attributed to the fundamental investment philosophy of Disney. Beyond the turnaround strategies that Disney used to rejuvenate the park in Paris, Disney emphasises a complete family environment – a strategy that attendance figures suggest is working. Not only is Disney opening a second theme park in 2002, but the company has plans to double attendance in Disneyland Paris by focusing on new markets and emphasising rail and charter links.[4] As remarked by a spokesperson for the Paris tourist office, Disneyland 'now makes up part of the package of visiting Paris, for both the French and foreigners'.[5]

However, for placemarketers, the Disney archetype presents a major challenge. First, Disney sets very high standards for the fundamentals – design, service, cleanliness and safety. Any place in Europe that wishes to attract the visiting public needs to benchmark their project against the Disney standard. Second, Disney has an ability for taking real-life events and converting them to a shorthand plastic reality. This very believable illusion makes real-life events pale by comparison. The placemarketer with a historical or natural attraction needs to find communication mechanisms to make their attraction interactive and meaningful to the public – a way to make Donald Duck blink.

Sources: 1. 'EuroDisney ends year in black', *Los Angeles Times*, 15 November 1995 (Lexis Nexis).
2. Tim O'Brian, 'EUROPE: theme park industry', *Amusement Business*, 17 August 1998 (Lexis Nexis).
3. Charles Masters, 'French fall for the charms of Disney', *Sunday Telegraph*, 14 April 1997, p. 21.
4. 'Disney to look beyond top European markets', *Travel Trade Gazette Europa*, 10 December 1998; 'Disney plans second theme park in France', *Agence France Presse*, 11 January 1999 (Lexis Nexis).
5. Masters, *op. cit.* p. 21.

Consider Ireland, which continues to attract many tourists, not only ethnic Irish from North America, but also many Europeans. The Irish Tourist Board observed that although an increasing number of young European hikers and campers were visiting the Emerald Isle to enjoy its natural unspoiled beauty, they spent little. A serious question for Ireland was whether the Irish Tourist Board's tourism scorecard should be based on the number of tourists attracted (the prevailing standard) or the spending quality of the tourists. A consensus emerged that Ireland was better off attracting fewer but higher-income tourists who stay longer and spend more.

Towards this end, the Irish Tourist Board now touts not only Ireland's mountains, water and ancient buildings but also its literary giants. They want to induce high-income culture-seeking tourists to visit Dublin where the legendary Irish sparkling repartee and wit can be experienced. The Irish are also improving Dublin's hotel and restaurant facilities as an act of investment marketing. A downside to the upscale strategy is the persistent problem of litter that dissuades tourists from enjoying the city. The litter problem is an issue so intense that Deputy Jim Mitchell, chairman of the accounts office, said Dublin 'is a dirty place' and litter 'will jeopardise our tourism industry'.[5]

Whatever tourist segment a place aims at, it needs to be very specific. True, a ski area attracts skiers; swimming and natural reefs attract snorklers and divers; art attracts the culture seekers; gambling attracts gaming tourists. Yet, even with such givens, places must segment tourists according to additional characteristics. Tourists to the Alps are offered very specific target packages: Montreux-Vevey with its *high-level tourism* in the famous hotels – the Montreux Palace, Eden au Lac or Royal Plaza Intercontinental; *mountaineering* in places like Zermatt or Grindewald; *downhill skiing* in places like Davos and Albertville. But segmentation will go much further in the future. The relatively small Alpine region will need to expand its market vision to include a wider array of attractions. Thus, various places can distinguish themselves by marketing cycling, horse-riding, health spas, theme parks, and other specific characteristics.

Markets and attractions change over time. However, some places manage to keep the same tourist image for decades. One such example is Montreux in the Lake Geneva region where many people return decade after decade. Montreux is marketing itself via famous persons having resided there. Charles Chaplin, rising from his comic resting place, introduces the place by saying: 'In the midst of such happiness, I sometimes sit down on our terrace as the sun goes down and contemplate the great expanse of green lawn and the lake in the distance with the reassuring presence of the mountains beyond the other shore'. The Montreux Festival – also called '*Festival of Festivals*' – puts Montreux regularly in the world focus. Montreux, claiming to be a place of '*Artistic inspiration*', exemplifies a certain degree of stability in a placemarket subject to intensifying competition. However, Montreux must maintain its hard-won turf. Competition is intense, as festivals have emerged on all types of themes: classical music, jazz, movies, fine art, theatre and dance, and anniversaries. Tourists now have many options, and long-time leaders, such as Montreux, are under increasing pressure to maintain market share.

European cities can be compared on a number of tourist performance indicators (see Table 9.2).

In Table 9.2 the first thing one notes is the dominant position of London and Paris, which puts the two cities in a class by themselves. The second observation concerns the huge differences in average stay. According to Arie Shacher of the Institute of Urban and Regional Studies, Hebrew University, London offers a special combination of tourist attractions such as historical sites, museums and theatre in many forms.[6] As a centre of international conferences, London combines all the most important attractions: high-quality accommodation, effective transport infrastructures and a huge variety of cultural offerings. All of these advantages work to lengthen the average stay.

Places must be ready to respond to changing demographics and lifestyles.

Table 9.2 ◆ Competition results in some major European cities

City	*Arrivals*	*Nights spent*	*Average stay (days)*
1. London	14,700,000	82,600,000	5.62
2. Paris	12,602,168	28,269,280	2.24
3. Munich	3,242,743	6,607,551	2.04
4. Rome	2,683,895	12,018,523	4.48
5. Vienna	2,637,572	6,717,752	2.55
6. Berlin	2,542,446	6,405,098	2.52
7. Milan	2,135,197	5,579,129	2.61
8. Brussels	2,045,800	3,035,000	1.48
9. Frankfurt	1,863,168	3,442,828	1.85
10. Barcelona	1,818,609	4,089,509	2.25

Source: Van den Berg *et al.*, *Urban Tourism*, Euricur, Erasmus University, Rotterdam, 1994, p. 153.

The smaller the place or city, the more vulnerable it is. What new opportunities will the ageing European population offer to places like Baden-Baden, Belgian Spa, or the medicinal springs in Hungary with their oily and mildly radioactive water rich in hydrogen carbonate? Which new strategies should a place work out as a response to increased ecological interest among tourists? How can a place capitalise on the trend towards more short visits by two-career families who have less time to spend away from home? And what can be done to exploit the opportunity that opens up when a place is suddenly connected to a new high-speed railway?

Changing demographics and lifestyles present a continuous challenge to the tourism industry. The high-living baby boomers of yesterday are today's older baby boomers. Where baby boomers once opted for status destinations and elaborate accommodations, older baby boomers now opt for all-inclusive resorts and package tours that promise comfort, consistency and cost-effectiveness.

Tourist strategies and investments

In the face of growing tourist competition, places must be prepared to maintain and indeed upgrade their place investments. A major trend today is heritage development, the task of preserving the history of places, their buildings, their people and customs, and other artifacts that portray traditions. Typical examples are to be found in the city of Vilnius, Lithuania, and the city of Riga, Latvia. In the case of Vilnius, a careful restoration is now taking place in order to portray its proud historical traditions. The city, on the UNESCO World Heritage list, has one of the greatest collections of European architectural styles in Europe: gothic, renaissance and baroque.[7] The city of Riga has also come to life again after half a century of communist domination.

Restoration programmes are ambitious – one of the first buildings to be returned to its former glory being the Opera House. The art nouveau architecture of the old inner city of Riga is today marketed as a top European attraction. As a result the slogan from the 1930's, '*Little Paris of the North*', has come back into use.[8]

Countless examples exist of places rediscovering their past, capitalising on the birthplace of a famous person, an event, a battle or other 'hidden gems'. Places rely on various monikers for identification: Dijon as '*the City of Mustard*'; Lübeck as '*the City of Niederegger Marzipan*', Amsterdam as '*the Place of Liberty*', Florence as *the Centre of the Renaissance*. Exhibit 9.5 describes how Romania is repositioning itself to capture the myth market.

Can Dracula save Romania?

EXHIBIT 9.5

While Bram Stoker's novel *Dracula* inspired myth and legend for over 100 years, the novel – and the 250 films it spawned – went virtually unnoticed in Romania and in its legendary region of Transylvania.

Instead, Romanians have struggled to overcome the legacy of their own, modern-day Dracula: communist dictator Nicholae Ceauşescu who was overthrown and executed in 1989. Fearing that the vampire legend would give Romanian peasants a bad image, Ceauşescu's communist regime never allowed the publication or translation of Stoker's novel, and it has only been in the past decade that Romanians have learned of the Western fascination with the Dracula myth.

The tourist picture is still marred by years of neglect and destruction of historical buildings. Once called the 'Paris of the East', Romania's capital, Bucharest, became a 'suffocating jungle of concrete'[1] as Ceauşescu razed homes, churches and city blocks to build countless drab, socialist-style apartment buildings in the early 1980s. But outside Bucharest, pastoral villages still exist. And it is on this idyllic scenery that Romania's tourism bureau is trying to capitalise. 'Once a strong summer-sun destination',[2] with its Black Sea resorts and Danube Delta, Romania's tourist industry has fallen into jeopardy. Plagued by poor hotels, undependable transportation and telephone service, and a tourist-deterring, cash-only society, Romania now relies primarily on its ski resorts for tourist currency.

Dan Matei, Romania's minister of tourism, is trying to reignite the country's appeal: 'We need more visitors, and if tourists want hands coming out of coffins, we'll give it to them'.[3] Beginning with the first World Dracula Congress in 1995, Romania has begun to embrace the Dracula myth in the hope that it will boost its sagging tourist industry. Romanian tour companies have begun to organise tours and trips revolving around the life of Vlad Tepes (Vlad the Impaler), the ruthless and legendary Transylvanian ruler on whom Stoker based his 1897 novel.

While Vlad Tepes is still revered by the Romanian people as an Orthodox crusader for his fearless (and ruthless) defence of Romania from Turkish invasion in the fifteenth century, the marriage of legend and history is quickly becoming a potent antidote to Romania's tourism ailment. It is certainly not ideal for most Romanians that their country's primary image in the West consists of Ceauşescu and Dracula, but it is a starting point. By luring tourists with an interest in legend and history, Romanians can then begin to introduce tourists to its pastoral country and resort areas.

Sources: 1. Valerie Voss, Steve Nettleton, Stephanie Oswald, 'A trip to Romania', *CNN Travel Guide*, 8 November 1997, transcript no. 97110800V31 (Lexis Nexis).
2. 'Mountains are top draw', *Travel Trade Gazette UK & Ireland*, 4 March 1998, p. 45 (Lexis Nexis).
3. Richard Gilbert, 'In the teeth of history', *The Independent*, 27 August 1995, p. 47 (Lexis Nexis).
Virginia Marsh, 'Romania prepares for Dracula without tears', *Financial Times*, 22 May 1995, p. 3 (Lexis Nexis).
Hugh Pitt, 'Living in the shadow of Count Dracula', *The Times*, 4 January 1997 (Lexis Nexis).

Investors in cross-border tourist projects may apply for financial support from the EU. '*The European Vineyard Routes*' is one such example. Six member states – Germany, Greece, Spain, France, Italy and Portugal – have joined forces to develop tourism in the European wine regions. A multilingual guide/tour list encourages the exploration of these regions and also assists in the exchange of experiences between vineyards. Other activities include press information, inter-regional training missions, permanent liaison offices and the creation of a quality chart and label. As another example, there is a *cross-border sport fishing* project which aims to attract people to sport fishing in the Hautes-Pyrénées intersecting the borders of France and Spain. Another widely promoted event is a *cross-border cycling tour*. An even more specialised theme is found in the '*Asparagus Tour*' project. The Dutch–Belgian border region, Limburg, with its rich agricultural and rural heritage, has developed the so-called asparagus tours. The area has organised local fairs and produced brochures and posters.

With the current European trend towards shorter but more frequent vacations, many places within two hours travel of major metropolitan areas have found new opportunities to access the tourist market. The renewed growth of the family vacation market also has redirected some places towards a 'family friendly' image. Many European theme parks, hotels and vacation facilities are within easy reach of the metropolitan areas. A place with such a location can exploit its new strategic position.

Another dimension in tourist attraction is how much language and intercultural understanding a place can provide. The English, who tend to be generally more adventurous when choosing holiday destinations, find their native tongue understood almost anywhere in modern Europe. Luther Buss, vice-president of German tour operator NUR (Neckermann & Reisen) observed the tendency for large groups of Germans to holiday in the same resort and to create a 'German cluster'. The majority of Germans prefer to eat in restaurants where the menu is in German and to stay in hotels where the staff speaks German. Buss paints a picture in which the Balearic Islands are transformed into a little Germany during the summer and he claims, 'There is a street in Playa de Palma known locally as Bierstrasse where every second building is a tavern. In the height of the season about 15,000 Germans, nearly all men, drink there every evening. And I swear that on those nights more beer is drunk in that one street than in the whole of Frankfurt'.[9]

Such intercultural observations can be actively used by places trying to attract certain foreign target groups to *their* place. Certain places in Northern Europe in need of an increased tourist market have consciously invested in improved language knowledge among staff in the hospitality business as well as elsewhere in society, for example the civic leaders.

The environmental movement has compelled the travel industry to adapt more earth-friendly approaches, and places are seeking to develop '*green*' images. Tourist places have become more sensitive to zoning, density, land use and the problems of overbuilding. In some places, regional and local tourist agencies, airlines, railways and hotel chains are all talking about green issues, and how best to accommodate growth while respecting environmental values. The German Travel Agents Association (DRV) has worked out environmental recommendations that provide practical tips and suggestions for better awareness on how environmentally-minded management ultimately pays off. Green images are more common in Western and Northern Europe where tourism is more developed. In Eastern and Southern Europe around the Mediterranean we find fewer cases of green consciousness. This lack of green images presents marketing opportunities for places in these areas to develop an environmental marketing strategy.

Event-based tourism has become a vital component of tourist attraction programmes. Small or rural places typically begin with a festival or event to establish their identity. Urban newspapers frequently publish a listing of events, festivals and celebrations that occur within a few hours' drive. Local and regional tourism offices make sure that travel agents, restaurants, hotels, airports, and railway and bus stations have event-based calendars for posting. Many European countries now have free numbers to call in the USA to request a listing of their forthcoming events.

Tourism investment ranges from relatively low-cost market entry for festivals or events to multimillion ECU infrastructure investments for stadiums, transit systems, airports, railway stations and convention centres. Today, urban renewal planners seek to build tourism into the heart of their city's revitalisation. The *Cardiff Bay Project* and the *Civic Centre* in Cardiff, *Akers Brygge* in Oslo, and the *Kop van Zuid* project in Rotterdam are all examples of urban renewal where the old and new are merged to create attractiveness for residents, businesses and tourists. These examples also illustrate the advantage of jointly developed projects between the public and private sectors. The public sector can be the overall catalyst with the private sector as the actual operator.

Investments in various tourism projects can be supported by the EU. The structural funds are sometimes a major contributor to tourism development. Aid tends to go to 'underdeveloped' regions (objective 1), those affected by the decline of industry (objective 2) and those concerned with rural development (objective 5b). Actions are also taken under certain community initiatives (such as LEADER, INTERREG, REGIS). Opportunities for tourism to implement joint measures, set up networks and try out new actions are planned under the community's ENVIREG, RECITE, PACTE and OUVERTURE programmes. During the period 1989–1993, the tourist industry received a total of ECU3 billion for investment and infrastructure projects for tourism.[10]

Positioning and niching in the tourist market

To attract tourists, places must respond to the travel basics of *cost*, *convenience*, and *timeliness*. Tourists, like other consumers, weigh the *costs* against the benefits of specific destinations – and investment of time, effort, and resources against a reasonable return in education, experience, fun, relaxation and prospective memories. *Convenience* takes on various meanings in travel decisions: time involved in travel, airport to lodging distance, language barriers, cleanliness and sanitary concerns, access to interests (for example beaches, attractions, amenities), and special needs (elderly, disabled, children, dietary, medical care, fax and telecommunication, auto rental). *Timeliness* embraces those factors that introduce risk to travel: wars, terrorism, civil disturbances and political instability, of tourism currency fluctuations and convertibility, airline and transit safety, and sanitary conditions.

As a general rule, all places and tourist businesses seek to be competitive in costs, minimised risks, and maximised conveniences and amenities. Tourist packages range from total planning of hour-by-hour detail to multiple options and choices. To accommodate multiple tourist needs, packages range from destination-to-destination no-frills to site-and-event-based full-frills luxury. Beyond basics, travellers make comparisons about the relative advantages and disadvantages of competing destinations: geographical (local, regional, national, European or non-European), special interests (hiking, snorkeling, mountaineering), and amenities (music, art, entertainment). Should I ski in the Alps or in Scandinavia? Should we go to some of the 'new' places in Eastern Europe or continue our return trips to old England? Tourists, like other consumers, constantly make trade-offs between cost and convenience, quality and reliability, service and beauty, and other choices. Depreciation of a country's currency, for example, can immediately attract tourists from another country.

Places must market not only their *destination* in general, but also their specific *attractions*. Places must provide easy access to their attractions by bus (as in London), trams (as in Vienna), underground railway (as in Moscow), boats (as in Venice), and planes (as in Schiphol with its 25 million passengers a year). Places can distribute brochures, audiotapes and videotapes, postcards and Internet pages. Most major hotels now provide in-home video packages to assist visitors in planning local tours, booking events or in seeing various sites. City bus or boat companies offer half-day, full-day and evening tours to highlight the place's major attractions. A transportation breakdown can ruin a visit (see Exhibit 9.6).

'Just run'

EXHIBIT 9.6

The day did not start well. The passenger was flying a European carrier from Stockholm to Leipzig with a stopover in Munich. It was November and the plane was parked on a remote runway at Arlanda Airport. The plane's temperature seemed about 30 degrees Fahrenheit as the shivering human cargo waited for the frozen plane to warm up. That experience turned out to be the most pleasant part of the trip.

En route to Munich, the crew announced that the flight would arrive late and that a special van would rush passengers to connecting flights. Our passenger's flight to Leipzig was for some reason not included. When the passenger explained the oversight to crewmembers, he was informed that if he was not on the special arrangements list, he must board the regular buses, not the special van. There would be no exceptions. With the snow blowing furiously, the passenger ignored the admonition and ran out to the van where, pounding on the window, he begged for a ride. The driver of the half-empty van looked at him with disdain and drove off in a cloud of snow. The passenger was left to board a slow bus to the terminal.

The situation did not improve in the terminal. After a frantic search for the departing flight to Leipzig, three minutes to go, and a missed meeting on the horizon, he found an attendant. The attendant informed him that his gate was at the opposite end of the airport. Hoping for a hurried phone call to the gate and fast ride on a cart, the passenger asked plaintively, 'How should I get there?' The response: 'Just run.' He did, arriving at the gate after a long tortuous sprint carrying a heavy suitcase. 'We were wondering where you were', said the gate attendant with a stiff smile.

The possible explanations

- Leipzig officials: Munich dislikes Leipzig and is punishing passengers.
- Airline officials: A breakdown in computers – 'Send a bottle of Moët et Chandon'.
- Psychiatrists: A combination of latent hostility and an inability to adapt to unanticipated glitches.
- Placemarketers: A training programme emphasising people skills and adaptation to crisis should be implemented.

Places need to monitor closely the relative popularity of their various attractions by determining the number and types of tourist attracted to each location. The popularity of Ferrara the '*City of Renaissance*', *the medieval city of Rhodes*, *the Vatican City* or *Cologne Cathedral* can suddenly or gradually change. Places must therefore seek to deepen the quality of their attractions. The search process should never stop. The *Luther Memorials* in Eisleben and Wittenberg or the *Hanseatic City of Lübeck* must gradually develop new attractions. In the case of Lübeck, for instance, it is of great importance to exploit the opportunities which have opened around the Baltic Sea and to give a contemporary context to the old Hanseatic concept.

However, concepts alone do not attract tourists. Places must seek to enhance the travel experience by providing greater value and making the experience more significant and rewarding. Such appeals may be couched in terms of culture, tradition and people. A city can develop itself in a more foreigner-friendly direction. This can be done by creating tours that emphasise nationality interests, designing brochures in a variety of languages and providing hassle-free currency exchanges. By providing such customer-centred elements a place can deepen cultural bonds and ties.

Competition for place advantage in tourism extends to restaurants, facilities, sports, cultural amenities and entertainment. There is a permanent struggle among European places to have the most four-star hotels; best wine and drink; best chefs; best and most museums and theatres; or best native, cultural or ethnic flair. The popularity of the Michelin Guide is a reflection of this struggle. Almost every corner of Europe is ranked by the Michelin Guide or various travel magazines according to best hotels, restaurants, and other tourist attractions. These testimonials and rankings, where favourable, are then incorporated into travel brochures, place advertising and travel guides.

Communicating with the tourist market

Tourist competition, like business attraction and retention, involves image-making. Place images are heavily influenced by pictorial creations of the place, often in movies and on television, postcards, sometimes by music, and in other cases by popular entertainers and celebrities. Decades later, these place images still persist. Ireland exploits the John Wayne/Maureen O'Hara film *The Quiet Man* as an idealised image of the Irish, while Heidelberg still benefits from Hollywood's version of *The Student Prince*. Lately, London has increased tourist access to William Shakespeare's work through the new *Globe Theatre*. Copenhagen focuses on *The Little Mermaid*. (It is said: 'This is one of the few statues where the photograph looks better than the real thing'.)

Places often discover hidden assets that have large tourist potential. Such assets can sometimes be communicated with humour and brilliance and even develop into cult objects. Figure 9.2 shows two posters that have attracted much attention. The French region Franche Comté markets their great '*Geniuses*' such as Louis Pasteur, the two brothers Lumière, and Victor Hugo. The other hidden assets are a number of products and attractions from the region that are challenging their American counterparts. The core message in both posters – underscored with an ironic touch – is the proud cultural heritage of Franche Comté.

Finally, effective place imaging requires a congruence of advertising and the place. Glossy photographs of sunsets, beaches, buildings and events need to have some relationship to what tourists actually experience; otherwise places run the risk of losing tourist goodwill and generating bad word of mouth. Travel agents are responsive to place feedback from customers, and they may not recommend a destination. Placemarketers should sample travel agents about the feedback they get from their customers.

Organising and managing tourism marketing

Making a tourist-friendly place is the task of a great many place-sellers. A necessity is a model for organising and managing tourism marketing. Table 9.3 illustrates the model used by Spain, one of the main tourist markets in Europe.

Source: Comité Regional du Tourism, Besançon.

Fig 9.2 ◆ Posters from Franche Comté

Table 9.3 ◆ Organising and managing tourism marketing – the Spanish case

Public institutions	
National level	**Role**
Intergovernmental body for tourism	Co-ordination between different government departments
Ministry for Commerce and Tourism	Co-ordination of the ministries and public administration
Secretariat General for Tourism	Implementation and administration of the government's policy
Directorate General for Tourism Strategy	Co-ordination between the autonomous communities
Directorate General for the Promotion of Tourism Strategy	Tourism promotion and marketing activities abroad
Spanish tourism offices abroad	Co-operation with the autonomous regions concerning their promotion overseas
Institute of Tourism Studies	Documentation, information and research Training and development of distribution systems
Official School of Tourism	National tourism school for the training of providers of tourist services
Regional level	
Administrative regional councils in the autonomous provinces	Tourism promotion and planning at the regional level. Control of tourist activities of companies
Local level	
Communities	Promotion of tourist activities on a local level (Note that there are 8,056 communities in Spain)

Source: The Role of the Union in the Field of Tourism, Commission Green Paper, Commission of the European Communities, Brussels, 4 April 1995, pp. 62–64.

Even though the national structure in Spain seems dominant on paper, the main promotion takes place regionally and locally. Furthermore, at the regional and local level, public and private institutions have joined forces to a great extent. In the southern parts of Europe, local chambers of commerce are heavily involved in tourism strategies and promotion. Several major European cities have significantly more economic resources for tourism marketing than the regional and national tourist promotion agencies.

One can conclude that the public and private sectors, especially during the 1990s, have improved their collaboration in tourism. The competitive climate in Europe has pushed the public and private sectors closer together in many places. More commercial considerations are being recognised as important. The American way of joining forces, especially on local and regional levels, has spread to Europe. Bridge-building between the sectors is occurring. One example of this is the closer co-operation between the public body World Tourism Organisation (WTO) in Madrid and the private World Travel and Tourism Council (WTTC) in London.

Business hospitality market

Europe has witnessed a huge increase in business travel. Two main categories can be identified. *First*, millions of small and regular business meetings are increasingly taking place in a cross-border context. *Second*, there is a growing market for trade shows, conventions, assemblies, conferences and consumer shows. In both cases the key revenue factors are the size of the group, the length of the stay and its service demands.

Table 9.4 shows comparative figures for certain European cities of the share of business travel versus leisure travel. In all the cities, apart from Edinburgh, the business share is much higher than that of leisure.

Table 9.4 ◆ Business and leisure tourism in selected cities, 1991

	Bed, nights in hotels (millions)	*Business*	*Leisure*
Antwerp	NA	65	35
Copenhagen	2.9	62	38
Edinburgh	4.4	30	70
Glasgow	NA	75	25
Lyons	2.7	92	8

Source: Van den Berg *et al.*, *Urban Tourism*, Euricur, Erasmus University, Rotterdam, 1994, p. 161.

Edinburgh attracts large numbers of holiday tourists because of its famous festival. The other cities benefit mostly from business travellers who greatly outnumber the leisure tourists. Yet it must be remembered that business travellers who stay overnight expect leisure type offerings such as entertainment, historical attractions or natural beauty. This means that each place must be able to offer comprehensive and specific target packages (STP) including business and leisure offerings.

Developing competitive meeting facilities

As the meetings market has grown, so has the number of places and facilities competing for the business. European places are boosting their capacity to handle huge meetings. A mega-event such as the International Rotary Meeting at the International Exhibition Centre in Birmingham attracted 23,000 participants. It has been calculated that almost £20 million was spent in Birmingham during this single meeting. (The figure does not include travel costs.) This contribution to Birmingham can hardly be overestimated since most of the purchased services and products originated from the local market.

Convention facilities in Europe improved immensely in the 1990s. Of course, there are some leading and classic meeting places, such as London or Paris. However, many other places also offer attractive world-class packages: Brussels, Luxembourg, Strasbourg, Berlin, Amsterdam, Geneva, Vienna, Milan, Nice and Madrid. Many others are lining up: Helsinki, Stockholm, Copenhagen, St Petersburg, Moscow, Leipzig, Prague, Budapest, Munich, Cologne, Düsseldorf, Essen, Frankfurt, Hannover, Hamburg, Nuremburg, The Hague, Utrecht, Manchester, Birmingham, Glasgow, Cardiff, Toulouse, Lyons, Cannes, Bordeaux, Bologna, Florence, Lisbon, Barcelona, Granada, Seville and Valencia.

A successful convention place offers not only an attractive price. A world-class package must also contain a competitive combination of physical meeting facilities and a number of exciting unique offerings. As a consequence European places are trying to specialise in certain types of conventions, congresses and exhibitions. The competitive climate and specialisation are now heightened as Eastern Europe is entering the convention market. For instance, Belgrade has managed to attract a convention for the computer and communications industry, Moscow has attracted pharmacology and radiology, and Leipzig has focused on a medical trade fair and congress.

The European market also includes thousands of small places competing with their very specific packages. Åland, an autonomous part of Finland in the middle of the Baltic Sea, is surrounded by 6,500 small islands and offers a unique setting. Other small places with easily identifiable positions are: Isle of Man, Gibraltar, Liechtenstein, Monaco, Malta and Andorra. They are all meeting places with a very special flavour, but are facing competition offering more amenities and benefits. Malta, with the advantage of a financial cluster, is planning a new Hilton hotel and an international casino. Andorra, with its unusual ratio of 60,000 inhabitants and 30,000 hotel beds, can provide attractive combinations of business meetings and leisure.

The competition for hospitality business begets a certain spiralling 'space race' among competing cities. There are both internal and external dynamics. The *internal* dynamic stems largely from hotel and hospitality business expansion which builds or overbuilds to meet prospective demand from conventions and trade shows. When hotel occupancy rates fall below a profit level – roughly 60 per cent occupancy – pressure mounts to expand exhibition and meeting space in order to increase hotel occupancy rates.

The *external* dynamic comes from competitors' space expansion plans. Several European cities have recently expanded their exhibition space and many more projects are in the planning stage. The European dimension has been much more manifest following the EU's move towards a single market. Today, exhibitions, trade fairs, conventions and conferences are being organised in a greater context for the larger European market.

Strategies for winning in the business hospitality market

Conventions, conferences and the trade show business, in contrast to tourist attractions, involve dealing with dedicated specialists such as trade association directors, site selection committees and convention specialists who make site selection recommendations based on price, labour costs, facilities and various amenities. Facilities are critical to accommodating association needs – which often means the capacity to run multiple shows concurrently – and providing Class A space at reasonable rates. Discounted hotel, restaurant, theatre, airline, car rental, transport, and other amenities are all part of competitive packaging. Such customer targeting requires co-operation between the place-sellers in a specific place.

Facilities must also be upgraded to meet aesthetic and convenience needs – restaurants, shops, rest-rooms, greater cleanliness, speed of set-ups and take-downs, security, and proximity to central shopping areas and restaurants. Central and convenient communication is not so easily managed within European cities of the old urban design. Since these urban traditions – and bottlenecks – are part of the unique product, they often cannot be easily changed. The new European Parliament building in Brussels – '*The most expensive building in Europe*' – is an example of how much a place is willing to invest in a project to improve convenience for a few in order to safeguard its position as a top European meeting place. Located in the inner city of Brussels, the building creates traffic problems and is architecturally inconsistent with the surrounding environment. Because of competition to host the European parliament, Brussels stuck the building in a location that is attractive to the members despite these issues, but this move risked numerous inconveniences to the public.

Each convention centre has its competitive advantages and disadvantages. Some convention places in Northern Europe have bad weather during autumn and spring, whereas others in Southern Europe, such as Seville or Athens, are too hot in the summer to be competitive. In some cases, for example Oslo and Moscow, hotel prices are too high to attract convention place-buyers. The dream of all places is to attract customers during the off-season and the inducements include cut prices and free services.

In recession periods, organisers cut back on travel for professional development, trade shows and even sales contacts; some travel is replaced by video conferences, teleconferences, and fax machines. Like tourism, the meetings market experienced some difficult years in the beginning of the 1990s in Europe. Yet despite the recession, more investments in professional meeting facilities were planned than ever before. This commitment to development reflects the belief that the European market will expand in the long run.

Conclusions

Tourism and the business hospitality market have emerged as viable place development strategies on a footing equal to business retention and business attraction. In service-driven economies with ageing populations, these two businesses are generally expected to grow at rates ahead of the national economy.

Several tourism/travel related trends are worth noting:

1. The economic development plans of places will increasingly emphasise the contribution of the tourism and travel industry.
2. Greater market segmentation will follow from better marketing information, and tourism strategic marketing and management will receive increased emphasis.
3. Travellers will more often combine business and personal travel with emphasis on cultural and recreational activities requiring places to adapt to cross-marketing.
4. Greater interest in certain sports and recreation will require places to invest more in open space and recreational facilities and to develop lower-key, environmentally sensitive experiences.
5. The opening of Eastern and Central Europe will create a boom in European tourism.
6. Shorter working weeks in Europe will increase short-trip tourism. Smaller places, within a convenient travel distance from the big cities, can be real winners if they adopt a proactive marketing strategy.

Smaller places can promote tourism and business meetings at relatively little cost. However, as they seek access to broader markets, the cost for public and private investments rises rapidly. At the upper end of the scale, large capital investments are required for airports, convention centres, basic infrastructure and public services. Private sector investment in hotels, shopping areas and restaurants need to be carefully co-ordinated and planned with public investments so that one does not proceed without the other. Physical assets must be continually upgraded and new products and concepts developed. Exhibit 9.7 offers a test that places can use to assess their visitor friendliness.

A test of visitor friendliness for places

EXHIBIT 9.7

Although not an exact measurement of a place's visitor friendliness, the following ten questions can provide a rough estimate. With 10 points for each favourable answer, a passing score is 60. Anything lower probably spells trouble for the place.

1. Are the central access points to your community/place equipped with visitor information centres (road, rail, plane) or do they at least provide instructions on where to find information easily?
2. Should an airport or a railway station be the primary access point, does it provide a full range of visitor information services (e.g. accommodation, tourist booth, visuals on sites, listing of events and what to do, specialised information for the elderly, foreigners and families)?
3. Do visitor facilitators – cabs, buses, airline/railway personnel, security airport/railway operators, reservation personnel – receive any formal training, and does a system exist to monitor the quality of visitor facilitator services?
4. Do hotels/motels offer in-house television access channels for visitors with information on events, attractions, restaurants and things to do?
5. Is a single organisation/agency responsible for visitor business and are public funds provided for its activities?
6. Does that organisation/agency have a marketing profile of visitors and is this profile used in its marketing activities?
7. Does the place's hospitality industry accommodate foreign visitors' needs (language, directions, special interests, etc.)?
8. Does a range of accommodations exist to meet actual or expected visitor needs (by price range, size, facilities, access to sites, etc.)?
9. Is access to sites, attractions and amenities (events, recreational, central location) easily available at reasonable costs?
10. Does the place welcome visitors and accommodate their needs (commercial hours, credit cards, language, signage, traffic, parking, public services, etc.)?

10

Attracting, retaining and expanding business

Every place performs particular economic functions. Some place economies are diversified, whereas others are dominated by a single industry. Some are service centres and others are agricultural communities. However, a place's economic activities are not necessarily constrained by their surrounding economic boundaries. In the enormous European market – the fifteen EU countries along with their 380 million inhabitants – the smallest place can expand its business on an international market with fewer and fewer administrative obstacles. By viewing a place through a cross-border European lens, one can better understand how a place functions in an international context.

A place's ability to compete changes over time. At one time, Venice and Bruges were thriving as dynamic hubs for international trade, but some centuries later they had become minor players in the trade world. Once again they have become dominant leaders, but now in the tourist market. This history illustrates that places, just like corporate giants and entire industries, may rise and fall with new technologies, new competitors and shifting consumer preferences.

Over the last century, a general pattern can be identified in European place strategy. From the beginning of the twentieth century until the Second World War – a period which can be classified as *European industrialisation* – places used specific raw materials and other competitive factors as an incentive for industrialists to establish new manufacturing plants. Greenfield projects dominated during this period. After the Second World War, between 1945 and 1960, when Europe entered a long period of reconstruction, place strategies focused on rebuilding, modernising and expanding diminished industrial capacities, in several cases with support from the Marshall Plan. Manufacturing was still first on the list.

With the deep European crisis in coal and steel during the 1970s, for example in the Ruhr area, and Wales, a new focus emerged to replace lost jobs.

But the basic strategy was to struggle to keep the current structure alive as long as possible. However, by the end of the decade new growth niches emerged, especially in the service sector. As a result that sector attracted more attention.

In the 1980s, many places started to focus on encouraging new business start-ups. Inspired by the high growth figures in American high-tech centres, research parks and clusters, European places worked out their own *'Silicon-strategies'*.

In the 1990s, many European places were trying to attract international investors interested in mergers and acquisitions expansion, and greenfield projects. The underlying assumption was that new investors could revitalise otherwise declining business. Even the most foreign sources of capital were often welcomed as long as they invested in new networks and business expansion. Most places were dreaming of huge greenfield projects that were popular at the beginning of the century.

Today, places can use one or more of six generic strategies to improve their competitive positions:

1. Attracting tourist and business visitors.
2. Attracting business from elsewhere.
3. Retaining and expanding existing business.
4. Promoting small business and fostering new business start-ups.
5. Expanding exports and outside investments.
6. Expanding the population or changing the mix of residents.

We have already examined the first strategy – attracting tourist and business visitors – in Chapter 9. We will examine the last two strategies, expanding exports and investments and altering the residential population base in Chapters 11 and 12. Here in Chapter 10, we will focus on place strategies for attracting, retaining, expanding and starting new businesses.

Attracting businesses from elsewhere

European places have a long history of attracting businesses from elsewhere. The subject of attracting new businesses was made a top priority after the 1970s when many places experienced the negative consequences of low rankings and bad images in the placemarket. In response international competition became intense. The spectre of mass unemployment again haunted European citizens and politicians.

How businesses select locations

Places should begin their business attraction planning with an assessment of their economy and an audit of their locational characteristics (their local business climate). Accurate and frequent updating of operating conditions, cost factors, and quality-of-life features provide an understanding of how well one place compares with others. Table 3.3 (Chapter 3) offered a list of *hard* and *soft* attraction factors which businesses consider important in most site designations.

These attraction factors change over time and from project to project. During the past three decades, place competitive advantages, strengths and weaknesses changed. As Table 10.1 indicates, new non-economic factors – or *soft factors* – have become increasingly important in location-expansion decisions.

Table 10.1 ◆ Locational characteristics: old and new

Characteristics	*Old*	*New*
◆ Labour	Low cost, unskilled	Quality, highly skilled
◆ Tax climate	Low taxes, low service	Modest taxes, high services
◆ Incentives	Least-cost production, cheap land and labour	Value-added adaptable labour force, professionals
◆ Amenities	Housing and transportation	Culture, recreation, museums, shopping,airport
◆ Schools	Availability	Quality schools
◆ Higher education	Not key	Quality schools and research facilities
◆ Regulation	Minimum	Compatible quality-of-life and business flexibility
◆ Energy	Cost/availability	Dependability/reliability
◆ Communication	Assumed	Technology access
◆ Business	Aggressive chamber of commerce, etc.	Partnerships

Various soft factors have gained prominence and assumed multiple forms: quality of public education, skilled labour force in the relevant niche, political stability, a trustful local business climate, modern telecommunications, local access to support services such as marketing and banking, recreational activities and sports teams, shopping facilities, cultural institutions and other general quality-of-life considerations. Environmental considerations also grew in importance, such as clean air and facility compliance with stronger air, water, and chemical and waste disposal regulations.

In a market characterised by many place-sellers and few place-buyers, place-sellers primarily compete on place inducements. However, place inducements are not always the crucial determinant. In increasing numbers, buyers are shifting in their interest towards places that offer firm-specific and especially non-cost factors. Places with universities, related research facilities, international partnerships, and good quality-of-life factors have an advantage over places that lack these features. In many place decisions a dynamic local leadership can be more valuable than cheap land or public subsidies. Michael Porter adds the competitive environment as a critical place building factor (Exhibit 10.1).

The race for high-tech industries

During the first part of this century, European communities focused solely on attracting basic heavy manufacturing industries. Today, they seek 'clean' factories. The race is to build an attractive local climate to attract high-tech industries. This 'Silicon strategy' is symbolised by places like Silicon Glen, Cambridge, Sophia Antipolis and Grenoble. Thousands of small places are also establishing their own high-tech strategies. They are struggling to keep a critical mass and to support 'their' knowledge-based firms. Both small and big Silicon Valley clones are promoting science and business parks, research centres, and buildings designed to house two or more knowledge-based companies.

Marketing clusters: a competitive model

EXHIBIT 10.1

Places that have a number of similar industries are more likely to attract companies in comparable businesses. Michael Porter argues that these competing or complementary companies form clusters of excellence that build productivity through rivalries and asset sharing. In Porter's view places should encourage competition because it forces companies to innovate in order to stay ahead and also attracts world-class talent. What do Porter's insights mean to the thousands of European communities that are seeking to expand their workforces and create a higher standard of living?

- The place that already has a cluster needs to expand its financial and skills base. The task here is to anticipate the needs of clusters – for example, communication, human resources, and transportation – and deliver higher quality support. In some cases, such as Cambridge, the cluster is being expanded to surrounding communities; this move can improve competitiveness and secure a critical mass.
- Many European places are in what can be termed the pre-cluster stage. These places might consider targeting promising industries in order to create full-fledged clusters. The place may have only a few companies or a number of companies without any real similarities. In this case, the place's task is to inventory the marketplace, assets, and workforce to determine the right combination of companies to locate in the area. Many success stories abound of places, such as Ennis in the West of Ireland and Oulu in Northern Finland, that built clusters in the telecom industry. In software, Riga is building a software cluster, and Cyprus is trying to become a leader in financial services. In each case the places benefit from technology, an educated workforce, and targeted development.
- For some places in the very early development stage, a practical approach might

involve practising strong attraction strategies and casting a wider net. Corby, England, a formerly run-down steel town of 50,000, is a good example of a town practising a strategy that concentrates on making deals. The town leaders have constructed a model that combines an aggressive use of grants, incentives and subsidies with first-rate execution. Corby has attracted an eclectic array of new businesses to its industrial parks, including steel, food, and automotive companies. This cluster is not product specific, like shoes or glass, but could be labelled entrepreneurship. The Corby focus is buttressed with a careful attention to promotion, willingness to cut through red tape, and a risk mentality.

In the cases described above, the common denominator, irrespective of whether the place is a cluster, pre-cluster, or early developing model, is that strategic market planning is crucial.

Sources: Michael E. Porter, 'Clusters and the New Economics of Competition', *Harvard Business Review*, November/December 1998, pp. 77–90. See also Porter's 'On Competition', Harvard Business School Press, Boston, 1998. For a complete discussion of Corby's re-emergence see Terry F. Buss and Robert Bartok, 'Corby, England Leads Economic Development in Europe', *Economic Development Review*, Vol. 12, No. 3, pp. 83–87.

Yet today, many 'Silicon strategies' are in trouble. During years of European recession in the beginning of the 1990s, many high-tech centres lay underdeveloped, and they have since become subsidised research parks and incubators. A major problem is to achieve a critical mass that gives the place a sufficient quality image or niche leadership position. Many places suffer from 'brain drain' and the need to develop education and quality-of-life incentives to keep clusters of talent. Another problem is that the potential number of high-tech companies and jobs has probably been overestimated. Compared with Japan and the USA, Europe has a smaller proportion of high-tech jobs (Figure 10.1).

As can also be seen in Figure 10.1, European industrial employment figures are closer to the US and Japanese as a consequence of the decline in these two countries. Unfortunately, this is due to a much sharper productivity increase in the USA and Japan; and place-buyers are buying productivity. From a place-selling perspective, European sites must develop more competitive strategies and offerings. European high-tech offerings must be of a long-term character in order to inspire enough confidence to compete with US and Asian placemarkets.

Attracting service industries and corporate headquarters

The impact of European service industries fluctuates dramatically between nations, regions and especially communities. At a national level we can contrast several European countries with the highest and the lowest proportion of employment in the service sector (Table 10.2).

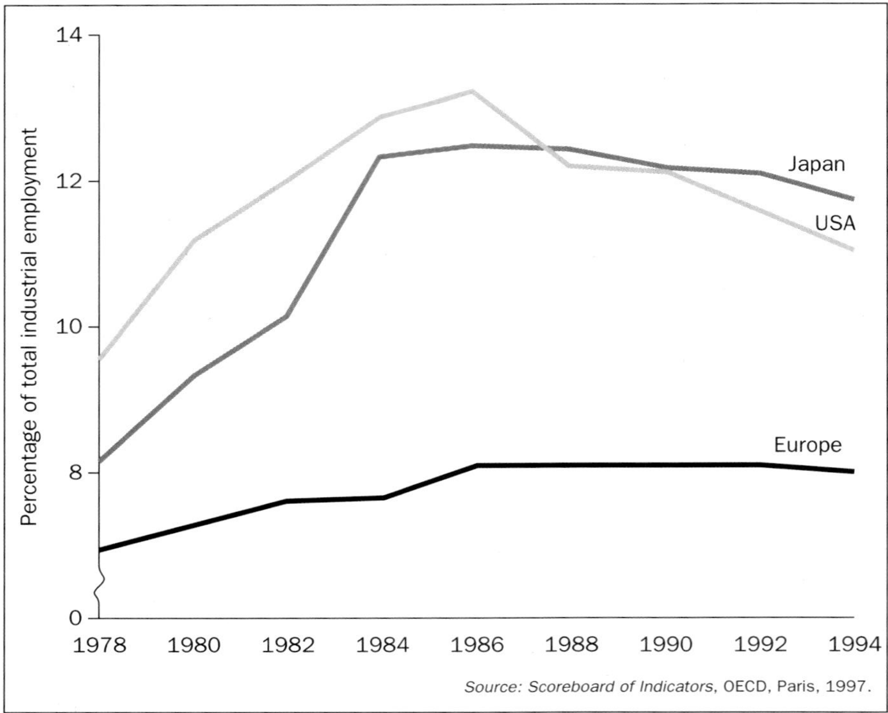

Figure 10.1 ◆ Employment in high-tech industries

Table 10.2 ◆ Percentage of employment in the service sector

Highest		*Lowest*	
Netherlands	73.0 %	Poland	44.1%
Sweden	71.6%	Czech Republic	50.1%
Norway	71.3%	Portugal	55.7%

Source: The OECD Observer, OECD, Paris, 1997 edition.

Differences are actually much larger if we examine specific communities. Bank services in the inner city of Frankfurt represent a whole service world forming a competitive cluster. Many places within the German Ruhr region, as well as many Polish, Czech and Portuguese cities, are struggling to increase their service industry.

Conventional European views saw service-sector employment as providing low-paying, low-skilled work, exporting little, and having a low economic multiplier. However, this attitude is being re-examined as Europeans confront high unemployment and no growth in the manufacturing sector. The old view that 'real jobs' are available only in the manufacturing sector is quickly disappearing.

Places today recognise that services account for well over 50 per cent of the world's economic output and that it is the value-added relationship between services and manufacturing (and vice versa) that is critical to job creation. These places have also noted how the service sector within the EU has grown from 42 per cent of GDP in 1970 to 63 per cent of GDP and 62 per cent of employment today. Naturally, such deep and dramatic figures push places into a healthy increased interest in service industries. Places are developing new strategies to attract entrepreneurs.[1] Pauli has analysed a number of European service entrepreneurs (see Table 10.3) and observed that they have generated some 750,000 jobs and ECU 25 billion in turnover.

Table 10.3 ◆ Top 25 European service entrepreneurs

Entrepreneur	*Business*	*Starting company*	*Nation*
Paul Andreassen	Cleaning	ISS	Denmark
Pierre Bellon	Catering	Sodexho	France
Silvio Berlusconi	Media	Fininvest	Italy
Richard Branson	Entertainment	Virgin	UK
Miguel Duran	Lotteries	ONCE	Spain
Tom Farmer	Car repair	Kwik Fit	UK
Ph. Foriel-Destezet	Temporary employment	ECCO	France
Giorgio Guigiario	Design	Italdesign	Italy
Frits Goldschmeding	Temps/security	Randstad	Netherlands
Bertil Hult	Language training	EF	Sweden/USA
Serge Kampf	Software	Cap Gemini Sogeti	France
Bessel Kok	Financial telecoms	SWIFT	Belgium
Henry Lavanchy	Temporary employment	Adia	Switzerland
Robert Maxwell	Publishing	Bertelsmann	Germany
Claus Møller	Training	TMI	Denmark
Werner Otto	Mail order	Otto Versand	Germany
J. Philip-Sørensen	Security	Group 4 Securitas	Netherlands/Sweden
Jan Pierre	International moving	Arthur Pierre	Belgium
Glen Renfrew	Electronic publishing	Reuters	UK
Hildson Ryan	Fast consumer services	Minit Int'l	Belgium/Switzerland
Clive Thompson	Pest control	Rentokil	UK/Denmark
Gilbert Trigano	Tourism	Club Med	France
Nicholas Wills	Business support services	BET	UK
Egon Zehnder	Executive search	Egon Zehnder	Switzerland

Source: Gunter Pauli, *Double-digit Growth, How to Achieve It with Services*, Pauli Publishing, *Berlaar*, 1997, p. 29.

A place can attract service industries and entrepreneurs such as those listed in Table 10.3 if the place targets entrepreneurs early in their search process. Being an early host place for EF, Club Med or Reuters can establish a positive place image and new job opportunities and networks. These networks open unexpected contacts and create positive spirals. But place-sellers need a systematic approach. In most European countries, service business associations have a comprehensive knowledge of service structures, individual actors and areas in which new businesses will emerge. Place-sellers need to establish contacts with such associations and networks.

Many urban redesign projects are planned from the very beginning to suit certain service businesses. Such a project can be a city district specifically designed to attract insurance companies, a pedestrian street where travel agencies can gather, or a shopping area with a certain service profile. It can occur in connection with the implementation of many conversion programmes. It can be a closed hospital, a downsized industry, or a previous military campus which has been converted into various service-related clusters. It may take the form of an incubator for small service companies or a full-scale service centre, specifically loaded with information technology and other built-in attractions.

A primary target for many larger places is to attract company headquarters. Yet, one should recognise that headquarters relocations are generally infrequent. Places cannot lure or entice a move if the company is not looking to move. Relocation is most likely to occur if the company is under pressure (for example takeovers, mergers, break-ups, reorganisations) or when the local business climate has become burdensome (for example higher operating costs, heavy taxes that cause staff recruiting problems, declining quality of life, or a bad place image in general). Europe has witnessed a number of headquarters being established during the 1990s, primarily by non-European companies wanting to establish a presence within Europe. Exhibit 10 .2 describes a search process for a European headquarters.

European headquarters – a place-buying case

EXHIBIT 10.2

The US software company Computer Associates decided in 1995 to establish a European headquarters. Lisa Mars, senior vice-president, explained that the new headquarters 'would reflect the corporate culture of our New York world headquarters – open spaces to allow staff to exchange ideas freely, and childcare and leisure areas. We knew we would have to build a greenfield to achieve this.'

The placebuying process consisted of the following steps:

- Lisa Mars and the real estate manager, Walter Imperatore of Computer Associates, contacted local economic development offices in Europe to gather information.
- Mars and Imperatore made approximately twenty trips to Brussels, Paris, Frankfurt, Dublin, Rome and London to look at several sites around each of these cities.
- By August 1996 an informal shortlist was ready.
- Mars observed, 'We preferred the UK even though it was not the cheapest option. French sites offered cheaper land. In Ireland low corporate tax rate and incentives were a draw. But the UK's English-speaking and deregulated workforce was important for us ...'

- Mars and Imperatore looked at eight sites in the corridor along the M4 motorway running west of London, where the UK headquarters was already located. They also looked at six sites around Edinburgh and Glasgow to get a cost comparison. They determined that locating in Scotland would be much cheaper particularly with the incentives that the area offered.
- But costs were not the sole consideration. The search process ended in January 1997, with the decision to build a $150 million headquarters at an environmentally protected site in the Royal Borough of Windsor.

The final site is located in a rurally protected greenbelt zone. A seventeenth century manor house also enhances the property. Mars said of the final choice: 'I am not too worried about local stories that the house is haunted. A poltergeist is said to switch lights on and off, open doors and rattle the huge shutters on the windows. And a scientist killed in World War II is occasionally spotted walking around. As an American, I find the whole thing quite thrilling.'

Hard and soft attraction factors in a unique combination made Windsor the winner. Conventional wisdom says that hard factors, such as costs and financial incentives, are always decisive. In this case, the winning site possessed an overwhelming soft factor – a fully-developed ghost package in a convenient greenfield location.

Source: Lisa Mars, 'Euro HQ goes to historic site', *Corporate Location*, September/October 1997, p. 160.

As suggested in Exhibit 10.2, there were large cost differences between, for instance, areas around Edinburgh and London. This means that places in and around London must provide enough additional attractions to compensate for hard factors such as higher real estate costs and higher salaries. How such a London attraction can be positioned was summarised by Tony Travers, director of the Greater London Group, a group of academics at the London School of Economics: 'It's clear that what encourages business to decide to move here is in part the hard-nosed business thing, but in part softer things which are heavily based on perception.'[2] Such perceptions include the view that London is a long-term secure place to run a business. In addition, London has the huge, immeasurable advantage of being English-speaking. It is no surprise that London scored well (second only to Toronto) on Arthur Andersen's list of '*Best cities for work and family*' published in *Fortune* magazine's November 1996 issue.

In a world characterised by increasing opportunities and shifting resources, places need to provide regional barometers that reflect different housing costs, salaries, taxes, energy costs and other expenses. In the first stages of a search process, place-buyers in the service sector rely heavily on such regional barometers. However, as the search progresses, the final decision to change is often a combination of factors that can be both emotional and quantifiable.

Attracting shopping malls, retailers and wholesalers

Probably no single business location phenomenon has transformed a place's landscape and economy more than changing retail and wholesale forces.

There has been a long evolution beginning with itinerant pedlars replaced by department stores; then came large retail-anchored suburban malls, anchorless malls and mini-malls of speciality stores. The current trend is towards factory outlet malls, discount warehouses and virtual sales. Retailing patterns have radically transformed many places.

Today the retail distribution sector represents about 14 per cent of output and employment in the EU.[3] The sector can be separated into two major categories: *wholesale business* (defined as units engaged in the resale of goods to manufacturers and others for further processing) and *retail businesses* (defined as distribution to final consumers). Some places have allocated vast resources on place-selling efforts focusing on wholesale and retail businesses. Urban redesign effort is directed to attracting these place-buyers. The potential contribution of the distribution business makes it worthwhile, from a place-selling point of view, to understand the following current European trends in distribution:

- Reduced number of larger operators.
- Closer vertical and horizontal links between manufacturers, wholesalers and retailers.
- Slower increase in the number of hypermarkets.
- A rise in franchising.
- Increased distance selling.
- Networks of multifunction distribution centres.
- Increased use of automation and information technology.
- New concept stores being introduced.
- Moves towards internationalisation and cross-border networks.
- Growth in the Europeanised dimension.

These trends, increasingly fuelled by new media and communication technology (like the Internet), create turbulence in employment within the distribution sector. We can anticipate that of the 14 per cent employed today in this sector, some jobs will shift towards transportation and logistics flows which have resulted from the growing ease of ordering and selling via international communication networks, while others will shift towards activities facilitating these flows, that is, IT and communications sectors.

Despite the shifts in retail distribution, places still benefit from high-profile retail institutions. Famous stores in Europe can act as magnets to attract new businesses. Consider such department stores as *Magasin du Nord* in Copenhagen, *Harrods* in London, the new *Kulturkaufhaus* in the Berlin Friedrichstrasse, the classic *GUM* in Moscow, *Fiorucci* in Milan or the famous fashion stores *Gucci*, *Prada* and *Marino*. Brussels offers *Inno* and the well-known *Virgin* for music enthusiasts. Paris has its mecca for music lovers in *Fnac* in rue de Rennes. The biggest department store in Northern Europe is *Stockmann* in

Helsinki. These stores are considered the great treasures of European retailing and brand the entire shopping area.

Many places would like to attract stores that can contribute to an important retail cluster. To do so, places have to ask such fundamental questions as, how can we attract retailers such as IKEA, Carrefour, H&M, or Corte Ingles? More specifically, how can we combine them in a shopping mall? Or on a much smaller scale, how can we attract McDonald's, Burger King or even 7 Eleven? The answers may be a combination of incentives, tax breaks, road construction or myriad other factors. The key issue for the place-seller is to seriously improve the negatives, deal with the inevitable threats, and market aggressively the new position.

There are two major threats to the European retailing picture: discounters and virtual sales. One is the trend of large speciality operators moving into the fashionable and often higher-priced city centre shopping areas. Another is the growing number of consumers willing to buy from mail order and the Internet. The discount threat demands that places decide their markets and themes and work forcefully to maintain them. In New York City the large discounters are buying factories and converting them to stores, placing pricing pressures on department stores and small shops. Countries with many virtual stores, such as Ireland, are selling massive amounts of clothing and computers from call centres and the Internet. In response to the threats, places will have to design their retail stores in such an attractive manner that customers will want to visit the stores and pay for the experience, selection and service. This demand on retail service means more attention to training of personnel, depth and quality of stock, and commitment to the place's image and long-term viability.

A critique of financial incentives

The European recession, the lack of growth, and high unemployment have quite naturally raised the willingness of European places to use financial incentives to attract businesses. Virtually every nation, region and community in Europe is using some sort of financial incentive. It may be large or small incentives: tax exemption, no rent periods, completely free or subsidised workforce training, special electricity discounts, marketing projects paid by the place, free parking space, accelerated depreciation, special tax-free reserves, interest subsidies, and other inducements.

There are no limits for national, regional and local innovation in the incentive area. There are regions where structural challenges and economic crises, combined with a lack of local leadership, have left places bereft of any strong attractions. The only remaining attraction is financial incentives. Some regions in Europe have become '*incentive paradises*'. If these places could generate true attractions, they would have less need for financial incentives.

Europe is not alone in using financial incentives. In the USA, cities and states have been in competition to provide tailor-made packages for various inward investors. BMW and Mercedes were the benefactors of biddings for their plants and found favourable deals in South Carolina and Alabama. Japanese companies also used the bidding wars to their advantage.

Financial incentives offer a temporary advantage, a competitive edge, a kind of 'early bird gets the worm' reasoning. As more nations, regions and communities join the incentives contest, competitive advantages diminish. The question in Europe is, what will happen to financial incentives in the years to come? Several factors are pointing towards a change:

1. Disappointed expectations when bidding wars indicate that financial incentives are not enough.
2. Negative media treatment of the players in the bidding wars. When the Hoover Company moved from Dijon to Glasgow and received a financial package of ECU 10 million, Hoover received bad publicity throughout Europe.
3. A slow shift in EU support and programmes towards Eastern Europe and away from Western Europe. Objective 1 status – the highest category for assistance – will be tightened before the accession of new member states. Certain regions will drop their Objective 1 status: Lisbon, Valencia, Corsica; Valenciennes in France, Sardinia and Puglia in Italy, Hainaut in Belgium, Flevoland in the Netherlands, and the Republic of Ireland.
4. A growing recognition of hard and soft attraction factors other than just financial incentives.
5. The emergence of more professional placemarketing strategies in Europe.

Exhibit 10.3 outlines the pitfalls of incentive offers.

Russian roulette: a guide to incentives

EXHIBIT 10.3

The changing competitive environment adds up to a different future environment for inducements. However, in the short term, places that do not have a straight-up competitive advantage will continue to offer companies incentives to move. There are four major issues for the place-inducers to consider:

1. Always study the company for its ability to sustain and market its products. When the state of Pennsylvania gave up its entire training budget to attract Volkswagen, it was betting on the company's ability to sell its new model, the Rabbit. But sales in the USA bombed and so did the state's massive commitment when Volkswagen pulled out of the plant.
2. The best inducements are aimed at companies that will find similar companies in your area. A large concentration of companies will encourage others to be attracted to the labour pool and the supportive community. The implementation of bio-regions in Germany is a good approach because it encourages a core of companies to establish a beachhead. It also

enables banks and other financial houses to specialise in lending money to these enterprises.

3. A bad environmental product will bring short-term jobs and long-term misery. Places that have attracted chicken plants, for example, frequently find that environmental effects are so devastating that desirable companies are not interested in moving in, and mobile and capable labour will leave.
4. Offering incentives may be a zero-sum game for some places. If an inducement is offered, it needs to be strategic and not merely for the sake of increasing the pot. To high-tech start-up companies, available loans for non-collateral assets are essential. In most cases, without that one piece of financial support, offers of cheap electricity or water are of little value.

In the real world of place attraction, how much you have to give up is generally related to how little you have. A place that wants to compete for targeted industries and services needs to build up its core infrastructure, invest in worker skills, ensure citizen and financial support, and select targets that have a reasonable chance of survival after the year 2000.

Retaining and expanding existing businesses

Most communities and various regional bodies recognise the importance of retaining and expanding their existing businesses. They see this as their first line of defence. They know from today's challenging business environment that local business expansion does not occur automatically. They also know that external businesses might interpret bad performance among existing local businesses as an indication of a poor local business climate and anticipate that taxes will rise to compensate for revenues lost by move-outs or poor performers.

The active retention and expansion of local businesses is obviously a place-marketing act. Retention strategies are usually less manifest and dramatic than attracting external businesses. The strategies are normally more of a 'drip-drip' character, without attracting much local media attention. However, sometimes the retention process can explode and become media driven because of events such as:

- Reduction in the number of production shifts.
- The announcement by an existing company of its decision not to invest in a previously planned project.
- No new employees recruited.
- A business deciding to downsize or restructure.
- The business closing its plant and relocating.

Before such situations occur, many preliminary events take place. Local representatives, if they are alert, can read signs of impending problems. They need to meet these businesses and assist them if possible. Each day a place should be continually place-auditing to monitor existing businesses. The local business climate, constituted by hard and soft factors, must be protected and improved by the place-sellers. Relationship-building is an important element in the process. The main aim is to integrate businesses maximally. The more integrated they are, the less mobile the businesses become. Integration programmes are a tool to encourage existing investors to grow, to reinvest and to create more jobs.

The strategy to integrate existing businesses maximally is probably one of the strongest trends in Europe. It takes place in millions of small day-to-day decisions within the local placemarket and they could be called *integration programmes*. Typical actions include:

- An informal dialogue takes place between a manager of an enterprise and a community representative where the former may complain about local students' language skills. Such dialogue should lead to introducing new or stronger language programmes in the local schools.
- Existing businesses are invited to participate in developing the placemarketing strategies. Participation has two effects: (1) New ideas may emerge, and (2) Participation provides an opportunity to integrate and develop a role and feeling of responsibility.
- The 'keep in touch' dialogue can reveal a need to find appropriate housing for certain categories of existing staff. The community can quickly set up a taskforce to find new attractive land to build on. The quick response would be interpreted positively by the company and its staff. If good housing results, this is of course another positive factor.
- An important company informs the community about some dangerous threats on the horizon, and consequently, the community joins forces with the company to handle the threat. For example, wine producers from Spain, together with their community and regional leaders, are lobbying in Madrid and Brussels for favourable export treatment. Other mutual lobbyists are the many places involved in the European Airbus consortium, and their active promoting of a further commitment to Airbus development.

In spite of close dialogue between existing businesses and a place, a company might decide to close a plant or to relocate. Even here, the place may manage to intervene. For instance, when the giant potato chip producer OLW announced its plans to move out from the small Swedish city of Filipstad with the loss of 120 jobs, a period of intensive lobbying started with the aim of providing an attractive package that OLW could not resist. After a period of negotiation, the city managed to work out an offer that stopped the planned move. The company still resides in Filipstad.

While business retention and expansion strategies offer more potential than conventional business attraction strategies, they also invite abuses. Retention policies and programmes should be compatible with market forces and trends rather than be anti-market or cater to special interests.

Promoting small businesses and fostering new business start-ups

Many European communities run initiatives, plans and programmes to promote small businesses and start-ups. Small and medium-sized enterprises (SMEs) were a priority during the 1990s. On an overall European level, this new focus was visible during the 1997 EU Summit when employment issues were the main theme. The heads of governments expressed deep concern over the weak performance of the European economy and advocated the creation of 12 million new jobs over the next five years. Such a move would decrease unemployment from 11 to 7 per cent. One of the main proposals called for improving the business climate for SMEs and start-ups. Under this plan, costs and administrative burdens must be decreased, risk capital must be easier to find, and taxes and charges of SMEs must decrease. Some places and regions are seriously trying to adopt far-reaching SME measures and start-up programmes.

In 1994 the European Commission produced a number of recommendations to improve the legislative and fiscal environment for SMEs. By highlighting existing *best practices* in the EU, the Commission hoped to inspire member states that were lagging behind. Taxation of SMEs, transfer of enterprises from one generation to the next, and deferred payment in business transactions were some of the recommended tactics. Another SME activity is called the BC Net (Business Co-operation Network) aiming at better collaboration between large and small enterprises. The Commission also assists SMEs through Euro Info Centres, Europartenariat, and Interprise programmes for subcontracting. On top of this there are many regional and local SME initiatives co-financed by the European Regional Development Fund (ERDF). For instance, the German region of Sachsen Anhalt has received ECU 35 million from the EU with the aim to support SMEs. Key measures to increase competitiveness and create jobs are: skills upgrading, technical assistance, quality management, and organisational and personnel management.

All these initiatives can be adopted in various ways at local and regional levels. Every place has its own unique SME and start-up culture. This can be illustrated by the fact that there are now more options available regarding how to approach SMEs and starts-ups. There are ambitious EU programmes, national policies, regional strategies and local plans. Their combination in a local setting is unique. How local strategies are worked out depends greatly on the type of local leadership present in a place. In some of the small villages in Emilia Romagna in northern Italy, SME traditions are extremely strong and can therefore act as the best practice in a wider European context. Since each country or region has its own best practices, other place strategists need to visit those regions to learn possible improvement strategies.

Whether or not a place is actively supportive of new business development can be better assessed by answering the questions developed for places shown in Exhibit 10.4. Anything less than a passing score indicates that a place should reassess its commitment to new business development.

Business climate test: measuring your place's entrepreneurial climate

EXHIBIT 10.4

During the 1990s most places embraced a strategy of promoting SMEs and starts-ups. The following ten questions inspired by *Inc.* magazine provide a rough approximation of where a community stands. With ten points for each favourable answer, a passing grade is sixty points. Places can use the test to measure goals and achievements in new business developments.

1. When local civic leaders meet business leaders, are there as many chief executive officers of SMEs as bankers and corporate executives?
2. Are SME chief executive officers invited to join important events within the community?
3. Do local newspapers follow the fortunes of start-ups and growth of SMEs with the same intensity as they do large corporations?
4. Are innovative SMEs able to recruit nearly all their professional workforce from the local arena?
5. Do SME representatives often refer to easy access of venture capital?
6. Does the local college encourage its teachers and students to participate in entrepreneurial spin-off?
7. Do CEOs from local SMEs hold even one-quarter of the seats on the boards of the three largest banks?
8. Does the city's economic development department spend more time helping local companies grow than it does chasing after branch facilities for out-of-the-region corporations?
9. Is there decent, affordable office and factory space available for businesses in the central business district?
10. Can you think of ten recent spin-offs – SMEs started by entrepreneurs – which have left larger companies?

Source: Inspired by the 'Business Climate Test, *Inc.*, March 1988, p 81. Reprinted with permission, *Inc.* magazine, March 1988. Copyright 1988 by Goldhirsh Groups, Inc., 38 Commercial Wharf, Boston, MA 02110.

Conclusions

The worldwide competition for attracting and retaining business has passed through four phases in European place-development practices.

In the *first phase*, after the Second World War between 1945 and 1960, Europe entered a period of reconstruction. Key concepts were modernisation and expansion within manufacturing industries.

In a *second phase*, starting in the 1970s, sweeping restructuring plans, relocations and plant closures in the European heartland led to a strong public demand for government action. Most demands were directed upwards to governments and relevant departments in national capitals. New compensatory packages were sought. Local attraction strategies were unknown or scarce at that time in Europe. For many places, it was a time of painful economic transition. The microelectronics revolution was felt as well as global competition. Places, in joint effort with governmental incentive packages, rushed in to replace lost jobs and businesses. The priority for solving place dislocations was primarily a national concern and few places looked internationally for solutions.

In a *third phase*, which can be linked to the 1980s, a more complex place strategy developed. Key concepts became new technologies, employee education, intellectual infrastructure, high-tech centres, research parks, and 'Silicon strategies' often inspired by the USA.

A *fourth phase*, Europe in the 1990s was actively attracting international investors to move into all types of niches. Manufacturing was only one place-selling platform. Key concepts were mergers and acquisitions, and expansion and development of the local business climate. Thus, retaining and expanding existing businesses was a top priority. This led to vast experimentation with new programmes. Intensive relationship-building between the community and existing companies was more common. Integration programmes appeared in which existing businesses participated in place actions. Public and private sectors learned from each other. These learning processes included new partnerships, new institutions, and new approaches to carry out multiple, complex place-development activities.

In this multiple and complex place-development climate, financial incentives are one of several hard and soft factors. Bidding wars between places – offering mainly financial incentives – can be counterproductive for the image of the winning place. The real place winners are instead using long-term placemarketing strategies that can add new commercial value to existing businesses as well as to external place-buyers.

At the beginning of the new millennium a *fifth phase* can be identified on the European placemarket. This phase will be dominated by the fact that what has been termed Euroland has grown from a vision into a reality that affects the daily lives of its citizens. Unified Europe, with its European single currency, started with eleven countries with a total population of 300 million and now represents the world's second largest economy. When the remaining four members of the EU join the Euro area, the combined forces will overtake the USA in terms of GDP. This growing confederation, containing comparable prices and a growing number of comparable standards, pushes and inspires European places and regions on a massive scale to offer competitive attractions. Therefore, in the fifth phase, places are professionalising their placemarketing. Reaching a leading *European* place position today is as natural as it was only ten or twenty years ago to reach a leading *national* position. In this competitive marketplace, effective targeting of specific groups can make the difference between winning and losing. Places need to examine their histories, adventures and attractions to package the most compelling message for their market. In Chapter 11 we examine how places can expand their markets through export and foreign investments.

4. What strategies can a place use to enhance the image of its exportable products and to transfer a positive place identification to these products?

How important are exports to a place's economy?

A place without exports is almost unimaginable. Consider a place that grows only apples and consumes all of the apples locally. Such a place needs to import goods that it does not produce: food stocks, computers, automobiles and other products. But then, how is this apple-growing place to pay for the goods it imports? Ultimately, the place would have to develop some exports to pay for its imports.

For most cities, regions and nations in Europe, exports are their lifeblood. The EU is the world's biggest trading power. In 1997, it claimed 19.6 per cent of all world exports.[1] The single market has been estimated to have increased intra-European trade by around 20 per cent.[2] Historically, the living standards in EU nations are closely linked to their export performances. One can identify places where export achievements have been extraordinary and where living standards are extremely high. The challenge in such places is to promote a climate where the existing export-driven companies can flourish.

The benefit that a place gets from foreign trade depends largely on whether its industries are export-oriented or import-competing. Places strong in export-oriented industries – aircraft, business services, lorries, chemicals and computers – benefit through the ripple effects of these exports on local employment and purchasing power. Places strong in import-competing industries – autos, textiles, consumer electronics, metal products and tyres – are likely to be hurt by growing imports. Some places seek to export more (export promotion). Others seek to reduce current imports by producing the same goods and services at home (import substitution).

From an individual place point of view, export and import flows can be dramatically influenced by the European rules on public tender. Public contracting accounts for around 12 per cent of the EU's GDP. In monetary terms, this amounts to ECU 690 billion annually. In the past, the awarding of public contracts was often based on political or economic favouritism. Now, new rules established by the EU on public procurement provide more genuine competition and thereby lowered costs. At least theoretically and irrespective of geography and borders, every place or business in the internal market should have the same chance to export or import. How the public sector in Europe has been further opened for competition by the use of Tender Electronic Daily (TED) is discussed in this chapter's section on brokers.

Some European nations are more export-driven than others. Among the most obvious examples are the Netherlands, Belgium, Denmark and Sweden. But differences are even greater if we study regions and cities. Examples of such places with excellent export performance are Hamburg, Ile de France, Darmstadt, Greater London, Bremen, Oberbayern, Stuttgart, Lombardia, Valle d'Aosta, Groningen and Luxembourg. On a micro level we can find very small communities or even individual villages where export is everything. One such small place is the north Italian community of Agordo with 4,000 citizens, 2,000 of whom are working in 'their' company Luxottica where they produce and ship exclusive glasses – 18 million in 1996 – to the world market.

'*Hot export spots*' where exports are totally dominating a place's economy can be found throughout Europe: the Swedish community of Södertälje with 83,000 inhabitants hosts the huge Scania factory which is a dominant global supplier of heavy trucks. The seldom heard of German city of Herogenauchrach in Bavaria is home for two of the most powerful sporting goods brands in the world: Adidas and Puma. The inhabitants of the small island of Arran off the coast of Scotland have been producing unique jumpers for centuries using wool from their own sheep. From a placemarketing perspective, it is important to note that the jumpers are named after the island.

Developing into a 'hot export spot' is a desirable goal for most places. Higher living standards, low unemployment and a stable tax base are the inevitable rewards.

Assessing a place's export potential

Export promotion begins with identifying who exports and who can potentially export. One tool, *economic base analysis*, measures the relative presence of a particular industry in a place compared with the nation or some other relevant part of Europe. If the *export base ratio* in a place is greater than unity, it suggests that the industry exports its goods or services; a ratio less than unity suggests that the industry's goods or services are partly imported. Thus, if almost 90 per cent of Agordo's workers are in the glass industry, and only 0.5 per cent of Italy's workers are in the glass industry, we can assume that Agordo's glass industry is a major glass exporter. This rough measuring device provides some indication of the export side of a place's economy as well as where it might have a competitive advantage.

The other task is to identify non-exporting companies and industries that have export potential. These companies can offer products or services that would possess some competitive advantage in another market, such as unique features or styling, high quality, high value for the money or brand image strength. Some of these companies start exporting on their own for a variety of reasons: excess capacity, unsolicited orders from abroad, a competitive attack from abroad or the pursuit of production economies of scale. At the same time, some managements hesitate because of perceived high costs, risks or lack of export management know-how. Here place-sellers can play a positive role.

They can help to identify foreign opportunities for companies, assist them in finding distributors or importers, provide export training, and offer export insurance and credit. Such efforts can work as a springboard for both large and small companies to improve their export performance.

Ways to assist companies in promoting exports

Local, regional and national export promotion networks and agencies face a difficult task in both converting non-exporters to exporters and getting current exporters to expand their activities.

Export promotion agencies can play at least ten roles in assisting and stimulating exports. They act as informer, broker, expediter, trainer and counsellor, financier, host, targeter, promoter, facility developer and new technology developer.

Informer

Place developers can systematically provide existing businesses with information about export marketplaces. A network of export-experienced people can be gathered within the place. Such networks are never established by themselves; there must be a place-bound catalyst in the middle. In Europe it may be the chamber of commerce or the economic development unit of the community that acts as a catalyst, at least on the local and regional levels. Where there are stable clusters – consider for example, the shipping clusters of Norway or the textile SME clusters in Italian Tuscany and Umbria – much of the export-related information is distributed within local and complex networks.

Broker

A place can also perform a brokerage function in relation to export promotion. This could involve more specialised services for small exporters as well as larger companies. Brokering may entail finding names of specific contacts, agents, and distributors. A special service such as Tender Electronic Daily (TED) is often appreciated in times when many companies lack competence to understand what is going on in various electronic marketplaces.

The TED is an online service distributing calls for tenders, contract awards and pre-information notices. Approximately 500 European government tender notices are posted each weekday on TED. The tender opportunities originate from local, regional and national public bodies throughout Europe as well as EU institutions. TED contains all tender notices for public procurements and other purchases of the EU above a certain threshold value (more than ECU 200,000 total value of a contract). Notices are also included for other WTO/GATT countries such as Japan, USA, Switzerland and Norway. TED Alert is a service offered whereby search profiles are established for corporations, trade consultants and other subscribers to identify all government tenders relating to individual interests. Each day, TED is queried for matches generated from each profile. These hits are sent to each subscriber via email or fax the same day the government notice is posted on TED. A place looking to be competitive can improve its chances by using a broker to find the best matches. For more on TED see http://www.tenders.com/interest.htm.

Expediter

Export promotion also involves matching local businesses with foreign trade missions and trade shows. A place can invite specific companies to participate, offering, for example, to defray part or all of the costs of travel, displays, interpreters and other required services. During trade shows and trade missions, places have the opportunity to integrate placemarketing messages and business offerings from the same place. Such integration could provide added benefits for all participants. Classic examples are European trade shows where places are organising a total products concept within which various tourist and travel operators participate.

Trainer and counsellor

Places can conduct their own seminars, workshops, conferences and training sessions by working with existing export-driven enterprises, chambers of commerce and independent business experts. Education, training and counselling have all become an integral part of trade promotion services offered by places seeking to promote export growth. The introduction of EMU has increased local and regional efforts to learn more about export markets.

Ireland has turned its counselling expertise into a marketable export. The Irish export *target marketing*: they have advised countries such as Costa Rica, Pakistan, Nigeria and Panama about where and to whom they should sell their products. For example, they suggested that Panama should market food-processing and lower-level electronics to Spain, Italy and France.

Financier

European countries in general, as well as the USA and Asia, have established systems for export loans and guarantees. Export credit has been an important factor in international trade for several years. Export credit agencies, some of which have been in existence for over fifty years, can have a decisive role in export trade. Official support may take the form of 'pure cover' which means giving exporters or lending institutions insurance or guarantees without financing support. It may also be given in the form of 'financing support' which is defined by OECD as including direct credits to the overseas buyer, refinancing and all forms of interest rate support. One of the earliest practitioners of 'pure cover' was France, which offered generous financial packages to support important projects. (Such packages were sometimes coordinated with a presidential visit to other countries.) Today, OECD has worked out certain guidelines for officially supported export credits.

A place needs to have a workable knowledge of the range of financial schemes such as loans, guarantees and insurance. Financial know-how is a valuable competence in the highly competitive placemarket. In some places, a local bank can play a key role providing financial know-how on a specific export market. In the small Norwegian town of Kirkenes, a short distance from the Russian border, the local bank, Den Norske Bank, is playing an active trade and export role.

Host

Being a good host includes attracting foreign business visitors, sponsoring delegations and cultivating partner-city relations. The benefits of the tourism and hospitality business are multiple spillovers into trade and foreign investment as some places seek to convert tourists and guests into traders and investors. Places can actively promote foreign business visits to local trade shows and exhibitions and arrange meetings and contacts with local business counterparts.

Dating from the post-war period, partner-city relationships have expanded from a ceremonial and cultural exchange into place-to-place relationships where formal agreements focus on mutual trade opportunities, tourism, technology transfer, EU projects, education and culture. Partner-city arrangements are also supported by the EU as a method for broader European integration, which has been especially productive for Eastern and Central European communities. For example, the city of Jena (previously in DDR) and Erlangen in Bavaria partnered and as a result Jena has experienced a revival in business development.

One such example is the programme ECOS-Ouverture (External Interregional Co-operation Projects) which aims to improve co-operation with communities outside the EU, focusing on Eastern and Central European places. Such co-operation can open doors for innovative new contacts and business networks.

Targeter

Rather than being all things to all businesses, more and more places are developing lists of target industries and companies to pursue. Depending on organisational structure and resources, targeting can be by geographical area, local clusters of industries and products, and by matching export market opportunities to specific companies and their products. Many European places are promoting local products such as wine (France), whisky (Scottish Highlands), or olives (Spain).

A basic precondition for effective local targeting is that there exists a local placemarketing strategy.

Promoter

While all the above-mentioned activities and programmes involve trade stimulation, places also need an overarching programme for expanding public awareness of export opportunities. Just as some places invest heavily in tourism promotion, that same investment is required to reach broader audiences on trade. Such services include general ads, hot-line services, billboards, videos, Internet services, newsletters and promotional pieces. The marketing aspect of trade promotion is, in many cases, the weak link in export development strategies. Places tend to overinvest in providing services and underinvest in the actual marketing of them.

The accession countries to the EU have been particularly eager in promoting export strategies and at the same time marketing their services to place-buyers. For example, the message from the Hungarian Investment and Trade Development Agency (ITD) is: '*We Make it Our Business to Make Yours Grow in Hungary*.'[3] The Baltic states are also aggressively marketing their trade and export role.

Facility developer

Some places are better positioned for trade than others. They share a border with a co-operative nation or possess a basic international trade base with ports or airfields. Some places have exploited these advantages better than others: Rotterdam, Lille, Tallinn, St Petersburg, Trieste, Barcelona and certain suburbs of London. In some cases, places have managed to simplify customs procedures and to retrain customs staff.

The case of Calais is interesting since there were real fears that with the coming of the Channel Tunnel, many tourists would just bypass Calais on their way to the Côte d'Azur. But a new trade industry has sprung up – the 'duty-free day tripper' (DFDT). For example, to save more than 50 per cent of the UK price, the DFDT's flock to the new boutiques in Calais to stock up on drinks requirements. Another place with high trade ambitions is Gelderland in the Netherlands which is strategically situated between Europe's largest port (Rotterdam) and its largest market (Germany). Europe's main north–south and east–west motorways cross through or close by the region of

Gelderland. To take advantage of this positioning, a billion dollars is being spent on a multimodal transport terminal that will reinforce Gelderland's image as a trade and logistics centre.

In 1997, European airports handled 64 per cent more freight than in 1996.[4] In order to facilitate export, it is of strategic importance for the place to host an air traffic hub. Amsterdam with its huge Schiphol Airport is a classic illustration of how a European hub can improve place competitiveness. Many smaller places are eagerly promoting their regional air hub as a gateway for trade and export.

But it is not sufficient for such trade meccas to offer only ports and airfields. In order to attract buyers, places need an attractive combination of banks, consultants, export expertise, trading companies and support services such as language and intercultural and legal competence.

New technology developer

A place can systematically provide its companies with test grounds for various innovations. Such tests can then develop into important showcases for the export market. Investors and customers are encouraged to visit the pilot place in order to get an on-site and full understanding of the product or service. Pilot projects of this kind have become quite common as a result of the growing complexity of products and services. The pilot approach has developed particularly well. For instance, in 1998, two new railway systems were inaugurated: one between Copenhagen and Kastrup Airport and the other between Oslo and Gardermoen. Adtranz, which produces high-speed trains and other rail-related products, aggressively promotes visits to Gardermoen and Kastrup to witness the crafting of communication solutions. The Adtranz customer magazine resembles a place-marketing pamphlet and could as well be produced by the city of Oslo or Copenhagen. Here place and enterprise are jointly hoping for visits and export opportunities.

Another example is the export promotion which took place in the autumn of 1998 when the French president Jacques Chirac inaugurated the new underground Line 14, the Meteor, in Paris. The new system was promoted as a revolution in urban transport. The Paris transport authority, in its invitation to many of the decision-makers from the world's urban subway community, described the new automatic system as a window on state-of-the-art rail technology with a potential for Berlin, Düsseldorf and Singapore.[5]

Pilot projects are uniting places and enterprises. We have already discussed the Bangemann Challenge in Stockholm where IT businesses are developing new products and services in close contact with the city. Another example is the city of Ennis which in concert with Telecom Éireann is developing new IT solutions designed to be showcased in the international export market. The complexity of IT applications opens opportunities for full-scale pilot projects of this sort in many European cities. This is probably one reason behind the overwhelming response to initiatives such as TeleCities (more than 60 European cities participate) and Infoville.

To stimulate IT applications, the EU offers research programmes as well as integrated regional development programmes. One example of an initiative aimed at the wide use of IT applications is the establishment of the ISAC (Information Society Activity Centre), a joint collaboration between Directorate Generals III and XIII. The centre aims at the establishment of the information society at all levels in society. Within this framework, European places and communities use the large potential of marketing themselves as a pilot region for innovative IT applications. The aim is to promote the best possible preconditions for enterprises and citizens as well as the creation of an image as a forward-looking and export-oriented place. There are a number of locally based network programmes (Exhibit 11.1).

A competitive place service: international trade networking

EXHIBIT 11.1

Networking on the international market can add a highly competitive edge to a place. In this exhibit we show four different approaches with four different actors. In each case, the service is tailored to the problems and the needs of the companies.

1. The World Trade Centre (WTC) in Sophia Antipolis provides sophisticated telecommunication systems, worldwide Internet and direct Internet access. The networking service is linked to more than 300 world trade centres in over 90 countries. Its global network contains more than 500,000 companies. Banking and electronic payments are also part of the service package. Anders Berner, head of the WTC in Sophia Antipolis, believes that the service may be particularly important to SMEs and start-ups in the park. It enables users to exchange and review trade opportunities.[1]
2. The Tyrol region in Austria has managed to attract a number of high-tech industries from Switzerland, Germany and Italy. As an important service the Tech-Tirol Technology Centre provides 'aftercare' (after the introductory investment) support of various types. As a key element the centre offers networking nationally and internationally.[2]
3. Many banks are offering international networks that can be of great value for trade. ING Barings with a strong presence in Eastern Europe offers trade and investment services. ABN Amro, ranked as the number one bank in foreign direct investments, focuses on emerging markets. ABN Amro managed, for example, to work out a US$ 50 million financial package for the renovation of Lithuania's Klaipedo Nafta oil terminal. This project was covered by export credits from the Netherlands, Sweden, Germany and the USA. For Laipeda such an international bank networking was vital for the implementation of the project.[3]
4. Euro Info Centres exist throughout Europe. In 1998 the number of places with a centre had reached 233. The intention is to provide information for SMEs in business matter related to internationalisation, the euro, trade and innovation. The Euro Info Centres form a European Commission network, operating under the auspices

of Directorate General XXIII which co-ordinates, manages and co-finances them. They are active in the field of public procurement, they publish their own news bulletins and many of them have their own Website. In, for example, Glasgow, Scotland, their info centre offers local companies a one-stop shop for European information. On its list of services one finds the following:

- Daily searching of the supplement to the *Official Journal of the European Communities* for public tender opportunities in their specific line of business. During 1998, users of the service in Glasgow won in excess of £50 million of contracts.
- A tailored Alert service specific to local clients' needs, keeping them updated of new and amended guidelines, regulations and legislation as they affect their own business sector.
- Personalised grant searches to identify the European grant schemes best suited to their individual project.
- Access to market intelligence reports from one of the most extensive databases available.
- Seminars for local organisations on bidding for public tenders, preparing for the euro, as well as taking part in local trade fairs, small business shows and exporters' workshops.[4]

A place that can incorporate a networking service into its place structure will have an advantage, especially in the future when access to trade and export intelligence will be even more decisive for a place and its enterprises.

Sources:

1. Interview with Anders Berner, head of World Trade Centre, Sophia Antipolis, 28 October 1998.
2. Tech-Tirol, 'Tyrol – a peak location for business', Advertisement, *Corporate Location*, September/October 1998, p. 84.
3. 'The good bank guide', *Corporate Location*, September/October 1998, pp. 38–39.
4. Interview with Steven Ross, Euro Info Centre in Glasgow, 2 November 1998.

Exploiting the place-of-origin image

If all the brands within a particular product category were perceived by consumers to be equal in quality and price, buyers would probably favour buying the brand that is locally or domestically produced. In this way, consumers would receive faster producer redress if dissatisfied and, at the same time, support local income and jobs. However, different brands in a product category are rarely perceived as delivering equal value. In fact, buyers make distinct brand evaluations based on their image of the place of origin (see Exhibit 11.2).

Swiss knife quality: a launching pad for other products

EXHIBIT 11.2

For less than $30 anyone can buy the Soldier, the original, standard issue Swiss knife manufactured by the Victorinox Cutler Company for the Swiss Army since 1891. The Soldier is one of over 400 different models of almost indestructible pocketknives made by Victorinox and sold throughout the world. Swiss Army knives can be used for a number of different purposes such as sawing wood, trimming fingernails, picking teeth, driving screws and opening cans. The models range from a slim, simple, twin-bladed economy model to the full-featured SwissChamp, an eight-ounce model with thirty-three different functions.

In a typical day close to 70,000 knives are manufactured by Victorinox and Wenger, the two companies with exclusive rights to worldwide production and display of the white cross. Victorinox, Europe's largest knife manufacturer, and Wenger, which exports 30 per cent of its output to the USA, have a product with cult status as heroic knife stories build credibility without the necessity of advertising.

Switzerland, the country of origin, is regarded as a major factor of appeal for this brand. More recently, the strength of the brand's name has spread to the sale of Swiss Army watches, compasses and sunglasses and demonstrates how the knife's image can transfer to other items. All of these products are made in Switzerland. The manufacturer is vigorously prosecuting brand infringements by manufacturers making inferior imitations in other countries. The success of the Swiss Army name in marketing a range of products is owing to the company's ability to manufacture a high quality product that defines its country's image. The 'Swiss made' image is evident in watches, confectionery and machinery, but it is the usefulness and reliability of the Swiss knife that has become the key to promoting other products.

Source: Giles Laffon, 'Copies', *Agence France Presse*, 13 June 1997 (Lexis Nexis); Fleming Meeks, 'Blade Runner', *Forbes*, October 1990, pp. 164–167.

A product's place of origin can have a positive, neutral or negative effect on non-resident as well as resident buyers. Most buyers – at least those interested in fashion – are favourably disposed to clothing bearing the label 'Made in Italy'. The 'Made in England' origin for luxury cars in the USA was a negative image until the recent revival of Jaguar quality. Place-images can sometimes change or develop quickly. Only a few years ago, a product with 'Made in Poland' or some other Eastern European country brought negative quality signals. Today, new images have been created, as illustrated by the growing reputation of Volvo buses from the new Warsaw plant.

Consumers form preferences for products from certain places based partly on personal experience but also through inferences about quality, reliability and service. Johnny Johansson contends that consumers use the 'made in' label as a cue to draw inferences about the product's worth.[6] Thus, buyers assume that a printing press made in Germany is of a higher quality than one made in Bulgaria. Several place-of-origin studies have found the following:[7]

1. The impact of place-of-origin varies with the type of product (for example, car versus oil).

2. In highly industrial countries, consumers tend to rate their domestic goods highly, whereas consumers in the developing countries tend to have a bias against products produced in their own or other developing countries.
3. Certain countries and places have established a generally good reputation regarding certain goods: Milan for fashion, Paris for perfume and fashion, Bavaria for high-quality cars, Parma for dried ham, Belgium for chocolate. This reputation stems not only from a product's characteristics but also from accessibility, history and service reliability.
4. The more favourable a place's image, the more prominently its name should be displayed in promoting the brand.
5. Attitudes towards place of origin can change over time.

What can a place do when its products are competitively equal or superior but its place of origin turns off consumers? The place may resort to co-production or even a joint venture where the product is to be finished at another place that carries a more positive image. Thus South Korea makes a fine leather jacket that it sends to Italy for finishing. The final jacket is then exported with a 'Made in Italy' label and commands a much higher price. In a twist of snobbery, the French icon Chanel bag, coveted by fashion-conscious women, is often manufactured in Italy. It has become commonplace to label certain products from some European places with 'Made in Europe' to take advantage of the goodwill of the European dimension.

Another strategy a place may pursue is to hire a celebrity to endorse the product to overcome consumers' apprehensions. In seeking to introduce athletic footwear to Europe, Nike used America's best-known professional basketball star, Michael Jordan, to attract huge crowds to his performances at Nike's exhibits. Even a visit by Microsoft's Bill Gates can lend instant credibility to a place's stake in the IT arena. A variation of this approach is the iconic political visit. Boris Yeltsin's visits to Western European countries and elsewhere have been conscious steps to build goodwill. Following in his wake are Russian delegates trying to establish new business contacts to attract direct inward investments. Places and their companies often use similar strategies to upgrade their country-of-origin image such as sponsoring art exhibits, artistic tours, sports events and cultural shows.

In *The Competitive Advantage of Nations*, Michael Porter argues that nations succeed in particular industries because their home environment is the most forward-looking, dynamic and challenging.[8] Based on a four-year study of competitive successes in the leading trading nations, Porter found that companies facing tough, effective competition at home are more likely to be successful abroad. Competitive advantages are generated whenever rivals are geographically concentrated and are vying for supremacy in innovation, efficiency and quality. This competition allows places to align a name or region to its products: Italian jewellery companies around the towns of Arezzo and Valenza Po; cutlery companies around Solingen in Germany. Porter's argument accounts for how places' names become associated with consumable products like French wine, Irish whiskey, Danish ham and cheese, German beer, and Russian vodka.

Various consumer groups have their own identification images and preferences. This was clearly illustrated in a survey made by the European Commission in 1996 (Exhibit 11.3).

Place-of-origin images in Europe

EXHIBIT 11.3

The European Commission asked young Europeans to write down the first five things that came to mind when they thought about a particular country. Here are the associations that European youth identified with various countries.

Country	First five images
Belgium	Brussels –Chocolates –Tintin –Beer –Capital of Europe
Denmark	Vikings –Hans Christian Andersen –Copenhagen –Lego –Football
Germany	Beer –Berlin –Motorways –Goethe –Serious
Greece	Islands –Parthenon –Onassis –Socrates –Moussaka
Spain	Barcelona –Bullfighting –Paella –Art –Juan Carlos
France	Paris –Wine – Gérard Depardieu –Food –Fashion
Ireland	Green –The Irish pub –James Joyce –Celtic design –U2
Italy	Rome –Pasta –Art –Shoes –Pavarotti
Luxembourg	Castles –Banks –Small –Court of Justice –The Echternach dancing procession
The Netherlands	Van Gogh –Tulips –Drugs –Amsterdam –Flat
Austria	Vienna –Klimt –Sissi –Skiing –Mozart
Portugal	Port wine –The Cock of Barcelos –Lisbon –Explorers –Algarve
Finland	Lapland –Santa Claus –Forests –Saunas –Telecommunications
Sweden	Blondes –Cold –Nobel Prize –Ingmar Bergman – Pippi Longstocking
United Kingdom	Shakespeare –London –BBC –The Royals –Beatles

Source: *Europe on the Move: Exploring Europe*, European Commission, Brussels, 1996.

It is easy to distinguish the many place-bound links behind the answers in Exhibit 11.3. The list in Exhibit 11.3 reveals important place potentials. Place-marketers can often use such answers to exploit their brand assets, such as Portugal's creating more public access to its waterfront. Once a place's name becomes identified with a product or service category, it can seek to protect the integrity and exclusiveness of the product's benefits through regulatory and legal protections.

An important variation of aligning a place's name with its products involves cross-national ethnic marketing. Owing to historical, cultural and current ties between certain European places and their American counterparts, places target their export promotion and foreign investment strategies to these American places: Ireland to Massachusetts, Germany to Wisconsin, Sweden to Minnesota. Such marketing currently operates in both directions. Ethnic identification with products and place of origin can be a positive force in cross-national sales and marketing also within a growing and multicultural European home market.

Conclusions

Promoting foreign trade and investment has emerged as an important place development strategy that has gained equal footing with business attraction, retention, start-ups and tourism/hospitality activities. Export place development strategies will increasingly require more global thinking and strategic marketing to set apart a place, its people and businesses from other places or regions.

As in other aspects of place development, businesses have responded to globalisation and economic interdependence faster than most public organisations. However, European civic leaders have started to act on the European placemarket as well as overseas. They have become advocates, surrogates and brokers for making places more competitive. The successful place exporter will take advantage of these services and customise them to meet specific needs.

Places can gain an advantage by becoming known as the source of certain high-quality products and services. Many such examples can be identified on the global market and include transport, energy, banking, insurance, and manufacturing of jewelry and watches. Place-bound links are especially common in the food and drinks business. Textiles, music and entertainment are other types of business where fashion may be integrated with a specific place. A place that is able to co-promote its location and exports has the advantage of consumer awareness when the product is on the shelf or in use.

Places can develop into hot export spots where place-buyers and place-sellers have managed, step-by-step, to establish trade excellence. In one case, a small town might be rescued when a company moves successfully into exporting. In another situation, an entire region may become known for a particular product. The rewards for places are considerable but require strong public/private partnerships, cutting of bureaucratic obstacles and a commitment to supporting local companies.

We conclude with a test that places might use to audit how they measure up to the challenge of export promotion (see Exhibit 11.4). With ten points for each favourable answer, a passing grade is sixty points.

A way to measure your place's export climate

EXHIBIT 11.4

1. Can you name your place's leading manufacturing and service industry exporters?

2. Does your local chamber of commerce or similar promoting body offer a programme on export trade for members at least annually?

3. Does your local college or university provide any help to would-be exporters on identifying overseas markets and opportunities?

4. Is your major financial institution familiar with export financing, letters of credit and foreign exchange protections?

5. Does your local economic development agency sponsor trade seminars, trade shows and catalogues or provide marketing assistance?

6. Does your local export development agency or organisation identify, target and contact potential export companies to support trade facilitation?

7. If your place has a partner-city relationship, has it produced any new contacts or business ties between them?

8. Does your mayor or other local officials organise trade missions to visit Europe or to travel overseas to promote contacts and trade?

9. Does your community or place have a well-defined understanding of its local economy as to trade composition or potential?

10. Can you identify any trade facilitation strategies of your business community and/or economic development agency? Does it have a plan?

12

Attracting residents

Places not only try to attract tourists, businesses and investors, but they also undertake to shape a policy towards attracting and keeping residents as part of building a viable community. Places seek to appeal to certain groups and to discourage others. The targeted groups typically include professionals, investors, the wealthy, young families, students, retirees, and workers with special or relevant skills. At the same time, places may try to discourage low-income families, the unemployed, the homeless and certain immigrants. Understandably, efforts to attract certain people and exclude others remain controversial and are not always publicly discussed.

Consider the following facts on the European level:

- 2.9 per cent of all EU citizens are from non-member countries.
- Germany hosts approximately two-thirds of the immigrants in EU countries.
- Of the immigrants to EU countries, 35 per cent are citizens of another EU country.[1]

One basic goal for the EU has been to increase cross-border mobility. This goal creates new opportunities for place-sellers to attract first-rate talent. To provide potential residents with professional services is a growing priority. We can think of this in terms of *residential place strategies* initiated by place-sellers.

As enterprises move across Europe, residential preferences and conditions are becoming vital issues for more and more people. Place-sellers, place-buying companies, and special relocation service companies are all trying to help the residential market to answer questions related to hard and soft factors. The ability to provide quick and relevant answers to such questions is in itself an important attraction factor.

Settling down and building a new life in new surroundings is no easy matter. Each place raises its own set of relocation challenges for the potential resident. Therefore, a well-planned residential place strategy is often welcomed by place-buyers. It gives rise to appreciative comments and good word-of-mouth recommendations, as the buyers may talk of their buying experiences to others. Such information can play a decisive role for other persons considering a residential move.

In discussing resident attraction, this chapter addresses the following:

1. Why has resident attraction become important for placemarketing?
2. Whom do places want to attract and why? Within applicable laws, whom do places wish to encourage to relocate elsewhere?
3. What policies and programmes can places use to attract or discourage certain population segments, and how do they market them?

Why resident attraction is important in placemarketing

Places have always competed for certain people. For instance, Northern Europe actively tried to attract labour from Southern Europe during the 1950s and 1960s when industry was booming in the North. Targets were Italians and Yugoslavs, and they were enticed by a relocation service. At that time the system was based on relatively standardised and primitive mass-service.

Today, the old relocation mass-service has developed into a highly selective service similar to headhunting and management career planning. One can say that headhunting and placehunting go hand in hand. Many fast growing European communities are offering professional relocation services to the target residents and their families.

The free movement of goods and people on the internal market and the opening of new markets in Eastern Europe have led to more intensive competition for talented persons. Local access to intellectual capital represents one of the most important factors in place development. With the fierce competition in the development of sophisticated products and services, the race actually concentrates on the quality of the labour force. To attract people is therefore a strategic place investment.

A world problem: competing for talent and identity

Places should be concerned with their population size and composition. Losing population can be a serious economic threat. Not only is the tax base of the place eroded, but an annual drop in population quickly creates a negative image. Therefore, a high priority for a place should be maintaining or increasing the current number of citizens. Nations and places are positioning themselves strategically on their ability to attract talented people.

On the world placemarket, Europe is competing with thousands of places, regions and nations on other continents. For instance, Singapore aims to be the '*Brain Capital of Southeast Asia*'. It advertises around the world to attract professionals. The objective is to cement Singapore's future as an exporter of expensive services to the rest of Asia.

Europe is not homogeneous in terms of population. While some places are struggling with congestion owing to a serious lack of land, other places are confronted with growth restrictions owing to a low population density. In the latter case, existing infrastructure investments are not used enough, and the local market may be too small to attract place-buyers. European differences are revealed in Table 12.1.

Table 12.1 ◆ Europe's heterogeneous population map (people per km²)

Low density (0–49)		*Medium density (50–99)*		*High density (100–149)*		*Very high density (150 and above)*	
Iceland	3	Belarus	50	France	106	Luxembourg	154
Russia	9	Ireland	51	Portugal	107	Switzerland	167
Norway	13	Lithuania	58	Slovakia	108	Italy	190
Finland	15	Macedonia	75	Hungary	113	Germany	228
Sweden	19	Turkey	76	Albania	118	UK	237
Estonia	35	Bulgaria	77	Armenia	121	Belgium	328
Latvia	42	Spain	77	Denmark	121	Netherlands	371
		Greece	79	Poland	123		
		Croatia	85	Moldova	131		
		Ukraine	87	Czech Republic	133		
		Austria	95				
		Romania	99				
		Slovenia	99				

Source: 'OECD in Figures', *OECD Observer*, Paris, June/July 1996, pp. 6–7; European Bank for Reconstruction and Development, *Transition Report 1996*, EBRD, London, pp. 185–209.

Europe's population is distributed unevenly. Low density is a typical Northern European phenomenon. Several Eastern European countries, now opening for cross-border mobility, have a medium density with huge areas and too few residents. Nearly one-third of the EU population is crowded into regions with 500 or more inhabitants per square kilometre. Irrespective of current density figures, all European countries are marketing their attractions to skilled professionals.

Low or medium density places can easily be hurt in periods of recession or structural change. During the recent recession in Europe, many small and rural areas were severely hurt. In Finland several communities in the east and north have lost population in unprecedented numbers as residents, especially the younger generations, have moved out. The result is that community viability is threatened. In spite of higher living costs in the larger cities of the south and west, people leave because jobs are scarce, and prospects in the place are bleak.

The surprising fact is that so few places really try to work out proactive residential place strategies to combat depopulation trends.

Resident attraction approaches

Every place wants to boast of a high inflow of professionals, managers, technicians, senior officials, administrators and connected families. Parallels can be drawn between marketing to attract direct foreign investment and marketing to attract new residents. Integrated approaches, where business and person attractions are mixed together in the same message, are common. This is how such integration is promoted by the placemarketing agency Copenhagen Capacity: 'Add to that low corporate tax rates, expatriate tax breaks, a well-educated workforce and 75 per cent fluency in English, and you start to understand why more and more international corporations call Denmark their home'.[2] Thus, residential offerings, i.e. expatriate tax breaks and fluency in English are integrated into the overall place-selling package.

In the battle for talented persons, places try a number of appeals. *First*, places can market their own unique access to talented people. One illustration is Northern Ireland's claim: 'Interviewing IT literate graduates takes a little longer in Northern Ireland. Universities in Northern Ireland are turning out 600 IT literate graduates every year, so take your pick'.[3] This type of theme has become very popular throughout Europe and companies are increasingly selecting well-trained workers over other factors. John Ritchinson, CEO of the American Delco–Remis Portuguese plant, a manufacturer of electronics components for vehicles, in discussing the company's decision to build a plant in Portugal: 'We chose Portugal after scanning nineteen different European sites. Access to a qualified workforce was decisive. Our staff is young, energetic and eager to learn. Average age is only 27 and they are very adaptive to new ideas'.[4]

Second, places can offer target packages directed towards targeted people and their families. Such packages can include various mixes of hard and soft factors (see Figure 12.1). At one extreme, a place may offer very hard factors: no taxes. At the other extreme, a place may emphasise soft factors: a lifestyle.

Third, a place can offer different levels of relocation services. Sometimes the service is organised and offered exclusively by a public place-selling agency. On the other hand, it may be organised independently via a private company or with a certain alliance to a public agency. A typical private example is shown in Figure 12.2.

Come to where the quality of life still counts and residential entry in simple. Free property pack available.

29 High Street,
St Peter Port, Guernsey.
Tel: +44 1481 713463
Fax: +44 1481 700 337

MARTEL MAIDES

Example one: no taxes!

SWITZERLAND - VERBIER

Residences Palasui & Ivouette
Outstanding apartments of immense charm & character

A unique residential development of two chalets situated in the heart of Verbier, with unsurpassed sunny views and within easy walking distance of the resort's cable car and amenities. Built with your every need in mind the apartments have living areas from 138m2 finished to the very **highest Swiss standards** and comprise of 3 to 4 bedroom suites, spacious living rooms, generous terraces and parking for 2 cars in the basement garage.
PRICES FROM SWISS FRANCS 1,290,000

DAVID DE LARA & PARTNERS
The Swiss Property Specialists
TEL: UK 018-742 0708 FAX: UK 0181-742 0708

Example two: charm and character!

Sources: The European, 27 November–3 December 1997, p. 54; *Financial Times*, Residential property, January 1997.

Fig 12.1 ◆ Two very specific target packages attracting certain people

PME Sarl

Personnel Management Excellence
A Global Relocation Partnership Company

International Relocation Management

Career Transition

A Global Partnership

The partnership covers 56 countries throughout Europe, Australasia, The Americas, Africa and the Middle East.

Your answer to an International Move

A Local Presence

5, chemin Malombré - C.P. 2 - 1211 Genève 12
Tél. (022) 346 74 84 - Fax (022) 346 76 15

For further information please contact:
Anne-Claude Beaumont

Source: Newsweek, 1 May 1995.

Fig 12.2 ◆ A private relocation service

Relocation services will increase in importance in Europe and will be an integral part of other place attraction programmes, but there is no single model for organising the service.

Defining the population groups to attract

Places vary in the target groups they can and choose to attract. In some cases they may reach out for the growing retirees market; more common is for places to seek skilled professional and high-income earners. Lately, students have become another target group. Here we examine efforts to attract skilled professionals and certain lifestyle groups.

Targeting skilled professionals

A precondition for world-class production and services is the availability of skilled professionals. A place seeking excellence must therefore provide a maximum of attractions for this target group.

The following attractions will make a place desirable to this group: reasonable local taxes, attractive housing options, high educational quality, access to daycare centres, competitive social security costs and conditions, a positive attitude to newcomers, and relocation services that include efforts to find job opportunities for family partners. This last type of service is often neglected. Since in most families today both adults are working, an unhappy partner could discourage the move. Many places also worry that the 'brain drain' will counter efforts to attract talent (see Exhibit 12.1).

Reversing the brain drain

EXHIBIT 12.1

A raging controversy in Europe revolves around the battle for highly skilled workers. The term 'brain drain' suggests a place being sucked dry of its most talented and able people. The problem is severe in information and science technologies, but even in occupations such as chefs there are shortages. Consider these facts:

- Britain claims an erosion of talent to Eastern European countries – the 'Wild East' phenomenon – which offers upward mobility because of escalating salaries and promising business opportunities. The British IT industry, according to the European InformationTechnology Observatory, needs an additional 50,000 skilled workers to prevent a downturn in British industry performance.[1]
- France is irritated that Britain is draining away its talent pool. Professor Charles Morrison of the University of Paris claims that fleeing talent is the result of problems with high taxes, political disenchantment, increased unemployment, and 'a society of protected privileges, from which the young are excluded'.[2] The situation is so grave that Morrison compares it to the great talent

uprooting during the French Revolution of 1789.

- The USA, a big-time net talent importer, has now acknowledged an emerging brain drain and is asking for a change in immigration policies to facilitate more IT and science talent.

A worldwide battle for talent is on and the most gifted and mobile are looking for the best deals. A British MBA graduate looking for employment in the Eastern Bloc, Jeremy Moore, expressed the competition succinctly, 'I don't want to be Czech, I just want to do business'.[3]

In such a competitive environment for talent, what can a place do to plug the drain? There are places that are successfully addressing market needs and finding solutions. Sophia Antipolis is attracting large numbers of US companies because of its skilled, competitively priced workforce, international environment, wide-open spaces and sun. Science parks like Sophia Antipolis offer companies ready-made technical communities and make the new captures comfortable in moving to another country.[4] Ireland has reversed its brain drain through serious economic reform and by actively campaigning to convince young talented emigrants to return. During the Christmas holidays of 1996, Irish employers mounted a recruitment campaign to lure homecoming emigrants to stay.[5]

The irony of the brain drain situation is that the EU has 17.5 million unemployed people. The Semiconductor Equipment and Materials International (SEMI) has launched what it calls a 'skilled technology workforce' initiative[6] in collaboration with eight other trade associations. Its purpose is to match available jobs with the labour pool. In doing so, it is committed to convincing workers to pursue careers in areas that are in short supply of talented labour.

There is no sure cure for brain drain. In a fast-moving economy, places need to find ways that ensure incentives for attracting and maintaining a talented workforce.

Sources:

1. Paul Gosling, 'Bean counters make way for button pushers', *The Independent*, 19 March 1998, p. F6.
2. Ben Macintyre, 'Flight of young as Britain lures French talent', *The Times*, 20 May 1998 (Lexis Nexis).
3. Rosemary Behan, 'Big salaries prompt new brain drain to East Bloc', *Daily Telegraph*, 3 August 1998, p. 5.
4. Allan Tillier, 'Forget Silicon Valley, try the low-cost south of France', *The European*, 10 August 1998 (Lexis Nexis).
5. Brendan Walsh, 'Celtic Tiger: Ireland's economic boom is reversing a brain drain and bringing its education home', *The Gazette*, (Montreal), 18 August 1997 p. B3.
6. 'Europe high-tech industry faces skilled shortage crisis', *Agence France Presse*, 31 March 1998 (Lexis Nexis).

The increasing number of expatriates in Europe makes up one special target group. Since places want to attract expatriates, a number of place-bound personal tax concessions are offered by such countries as Belgium, Denmark, France, the Netherlands, Spain, Switzerland and the UK. These concessions are applicable only under certain conditions, such as a required length of stay in the country. This development has taken place in spite of efforts to harmonise the general tax levels in Europe, which vary considerably. Among the lowest are taxes in the UK and Portugal (40 per cent), while rates elsewhere can reach 60–65 per cent. The American Chamber of Commerce (ACC) in Germany conducted a study that argued that multinational companies are handicapped in retaining key staff because of stock options being aggressively taxed. Kim Eger, a manager at ACC, said of the problem, 'When executives face tax rates of up to 60 per cent on options, there is a strong incentive not to be located in Germany'.[5] Local and regional taxes also differ considerably and can become a major bargaining chip for retention of companies. While taxes are often a primary factor in moving situations, many smaller factors such as conditions at the airport can influence newcomers (Exhibit 12.2).

First impressions: taxis in Stockholm, paint jobs in Portugal

EXHIBIT 12.2

The critical first impressions of a visitor are often permanently etched by the experience at the airport. A negative occurrence can taint an otherwise beautifully constructed visit. The taxi service at Arlanda Airport in Stockholm gave new meaning to the term free market. Any unaware visitor found a long queue of taxis seemingly stretching a city block. Many drivers had different prices as the rules allowed for renegade taxis to charge what they could extract from exhausted and confused travellers. Customers often arrived at their destinations and were greeted with the rude jolt of paying as much as $150 for a ride to central Stockholm. No one would concoct such a devilish arrival unless the tourism and convention needs were not as important as political infighting. When asked of the problem at the airport, Swedish officials looked blankly and blamed the free market. Finally, after a protracted consumer revolt, the drivers' rates were standardised at a modest $40 and Stockholm was saved from travellers' ire.

Consider the conditions for arriving visitors at Lisbon airport in Portugal. After a long overnight flight, the visitor was herded into an institutional-looking, high ceilinged hall for entry. The walls were painted in drab colours and were devoid of pictures or posters. The signs were not welcoming, but terse and unclear, as they ordered people into lines. When asked about the problem, an airport official saw little wrong in it and questioned why they should fix the current airport since they would build a new one in ten years' time. Besides, he told the American visitor, 'Things are as bad at Kennedy Airport in New York City'. Stockholm needed a one-price plan and got it; Lisbon needed a renegade painter with 100 gallons of paint.

Place-buyers' children are often an important consideration within the family. Therefore, place-buyers rank the local availability of top quality schools very high. This is one reason why so many local and regional schools are vying to develop better images. The number of international schools in Europe is increasing, and a place with an international school has a distinct advantage. Table 12.2 indicates the number of international schools in different European countries. Many new schools are now in the planning stage.

Several places have established the International Baccalaureate (IB) in order to provide a competitive curriculum at the upper secondary level. The founders of the IB were convinced that students needed much more international experience to meet international challenges. In an international community, it is also necessary to have standardised examinations that have worldwide acceptability. Today, 660 schools in over 80 countries have received accreditation to participate in the programme headquartered in Geneva.

A place must also have a good reputation for educational networks, competences and educational mobility. The Erasmus programme (European Community Actions Scheme for the Mobility of University Students) ensures the ability of students to study across linguistic and pedagogical frontiers with full

Table 12.2 ◆ An important place selling factor: number of international schools

Country	*No. of schools*	*Country*	*No. of schools*
Albania	1	Luxembourg	2
Austria	5	Netherlands	22
Belgium	12	Norway	6
Bulgaria	1	Poland	3
Croatia	1	Portugal	12
Czech Republic	2	Romania	1
Denmark	5	Russia	3
Finland	4	Serbia	1
France	18	Slovakia	1
Germany	15	Slovenia	1
Greece	8	Spain	41
Hungary	3	Sweden	6
Ireland	4	Switzerland	35
Italy	28	Turkey	15
Latvia	1	UK	26
Lithuania	1		

Source: Ernst & Young, *Regions of the New Europe*, London, 1995, p. 96. The international schools in the table are only those which are members of the European Council of International Schools.

equivalency for the credits they may earn in foreign institutions. Other programmes include Tempus (TransEuropean Mobility Programme for University Studies) and TEXT (Trans-Europe Exchange and Transfer Consortium), and COMETT (European Community Programme on Co-operation between Universities and Industry regarding Training in the Field of Technology). Exploiting such possibilities can lead to increasing a place's profile with education-seeking target markets.

Targeting life-style groups

In the Information Age, people have more ability to choose where they want to live. As Peter Drucker observed, 'It is now infinitely easier, cheaper and faster to do what the 19th century could not do: move information, and with it office work, to where the people are'.[6]

In his book *Life Style: Your Surroundings and How They Affect You*, Peter Marsh concludes that in today's large-scale societies, to a great extent '*you are where you live*'.[7] Our place, housing, furnishings and possessions communicate our identity and reflect our values and ideals. This is, according to Marsh, particularly important in large-scale, fluid societies where it is more difficult to categorise individuals reliably in terms of accent and clothes; their neighbourhood then becomes an important clue to what they are like.

Based on an understanding of lifestyles, a place must learn how to market itself to various individual lifestyle segments. Demographics and lifestyle proliferation have led to an entire language characterising attitudes and behaviours. What was a *hippie* culture – often with a rural and idealistic set of preferences – in the 1960s and 1970s, turned into a yuppie culture (young urban professionals) in the 1980s. The *yuppies* had a strong residential preference for city life. Small cities and towns were certainly not on the shopping list. *Dinks* are the family version of yuppies (dual income, no kids), who, when they have children, become *dewks* (double earners with kids).[8] More lately, the *puppies* – poor urban professionals – have entered the picture during the European recession in the beginning of the 1990s. According to the Popcorn Report,[9] we can define another powerful lifestyle group: the *woofs* (well-off older folks). These middle-aged and wealthy people, born in the boom of the 1940s and drastically increasing in number, can be a highly attractive target group for many places.

Another issue involves the impact of information technologies on lifestyles. Futurists ponder on a world consisting of an officeless city where more people are employed at home as independent contractors or teleworkers. The exodus from cities to suburbs as places of residence and work is a phenomenon in most European cities and regions. The marketing challenge for large cities is how to slow the exodus and retain certain segments of urban dwellers. In addition, large cities seek to capture a share of the city-to-city migration of professionals and bring certain suburbanites back into the city.

Places must adapt to a Europe of movers. While in the past, migration tended to result in rural depopulation, more recent evidence indicates a more complicated pattern.[10] Young people entering the labour market tend to migrate from rural areas to regions with more dynamic labour markets and cultural life. For those same people at around 30 years of age, there is some reverse migration to native regions. This could give a place – even a remote one – opportunities if there is a strategy to provide specific target packages.

Placemarketers must constantly segment markets according to consumer attitudes, behaviour and lifestyles. Changes in attitudes must also be monitored. Here are some examples:

- A drift back to France is reported in 1997 where a weak property market had attracted many British place-buyers. (*Interest in business.*)
- The European attraction to gardening increased buying and moving to places where there was a garden tradition. (*Interest in gardening.*)
- The massive European golf interest pushed places and huge regions to exploit special offerings where golf and residential attractions are com-

bined. A Spanish region traditionally called the Costa del Sol now markets golf and residential packages to such an extent that one talks in terms of a 'Costa del Golf'. (*Interest in golf.*)

- New towns in Cumbernauld, East Kilbride, Glenrothes, Irvine and Livingston in Scotland were successfully built with a clear target group: people formerly living in overcrowded inner-city tenements. Today, these places are marketed by Scotland's Foreign and Commonwealth Office. (*Interest in quality of life.*)
- The trend towards 'village life in the heart of the big city' is meeting the needs of many young urban professionals. But there are also many older, empty nesters ('woofs'), wanting to combine city living with some of the best aspects of village life. (*Interest in inner city life.*)
- Many professionals are looking for residential solutions which can combine a central European position and at the same time provide all necessary family conveniences. For example, Düsseldorf offers a selection of international educational institutes with five foreign schools, a shopping location of first-class standard, 2,000 restaurants and pubs, and residential offerings close to the World Trade Centre.[11] (*Interest in convenient family life.*)
- The British government's attempt to rebrand the country's image with the slogan 'Cool Britannia'. (*Interest in popular culture.*)

Conclusions

On the world placemarket there is a silent war to attract professionals of all sorts. Europe is part of this global competition, where thousands of overseas places, regions, nations and continents are trying to promise residential paradise. The stakes are enormous as the future of community development rests on the ability to target and attract workers who can staff industries and provide vital services.

People attraction is likely to become an even more important component in place competition in the years ahead. Yet, unfortunately in practice, a systematic approach is generally lacking among European placemarketers. To be a winner in this competition place-sellers need to understand the underlying dynamics and lifestyles present on the residential market.

13

Organising for change

In this book, we have argued that many European places – cities, communities, regions and entire nations – are facing growing crises. As people and businesses become more mobile, they will move towards attractive places and evacuate unattractive places. The shrinking of time and distance in the global marketplace means that developments in other parts of the world can impact the fortunes of a place once thought to be competitive. This raises fundamental questions about what places can do not only to survive, but also to prosper.

Places must routinely reassess whether they are meeting the needs of their citizens and businesses. Each place must be continually involved in a value-added process. What benefits and attractions need to be added? How is the place helping local citizens and businesses find and create new value? Is the place providing distinctive benefits compared with other places?

Places have to visualise clearly the roles they play in the local, national and global economy. They have to answer: who will want to live and work here, under what conditions, and with what expectations? A place that fails to examine critically its prospects and potential is likely to lose out to more attractive competitors.

In this last chapter, we summarise the key challenges facing places and suggest ways in which they might meet these challenges. We specifically address three issues:

1. What key challenges are places facing?
2. How can places respond positively to these challenges?
3. Why is market-oriented planning necessary?

What key challenges are places facing?

European places face four major challenges.

Challenge one: *Places are increasingly at risk as a result of the accelerating pace of change in the global economic, political, and technological environment.* There was a time when place residents expected their city, community or region to maintain a permanent business and industrial character. Tomorrow would be much like today. Hamburg would remain a European centre for civil aviation engineering, Strasbourg a European meeting place, Clermont-Ferrand in the French region of Auvergne a centre for European vehicle tyre production. Today, however, place residents have learned that change, not stability, is the only constant. As a result, Hamburg, Strasbourg and Clermont-Ferrand are in a constant battle to protect their heritages.

The fact is that locations of global industries, as well as important institutions, keep shifting. Mobile companies are drawn to places with lower costs, better skills and a higher quality of life. Western Europe is now feeling pressure as investments in Eastern and Central Europe grow. Poland, Hungary, the Czech Republic and Estonia represent a new European investment market. Many others are lining up: Slovenia, Romania, Bulgaria, Slovakia, Croatia, Lithuania and Latvia. Privatisation has moved quickly in some of these countries, and this new network has welcomed strategic investors. The former communist countries are experiencing new life from an inflow of greenfield investments. In Hungary, for instance, General Motors, Ford, Suzuki and Audi have established motor plants. More will certainly come as the European map is redrawn.

Local companies may move elsewhere not only when they are searching for lower costs and higher productivity but also when they are outperformed in their local area. Companies that once had assured markets now face tough competition from invading multinational organisations which possess greater resources and offer better products at lower prices.

The heightened mobility of industry is due largely to dynamic advances in information systems; these, in turn, have facilitated the movement of goods, services, technology and capital across European borders. The result has been a dramatic weakening of time and distance barriers. Places can no longer expect to retain all of their major industries and businesses. They must be ready to abandon shrinking or non-competitive ones and replace them with new and more productive businesses. When places suddenly discover that there is no way to rejuvenate old steelworks or shipyards, the impact can be traumatic. They must take action before it is too late *and* develop new strengths in advance of reversals.

In the old economy, goods were produced in certain places that enjoyed least-cost advantages. They had distinctive national and often even specific place identities. In the new, complex economy, goods can be produced in several locations and then assembled in even more places. Robert Reich observed: Precision ice hockey equipment is designed in Sweden, financed in Canada, manufactured out of alloys whose molecular structure was researched and patented in Delaware and fabricated in Japan, and assembled in Cleveland and Denmark for distribution in North America and Europe.[1]

In these complex production links, the main owner of the ice hockey brand has the potential to co-brand to one of several places. As Rolex of Geneva has accomplished successfully with watches, the ice hockey brand can link to a place with a natural sports image.

While processing, interpreting and analysing the information in other places, service producers can also draw information from multiple places and disseminate the information to still other places. Before closing time on any day, the Anderson & Lembke advertising agency in Amsterdam transfers the day's information to its New York offices so that work may be continued. The initial trend was for corporations to move their back-office operations from cities to suburbs. In the next trend, they moved these offices to low-cost regions. Many of these regions have managed to provide high productivity and even world-class excellence in their new niche. Clusters of back-office companies have settled in certain peripheral parts of Europe and given these places a new industry and a new image. An increasing number of large companies are outsourcing their information systems to capture value from specialised firms and technologies. This move opens additional opportunities for places with excellent service clusters.

Places are further influenced by significant political developments. The end of the cold war means that hundreds of defence-dependent places, with military bases or heavy defence production, have to develop new strategies and programmes to soften the impact of a shrinking industry. Since 1984, 600,000 skilled jobs have been lost in the defence sector, and employment in the industry has fallen by 37 per cent within the EU.[2] In order to accelerate the diversification of economic activities in places dependent on the defence sector, EU has initiated the Konver Programme. Since the intent is to shift the military industry in a civilian direction, here again strategic placemarketing is essential and new niches must be developed.

The fundamental point is that external forces change rapidly and often unexpectedly and therefore transform the fate and fortunes of places. Industry cycles, trade policies and fluctuating national currencies add to these uncertainties.

Challenge two: *Places are increasingly at risk as a result of the inevitable process of urban evolution and decay*. Most places started off as rural agricultural communities, became towns, and then grew into cities and metropolitan areas. In the modern period, cities transformed from trade centres to industrial centres and then to service producers. As problems within the city expand – pollution, crime, congestion, traffic gridlock, poor schools and services, higher taxes and unemployment – movement to the suburbs increases. However, as a result of ambitious public and private urban redesign projects, more recent trends in Europe suggest a return to the inner cities.

Meanwhile, metropolitan growth continues from inner-ring suburbs to outer-ring exurbs. Factories and offices move further out, and soon clean, well functioning 'edge cities' emerge around the core city. In many cases, such edge cities have begun forming their own urban identity.

A century ago, major technological changes occurred that transformed and benefited urban growth: electricity, the internal combustion engine, subways, indoor plumbing and sanitation systems, elevators and steel structured buildings. Today, new technologies have emerged that allow economic activity to occur almost anywhere: satellite communications, fibre optics, mobile phones, the Internet and microcomputers. Several of the European places that adopted these technological breakthroughs early on have managed to turn the challenge into a competitive edge.

Challenge three: *Places are facing a growing number of competitors in their efforts to attract scarce resources.* In the face of mounting problems, places have responded by establishing specialised economic development agencies – planning, financing, marketing, tourism, exports – all related to place improvement. At least one thousand regional and national agencies operate in Europe today. Nobody has managed to calculate exactly how many there are at the local community level. As a rule, however, one can safely say that there is at least some rudimentary organisation within most communities. These agencies and units spend public funds for advertising and send salespeople on missions at home and abroad to attract resources to their area. But other places, as they soon discover, are matching or exceeding their own efforts and level of sophistication. The stark reality is that there is a superabundance of place-sellers hunting for a limited number of place-buyers.

Place-buyers have access to a growing amount of information about places, including place-ratings, real estate interests, consultants, and new software technologies that provide highly sophisticated and usable data. They make careful comparisons of what each place-seller offers in the way of costs of doing business, inducements, and quality-of-life benefits. Place-buyers may end up demanding such high concessions from a place that what appears to be a final winner may in fact turn out to be a loser. Place-inducement battles occur on all continents. In Europe, such battles have exploded as one of the consequences of the internal market. The free movement of goods, capital and persons throughout Europe was the main issue covered in the influential book by Paolo Cecchini, *The European Challenge 1992 – The Benefits of a Single Market*,[3] and we are now seeing how places respond to a competitive marketplace.

Places have to rethink the premises upon which they base their future. More importantly, they have to learn more about targeting customers if they are to be successful in attracting and retaining businesses and people, exporting their products, and promoting tourism and investments. Every place must recognise the nature of a free market rivalry and hone its skills as a competitor.

To win, places must respond to change rather than resist; adapt to rather than ignore market forces. This is not an easy task for community organisations which, traditionally in Europe, have very little experience with market orientation, investment climate and business life in general. In many cases the local public sector tends to live a separate life from the private sector. This is often considered to be the classic European situation.

Challenge four: *Places have to rely increasingly on their own local resources to face growing competition.* Current trends and forces pull businesses, much like nations, in two directions simultaneously. '*Think globally – act locally*' represents the new paradigm in which businesses must practise and apply globalism in outlook and operation, and localism in business practices and market differences. European nations are pulled together by the imperatives of trading blocs and the need for common rules, but they are pulled apart by inward pressures and provincial needs. Places also encounter the full force of these centripetal and centrifugal forces from business and higher government levels that end up producing a reversal of the preceding maxim: 'Think locally – act globally'. The place paradigm requires first an understanding of what a place has or can have that someone else needs or wants, and second a translation of these advantages to broader selected audiences.

Because many European governments are preoccupied with a huge debt burden – which cannot be increased because of EMU rules and many other reasons – they are less able than in previous decades to provide substantial direct aid to local communities. Even if such resources existed, the ability of national government and other central bodies to target and tailor specific resources to meet individual place needs is fraught with distribution and equity considerations. Furthermore, since all business originates in a specific place, it is impossible to grasp such combinations from a central position outside the relevant place. Business intelligence can be generated on a global level, but its commercial exploitation is always made locally. How a place meets these global opportunities can be called the 'business intelligence' of a place.

How must places respond to these challenges?

We have seen how places can be transformed: the German Ruhr from heavy industry to light industry and a positive development of the service sector; Wales from coal and steel to an electronics industry and even film industry; Provence–Alpes–Côte d'Azur from a one-sided dependence on tourism to a broadened industrial base with a high-technology sector. Such European lessons are quickly disseminated and serve to substantiate the fact that places can deliberately affect their mix of business.

A place's condition need not be hopeless; all places have some actual or potential resources to exploit. To turn fortunes around, places must think longer term and choose their short-term actions to deliver their long-range perspective.

To assist European place development in the years ahead, we propose the following ten responses that constitute a framework for navigating place development in the twenty-first century.

Response one: *Places need to establish a strategic vision to face these challenges.* Few places today can articulate a strategic vision of what they are aiming to be in the next ten or twenty years. All of the 100,000 or more communities in Europe want prosperous industries, rising real incomes and a better quality of life. But this is a wish or hope, not a vision. A vision must define a realistic picture of what they can become in the next decade and beyond as a place to live, work and play. A vision goes beyond simply targeting specific businesses that the public would like to see locate in a place. On the other hand, a strategic vision should not be so general that it fails to create a precise goal around which people can organise. The articulation of the vision should be localised to the specific place. If most other European places can identify with the same vision, it is in some ways meaningless for the specific place, even if it 'sounds good'. Exhibit 13.1 is an example of a carefully crafted vision.

The Grenland case: a balanced vision

EXHIBIT 13.1

The Grenland region, south west of Oslo, is the busiest industrial area in Norway. The area is often referred to as '*Norway in Miniature*'. Four communities comprising 100,000 citizens make up the Grenland region. Grenland's vision for the next 5–10 years encompasses these concepts:

1. Grenland will develop into an *innovation centre* in Norway.
2. It will be a *Norwegian gateway to Europe.* Grenland has the ambition to enter the twenty-first century as an integrated transport and trans-shipment hub for the whole of southern and western Norway.
3. Grenland should have an *employment situation* that is above the national average.
4. The *educational standard* should be at least the same as that of the rest of the nation.

This vision for Grenland is straightforward, readily understandable, and, most importantly, well balanced between too detailed an approach and the obvious risk of being too general. The vision is also broken down into a number of strategies and there are specific resources earmarked to implement the vision. The region has established an operative body, the Vekst i Grenland A/S Growth in Grenland Ltd to fulfil the plan. All these elements combine to ensure that the vision is a serious effort.

Sources: 'Grenland, Nyskapningssenteret i Norge og landets brohode mot Europe', Vekst i Grenland A/S, 1996; *Introducing the Grenland Region: A Great Place to Do Business*, Vekst i Grenland A/S, 1996–1997 Handbook, pp. 1–12.

Response two: *Places need to establish a market-oriented strategic planning process to face these challenges.* All places engage in some form of planning whether driven by fiscal, physical or social needs. Some places suffer from too many plans and planning groups. Overplanning can occur when planning replaces leadership. So long as 'plans are being made', some organisations can avoid dealing with real problems and conflicts of implementation, and consequently never become fully and effectively market-oriented.

Fundamental differences exist between the public and the private sectors in their relation to resource allocation. Most public organisations get their resources via complex budget processes with little or no direct dialogue with customers. Businesses, on the other hand, are influenced by their customers every day. Elected public officials receive their customers' opinions every third or fourth year, and in many cases these opinions emanate from organised groups with specific interests. These characteristics of public organisations can work against long-term planning and a broader place perspective.

Consequently, in a place's desperation to find planning answers, various quick-fixes emerge to span a short-term planning horizon and placate various interest groups. The most common ones are business attractions such as a new plant; major capital projects from sports stadiums to convention centres; a new tourist attraction such as a festival market; reorientation of retail operations into a mall; or casino gambling or theme parks. Often such projects are initiated by certain interest groups, a developer, an entrepreneur or a potential place-buyer. When the prospect of lost opportunities is felt, it is tempting to take immediate action.

These initiatives have the virtue of appearing to address one or more problems. They often deliver symbolic comfort to the citizens that specific action is being taken to secure a better future. After all, the message of immediate jobs is far more persuasive than the message of receiving durable or higher paying jobs in the future. Yet, many such actions turn out to be white elephants. More often than not, they fail to meet most tests of a viable plan for improving the community. Often such stop-gap measures offer a vague hope for triggering a host of other improvements that may or may not follow. Yet 'build and they shall come' makes no more sense for real estate development than it did for overall place development in the 1980s. Rarely do these proposals deliver a full solution to the community's problems. They do not deal with, but seek to avoid, more basic issues such as suburban flight, rural depopulation, increasing unemployment, deteriorating educational and transportation systems, and inadequate housing.

Clearly, places need to assign higher importance to the strategic planning process that moves beyond meeting electoral needs of the moment to incorporating the broader perspectives of the marketplace into place planning. Strategic market planning can serve as the guiding force in developing a place's future – a screen for both filtering and ranking specific actions or proposals that inevitably arise. Places need to keep themselves from habitually reacting to proposals for change and strive to be proactive in what they can do. This is not to ignore the reality of politics but rather to balance political needs with market forces. The place needs to identify its resources, opportunities and natural customers. The place must envision its future potential and adopt realistic plans that will enable it to achieve a competitive advantage.

Response three: *Places must adopt a genuine market perspective towards their products and customers.* Europe is moving towards a more market-oriented, consumer-driven economy. Each place must try to understand its potential customers' needs, perceptions, preferences and buying decisions. Even publicly owned airlines, telecommunications companies and energy utilities are becoming increasingly market-driven. The speed of change is even more dramatic in some Eastern European countries.

In an era when the public sector is asked to do more with less, governments and communities are compelled to think and plan more like businesses. They need to calculate the actual costs of their services and apportion them through prices to determine demand levels. They must generate more of their own resources through sale of services and seek to reduce costs but not quality through user fees and contracted services. They may also need to get out of certain public businesses and eliminate programmes that no longer meet the public's needs. They are learning the business of converting *spending-thinking* into *investment-thinking*, whether through preventive actions to avoid more costly remedies later or through allocating resources where they have highest returns. With a market orientation, a place sees itself as serving and meeting the needs of customers and directing resources towards citizens' welfare.[4]

Places ultimately thrive or languish on the basis of what they do to create skilled, motivated and satisfied citizens. Human capital is emerging as the most vital resource that places possess or can develop in place competition. Places that turn unskilled workers into skilled labour, promote innovation and entrepreneurship, and provide lifelong education and training gain a competitive advantage in the new economic order. The important industries of the future that specialise in commercial application of new technologies will locate in places that have a supply of skilled workers. Places that do little else but nurture an educated and trained labour force may do far more to enhance their competitive advantages over the longer run than those making a series of one-time investments in a single employer or a single capital investment.

A wholehearted marketing commitment must underly the placemarketing strategies. This can be difficult when market orientation has such a short tradition and where a market approach might be greeted with political distrust. Such distrust can still be found within many European places where the classical state-subsidised regional policy is dominant.

Response four: *Places have to build quality into their programmes and services to compete with other places.* On a day-to-day basis, people judge a place by the quality of its everyday services, not so much by its grand vision. Their impressions come from how easily the traffic moves, how clean the city air and streets are, how good the education system is, and how accessible cultural and recreational amenities are. Quality services are noted not only by the residents and business firms but also by those considering moving to, visiting or investing in a place. The same principle holds true for the tourism/hospitality business where competition intensifies as more places make the physical investments necessary to enhance their relative attractiveness. Beyond infrastructure, success turns increasingly on the service quality provided by industry and public sectors alike.

When standards of living rise, citizens generally develop higher expectations of performance. In weighing relocation decisions, businesses place increasingly more value on quality-of-life considerations than on cost factors alone. Service quality, therefore, requires continuous investments in infrastructure as well as in various amenities – museums, theatres, sports, entertainment, libraries, recreation – to maintain a competitive posture. The fact that tax revenues and borrowing often do not accommodate such needs means that there is even more need for a market planning perspective. Those places that figure out how to create and deliver high quality in their various services are much more formidable competitors in place competition. It is striking how small a role quality service has taken in European placemarketing strategies. In local community organisations there appears to be little attention paid to personal service, the handling of cases, applications, requests for assistance and information, and other daily services. Quality in these instances is important in setting the image of a place.

For many places, the transition to a strategic market planning perspective is an evolutionary one. It often begins with opening up public services to competition, moving to some privatisation and adopting total quality management (TQM) principles in service delivery. Once the skills of greater competitiveness and customer orientation are internalised, places are far more likely to adopt a customer orientation in marketing themselves externally. Not that the former necessarily leads to the latter, but rather the mind-set of markets and the meeting of identifiable needs can carry over from one to the other (see Exhibit 13.2).

Improving public sector service quality

EXHIBIT 13.2

Public organisations, being largely monopolistic in character, often have problems with being responsive to the needs and service requirements of its citizens. A number of mechanisms can help the public sector become more responsive:

1. *Outsourcing* of various public service functions in order to buy the best available solution on the market. One such area is the community switchboard. A dramatic improvement in service quality can be secured via the city call centre, which can be turned into a professional call centre. To the delight of citizens, public services can be delivered even after 5 pm. The call centre can provide a multitude of services in a coordinated way: questions regarding building codes, information about community meeting minutes and protocols, elderly care, daycare, utility bills, and other services. Tourism information and reservations – in different languages – are other quality improvements within reach via a place-related call centre.
2. '*Voucherisation*', where citizens receive a basic credit that they can choose to spend on the public service or a competing private service. With Internet access, citizens are able to scan the regional or local market in a much easier and more convenient way.
3. *Warranties*, where a public agency is required to compensate aggrieved citizens for personal losses or inconveniences ▶

caused by the agency. Some warranties that set standards for Europe are:

- If any part of the Railtrack network in Britain cancels trains or runs them excessively late, passengers may be compensated for their ticket cost by receiving a voucher for off-peak travel.
- If rubbish is not collected in a timely fashion in some Swedish communities, households can call in private contractors at the city's expense.

4. *Decentralisation*, the classic approach to improving service quality. Quicker and more flexible responses are major advantages flowing from decentralisation.
5. *Total quality management* (TQM), sometimes introduced in a systematic way within communities.
6. *Quick service*, an appreciated way of giving a public authority a positive image. One such example is the efficient handling of new passports by the police authorities – only 15 minutes – at Arlanda International Airport outside Stockholm.

Response five: *Places need skill to communicate and promote their competitive advantages effectively*. Having quality and being attractive is one thing, communicating the special quality of a place to others is quite another. Places must skilfully position themselves for those various publics who may wish to locate, invest, live or do business there. They must adapt their messages to highly differentiated place-buyers and at the same time develop a core image of what the place basically offers. The previously discussed concept: Grenland, '*A Norwegian gateway to Europe*' is carefully defined, realistic and supportable. For specific target groups such a concept has a distinct meaning. Another place-concept is '*Telecom Valley*' in France, which is not only a highly visual image, but also so well known that it is virtually a trademark.

As we have seen throughout this book, many European places have summarised their attractions in a concept that is consistently communicated. The concept must be built on a combination of unique place attractions and must be true to the place. A concept is most easily and effectively communicated when the images are based on reality.

A place-concept must be carefully communicated to take advantage of potential assets and tie-ins. As shown in product brands such as BMW of Germany, Chanel of Paris, Guinness of Ireland and Rolex of Geneva, a strong place-concept has enormous co-branding value. The effective place will build its slogans, themes and positions so that they are focused and recognisable to its important publics. In all cases communication programmes should be carefully planned and co-ordinated by a local or regional body with the understanding that successful images are the result of careful planning.

Response six: *Places need to diversify their economic base and develop mechanisms for adapting to changing conditions*. Places cannot rely on one or a few miscellaneous industries or businesses on which to base their future. Industries quickly rise and fall owing to technological changes, and they can respond quickly to productive advantages found elsewhere in Europe or on the global placemarket. Places must view their challenge as building a well-balanced portfolio of businesses.

Clustering has become a key concept for positioning a place's business mix. As Porter identified the challenge, 'Nations succeed not in isolated industries, but in clusters of industries connected through vertical and horizontal relationships'.[5] We must add that clusters are basically a question for places and regions to develop. Nations are usually too distant from commercial realities. It is also not the old clustering in which similar industries clustered in one place. Modern clustering involves sharing of new technologies, services and infrastructures across industries. Such sharing can be organised in a unique way and thereby create a set of competitive place advantages.

Places must identify trends and emerging needs that can influence new cluster developments. Effective local leadership must be concerned with the question of how competitive place intelligence can be stimulated and exploited.

Response seven: *Places must develop and nurture entrepreneurial characteristics.* Place development is spurred by entrepreneurial people and organisations. Irrespective of political alignment, most observers agree that in the shadow of high European unemployment and the lack of a dynamic labour market, places need to attract small business and entrepreneurship. Neil Peirce and Robert Guskind identified the ten best-managed cities in the USA, and the one main feature they isolated is the nurturing of an entrepreneurial spirit where city mayors and managers matched their private sector counterparts in market-driven thinking. 'Most important', noted the authors, 'all of the nation's best-run cities are characterised by managerial leadership that has set the stage for economic advances that make these cities masters of their own destiny'.[6]

The talent of local leadership is consistently found to be the key explanation behind winning place-positions in Europe. Some characteristics of entrepreneurial places and their public sector orientation are shown in Tables 13.1 and 13.2.

Response eight: *Places must rely more on the private sector to accomplish their tasks.* Increasingly, local and regional businesses are participating in strategic placemarketing processes. Not long ago in Europe, the most common scenario was, at least in practice, that the public sector worked within its own references. Of course, the business sector and its representatives had contacts with the public sector, but close and joint place development was not particularly common. Public/private partnerships emerged in the 1960s and 1970s in the USA In Europe, a cross-sector approach at the local and regional levels appeared as late as the 1980s. Today we can see joint approaches where public place representatives are forming partnerships with banks, utilities, leading local enterprises, chambers of commerce, real estate agents and other regional or local business organisations.

In 1984, after many years of slow growth in Europe, the Round Table of European Industrialists was founded as a body to initiate strategic projects throughout Europe. The aim was to enhance Europe's competitiveness as a

Table 13.1 ◆ Entrepreneurial places: characteristics

Place	*Characteristics*
Economy	Open, fluid, low barriers to start-ups
Social structure	Dynamic, mobile, outsiders welcome
Business	No dominant employer, competitive
Financial	Competitive banks, venture capital access
Labour	Skilled labour, professional workforce, support
Government	Support small business, start-ups
Innovation	Large university, corporate research centre
Media	Attention to entrepreneurs, new business
Jobs	Grow new businesses, small business growth
Amenities	Good quality of life, culture/recreation

Sources: David L. Birch, 'Thriving on adversity', *Inc.*, March 1988, pp. 80–84; Joel Kotkin, 'City of the future', *Inc.*, April 1987, pp. 56–60.

Table 13.2 ◆ Entrepreneurial public sector: characteristics

Public sector	*Characteristics*
Finances	Modest taxes, high bond ratings
Managers	Thinkers, visionaries, politicians, salespersons
Services	High quality, innovative, competitive
Culture	High citizen participation, open
Styles	Professional, results-oriented
Bureaucracy	Entrepreneurial, new ways to do things
Spending	Investments, performance, outcomes
Citizens	Consumers, shareholders
Planning	Anticipation, multiyear, strategic
Responsiveness	Good listeners, negotiators, accountability

Source: Adapted from Neil Peirce and Robert Guskind, 'Hot managers, sizzling cities', *Business Month*, June 1989, pp. 36–53.

base for industry and technological development. A dialogue with public sector leaders in Europe was established. The industrialists promoted industrial, technological, and infrastructural projects, for example the Channel Tunnel and IT-related systems. Such initiatives from the industrial sector marked the growing broader interest of businesses to participate, on a practical level, in areas that had traditionally been reserved for the public sector. A new climate has slowly developed where joint efforts – local, regional and national – have become more natural.

Such joint efforts are fairly common in Europe today. Yet there are still many places where public sector actors often cling to old roles as custodians of public works driven by outdated values inconsistent with today's economic and commercial realities. Risk-taking, competitiveness, entrepreneurship and leadership are neglected and even avoided. These things are too often assumed to be things 'taken care of by the business community'. In some nations and regions in Eastern Europe, far-reaching privatisation programmemes have changed the traditional roles completely.

Response nine: *Each place needs to develop its unique change processes as a result of differences in the place's culture, politics and leadership processes.* Different places cannot simply apply formulaic approaches to planning their future. Each place has its own history, culture, values, public bodies, institutions, leadership, and systems of public and private decision making. Strategic market planning inevitably takes different forms in Amsterdam and Gibraltar. Each place has to sort out how best to promote innovation, how to take the necessary actions to produce change, and how to form alliances that will get various publics to accept and support change.

Most places experience common barriers to change: inertia, lack of vision and political consensus, resource scarcity, and inadequate organisational machinery that will lead to change. Overcoming barriers depends on favourable events, trends and various catalysts for change – an election, new leaders, the media, and new organisations or evolution of older ones.

In spite of place differences, all places have to pay attention to certain basic imperatives:

1. Resource scarcity necessitates a certain *consolidation* of place development activities, both within the community organisation and between the community and the private sector. Consolidation provides opportunities to broaden participation, refine and focus place development strategies, and to pool and leverage transactions.
2. Places need greater *continuity and consistency* in their approaches to place development, which means institutionalising ways for leadership to emerge. Through consolidation, partnerships and the emergence of lead organisations, professionalisation of both public and private leaders can develop. Place development is frequently associated with recognised leaders who come from a variety of sectors.
3. Places need to reach *beyond their geopolitical boundaries* to leverage their resources, attack common problems and share collective benefits. Tourism, convention businesses, airports and bridges, for example, often extend activities beyond the immediate community areas. An individual region, or some regions in a joint effort, may support such a project. In some cases an individual project such as the Channel Tunnel has gone far beyond national boundaries. Concept-building, for example '*European Vineyard Routes*' (in several wine-producing countries), '*Kingdom of Crystal*' (a number of Swedish communities), the '*New Hansa Region*' (regions and cities

around the Baltic Sea), '*Star Region of Europe*' (Flanders in Belgium) has increasingly extended beyond an individual community because of the necessity to share resources and develop a critical mass. More complex structures are also emerging,for example '*The Four Motors of Europe*' which is a joint concept made up of Baden-Württemburg in Germany, the Italian region of Lombardia, Spanish Catalonia and the French region of Rhône-Alpes. Such Euro-regions, now formed into innovative networks beyond traditional boundaries, will certainly grow in number and importance in the future.

Response ten: *Places must develop organisational and procedural mechanisms to sustain place development and maintain momentum once it has begun.* Strategic market planning requires patience and persistence. It was many years before Frankfurt saw the results of investments in building and marketing its banking image and services into real place value. Even though it will take decades for Northern Ireland to change its image, we are witnessing the first fragile steps of investment in Belfast, its capital city. Another region undergoing change is southern Italy, which seeks to attract direct foreign investments. Such a transformation will require time and skilful organisational effort.

A danger exists when an impatient public becomes discouraged, changes elected leaders and reverts to preferences for quick-fixes. Because no panacea exists for place development, we can only learn from past successes and mistakes of others and ourselves. As historians have long noted, democracies tend to meet crises effectively which therefore enables leaders to lead and allows power to be temporarily concentrated. This pattern is apparent when we study local political leaders in places where huge structural crises have occurred. On the other hand, democratic institutions tend to work poorly in non-crisis places where checks and balances can create stalemates, if not paralysis.

Sustaining momentum can be difficult in the face of success. As a community experiences some initial progress, it may become complacent and relax its efforts. Soon longer-term goals are forgotten and momentum is lost. The challenge here is to keep the goal foremost in the public's mind, to allow them to revisit the strategic plan, and to provide a constant flow of information to the public on the progress achieved to date. Regrettably, implementation may be the least exciting aspect of change, but it remains the most important.[7] To sustain interest and approval means that the public must be convinced that various investments are producing results, accountability is being maintained and further progress will be achieved. An example of building on momentum is Exhibit 13.3.

Smaller European communities always face the risk of not attaining *critical mass* in their place development projects. Many ambitious plans and projects are started without sufficient consideration for building and maintaining resources, energy and organisational momentum. In order to reach critical

Valencia burns brightly

EXHIBIT 13.3

The *Fallas de Valencia* is the most spectacular fireworks festival in the world, lighting up the medieval city every March. Valencia's reputation as a place of irreverence and playfulness has been channelled into a highly competitive place development strategy.

The Spanish community Valencia is competing with Barcelona and Madrid to become the leading business and conference centre in Spain. Attractions in Valencia are skilfully designed and emotionally driven under the local leadership of the mayor Rita Barbera to meet her ambitious objectives. Her high visibility projects and plans cover all aspects of Valencian life from its local soccer team to inner-city renewal. She has made Valencia's passion crucial in her public role and branded it as the image of her administration.

Her commitment takes many forms. She loves soccer, at least the type of soccer played by the Valencian team. The mayor encourages the positive image the team reflects upon Valencia. She summarises her interest in the soccer team in three words: 'Passion, passion, passion',[1] and that rallying cry could stand for all of her enterprises. She wants Valencia to be 'a leading city – leading in culture and in quality of life. I want it to be a place with spirit and personality'.[2]

The campaign to reposition Valencia is carefully planned by Mayor Barbera in the city hall. For example, Valencia's status as an important commercial meeting place has recently been reinforced by the construction of the new congress centre designed by internationally acclaimed architect Sir Norman Foster. The mayor personally chose Foster for this crucial assignment, and she played an active role throughout the project planning stages.

Many more projects are being developed to sustain place development in the city. A new arts centre with an opera house is planned and a planet-arium/megacinema known as the 'Hemispheric' is under construction. An internationally renowned architect, Santiago Calatrava, was commissioned to design this complex. The entire project amounted to US$250 million. On top of this, a broad restoration of the medieval centre is under way as well as new public parks. A new linkage to the European high-speed train is also in the pipeline. Valencia has momentum as Barbera, in spite of controversies and detractors, fits one project on top of another.

Throughout her place development strategy, Barbera finds inspiration in the dramatic history of Valencia. The city has been the home of many cultures: Romans, Visigoths, Moors and the Aragonese. During the fifteenth and sixteenth centuries, Valencia became one of the most important economic powers on the Mediterranean, and these ancient traditions are systematically exploited and transformed into modern projects by the mayor. The mayor's vision was that Valencia develop into a modern business place – based on merchant traditions. Through her leadership she has managed to translate Valencia's core value into a powerful, competitive position.

Sources:

1. Internet: http://www2.combios.es/valenciacf/ValdeVac/febrero/rita.htm.
2. Hugh Pearman, 'Business shapes city life', *The European*, 13–19 July 1998, pp. 30–31.

mass, smaller places often need to associate with larger networks regionally, nationally or even internationally.

A last organisational aspect, often forgotten – is the issue of *aftercare*. The main aim of a place's aftercare programme is to help and encourage new and existing investors to adapt and grow, to reinvestment, and to create more jobs. According to Clive Vokes, formerly with the Welsh Development Agency

(WDA), an aftercare programme is a 'drip-feed process based on no quick-fixes'.[8] The programme must be systematic. All new investors should move into the aftercare programme immediately after they start operations. Continuity of contact is important, and the personal dimension should not be neglected. Since settling down and building a life in new surroundings is not easy, a place must meet both the investor and family members. Place-buyers rank aftercare efforts high.

The necessity of marketing places in Europe

As a place, Europe has been known for more than 2,500 years. The name 'Europe', first applied to the area before 600 BC, refers in poetic terms to a place in Greece somewhere between 'the rich Peloponnesus' and the 'wave-washed isles'.

Greece and its immediate hinterland were the market.[9] Now, 2,500 years later, Europe is the world's largest market. Never before in European history has there been such strong market pressure to be competitive.

In order to compete effectively in Europe, places must develop a marketing approach. Places must produce products and services that current and prospective citizens, businesses, investors and visitors want or need. Places must sell products and services internally and externally, nationally and internationally.

The task of marketing places undergoes constant change as new industries form, new technologies emerge, companies expand, and old businesses shrink, merge or consolidate. As conditions and customers change, products must be upgraded and refined and new products and services must be designed to meet new needs. In Europe, many places have responded to changing market demands: in Milan, the fashion industry; in Wales, the film industry; in the Ruhr area, sophisticated service companies; in Dublin, financial services. The European challenge is to become competitive not only throughout Europe but also around the world.

Opportunities for selling abroad are vastly expanding as global markets grow. Places are becoming more aggressive in assisting, financing and facilitating exports through information assistance, trading companies and trade centres. Entering the twenty-first century, European communities more than ever before need to help their local business firms develop market opportunities in specific national and international markets, to conduct online searches for buyers and agents, and to engage in cultural, scientific and educational exchanges. These communities need the support of 'their' commercial bank, chamber of commerce, trade clubs and other export intermediaries. Sister-city and partner-city relationships are growing throughout Europe, and encouraging an exchange of ideas, information and resources.

However, the single greatest challenge that places face involves marketing their various activities to their own residents and voters. Marketing to the internal consumers is not so much a technical marketing problem of methods, messages and targets as it is a political problem of embedding place development values in the public's mind.

Now we are back to the point at which we began. *All places are in trouble, if not now, certainly in the future.* The globalisation of the world's economy and the accelerating pace of technological changes are two forces that require all places to learn how to compete. European places must learn, in spite of very short traditions, how to think more like businesses and develop the local business climate, products, markets and customers. Joint efforts between public and private sectors must be more common in Europe.

The central tenet of *Marketing Places Europe* is that in spite of the powerful external and internal forces that buffet them, places have within their collective resources and people the capacity to improve their relative competitive positions. Their responses to the new bottom-up economic order are equally as important as national responses to the competitive challenge. A strategic market planning perspective provides places with the marketing tools and opportunities to rise to that challenge.

Notes

Chapter 1

1 *First Report on Economic and Social Cohesion*, Commission of the European Communities, Brussels/Luxembourg, 1996, p. 15.

2 Rosabeth Moss Kanter, *World Class: Thriving Locally in the Global Economy*, Simon & Schuster, New York, 1995.

3 *Growth, Competitiveness, Employment: The Challenges and Ways Forward into the 21st Century*, Commission of the European Communities, Brussels, 1993.

4 The following six countries are included in the enlargement, the so-called 'fast track': Estonia, Poland, Czech Republic, Hungary, Slovenia and Cyprus. However, the following countries have also applied for membership of the EU: Latvia, Lithuania, Bulgaria, Romania, the Slovak Republic and Turkey.

5 *Employment In Europe*, European Commission, Brussels, 1996, p. 3.

6 *Towards a Society for All Ages*, Commission of the European Union, Brussels, 1998.

7 Werner Weidenfeld, and Wolfgang Wessels, *Europe*, CD-ROM, EurOP, European Union Official Publications, 1997.

8 *World Investment Report 1997*, United Nations Conference on Trade and Development (UNCTAD), United Nations, New York and Geneva, pp. 2–13.

9 *Best Business Climate in Europe*, Welsh Development Agency (WDA), Cardiff, 1997, p. 2.

Chapter 2

1 Neil Buckley, 'Leading role at the centre of the EU. Survey – Luxembourg', *Financial Times,* 30 May 1996, p. 1.

2 Calculations based on information obtained from Internet: http://statec.gouvernement.lu/html en/portrait economique du luxembourg/index.html

3 Malta. Advertisement. *The European*, 10–16 July 1997, p. 35.

4 'The renovation market in Poland, 1996–2006', *European Construction Research* (newsletter), Copenhagen, 1997, p. 1.

5 *Portrait of the Regions*, Eurostat, vol. 2, Brussels/Luxembourg, 1993, p. 37.

6 *The Global Bangemann Challenge, Stockholm*, City of Stockholm, 1997, p. 3.

7 *Globalisation and Local and Regional Competitiveness*, OECD, Paris, 29 July 1992, p. 40.

8 *Europe in Figures*, Eurostat, Statistical Office of the European Communities, Luxembourg, 1995, pp. 64–67.

9 Martin Jacques, 'History Lesson at the Coronation of Blair', *The European*, 1 October 1997 (Lexis Nexis).

10 Philip Parrish, 'Money bag moves,' *Corporate Location*, January/February 1997, pp. 12–13.

11 'The European cities monitor, 1997', *Site Selection*, Conway Data, February/March 1998, p. 14.

Chapter 3

1 Francoise Hecht, 'Lille of the valley', *EuroBusiness*, February 1995, p. 68.

2 'Saarland, the German state with European skills', *Site Selection*, February 1995, p. 3.

3 'Saarland', Advertisement from Saarland Economic Promotion Corporation, Saarbrüken, 1997.

4 Timothy Shaw, 'Professors to tackle a tasty subject', *Financial Times*, 25 February 1997, p. 1.

5 Amon Cohen, 'The Euro may be good for you', survey – The Business of Travel, *Financial Times*, 20 November, 1997, p. 2.

6 *Jobs for the Millennium*, World Travel and Tourism Council (WTTC), London, 1997, p. 34.

7 *Europe in Figures*, Eurostat, Statistical Office of the European Communities, Luxembourg, 1995, pp. 330–333.

8 *EU Tourism on the Rise*, Eurostat, Luxembourg, 10 July 1998, pp. 1–2.

9 Interview with Mayor Antonio Cicchetti, June 1997.

10 Norman Crampton, *The Best Small Towns in America*, Prentice Hall, Englewood Cliffs, NJ, 1993, p. 394.

11 Gerald Cadogan, 'Not just in the springtime', *Financial Times*, 25 January 1997 (Lexis Nexis).

12 'Achieve competitive advantages in Ireland', Marketing material from Industrial Development Agency (IDA), Dublin, 1997.

13 *Competitiveness and Cohesion: Trends in the Regions*, Fifth Periodic Report on the Social and Economic Situation and Development of the Regions in the Community, European Commission, Brussels, 1994.

14 *Europe 2000: Outlook for the Development of the Community's Territory*, European Commission, Brussels, 1994.

15 Nicole Davison Atkins, 'The North–South divide,' *Corporate Location*, January/February 1998, p. 70.

16 Sari-Gilbert, 'North–South divide lingers,' *Financial Times*, 6 June 1991, p. 6.

17 Julie Wolf, 'Gardens can help property values blossom', *Wall Street Journal*, (Europe), 11–12 July 1997, p. 10.

18 Marcello Marin, General Secretary Fiera Milano, paper delivered in Malmö, Sweden, 20 August 1996.

19 Interview with Richard Leese, 14 April 1998.

20 Bernard Simon, 'A politician you can do business with', *Financial Times*, 26 July

1996, p. 10.

21 *'Trieste – Window on the East, Investment Guide to Trieste'*, Conway Data and the City of Trieste, 1997, p. 8.

22 David Owens, 'Pulling together at the heart of Europe', Survey – Rhône-Alpes, *Financial Times*, 20 May 1997 (Lexis Nexis).

23 'Europe's new leader in education', special advertising section on the Netherlands, *Newsweek*, 21 November 1994, p. 4.

24 *EuroFutures*, research report, Stockholm, 1997.

25 Tim Hindle, 'Monarchs of the glen', *EuroBusiness*, November 1994 (Lexis Nexis).

26 Jan Malmborg, 'Warsaw – the city that refused to die', *Dagens Nyheter*, 17 November 1996, p. 9.

Chapter 4

1 The Croatian government, being aware of the image, rejected participating in a Balkan investment conference aimed at attracting investors to the region as a whole. Mr Damir Ostovic, the assistant minister for privatisation, based in Zagreb, concluded: 'Inviting Croatia to take part in a Balkan's investment conference was like inviting Kuwait to participate in a Zionist fund'. Guy Dinmore and Anthony Robinson, 'Foreign Investments', *Financial Times*, 28 May 1997 (Lexis Nexis).

2 Jan Bielecki, 'Clean up your act, Central Europe', Central European Economic Review, *Wall Street Journal*, July/August 1997, p. 4.

3 Nicole Davison-Aitkins, 'Hunt for the centre of Europe', *Corporate Location*, May/June 1998, pp. 8–9.

4 *Michelin Green Guide: Scandinavia, Finland*, Michelin, Clermont-Ferrand, 1996, pp. 79–80.

5 *Portrait of the Regions*, Commission of the European Communities and Eurostat, vols. 1–3, Brussels/Luxembourg, 1993.

Chapter 5

1 'Saab to shift convertible production to Austria', *Dagens Industri*, 15 June 1999, p. 19.

2 Chris Butler, 'Money and jobs flowing out of Germany', *The European*, 4 June 1997, p. 1.

3 'Electrolux hit $113m loss in wake of shake-up', *Financial Times*, 7 August 1997, p. 1.

4 'Comment and analysis', *Financial Times*, 13 February 1997, pp. 12–14.

5 *Antwerp, Flanders*, Marketing booklet, Antwerp Tourist Information, Antwerp, 1996, pp. 3–6.

6 Andrew Hill, 'Sensitive barometer', Survey – Flanders, *Financial Times*, 4 May 1993, pp. 1–4.

7 'Star region in Europe', Placemarketing material from Flanders Investment Office, Brussels, 1991.

Chapter 6

1 Mary Hollingsworth, *Architecture of the 20th Century*, Bison Books, London, 1995, p. 127.

2 Guide Michelin, *Scandinavia*, 1996, pp. 198–199.

3 *Growth, Competitiveness, Employment*, White Paper, Commission of the European Communities, Brussels, 5 December 1993, p. 82.

4 'Spotlight on Spain: Buenos Noticias', *Site Selection*, August/September 1997, p. 662.

5 Charles Batchlor, 'Financial Times survey on investing in Central and Eastern Europe', *Financial Times*, 11 April 1997, p. 3.

6 *Regions of the New Europe, A Comparative Assessment of Key Factors in Choosing Your Location*, Ernst & Young, London, 1995, p. 12.

7 Bruce McDowell, 'Public works for tomorrow', *Intergovernmental Perspective*, Summer 1992, p. 23.

8 Herbert Girardet, 'Habitat 11: conserve and survive', *The Guardian*, 12 June 1996, pp. 4–5.

9 Birna Helgadottir, 'A great idea, but please, not just yet', *The European*, 18–24 September 1997, pp. 12–13.

10 Richard Wolffe, 'Manchester City plan', *Financial Times*, 6 November 1996, p. 10.

11 Renate Frank, 'Private security firms flourish as Germans worry about crime', *Deutsche Press-Agentur*, 24 April 1997 (Lexis Nexis).

12 'Germany. Election foretaste', *The Economist* (US edition), 13 September 1997, p. 50.

13 Renate Frank, *op. cit.*

14 Ernst & Young, *op. cit.* pp. 45–46.

15 'La vie, made in Geneva', placemarketing material from the Canton of Geneva, 1997.

16 Vick Hayward, 'Bilbao places its bets for a heroic gamble', *The European*, 2–8 October 1997, pp. 50–51.

17 *Ibid.*

18 Interview with Mayor Don Pedro Aparicio, June 1996.

19 Ariane Genillard, 'Survey of Baden-Württemberg', *Financial Times*, 29 April 1993, p. 39.

20 *High-tech Industry and Localisation*, OECD, Paris, 1989, p. 21.

21 Andrew Clark, 'The bad boy of Salzburg comes good', *Financial Times*, 11 August 1997, p. 11.

Chapter 7

1 Baha Gungor, 'Foreign Journalists in Turkey to be judged by "loyalty" of reporting', *Deutsche Presse-Agentur*, 5 August 1995 (Lexis Nexis).

2 Simon Brooke, 'How PR firms lobby for foreign governments', *The Times,* 25 September 1996 (Lexis Nexis).

3 'Turkey all out to boost tourism', *Xinhua News Agency*, 14 April 1998.

4 *Iceland*, Icelandic Tourist Board, Reykjavik, 1997, pp. 1–30.

5 Gregory Jensen, 'Glasgow – a city reborn', *Chicago Sun-Times*, 1 July 1988, p. 143.

6 *Ibid.*

Chapter 8

1 See Sidney Levy, *Promotional Behaviour*, Scott Foresman, Glenview, Ill. 1971. See Chapter 4 for more characteristics of advertising, personal selling and sales promotion.

2 *Panorama of EU Industry*, Eurostat, 1995/96, Brussels/Luxembourg, p. 24–11.

3 Thomas L. Harris, *The Marketers Guide to Public Relations*. John Wiley, New York, 1991.

4 *EuroBusiness*, October 1994.

5 Dennis Ellam, 'Capital punishment for the city that brought a smile to the world', *Birmingham Post*, 21 August 1998 (Lexis Nexis).

6 *Panorama of EU Industry*, p. 27-14.

7 Interview with Hans Sydow, International Marketing Manager, Andersen & Lembke, 17 August 1997.

8 Tom Walker, 'Irish rock band unites enemies', *Times Newspapers Limited*, 25 September 1997 (Lexis Nexis).

Chapter 9

1 Nicholas Woodsworth, 'Real hot spots in future world', *Financial Times*, 1 January 1994, p.VII.

2 Interview with Bengt Sahlberg, Professor European Tourism Research Institute, *ETOUR*, 10 July 1998.

3 *Financial Times*, section on Food and Drink, 1 October 1994, p. 12.

4 Armando Montanari (ed.), *European Tourism*, John Wiley, Chichester, 1995, p. 47.

5 Gavin Duff, 'Dirty old town image', *The Mirror*, 18 July 1998, p. 23.

6 Armando Montanari, *op. cit.*, p. 152.

7 'Welcome to Lithuania', Lithuanian Tourist Board, Vilnius, 1996.

8 *Latvia, Heartland of the Baltics*, Latvian Tourist Board, Riga, 1997, pp. 8–9.

9 Interview with Luther Buss, 10 July 1998.

10 *The Role of the Union in the Field of Tourism*, Commission Green Paper, Commission of the European Communities, Brussels, 4 April 1995, p. 11.

Chapter 10

1 Gunter Pauli, *Double Digit Growth, How to Achieve It with Services*, Pauli Publishing, Berlaar, 1997.

2 Alison Warner 'Capital working city', The Banker, *Financial Times*, 27 November

1997, pp. 25–27.

3 *Panorama of EU Industry*, Eurostat, European Commission, Brussels/Luxembourg, 1995/1996, pp. 20–1.

Chapter 11

1 'External and intra-European Union trade', *Eurostat*, no. 6, 1998, p. 14.

2 *European Regional Prospects*, ERECO, European Economic Research and Advisory and Consortium, Brussels, 1998, p. 38.

3 *Financial Times*, 9 December 1997, p. 3.

4 *European Regional Prospects, op. cit.*, 1998, p. 39.

5 'Chirac launches ghost riders on fast track to the future', *The European*, 19–25 October 1998, p. 23.

6 Johnny K. Johansson, 'Determinants and effects of the use of "made in" labels', *International Marketing Review* (UK) vol. 6, no. 1, pp. 47–58.

7 See Warren J. Bilkey and Erik Nes, 'Country-of-Origin Effects on Product Evaluations', *Journal of Business Studies* 13, Spring-Summer 1982, pp. 89–99; P. J. Cattin *et al.*, 'A Cross-Cultural Study of "Made-in" Concepts', *Journal of International Business Studies*, Winter 1982, pp. 131–41; and Gary M. Erickson, Johnny K. Johansson and Paul Chao, 'Image variables in Multi-Attribute Product Evaluations: Country-of-Origin Effects', *Journal of Consumer Research*, September 1984, pp. 694–99.

8 Michael Porter, *The Competitive Advantage of Nations*, The Free Press, New York, 1990, pp. 3–4.

Chapter 12

1 'Europe in figures', *Eurostat*, 4th Edition, Statistical Office of the European Communities, Brussels/Luxembourg, 1995, pp. 154–155.

2 Copenhagen Capacity, Advertisement, *Scanorama*, 27 September 1997.

3 'Interviewing IT literate graduates takes a little longer in Northern Ireland', The Industrial Development Board for Northern Ireland (IDB), Belfast, 1990.

4 'Success stories, Portugal', Portuguese Trade and Tourism Office, ICEP, Lisbon, 1997.

5 Doug Cameron, 'Give me a slice of life', *The European*, 29 June 1998 (Lexis Nexis).

6 Peter F. Drucker, 'Information and the future of the city', *Wall Street Journal*, 4 April 1989, p. 14.

7 Peter Marsh, *Life Style: Your Surroundings and How They Affect You*, Sidgwick & Jackson, London, 1990, p. 144.

8 Diane Crispell, 'Guppies, minks, and tinks', *American Demographics*, June 1990, p.51.

9 Faith Popcorn, *The Popcorn Report*, Harper Business, New York, 1992, p. 46.

10 *Europe 2000: Outlook for the Development of the Community's Territory*, Commission of the European Communities, Brussels, 1991, p. 156.

11 *Düsseldorf – Your Base in Europe*, Office for City Promotion and Economic Development, Düsseldorf, 1995, pp. 1–5.

Chapter 13

1 Robert Reich, 'The myth of made in America', *Wall Street Journal*, 5 July 1991, p. 14; see also Reich, *The Work of Nations: Preparing Ourselves for 21st Century Capitalism*, Knopf, New York, 1991.

2 Hans van den Broek, Member of the European Commission, symposium on One European Defence Industry, The Hague, 17 October 1996.

3 Paolo Cecchini, *The European Challenge 1992 – The Benefits of a Single Market*, Commission of the European Communities, Brussels, 1989.

4 David Osbourne and Ted Gaebler, *Reinventing Government*, Addison-Wesley, Reading, Massachusetts, 1992, Chapter 10.

5 Michael E. Porter, *The Competitive Advantage of Nations*, The Free Press, New York, 1990, p. 73.

6 Neil Peirce and Robert Guskind, 'Hot manager, sizzling cities', *Business Month*, June 1989, p. 38.

7 John Gunther-Mohr and Bert Winterbottom, 'Implementation Strategies, Turning Plans into Successful Development', *Economic Development Commentary*, Summer 1989, pp. 23–31.

8 Interview with Clive Vokes, 17 September 1997.

9 *Europe: A Thematic Atlas*, Economist Books, Glasgow, 1992, p. 12.

Index

Action plan
  developing the, 120–121
Athena, 125
Attraction marketing
  factors in, establishing the, 108
  importance of, 55–57
  trade fair wars in Germany, 56–57
Attractions, 140–153
  attraction chasing, 150
  buildings, monuments and sculptures, 151–152
  cultural attractions, 146
  festivals and occasions, 149–151
  history and famous personages, 142–145
  museums, 152
  natural beauty and features, 141
  recreation and entertainment, 146–148
  shopping places, 145–146
  sports arenas, 149
  Waterloo, 143
Audi, 49–50
Auvergne, 18–19

Barcelona, 203–204
Billboards, 192
Brochures, 190
Broker, 247–248
Budapest, 159
Business and industry
  attracting, 40–47, 225–242
    elsewhere from, 226
    factors in, 43
  Cambridge, 46–47
  corporate headquarters, 229, 232–233
  culture and language, 45
  entrepreneurs,
    climate for, 45, 240
    top service, 231
  financial incentives, 235–237
  Hannover, 43–44
  high-tech industries, 228, 230
  infrastructure for expansion, 44–45
  investment agencies, 42
  location advisory services, 40
  locations, selecting, 227–228
  marketing clusters, 228–229
  projects, strategic relevance of, 45–47
  retailers and wholesalers, 233–235
  retaining and expanding, 237–239
  service industries, 229, 230–233
    entrepreneurs in, 231
  shopping malls, 233–235
  small businesses, fostering, 239–240

Cambridge, 46–47
Change, organising for
  competitors, growth in, 274
  key challenges, 271–275
  local resources, looking to, 275
  pace of change, 272
  responding to, 275–286
    adopting a market perspective, 277–278
    change, managing, 283–284
    diversification, 280–281
    entrepreneurial characteristics, 281
    market-orientated strategy, 276–277
    organisational and procedural mechanisms, 284
    private sector, importance of, 281–283
    quality, building in, 278–279

skillful communication, deploying, 280
strategic vision, 276
urban evolution, 273–274
Valencia, 285
Communication
deploying, 280
managing, 2
Competition
global, 20–22
growth in, 274
Czech Republic, 169

Diversification, 280–281

Employment in Europe, 4
Entrepreneurs
characteristics of, 281
climate for, 45, 240
service industries, in, 231
top service, 231

European Commission
Employment in Europe, 4
Growth, Competitiveness, Employment:
the Challenges and Ways Forward into the 21st Century, 3
Towards a Society for All Ages, 5
European Marketplace
challenges in, 3–4
communication, managing, 2
competing and reinforcing megatrends, 1–2
convergence, 1–2
divergence, 1–2
five issues facing, 1–3
information technology in, 2
insecurity in, 4
places in difficulty, 13–16
Auvergne, 18–19
forces facing, 16–23
internal forces on, 16
Frankfurt, 15–16
Sheffield, 14–15
population of, 5
size of, 1, 8–10
stagnation in, 3
European Union
regional funds of, importance of, 22
Expediter, 248
Export market
assessing potential of, 246–247
assisting companies in promoting, 247–253
broker, 247–248
expediter, 248
facility developer, 250–251
financier, 248–249
host, 249
informer, 247
promoter, 250
targeter, 249–250
technology developer, 251–252
trainer and counsellor, 248
Audi in U.S., 49–50
expansion in, 47–50, 243–244
importance of, 245–246
international trade networking, 252–253
measuring climate for, 258
place of origin, exploiting, 253–257
Swiss knife, 254

Facility developer, 250–251
Financier, 248–249
Florence, 127
Frankfurt, 15–16

Grenoble, 117
Growth
bottom-up approach to, 3–6
patterns of, 5, 6
Growth, Competitiveness, Employment:
the Challenges and Ways Forward into the 21st Century, 3

Hannover, 43–44
High-tech industries, 228, 230
Holstebro, 120

Image marketing
contradictory image, 54
importance of, 51

negative image, 54–55
overly attractive, 51–52
positive image, 52
weak image, 52–53
Utsira, 53
Information search, 80–81
Empirica ranking, 91
influence of, 89–91
Michelin Guide, 93
Portrait of the Regions, 94
ratings services, other, 94
World Competitiveness Yearbook, 92–93
Information technology
growth in, 2
job creating power of, 19–20
Infrastructure
improving the, 130–137
environmental imperative, 134–136
intergovernmental planning, 133–134
management of, 133
needs assessment, 131–132
synchronising place development needs with, 136–137
trends in, 130–131
marketing the,
importance of, 57–59
Internet, 188–189
Investment
agencies, 42
places attracting, 10–11

Kop Van Zuid, 128–129

Magazines, 189–190
Marketing
necessity of, 286–287
perspective, adopting a, 277–278
Media channels, selecting, 187
alternative media, 192–193
billboards, 192
brochures, 190
choosing, 193–194, 194–196
direct mail, 192
Internet, 188–189
magazines, 189–190
newsletters, 190
newspapers, 189
radio, 188
telephone, 189
television, 188
Media results,
evaluating, 197–198
Media sources and messages,
managing conflicting, 199–200
Media timing,
deciding on, 196–197
Milton Keynes, 38–40
Monte Carlo, 163–164
Moscow, 175

Newsletters, 190
Newspapers, 189
Norway, 207

Paris, 127
Disneyland Paris, 207–208
People marketing
competent people, 63–64
enthusiastic local leaders, 59–63
entrepreneurial profile, 64
famous persons, 59
follow-me phenomenon, 64–66
Place auditing
action plan, developing the, 120–121
approaches to place development, 101
attraction factors, establishing the, 108
community service development, 101
competitors, identifying the place's main, 109
peer competitor, 109
superior competitor, 109
weak competitor, 109
conduct of, 107
economic development, 102–103
factors undermining places, 99–100
Grenoble's vision, 117
Holstebro, 120
implementation ability, 123–124
main issues, establishing the, 115–116

market planning process, 106–107
implementing and controlling the, 121–123
opportunities and threats, 114–115
Pamplona, 119
performance and importance matrix, 113
Sophia Antipolis, 107–108
strategic,
ability, 123–124
market planning, 103–105
strategy, formulating the, 119
strengths and weaknesses, analysing the place's, 111–114
Tallinn, 114
trends and developments, identifying major, 110–111
urban redesign and planning, 101–102
vision and objectives, developing, 116–118
Place buying
administrative dimension, 78–80
alternatives, evaluation of, 83
improving ratings of sites, 86
perceived values of sites, 85
rating of sites, 85
subjective, 83
geographical dimension, 76–78
identity of buyer, 88
information search, 80–81
Empirica ranking, 91
influence of, 89–91
Michelin Guide, 93
Portrait of the Regions, 94
ratings services, other, 94
World Competitiveness Yearbook, 92–93
place ratings,
compilation of, 94–96
reliability of, 96
value of, 96
post purchase,
actions, 89
behaviour, 88
satisfaction, 88–89
purchase decision, 86–87
steps to, 75–80
Place decay
forces involved in, 16
responses to, 23–24
Place excellence
importance of, 1
Place growth
dynamics resulting in, 17
European funding, impact of, 22
Place image
audience segment, selecting a, 162–163
change, openness to, evaluation of, 168
Budapest, 159
communicating a, 169
events and deeds, 172
positions, 169
slogans, 169–170
themes, 169
visual symbols, 171–172
Czech Republic, 169
designing the, 159
factors determining, 160–162
guidelines for, 167
marketing icons, 174–175
measuring, 162, 165
evaluative maps, 167
familiarity-favourability, 165
semantic differential, 165–166
Monte Carlo, 163–164
Moscow, 175
negative image,
correcting a, 172–176
removing the, 175–176
selling the, 177
advertising, 179
audience, clarifying with the, 177–178
broad influence tools, 178
cinema, role of, 185–186
direct marketing, 180–182
novelty icons, 186
personal selling, 184
public relations, 182–184
sales promotion, 182
song, 185

sports, 186
television, 185
Place improvement
aesthetic urban design, 126–130
Athena, 125
attractions, 140–153
attraction chasing, 150
buildings, monuments and sculptures, 151–152
cultural attractions, 146
festivals and occasions, 149–151
history and famous personages, 142–145
museums, 152
natural beauty and features, 141
recreation and entertainment, 146–148
shopping places, 145–146
sports arenas, 149
Waterloo, 143
checklist, 154–157
Florence, 127
infrastructure improvement, 130–137
environmental imperative, 134–136
intergovernmental planning, 133–134
management of, 133
needs assessment, 131–132
synchronising place development needs with, 136–137
trends in, 130–131
investments, types of, 125–126
Kop Van Zuid, 128–129
Paris, 127
people, 153–154
service provider, 137
programmes for improving education, 138–139
programmes for improving security, 138
St Petersburg, 127–128
strategies for, 125–157
Venice, 127
Place marketing
advertising and, 29–30
attraction marketing, 55–57
conduct of, 66–73
private sector actors, 68–73
public sector actors, 67–68
image marketing, 51–55
infrastructure marketing, 57–59
ingredients in, 3, 25
levels of, 27
main target markets of, 30–50
outside Europe, 6–8
people marketing, 59–66
planning group, role of, 26
success in, factors involved in, 27–28
value-added process, 26
Place ratings
compilation of, 94–96
reliability of, 96
value of, 96
Portugal, 266
Private sector
importance of, 281–283
role of, 68–73
Promoter, 250
Public sector
role of, 67–68

Radio, 188
Residents
attracting, 37, 259
approaches to, 262–264
importance of, 260
brain drain, reversing the, 264–265
competing for, 260
family, consideration of, 266
life-style groups, 267–269
Milton Keynes, 38–40
population map, 261–262
Portugal, 266
Stockholm, 266
targeting skilled professionals, 264
Retailers, 233–235
Romania, 211

St Petersburg, 127–128
Selling
methods deployed in,
advertising, 179
audience, clarifying with the, 177–178

broad influence tools, 178
cinema, role of, 185–186
direct marketing, 180–182
novelty icons, 186
personal selling, 184
public relations, 182–184
sales promotion, 182
song, 185
sports, 186
television, 185
Service Industries, 229, 230–233
entrepreneurs in, 231
Seville, 203–204
Sheffield, 14–15
Shopping malls, 233–235
Sites
alternatives, evaluation of, 83
improving ratings of, 86
perceived values of, 85
rating of, 85
subjective views on, 83
Small businesses
fostering, 239–240
Sophia Antipolis, 107–108
Stockholm, 266
Subsidiarity
principle of, effect of, 10

Tallinn, 114
Telephone, 189
Television, 188
Tourism
attracting, 207–210
Barcelona and Seville, 203–204
business hospitality, 219–221
communicating with, 216
Disneyland Paris, 207–208
electronic buying, 205
Europe, in, 204
importance of, 202
market, 201–202
segmenting, 205–207
meeting facilities, 219–220
Norway, 207
organising and managing, 216–218
positioning in the market, 213–216
Romania, 211
tourist strategies and investments, 210
visitor friendliness, test for, 223
Towards a Society for All Ages, 5

Unemployment
levels of, 4
Utsira, 53

Valencia, 285
Venice, 127
Visitors
attracting, 33–37

Waterloo, 143
Wholesalers, 233–235